HORSEMEN
— of the —
TRUMPOCALYPSE

HORSEMEN

— of the —

TRUMPOCALYPSE

A Field Guide to the
Most Dangerous People in America

JOHN NICHOLS

NATION
BOOKS
New York

Nation Books
116 East 16th Street, 8th Floor New York, NY 10003
http://www.publicaffairsbooks.com/nation-books
@NationBooks

Printed in the United States of America

First Trade Paperback Edition: August 2017

Published by Nation Books, an imprint of Perseus Books, LLC,
a subsidiary of Hachette Book Group, Inc.
Nation Books is a co-publishing venture of the Nation Institute and Perseus Books.

Editorial production by Christine Marra, *Marra*thon Production Services.
www.marrathoneditorial.org

Book design by Jane Raese
Set in 12-point DTL Albertina

Library of Congress Control Number: 2017946980
ISBN 978-1-56858-780-6 (paperback)
ISBN 978-1-56858-779-0 (e-book)

LSC-C

10 9 8 7 6 5 4 3 2 1

This book is dedicated to my mother,
Mary Kathryn Nichols,
and her friends in Burlington, Wisconsin,
in the heart of Paul Ryan's congressional district.
They live in the hometown of a great Wisconsin progressive,
Ed Garvey, and they delight in the resistance.

Contents

A Note on How to Use This Book

On January 20, 2017, Donald Trump the man became Donald Trump the presidency. This is a book on how to understand that presidency. It begins with a concept of governing that some in the chattering classes will struggle with, as their obsession with personalities often precludes them from discussing consequential matters. Presidents can often be inconsequential—or foolish, or erratic, or incomprehensible. But presidencies are never any of those things. They are powerful, overarching, definitional. They shape more than policies; they shape our sense of what the United States can be. Jefferson's presidency made America more expansive than even the most adventurous former colonists had dared to attempt, Lincoln's made America freer than all but the most courageous of the founders dared imagine, Franklin Roosevelt's made America fairer than Wall Street had ever been willing to permit, John Kennedy's made a mature nation young again. And Donald Trump's presidency will make America something different than it has ever been—something darker if his autocratic agendas prevail, something brighter if the resistance to those agendas coalesces into the welcoming, humane and aspirational America that Langston Hughes promised it could be.

The test of the Trump era is this: Will these United States go backward on a "Make America Great Again" journey that has everything to do with the word "again" and nothing to do with greatness? Or will they go forward with an honest and unencumbered recognition of the environmental, social and economic challenges of our time, and a bold and brave faith in our ability to meet them with the genius of science, the strength of humanity, the connectivity and liberating power of real democracy?

With his actions and his appointments, Trump has made it clear that he chooses to go backward. He intends for his to be the "again" presidency.

But it will not be Trump who makes the next America happen, just as it was not Jefferson or Lincoln or Roosevelt or Kennedy.

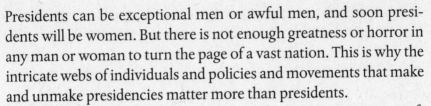

Presidents can be exceptional men or awful men, and soon presidents will be women. But there is not enough greatness or horror in any man or woman to turn the page of a vast nation. This is why the intricate webs of individuals and policies and movements that make and unmake presidencies matter more than presidents.

Pundits may choose to focus on presidents. Citizens cannot afford that luxury. When a moment raises questions of liberty versus autocracy, prosperity versus poverty, war versus peace, life versus death, citizens must tune out the gossip of campaigning and tune in on the essential issues of governing. This is only possible if they consider the whole of a presidency. Only an understanding of the whole of a presidency will allow them to determine whether to embrace or resist the possibility of an administration.

This is the essential leap—the one that took America from reverence for FDR to an embrace of a "New Deal," the one that extended from "all the way with LBJ" to a war on poverty and Medicare and Medicaid.

The men and women Trump chooses to surround himself with, and to empower, will determine the America that will emerge from his presidency. They will shape and implement the policies of this presidency. They will check and balance Trump's excesses, or they will steer this inexperienced and impulsive man toward precipices from which neither he, nor this nation, nor this world, can turn back. They will temper or incite Trump, fuel or still the cauldrons of racial and ethnic hatred and division. They will counsel against overreactions or they will make those overreactions inevitable, and incomprehensibly destructive.

But, for the most part, they will operate in the darkness of a media age when the major newspapers, broadcast networks and digital platforms are so absorbed with the pursuit of ratings and clicks that they refuse to put the spotlight on anyone but a "strongman" president.

Because the office of president has always been infused with a measure of majesty, and because it is afforded far more power than is enjoyed by the ceremonial presidents of most other lands, people in the United States and around the world have always struggled with the concept of an executive branch. They are attracted to the notion of an individualized, virtually monarchical executive—a soldier king making every decision, commanding every army, doling out every favor, collecting every emolument.

George Washington, the revolutionary commander whose countrymen encouraged him to serve as a king, struggled mightily to discourage such thinking. He accepted a system of checks and balances, distributed power to others and surrendered the mantle of authority willingly at the end of a second four-year term. With his democratically inclined secretary of state, Jefferson, he discouraged notions of an imperial presidency and counseled Americans to recognize themselves as sovereigns and their presidents as servants. In the early days of their republican experiment, Washington and Jefferson and their compatriots realized their visions with presidencies so small that they could be loaded up in stagecoaches and moved from city to city as the country sorted out the question of where it would locate its capitol. When it was decided that the District of Columbia would be the nation's center of government, the infrastructure of that government was so limited that Jefferson lodged in a rooming house on the night before his inauguration, walked on his own through muddy streets to the swearing-in ceremony, delivered a short unifying address and scrambled back to the rooming house in time for dinner.

Washington was an imperfect, yet serious man. Jefferson was an imperfect, yet visionary man. Trump is an imperfect man who is neither serious nor visionary.

"Only those Americans with no knowledge or who are self-deluded celebrate the start of the presidency of Donald John Trump, the most unqualified man ever to be elected to our highest office," wrote former White House counsel John Dean, our great philosopher of presidencies gone right and wrong, on the day of Trump's inauguration. "To wit: There is no evidence anywhere that Donald Trump has even a good newspaper or television news knowledge of the American presidency; nor is there any evidence he has ever read a single autobiography or biography of any of his forty-four

predecessors in our highest elected office. To the contrary, the evidence suggests he does not have sufficient concentration power to read a book, or even listen to an audio edition, not to mention receive an exhaustive briefing of the duties of his job."

With the exponential growth of the presidency in the twentieth and twenty-first centuries, the recognizable and defined executive branch of old has been transformed into something altogether foreign and exotic: an elaborate construct that historian Arthur Schlesinger Jr. began to identify the better part of a half century ago as the "imperial presidency." Constantly expanding, constantly extending itself, the presidency has become a labyrinth of intrigue and conflict, where even appointees who believe they are doing the bidding of the commander in chief may unwittingly take the nation in directions that the president did not intend. And it becomes a place where ideologues and con artists can, quite wittingly, launch initiatives about which the president knows little or nothing. That is more likely in the presidency of a Donald Trump than in those of his predecessors because Trump has the worst possible "experience" for the managing of a presidency: that of a reality TV–show star who has for decades played the role of a business executive. Corporate CEOs rarely if ever make a smooth transition from the private sphere to the public sphere; as the two most well-trained and experienced business executives ever to share the title of president, frequently failed oil executive George W. Bush and epically failed crony capitalist Dick Cheney, proved when they steered the United States into undeclared and disastrous wars and the worst economic meltdown since the Great Depression. But at least Bush and Cheney had familial and personal experience as governmental hangers-on. Trump has no such experience. He is, like the catastrophe that was Italian prime minister Silvio Berlusconi, a dilettante whose business career has never been much more than bad theater and whose governing experience is that of a grifter.

Berlusconi governed Italy from "the gut" as Trump says he will America. But Berlusconi governed in coalition, surrounded by a motley crew of partisans and ideologues and compromised souls who were at his service and at their own. The same is true of Trump.

This book groups the Trump circle into rough categories: ideological messengers, political hacks, military-industrial complex generals and dollar diplomats, and privateers and corporatists. Savvy readers will note that some of our subjects, like Steve Bannon or Sean Spicer, could have a place in more than one category. Savvier readers still will recognize that when a book is written at the opening of a presidency, some who were empowered initially will be disempowered eventually. Some who were on the scene at the start will disappear before the finish. Some who were nowhere near the corridors of power will suddenly appear in them. The full story of a presidency cannot be told until after it is finished. But a presidency can be understood, if explorers have a field guide. This book can be understood and embraced as such. More attention is paid to some lesser-known figures than to the celebrities among the newly empowered; that is because, ultimately, this book is more about power than personalities. There is a great deal of history in this book because history provides perspective, and perspective is what we need most of all in a moment so chaotic as this. And there is humor, because humor is required in a moment so daunting as this.

There is, as well, hope because this book is written in a period of resistance to an imperial and imperiling presidency. It proposes to strengthen that resistance by providing insight into the whole of the Trump enterprise. That fuller view, which extends beyond a president to examine a presidency, is essential. It is the wellspring of the popular authority that in a democratic republic can still check and balance the governing leviathan. James Madison, our imperfect and fretful, yet often visionary fourth president, was right in his prescription for America: "a people who mean to be their own Governors, must arm themselves with the power which knowledge gives."

—*John Nichols*, June 2017

Betsy DeVos and the Malice Domestic

AN INTRODUCTION TO THE TRUMPOCALYPSE

"Malice domestic" from time to time will come to you in the shape of those who would raise false issues, pervert facts, preach the gospel of hate, and minimize the importance of public action to secure human rights or spiritual ideals. There are those today who would sow these seeds, but your answer to them is in the possession of the plain facts of our present condition.

—PRESIDENT FRANKLIN DELANO ROOSEVELT, 1935

Even in America's post-truth moments, even in our ages of "alternative facts" and deliberate deception, the truth comes out. This is the eternal certainty, the promise across time that has sustained us in circumstances so dark as these. Franklin Roosevelt did not invent the notion of "malice domestic." He borrowed it from William Shakespeare, who recalled an ancient malice, and warned of those who might initially cloak their evil intentions in order to obtain authority over great nations. They might get away with it initially, but the damned spot is never washed away. As the wisdom tradition of the proverb writers assures us: "Their malice may be concealed by deception, but their wickedness will be exposed in the assembly." So it was that, in the transition period from the America that was to the America of Donald Trump, Betsy DeVos was exposed not just as an unsettling example of the "malice domestic" as it manifests itself in our times but as the very embodiment of the fraud perpetrated by a "billionaire populist" as he built an administration of greedheads and grifters, climate-change deniers and fake-news presenters, white nationalists and religious zealots, full-on neocons and blank-stare ideologues.

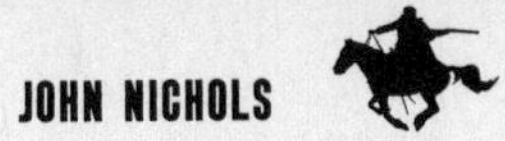

This book is not about Donald Trump, per se. This book is about Trumpism—the combination of propaganda and power, paranoia and plutocracy—that now grips America. Every "ism" needs a cadre of believers and buccaneers, and this book introduces you to the worst of the lot: the empowered elites of Donald Trump's inner circle who, by their actions and inactions, threaten to turn Trumpism into a Trumpocalypse for America and the world. This is the story of cabinet secretaries and assistants, commissioners and counselors, blood relatives and retainers, billionaire "advisors" and unindicted co-conspirators who make up a Trump administration that is absolutely unprepared "to form a more perfect Union, establish Justice, insure domestic Tranquility, provide for the common defense, promote the general Welfare, and secure the Blessings of Liberty to ourselves and our Posterity" but more than ready for a mission of provocation and plunder.

Despite his own ideological unsteadiness, Trump has surrounded himself with what Walter Dean Burnham, the great scholar of American political progress—and deterioration—refers to as "the most right-wing leadership cadre since Calvin Coolidge left the White House in 1929." The Trump administration is, Burnham warns us, a "wrecking crew" bent on reversing generations of American advancement, perhaps to a "primal date" in the Coolidge era. Hillary Clinton may have been injudicious in her 2016 campaign-trail consignment of Trump backers to a "basket of deplorables," but, surely, Trump's administration is a container so crammed with the contemptible that the very thought of exploring its contents can be overwhelming. Ignorance is no protection from this lot, however; they thrive on the confusion and exhaustion of good citizens and good chroniclers of our new condition. So we should appreciate moments of clarity.

Enter Donald Trump's designee to serve as secretary of education, the aforementioned Betsy DeVos, about whom Massachusetts senator Elizabeth Warren said: "It is hard to imagine a candidate less qualified or more dangerous." No less an authority than former president George Herbert Walker Bush's assistant secretary of education, Diane Ravitch, dismissed DeVos as "unqualified, unprepared, and unfit for the responsibility of running this important agency." The initial adjudicator of peril and possibility for the America experiment, George Washington, observed that education was so vital to the progress of a nation and its people that "without this foundation, every other means, in my opinion, must fail." So the fact that Betsy DeVos is an unmitigated and overarching fraud is a matter of considerable consequence. And the fact that DeVos was confirmed to serve as the head of so definitional a department, even after her fraudulence was revealed, tells Americans everything they need to know about the breakdown of the system of checks and balances that facilitates Trumpism. So it is only appropriate to point to DeVos as the best evidence of the broader crisis that began on January 20, 2017.

Like many of Trump's nominees and appointees, formal counselors and casual consiglieres, Betsy DeVos was an unknown entity to the vast majority of Americans when she was tapped for a cabinet post. Upon her nomination in November of 2016, a statement from the Trump transition team had the president-elect hailing the billionaire philanthropist as a "brilliant and passionate education advocate" who "will reform the U.S. education system and break the bureaucracy that is holding our children back so that we can deliver world-class education and school choice to all families." But that was just press-release happy talk from an administration that would soon affirm its determination to communicate "alternative facts." The truth is that Trump was so unfamiliar with his nominee to run an agency with a $70 billion budget, more than four thousand employees and responsibility for serving 50 million students in 16,900 school districts nationwide, along with 13 million post-secondary students, that, when he signed the paperwork nominating her for the cabinet post, the president looked around quizzically and asked: "Ah, Betsy. Education, right?" As it turns out, the only Trump administration insider who was more confused than the president about Betsy DeVos was Betsy DeVos.

In January 2017, at a hearing organized by the Senate Committee on Health, Education, Labor and Pensions, DeVos was supposed to make the case for her confirmation. Instead, she exposed herself. No, she did not have an education degree. No, she had never taught in a public school and nor had she administered one. No, she had not served on an elected school board. No, she had not sent her children to public schools. No, she had never applied for a student loan and nor had her children. But, yes, she did think that guns might have a place in public schools as a defense against grizzly bears. Asked about the basic measures of educational attainment, she struggled to distinguish between growth and proficiency in an exchange with Al Franken so agonizing that the senator from Minnesota felt it was necessary to speak very slowly and deliberately as he explained to the nominee for secretary of education that "this is a subject that has been debated in the education community for years." Toward the end of the many agonizing hours of questioning and attempts at answering on that January day, New Hampshire senator Maggie Hassan, the mother of a child with cerebral palsy, asked DeVos about programs and protections for students with disabilities.

DeVos, the nation's most urgent advocate of private-school voucher programs that educators and parents have identified as a particular threat to the educational prospects of children with disabilities, assured the senator that "I will be very sensitive to the needs of special needs students and the policies surrounding that." Yet, the nominee seemed to be unfamiliar with "the policies surrounding that" in general, and, more particularly, with the federal Individuals with Disabilities Education Act (IDEA).

"That's a federal civil rights law," Hassan explained to the flailing nominee. "So do you stand by your statement a few minutes ago that it should be up to the states whether to follow it?"

Grasping desperately for the most reassuring of the talking points she had been provided, DeVos replied: "Federal law must be followed where federal dollars are in play."

Hassan eyebrows rose. "So were you unaware, when I just asked you about the IDEA, that it was a federal law?" the senator asked. "I may have confused it," replied DeVos.

Americans who worry about maintaining the promise of public education for all students may at that point have been confused about how Betsy DeVos ended up in so embarrassing a circumstance, and about why anyone would think she was prepared to oversee education in America. Yes, DeVos had spent many decades and many dollars on campaigns to privatize and voucherize public education. But, as her Senate testimony revealed so glaringly and so egregiously, DeVos had not bothered, in all those years of self-promotional politicking, to familiarize herself with the essentials of the education system she proposed to "reform." How could someone who American Federation of Teachers president Randi Weingarten dismissed as a partisan automaton with "no meaningful experience in the classroom or in our schools" position herself to become "the most ideological, anti-public education nominee put forward since President Carter created a Cabinet-level Department of Education"?

The answer to that question came in the form of a question.

Vermont senator Bernie Sanders, who for years had warned of the danger that America was veering toward "of the rich, by the rich, for the rich" plutocracy, grilled DeVos on a host of issues, from school privatization to college costs. But he opened the discussion with an inquiry that resolved the mystery of DeVos's presence before the committee.

"Ms. DeVos," the senator began, "there is a growing fear in this country that we are moving toward what some would call an oligarchic form of society, where a small number of very wealthy billionaires control our economic and political life. Would you be so kind as to tell us how much your family has contributed to the Republican Party over the years?"

Resorting to the canned talking points that most of Trump's nominees used to avoid meaningful exchanges, DeVos responded: "Senator, first of all, thank you for that question. I was pleased to meet you in your office last week." Then she tried to dodge the question by saying: "I wish I could give you that number."

Sanders was having none of it. "I have heard the number was $200 million. Does that sound in the ballpark?"

DeVos gulped. "Collectively over my entire family," the billionaire campaign donor replied, "that is possible."

"My question is, and I don't mean to be rude, but," Sanders inquired, "do you think that if your family had not made hundreds of

thousands of dollars in contributions to the Republican Party that you would be sitting here today?"

A sheepish DeVos replied that "I do think there would be that possibility." But she could not muster energy for an argument that even she knew was comic. No one, not even Betsy DeVos, could have imagined, not for a minute, not even by the most remote possibility, that Betsy DeVos would be anywhere near a Senate hearing room, let alone the cabinet table, if she had not bought her way into the room.

That fact should have disqualified DeVos, as similar details should have disqualified the new president's nominees for the secretary of the treasury position once held by Alexander Hamilton, for the secretary of labor position once held by Frances Perkins, for the position of ambassador of the United States to the Court of St. James that was held in the last century by the likes of Averell Harriman and Joseph Kennedy (and in preceding centuries, and with the designation as "minister" or "envoy," by future presidents John Adams, James Monroe, John Quincy Adams, Martin Van Buren and James Buchanan). Unfortunately, neither DeVos nor her patrons were possessed of the sense of duty, or shame, necessary to derail the moneyed mandarins who were grasping for levers of power in the Trump interregnum. Sinecure after sinecure, position after position, was handed to this billionaire or that multimillionaire; those with fat wallets and fast pens were, again and again, assigned the power to define American policy by the man who had throughout his 2016 campaign dismissed recipients of big-money largesse as "puppets." In the first six weeks after his election, according to *Politico*, campaign donors accounted for "39 percent of the 119 people Trump reportedly considered for high-level government posts, and 38 percent of those he eventually picked." Trevor Potter, a lawyer who once advised Republican presidential nominee John McCain, suggested that Trump's penchant for picking major campaign donors for positions of major responsibility set up a disillusioning circumstance for "voters who voted for change and are going to end up with a plutocracy."

Unfortunately, aside from Bernie Sanders, members of the U.S. Senate often have trouble getting exercised about plutocracy. So it was that, on January 21, 2017, the Education Committee voted 12–11 to send the DeVos nomination to a full Senate where members of the Republican majority were prepared to rubberstamp another Trump nominee. There was no real system of checks and balances when it came to this president's picks, even when they were so manifestly inept and monumentally conflicted as Betsy DeVos. Despite the fact that many Republican senators positioned themselves as #NeverTrump men and women of principle during the bitter 2016 presidential race, those same senators fell in line behind nominees who had often donated not just to the Trump campaign but to the Republican Party that claimed their loyalty.

This is the nightmare scenario that James Madison feared when he envisioned the abandonment of the duties that extend from the swearing of an oath to "support and defend the Constitution of the United States against all enemies, foreign and domestic" by "a number of citizens, whether amounting to a minority or majority of the whole, who are united and actuated by some common impulse of passion, or of interest, adverse to the rights of other citizens, or to the permanent and aggregate interests of the community."

Madison, the designer of the drafting project that yielded the Constitution and an essential author of the Bill of Rights, was the most uneasy of the founders. Strikingly conscious of his own failings and those of his contemporaries, the man who would serve as the fifth secretary of state and fourth president of the new United States warned that "the essence of Government is power; and power, lodged as it must be in human hands, will ever be liable to abuse." He concerned himself with the dangers of militarism, observing that "of all the enemies to public liberty war is, perhaps, the most to be dreaded, because it comprises and develops the germ of every other." He worried about propaganda and how "all the means of seducing the minds" might be "added to those of subduing the force, of the people." He saw the threat of an imperial presidency, under which "the discretionary power of the Executive is extended; its influence in dealing out offices, honors, and emoluments is multiplied." Madison fretted about the "unequal distribution of property," about the

mingling of religion and government to establish a state church ("in no instance have they been seen the guardians of the liberties of the people") and, as a Virginia plantation owner, about the original sin of the American experiment (admitting, albeit too quietly and too late, that slavery was "the great evil under which the nation labors").

No member of the founding circle understood the weaknesses and vulnerabilities of the American experiment so well as Madison. It was for that reason that he advocated so ardently for a system of checks and balances that might serve as the "great security against a gradual concentration of the several powers." Today, Madison's fear of factions is often seen as the overly idealistic affectation of a man from another time; as the resistance of a romantic to the inevitable development of American variations on the British Tories and Whigs. But Madison was no romantic and nor was he a rigid nonpartisan; in fact, he was the essential lieutenant to Thomas Jefferson in his fellow Virginian's wrangling with Alexander Hamilton and in Jefferson's 1800 challenge to John Adams. Madison was a realist. He accepted the prospect of parties. But he was terrified by the prospect of excesses of partisanship as they might manifest themselves in a distant time when "the accumulation of all powers, Legislative, Executive, and Judiciary, in the same hands, whether of one, a few, or many, and whether hereditary, self-appointed, or elective, may justly be pronounced the very definition of tyranny."

Donald Trump is one man. A powerful man, to be sure, but still one man. He can only govern with the collaboration of other men and women, like Betsy DeVos. And, in the American system, he could not have established that collaboration at its highest and meaningful level without the acquiescence of Republicans in the U.S. Senate. Unfortunately, they did acquiesce. Even after they had watched Betsy DeVos melt down, and in full knowledge of the fact that her only "qualification" was her wealth, a sufficient number of Republicans (with an assist from Vice President Mike Pence) decided to give the woman who "may have confused it" control over education policy and practice in the United States.

Something is broken in America. The structures that were meant to protect and preserve the republic have been undermined. The

American experiment has been rendered vulnerable by the excesses of partisanship that manifest themselves not just in Trumpism but in the acquiescence to Trumpism by congressional charlatans who have traded away their consciences in order to align themselves with an unconscionable president who, in the words of the *Economist* during the 2016 campaign, "has prospered by inciting hatred and violence." The magazine described Trump as a man "so unpredictable that the thought of him anywhere near high office is terrifying." Most Americans agreed. Fifty-four percent of them voted for someone other than Donald Trump for the presidency. But an archaic system that allows the loser of the popular vote to be the winner of the Electoral College allowed the terrifying prospect of a Trump presidency to be realized.

To avert the greater terror that might extend from this presidency, Americans must move from the lesser fear of a man to a greater understanding of an administration where the high stations of influence are occupied not just by a Donald Trump and a Mike Pence, but by a Steve Bannon and a Jeff Sessions, by a Rex Tillerson and a Betsy DeVos. Fear can weaken people or strengthen their resolve, it can overwhelm or it can provide clarity, it can define us or define our determination to take our country back.

There is malice to be found in any survey of Trumpism. Democrats and Republicans, liberals and conservatives, have confirmed and condemned the threats that have arisen since Donald Trump assumed the presidency. But if history is our guide and guardian, then we know that exposing the malice, and examining how prominent (and not so prominent) members of this administration manifest it, is the key to averting catastrophe and restoring that measure of sanity that might steer the ship of state back toward a true course. Trump and the mandarins who conspire to do his bidding have seized the levers of power. But they have not pulled their grip tight enough to strangle America's promise. If it is our purpose to dislodge them before too much damage is done, then our answer to them is found, as FDR suggested, "in the possession of the plain facts of our present condition." If we separate ourselves from the frenzy of the moment, we are reminded, again and again, that this is the

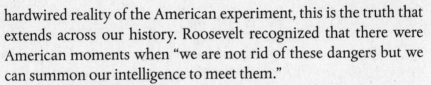

hardwired reality of the American experiment, this is the truth that extends across our history. Roosevelt recognized that there were American moments when "we are not rid of these dangers but we can summon our intelligence to meet them."

This is such a moment. Our charge, as in the past, is to arm ourselves with the simple facts of the Trump presidency. To use these facts to address the malice domestic. To avert the Trumpocalypse.

PART 1

Wicked Messengers

The American fascist would prefer not to use violence. His method is to poison the channels of public information. With a fascist the problem is never how best to present the truth to the public but how best to use the news to deceive the public into giving the fascist and his group more money or more power.

—VICE PRESIDENT HENRY WALLACE, 1944

The American presidency has never been at the whims of an authoritarian personality like Donald Trump. He is going to test our democracy as it has never been tested.

—JOHN DEAN, 2017

Donald Trump claims that he was elected with "a massive landslide victory," that he prevailed with "one of the biggest Electoral College victories in history," that his Democratic rivals "suffered one of the greatest defeats in the history of politics in this country."

House Speaker Paul Ryan says Trump "earned a mandate" for a "go big, go bold" agenda, while Trump "counselor" Kellyanne Conway does not just claim a mandate but gripes that critics of the billionaire are "attempting to foment a permanent opposition that is corrosive to our constitutional democracy."

"The left is trying to delegitimize his election," cries Conway. "They're trying to deny him what he just earned." Now, that's disciplined messaging.

So disciplined that Trump appears to believe it. When he was corrected on his electoral math by NBC reporter Peter Alexander during the first press conference of his presidency, Trump seemed

genuinely surprised. "Well I don't know, I was given that information. Actually I've seen that information around," Trump said. "But it was a very substantial victory, do you agree with that?"

Alexander was gracious. "You're the president," he said.

Trump should not have been surprised. The facts of this president's electoral malaise have, since November, been as plain as numbers on paper. Trump received 2.8 million fewer votes than his Democratic rival. He secured just 46.1 percent of the popular vote, a significantly lower percentage than "loser" Mitt Romney won in 2012. Only a narrow Electoral College advantage, based on razor-thin margins in a handful of states—Michigan, Pennsylvania, Wisconsin—made Trump the president.

But even if Trump's ego can't be wrapped around reality, his aides and allies know the truth they are up against. Ryan is a political careerist with more than a quarter century of in-the-trenches experience on Capitol Hill. Conway is not just a political animal; she's been a pollster and partisan pundit for two decades. These people know Donald Trump did not earn a mandate from the voters. They know that questions about his dubious legitimacy are rooted in entirely legitimate concerns about a mangled election that was narrowly decided after a race characterized by voter suppression, hacking and charges of manipulation from abroad.

Yet Trump's team stays on message. He won. He won big. He has the support of the American people. "Period!"

That's what White House press secretary Sean Spicer says when he wants to end a line of questioning that is about to get interesting. Spicer says "period" a lot with regard to the president's alleged "mandate." But the press secretary always spices his claim with something more than talk of election numbers. When he's challenged on some new policy move that's clearly unpopular, Spicer says something like, "I get what the press wants, but the American people have understood exactly what they're getting and they voted overwhelmingly for him. He has been very clear about what he owns, the role of his family and everything else since he announced that he was running for president, and they overwhelmingly elected him with all of that on the table."

White House chief strategist Steve Bannon does the same thing. Bannon claims with his very straight face that Trump, the former "New York values" donor to Democratic campaigns who talked up single-payer health care and infrastructure spending as he was winning over the Republican base, the thrice-married playboy who made himself the champion of evangelical Christianity, the billionaire son of privilege who claimed to be taking on the elites and then stuffed his cabinet with Goldman Sachs alumni, is . . . consistent. Bannon tells us that Trump's rambling campaign speeches were packed with "a tremendous amount of content" and that Trump "laid out an agenda with those speeches" and that he won a mandate to get that agenda "executed."

Bannon also claims that Trump is "probably the greatest public speaker in those large arenas since William Jennings Bryan." Bannon knows that is a ridiculous statement. But Bannon does not care. His purpose is not to get the history right. His purpose is to rewrite history in order to perpetuate the fantasy that Trump is making America great again.

What Americans witnessed in the first months of the Trump presidency was a classic bait and switch. Trump ran an erratic, chaotic, at times incoherent campaign that was consistent only in its appeals to the base instincts of a minority of Americans: xenophobia, sexism, racism and generalized fear of the future. As Evan McMullin, the former Central Intelligence (CIA) operations officer and Republican congressional aide who mounted an honorable if quixotic independent conservative presidential bid in 2016, explains it, Trump's campaign message was a toxic brew of authoritarian schemes that often disrespected democracy itself. "He had questioned judicial independence, threatened the freedom of the press, called for violating Muslims' equal protection under the law, promised the use of torture and attacked Americans based on their gender, race and religion," argues McMullin. "He had also undermined critical democratic norms including peaceful debate and transitions of power, commitment to truth, freedom from foreign interference and abstention from the use of executive power for political retribution."

All true. And Bannon, who is at once very smart and very calculating, knows this. He understands how very at odds the Trump presidency is with the American experiment. That is why he is so desperate to cloak it in the "legitimacy" of history and the false claim of consistency. Bannon, the Breitbart News boss who proudly announced that he made the incendiary conservative website into a "platform for the alt-right," and used that platform to inform and inflame Trump's candidacy even before assuming his successive roles as "campaign CEO" and "chief strategist," did much to insert authoritarian politics into the campaign. And he still does with his aggressive reference to a free and independent press as "the enemy." Yet, for public consumption, Bannon claims that Trump was elected on an agenda that involves whatever program Trump happens to be advancing on any given day.

This is wicked messaging. It reverses every equation and claims that a president who was elected to "take on the elites" is carrying out his campaign promises when he packs his cabinet with billionaires, bankers and lobbyists. It seeks to distract us from the fact that the president who patted himself on the back for recognizing the mistakes made in the Iraq War has begun his tenure by sending more troops to the Middle East, launching unauthorized bombing missions against Syria and generally dismissing the Congress as he inflames tensions around the world. It tells us that there is nothing wrong with a president who is supposed to be on the side of working people gutting the Department of Labor, and a president who promised to provide more and better health care pushing an agenda that would leave tens of millions of Americans without insurance.

This is the big lie, as told and told again by the Trump team. When it comes from Trump, himself, it is merely a mask for his own inexperience and insecurity. As former Nixon White House aide John Dean warns with regard to this president: "Not only does he not understand the job, he has been pushed to the hard right during the transition because he is a man with no firm political beliefs of his own." But those who work with Trump have beliefs. And among the messengers, spokespeople and strategists he has surrounded himself with and empowered, there is a great desire to advance those beliefs—to make of Trumpism something that extends less from Trump than from themselves. People like Steve Bannon and Kellyanne Conway realized early on that "Trump was an empty vessel into which they deposited ideas, which explains how some of his conflicting stances developed," notes Dean. And he adds: "Bannon and Conway are fronts for billionaire hedge fund operator Robert Mercer and his daughter Rebekah, who have strong beliefs."

"Trump's authoritarian personality is," John Dean warns, "very troubling." The authoritarian tendencies of the wicked messengers who have surrounded Trump are even more troubling. And the combination gives Dean nightmares because, he explains: "Authoritarianism does not work well in a democracy."

—1—

THE INVESTORS

Robert and Rebekah Mercer

A month after the November 2016 election, the people who had guided that year's campaign to the most unlikely of finishes—the finish they desired—gathered to celebrate at Owl's Nest, the sprawling estate on Long Island's North Shore where billionaire Robert Mercer makes his home. The "Heroes and Villains" costume party invited guests to appear as favorite film stars. But Kellyanne Conway, who would be taking a break from the presidential transition to attend as Supergirl, said: "I predict there will be an abundance of Hillary and Trump finery. We can't get enough of this victory."

The best Trump "costume" was not a costume at all. President-elect Trump arrived as himself to personally thank Mercer (who dressed as the hypnotic Mandrake the Magician) and his middle daughter, Rebekah (who wore a Black Widow costume), for "bringing some organization" to his campaign. It was a surprise appearance. When the man who was perhaps even himself surprised with his victory entered the lavish estate, the crowd chanted: "Trump won! Trump won!" But, of course, Trump was not the only winner in the room. One guest told the *New Yorker*: "I was looking around the room, and I thought, No doubt about it—the people whom the Mercers invested in, my comrades, are now in charge."

The funny thing was that Robert Mercer had not even wanted this president, at least not at first. His chosen contender in the 2016 Republican presidential race, the man who had attended the previous year's World War II–themed bash at the Mercer mansion in Winston Churchill drag, was Texas senator Ted Cruz.

"Robert Mercer hasn't invested in Donald Trump because he believes in Trump's campaign platform. He preferred Ted Cruz during the campaign, and Ted Cruz was clearly no fan of Donald Trump. Looking at Mercer's historical political giving patterns, Cruz is far more aligned with Mercer's worldview than is Trump," explained David Magerman, an employee of Renaissance Technologies, the investment management firm (currently managing $36 billion) where Robert Mercer serves as co-CEO. "So, what did Mercer's investment in Trump amount to? He was effectively buying shares in the candidate, and Robert Mercer now owns a sizeable share of the United States Presidency."

Trump's appearance at the party confirmed his appreciation of the investment by the Mercers, who backed his candidacy when many of the other billionaire masters of the GOP universe, including brothers David and Charles Koch, kept the obnoxious reality-TV star at arm's length. Another confirmation came when Rebekah Mercer got a place on the sixteen-member executive committee in Trump's transition team. But the real measure came when, at the party, Trump named the people the Mercers had assigned to his campaign: Kellyanne Conway, Steve Bannon and David Bossie, the president of Citizens United (yes, that Citizens United) and former deputy campaign manager for Trump's campaign.

As David Magerman explained: "Stephen Bannon came from Breitbart News, of which Mercer owns a significant percentage, and Kellyanne Conway came from Mercer's circle of political foundations. And, of course, Mercer's daughter Rebekah represents his interests and his worldview with her presence on the transition committee and her close relationship with Bannon and Conway. Mercer also has insisted that Trump use his company Cambridge Analytica, which uses its statistical models of voter psychology to get unpopular initiatives (like electing Donald Trump) through the electorate." The bottom line is undebatable: The Mercers have surrounded our president with his people, and his people have an outsized influence over the running of our country, simply because the Mercers paid for seats at that table.

The Mercers paid so much for so many seats that they may have run afoul of campaign-finance law. The Campaign Legal Center alleges that the Mercer-funded "Make America Number One" super

 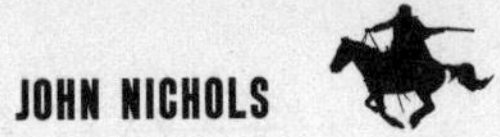

PAC illegally compensated Steve Bannon's work as Donald Trump's campaign CEO. "The evidence suggests a Mercer-backed super PAC secretly subsidized Steve Bannon's work for the Trump campaign by funneling $280,000 in payments to a firm described as a 'front' for Bannon," says Brendan Fischer, associate counsel at the Campaign Legal Center. "Once Bannon was taken on as CEO of Trump's campaign and continued to be paid by Mercer's entities, this became an issue," said Larry Noble, general counsel at the Campaign Legal Center. "It is especially concerning now that Bannon is White House chief strategist. Bannon's compensation shows the pervasive influence of the Mercer family of donors in the Trump orbit."

Pervasive influence? Yes, says John Dean, who knows a thing or two about how White Houses operate.

"The Mercer agenda is radical right-wing," argued the former Nixon counsel who has decried the GOP's lurch toward far-right authoritarianism. "It is not difficult to trace Donald Trump's sudden turn to the hard-right, which occurred during his transition. Rebekah Mercer is a direct link to the Heritage Foundation, the Koch brothers, Betsy DeVos and her family's foundation, along with countless other conservative causes. The Mercers' fingerprints can probably be found on nominations who want to abolish departments and agencies like EPA, the SEC, Department of Energy, Department of Housing, and the like. Because Trump has no strong feelings about any of these matters, and he needed all the help he could get during the transition, he has given those who came to his assistance at the end of his campaign to help him win a free hand in organizing his administration."

So why doesn't everyone in America know everything about Robert Mercer? And Rebekah Mercer? Why aren't they cues to start booing at Democratic rallies, like the Koch brothers? Or punch lines for politically inclined comics, like Sheldon Adelson? It is not that they don't have the kooky views that are required of right-wing billionaire campaign donors. When Steve Bannon starts raging about the "deconstruction of the regulatory state," he is in perfect harmony with Robert Mercer, a brilliant computer programmer who shares the Ayn Rand–influenced libertarian leanings of many in his field. It makes sense that Mercer and Bannon are singing in harmony. Bannon has worked for Mercer for years, as a paid political advisor and manager of a network of operations that now includes the West Wing of the Trump White House and various cabinet agencies. The concession is so extensive, and Bannon's managerial role is so consequential, that, when the strategist was supposedly frustrated with White House palace intrigues in early April, *Politico* reported that "Republican megadonor Rebekah Mercer, a longtime Bannon confidante who became a prominent Trump supporter during the campaign, urged Bannon not to resign. 'Rebekah Mercer prevailed upon him to stay,' said one person familiar with the situation."

The Mercers are owners of Breitbart, and major investors in Bannon projects such as the Government Accountability Institute and the Glittering Steel film production company. And it is from those investments that their influence extends. It is true that the Mercers donate money to Republican candidates and campaigns (more than $40 million over the past decade), but that's just hobby giving—and not always so successful, as was seen with the $10 million they invested in the Kellyanne Conway–run super PAC that was supposed to elect Cruz. But what makes them matter is the money they give to shape the issues that Republican candidates and campaigns, as well as the media and a lot of voters, end up talking about. "The Mercers' approach is far different from that of other big donors. While better-known players such as the Koch brothers on the right and George Soros on the left focus on mobilizing activists and voters, the Mercers have exerted pressure on the political system by helping erect an alternative media ecosystem, whose storylines dominated the 2016 race," wrote Matea Gold in a profile of the family for the *Washington Post*. "Their alliance with Bannon provided fuel for the narrative that drove Trump's victory: that dangerous immigrants are ruining the country and corrupt power brokers are sabotaging Washington."

Yes, it is absurd that billionaires with a $75 million luxury yacht called the *Sea Owl* (which *Newsweek* says "has a crew of 18, fingerprint-recognition keypads, a self-playing Steinway baby grand piano and a mural of a tree, carved from Peruvian mahogany, that spans

several flights of stairs"), a private-pistol range in the North Shore mansion (and a firearms company to provide weaponry if needed), a $2.7 million model-train set in Robert Mercer's basement and all the other arguments for more taxation of the rich imagine themselves fighting the elites. It is almost as absurd as adults dressing up as Mandrake the Magician and the Black Widow and Supergirl and Donald Trump for a costume party in the middle of a presidential transition that was not going very well.

But rich people can do that. And the Mercers are just getting started. Their associates say they've got a "Silicon Valley" view of politics that throws money around "to test various tactics to see which is most effective." It doesn't have to work every time. It can even be a little messy; maybe they didn't get a Ted Cruz. But they got a Donald Trump.

A president's a president after all, and when he puts your employees in the Oval Office and shows up for your costume parties, well, you've won.

—2—

THE JACKSONIAN DEMOCRAT

Stephen Bannon

White House Senior Strategist

Steve Bannon reads history. A lot of it. Bannon is of an age where he is more likely to be found with a book under his arm than one of the electronic screens into which his operations fed so much fake news before, during and after the 2016 presidential campaign. The former naval officer, special assistant to the chief of naval operations at the Pentagon, Harvard Business School graduate, Goldman Sachs investment banker, Hollywood mogul, new-media entrepreneur, right-wing propagandist, political Svengali and alt-president regularly reads his way into places no one ever expected to find him. Then, as the smartest person in the room, he rewrites the rules to make history of his own.

For most of his long career as a corporate, entertainment and political provocateur, Bannon has accomplished his literary and personal shape-shifting without being noticed by the people he does not want to notice him. He likes to be underestimated. "Darkness is good," says Bannon. "Dick Cheney. Darth Vader. Satan. That's power. It only helps us when they [the enemies] get it wrong. When they're blind to who we are and what we're doing."

Bannon's remarkable intellectual and organizational skills, and his sly strategies, were always too bold to be understood by the tired mandarins who minded the infrastructure of a money-and-media industrial complex that was designed to maintain the elite status quo of the twentieth century into the twenty-first. The actual elites had little to fear from Bannon, who had spent a lifetime in their service and now proposed to cut their taxes and end the regulation of their business empires. But the bureaucrats, the managers,

the commentators, the pundits, the consultants, the congressmen, the senators, the presidential candidates who for decades had made a nice living serving those elites had no idea what to make of the guy who proposed to kick them off the political playing field. So they ignored him, or ridiculed him, or condemned him. Bannon was embraced only by those desperate pretenders—fringe-hugging ideologues, socially awkward hedge fund managers, seemingly unelectable presidential candidates—who were willing to front for a modern Machiavelli who had no concern with titles, but a great interest in positioning himself as the new power behind the throne.

During the 2016 campaign, many commentators imagined that it was all a game for Bannon, and for Trump. This was the theory that launched a thousand speculative pieces by media writers who imagined that the haphazard race they ran after their billionaire mentors Robert and Rebekah Mercer put them together with Kellyanne Conway was part of some grand scheme by Bannon to jumpstart an alt-right challenger to Rupert Murdoch's flailing Fox News network. But Bannon had already done that when he took over the late Andrew Breitbart's bad-boy website and made it an even more politically incorrect battering ram—the online crazy uncle that told conservatives they should embrace their worst impulses and demanded that the Republican Party become precisely what it had been formed by Abraham Lincoln and John Fremont to oppose. Bannon, who burns through careers like smokers burn through cigarettes, was saying in 2014 that "quite frankly, we have a bigger global reach than even Fox." He was finished with media manipulation and ideological disputation. He was ready to take charge. And Trump was his ticket.

Impossible? Hardly. Bannon knew his history.

"I am Thomas Cromwell in the court of the Tudors," Bannon gleefully announced when writer Michael Wolff came to visit him at Trump Tower after the election. That was a telling reference, indeed, not merely to King Henry VIII's conniving chief minister but to the historical revisionism that since the 1950s, with the encouragement of conservative historian Geoffrey Elton and the BBC docudrama team, has reimagined Cromwell's conspiratorial power grabbing as a revolutionary grand plan for remaking the British monarchy. A conservative propagandist with "traditionalist" tendencies like Bannon would of course be attracted to the Cromwell myth, except of course for the part where Henry sours on Anne of Cleves and has Cromwell executed for treason and heresy.

An even more telling historical reference came a few weeks later, however, following what has come to be known as Trump's "American Carnage" inaugural address in January 2017. While listeners were visibly shaken by what University of Michigan professor Juan Cole described as "a chain of falsehoods, saber-rattling and scary neo-fascist uber-nationalism," Bannon was thrilled with the speech he had crafted with "you will obey" Trump loyalist Stephen Miller. The newly empowered White House "chief strategist" told the *Washington Post*'s Robert Costa that Trump's address was "an unvarnished declaration of the basic principles of his populist and kind of nationalist movement. It was given, I think, in a very powerful way. I don't think we've had a speech like that since Andrew Jackson came to the White House. But you could see it was very Jacksonian."

Bannon was not just engaging in the presidential name-dropping that is common on inaugural days when new presidents and their aides attempt to associate their projects with the legacies of predecessors. He was advancing a long-term project to make Trump Jacksonian. During the Trump transition, a senior aide to the president-elect told the *Daily Beast* that Bannon would "encourage [Trump] to play up the comparison" and push the theory that "Trump's campaign and message was a clear descendant of Jacksonian populism and anti-political elitism." Bannon, the aide said, "is why Trump keeps equating himself with Andrew Jackson."

Bannon and Miller have even, aides say, prepared Jacksonian reading lists for Trump. Unfortunately, by every account, Trump is having trouble keeping up. When Fox's Tucker Carlson asked what he was reading in early March, the president replied: "Well, you know, I love to read. Actually, I'm looking at a book, I'm reading a book, I'm trying to get started. Every time I do about a half a page, I get a phone call that there's some emergency, this or that. But we're going to see the home of Andrew Jackson today in Tennessee and I'm reading a book on Andrew Jackson. I love to read. I don't get to read very much, Tucker, because I'm working very hard on lots of different things, including getting costs down. The costs of our country are out of control. But we have a lot of great things happening, we have a lot of tremendous things happening." Trump's inability to focus on those Jackson biographies was confirmed in early May, when a Sirius XM radio interview revealed Trump ruminating about how, "had Andrew Jackson been a little later, you wouldn't have had the Civil War. He was a very tough person, but he had a big heart. He was really angry that he saw what was happening with regard to the Civil War. He said, 'There's no reason for this.' People don't realize, you know, the Civil War—if you think about it, why? People don't ask that question, but why was there a Civil War? Why could that one not have been worked out?" Jackson was a slaveholder who dispersed the abolitionist movement during his presidency, left the White House almost a quarter century before the Civil War began and died more than fifteen years before the first shots were fired.

So much for Trump the historian.

On the "Trump's so Jacksonian" project, like so many others, it still falls to Bannon to fill in the blanks, as he has done since even before he formally signed on with the Trump campaign. "A year before Bannon joined Trump's campaign staff, he described himself in the email as Trump's de-facto 'campaign manager,' because of the positive coverage that Breitbart was giving Trump. That coverage had largely been underwritten by the Mercers," noted a March 2017 Jane Mayer profile of Robert Mercer in the *New Yorker* titled "The Reclusive Hedge-Fund Manager Behind the Trump Presidency: How Robert Mercer exploited America's populist insurgency." In addition to providing "a public forum for previously shunned white-nationalist, sexist, and racist voices," noted Mayer, "Breitbart enabled Bannon to promote anti-establishment politicians whom the mainstream media dismissed, including Trump." Trump, in turn, learned the politics of anti-Obama "birtherism," immigration scaremongering and, above all, Muslim-bashing from Bannon's alt-right website.

Now that Trump is president, Bannon is teaching him what kind of president he should be. It's a troublesome process. Much has been made of Bannon's fascination with European neofascists and actual fascists, from the Italian philosopher Julius Evola, who thought Mussolini was soft but respected the style of German Nazis like SS head Heinrich Himmler, to French anti-Semitic author Jean Raspail, whose book *The Camp of the Saints* has been compared to Adolf Hitler's *Mein Kampf*. Then there's Bannon's own 2014 speech to a conservative Christian conference at the Vatican, where he mentioned Evola, decried "the immense secularization of the West," declared that "we're at the very beginning stages of a very brutal and bloody conflict" and announced that "we are in an outright war against jihadists, Islam, Islamic fascism." Those comments, when reexamined after Trump assumed the presidency, inspired headlines like "President Trump's right-hand man Steve Bannon called for Christian holy war: Now he's on the National Security Council." (Bannon was eventually edged out of a formal National Security Council role, though not necessarily out of the orbit, as photos from the Situation Room at the time of the early-April Syrian bombing mission revealed.) Conservative pundit Glenn Beck, who calls Bannon "quite possibly the most dangerous guy in all of American politics," compares the White House insider with Joseph Goebbels. John McCain's veteran aide, John Weaver, says: "The racist, fascist extreme right is represented footsteps from the Oval Office."

But the foreign ideological influences aren't the only troubling ones. So, too, are the grabs for shards from America's past, especially those that remain from when it has veered in racist, nativist and crudely nationalist directions.

The fact that Bannon is drawn to Andrew Jackson, of all presidents, ought to rattle Americans. There's a reason why millions of Americans were thrilled with the 2016 announcement that Harriet Tubman would bump Jackson from the front of the $20 bill. *Indian Country Today* recognized the 250th anniversary of the seventh president's birth with an article entitled "Indian-Killer Andrew Jackson Deserves Top Spot on List of Worst U.S. Presidents" and recalled that "in 1830, a year after he became president, Jackson signed a law that he had proposed—the Indian Removal Act—which legalized ethnic cleansing. Within seven years 46,000 indigenous people were removed from their homelands east of the Mississippi. Their removal

gave 25 million acres of land 'to white settlement and to slavery,' according to PBS. The area was home to the Cherokee, Creek, Choctaw, Chickasaw and Seminole nations. In the Trail of Tears alone, 4,000 Cherokee people died of cold, hunger, and disease on their way to the western lands."

Describing Jackson as "a disaster of a human being on every possible level," Vox's Dylan Matthews correctly noted that, in addition to "Jackson's role in American Indian removal—the forced, bloody transfer of tens of thousands of Native Americans from the South," Jackson "owned hundreds of slaves, and in 1835 worked with his postmaster general to censor anti-slavery mailings from northern abolitionists" and that "Jackson's small-government fetishism and crank monetary policy views stunted the attempts of better leaders like John Quincy Adams to invest in American infrastructure, and led to the Panic of 1837, a financial crisis that touched off a recession lasting seven years."

Jackson has his defenders, like Andrew Jackson Foundation CEO Howard Kittell, who told *USA Today* that "we need to remember our history, and history is messy." True. But John Quincy Adams, Jackson's predecessor, opposed the expansion of slavery and showed respect for native peoples, so it's fair to say that Jackson made things messy. And he did so with populist appeals that divided people against one another, attacked the free press, disregarded sound economic and scientific ideas, undermined the courts and diminished rather that strengthened democratic progress.

Donald Trump, who gripes about taking Jackson's image off the $20, knows only the bare essentials of the Jackson story. But when he appeared at the Hermitage to honor the anniversary of Jackson's birth in March 2017, the forty-fifth president was thrilled to make comparisons. Declaring that "he reclaimed the people's government from an emerging aristocracy," Trump said: "Jackson's victory shook the establishment like an earthquake. Henry Clay, Secretary of State for the defeated President John Quincy Adams, called Jackson's victory 'mortifying and sickening.' Oh, boy, does this sound familiar. Have we heard this?"

Trump argued that "the political class in Washington had good reason to fear Jackson's great triumph. 'The rich and powerful,' Jackson said, 'too often bend the acts of government to their selfish purposes.' Jackson warned they had turned government into an 'engine for the support of the few at the expense of the many.'"

Trump's speech in Tennessee highlighted the extent to which his inaugural address, as penned by Bannon and Miller, echoed Jackson's rhetoric. And how much the current president has, with prodding from Bannon (who helped to hang a Jackson portrait in the Oval Office), come to identify with his distant predecessor.

As the crowd laughed along with him, Trump mocked historical claims that Jackson's election, like his own, was a "calamity." But the thing is that, for millions of Americans, Jackson's presidency was a great calamity that spread slavery, undermined abolitionism, displaced Native Americans, destroyed lives and created financial ruin. Jackson, who lost his initial run for the presidency in 1824, committed many of his most lawless and destructive acts for reasons of politics: to sustain a populist movement that supported him as a champion of a minority—angry white men who could vote—over a majority made up of women, African Americans, Native Americans and others who were denied the franchise.

Steve Bannon, Trump's Jackson whisperer, does not speak of the dark side of "Jacksonian democracy." But he does speak, a lot, about building a Jacksonian movement in contemporary America. "Like Jackson's populism, we're going to build an entirely new political movement," he says, describing the rough mix of tax breaks and infrastructure-job promises that he thinks will work. Maybe. "We're just going to throw it up against the wall and see if it sticks," says the strategist. "It will be as exciting as the 1930s, greater than the Reagan revolution—conservatives, plus populists, in an economic nationalist movement."

What made the 1930s exciting was the determination of Franklin Delano Roosevelt and his "New Deal" administration to take on the plutocrats in order to make work for everyone, build out a social-welfare system and develop a regulatory state to protect those who

were most in need and most vulnerable. Bannon proposes the opposite with a narrower vision of "economic nationalism," promises to "let our sovereignty come back to ourselves," an apocalyptic vision of the threats facing the United States, visceral disdain for the "corporatist, globalist media" that he says really is "the enemy" and visceral excitement about "the deconstruction of the administrative state."

Steve Bannon's vision harkens back to the Democratic Party of the thirties. But it is not the 1930s and the Democratic Party of Franklin Roosevelt. It is the 1830s and the Democratic Party of Andrew Jackson.

—3—

THE SPINSTER

Kellyanne Conway

White House Counselor

Donald Trump was in trouble. It was a little over a month from election day and the *Access Hollywood* tape had finally gotten out. The *Washington Post* headline read: "Trump recorded having extremely lewd conversation about women in 2005." Actually, "extremely lewd" was putting it mildly. Here was actual tape of the Republican nominee for president of the United States, speaking as a fifty-nine-year-old married man about his techniques for "moving on" women other than his wife ("I moved on her like a bitch . . ." "I did try and fuck her. She was married . . ." "Grab 'em by the pussy . . .") The New York playboy who was trying desperately to reposition himself as a conservative-values candidate had gotten caught explaining in a hot-mic conversation that as a wealthy reality-TV star in America "you can do anything" to women.

It didn't help that the *Huffington Post* did the math and reported that "Donald Trump Made Lewd Comments While Melania Was Pregnant."

For top Republicans who had grudgingly gotten on board the Trump train, this looked like the last stop. Arizona senator John McCain said he could no longer support Trump, as did dozens of other top Republicans. House Speaker Paul Ryan said he could no longer defend Trump. Republican vice presidential nominee Mike Pence went into hiding and then finally announced that "as a husband and father, I was offended by the words and actions described by Donald Trump in the eleven-year-old video released yesterday. I do not condone his remarks and cannot defend them." Pence said he was praying for Trump. Former Utah governor Jon Huntsman summed up sentiments inside the party rather well when he said: "In a campaign cycle that has been nothing but a race to the bottom—at such a critical moment for our nation—and with so many who have tried to be respectful of a record primary vote, the time has come for Governor Pence to lead the ticket." (As punishment for this apostasy, President Trump would later name Huntsman to the most unenviable position in his administration: ambassador to Russia.)

It seemed that Trump was finished. If he did not drop out, he would lose—horribly, devastatingly, overwhelmingly—to Hillary Clinton in an election finish that pundits predicted could doom Trump-aligned Republicans nationwide.

Then came Kellyanne Conway.

Conway was Trump's campaign manager, and as such she was supposed to defend the guy. But she was also, as she often mentioned in TV interviews, the happily married mother of four young children. She had made her name as an up-and-coming pundit by ripping on Bill Clinton's scandalous behavior with White House intern Monica Lewinsky, to such an extent that the *Washington Post* explained her rise as a conservative commentator as a side effect of the Republican attempt to impeach Clinton. "Then Monica happened," explained the *Post*. "The Clinton-Lewinsky scandal created full employment for pundits of all stripes, with particular visibility to a subset of young, female conservatives—Ann Coulter, Laura Ingraham, Barbara Olson, Kellyanne Fitzpatrick (soon to be Conway). The 'pundettes,' as they came to be known, filled a market need: a telegenic group of anti-Clinton women."

Kellyanne's future husband, George T. Conway III, established a reputation, of sorts, as a conservative lawyer who hounded Bill Clinton. "When Paula Jones sued Bill Clinton for sexual harassment, [George] Conway wrote the Supreme Court brief, though his name never appeared on it," noted a *New Yorker* reflection on George, who aligned himself with the conservative Federalist Society that targeted the Clinton administration. "The Court, in a landmark decision, agreed with Jones's argument that a sitting President could face a civil lawsuit. During depositions in the lawsuit, Clinton denied having a sexual relationship with Monica Lewinsky, which eventually led to his impeachment trial. George Conway became deeply involved in getting out information from the depositions. During that period, he reportedly emailed Matt Drudge an infamous scoop about the shape of Clinton's penis."

The Conways dated during the Clinton impeachment and married at the dawn of the George W. Bush presidency. Kellyanne made it her mission to get women some respect in the Republican Party. Her niche survey research firm, the Polling Company, made money advising corporations about how to market American Express cards and Vaseline to women; but her major project was on teaching boorish politicians like Pence and Newt Gingrich how to close the gender gap. Conway even co-wrote a book with Democratic pollster Celinda Lake, *What Women Really Want: How American Women Are Quietly Erasing Political, Racial, Class, and Religious Lines to Change the Way We Live.*

This could not be good for Donald Trump. Surely, Kellyanne Conway, who made her name railing against the diminishment of the presidency by Bill Clinton, and wrote bipartisan books about women and politics, was not going to try to defend his atrocious verbiage and behavior. When Trump's campaign manager cancelled morning talk show appearances on the Sunday after the *Access Hollywood* tape was released, the rumor was that even Conway had a breaking point. And that it had been reached.

Or not.

That Sunday night, barely two days after the *Access Hollywood* fiasco began to unfold, Conway put an end to it.

Trump had turned in a typically convoluted, and just plain weird, appearance that evening during the second presidential debate in St. Louis. Afterward, Conway sat down with MSNBC's Chris Matthews to declare victory. Matthews asked about the tape. "I'm with the campaign until the bitter end, unless . . ." answered Conway. Sensing vulnerability, Matthews asked: "Unless what?"

Conway was wrestling with the question of whether another tape would surface, or that the next day's news would feature another victim of Trump words and deeds that Nita Chaudhary, the co-founder of UltraViolet, characterizes as "the embodiment of a culture that

normalizes sexual harassment and violence against women." Conway was not embracing the National Organization for Women's view that "Donald Trump Promotes Sexual Assault As a Rich Man's Perk." But she was clearly struggling with the prospect she might be signing on to a sinking campaign. Right there on national television. And then she remembered her higher calling: electing a Republican president who would serve the interests of her billionaire benefactors. "I'm sitting here as his campaign manager," she declared. "I'm sitting here with you where he just performed beautifully."

Suddenly, Conway was "on." She was spinning on all cylinders with the robotic precision that led a Pulitzer Prize–winning author who appeared frequently with Conway on pundit panels in the 1990s and early 2000s to describe her as "an absolute automaton for her wing of the Republican Party."

"I've made a commitment and I believe that he would be a much better president—first of all, he won the debate tonight, clearly," chirped Conway. "And the reason you know he won the debate is (a) you watched it or (b) everyone is going to talk about that he was standing behind her and in her space. I am committed to not letting Hillary Clinton appoint the next three or four justices to the Supreme Court."

From that moment forward, Conway was everywhere, as Trump Defender No. 1. Yes, of course, Conway argued, Trump's words were "horrible and indefensible," but she claimed, in a fact-free pivot, that some of the Republicans who were now trashing Trump had harassed her when she was "younger and prettier." Within days, she was jettisoning expressions of concern and sympathy and simply dismissing new charges of groping and harassment—no matter how valid, no matter how detailed—with a casual announcement that "I believe—Donald Trump has told me and his family, and the rest of America now—that none of this is true. These are lies and fabrications. They're all made up. And I think that it's not for me to judge what those women believe. I've not talked to them, I've talked to him."

That was all that was needed—not to sway backers of Hillary Clinton, or to attract moderate swing voters. It was what was needed to keep conservative women on board for Trump, and in so doing to keep Trump viable for the final month of a campaign that Steve Bannon and Kellyanne Conway had calculated could be won not with a majority of the vote, and perhaps not even with a plurality of the vote, but with a narrow Electoral College strategy that focused primarily on linking the conservative base with disaffected white working-class voters in a handful of battleground states.

"If Kellyanne had not been there when the firestorm hit, I don't know if we would have made it. She literally became a cult figure during that time period, just because of her relentless advocacy for Trump on TV," Bannon explained in an early 2017 conversation with the *Atlantic*, which reported that "Bannon says it was Conway's calm presence that led both wavering women and conservative voters to think: If she can still support Trump, I can, too."

Republican pollster Frank Luntz, who has known Conway for decades, and who has engaged in his share of intense political fights in the United States, Israel and other countries, says Conway saved Trump from political oblivion. "He owes her for standing up for him. I could not have done what she did," Luntz marveled. "I would not have survived it; I'm impressed that she did. In every possible sense, she won. I do not believe he would be president without her."

What Conway won was an opportunity to keep defending Trump in a way that historians will come to understand as a new form of political mendaciousness: spin rooted in absolute loyalty not to a man or a party but to an insider agenda that most viewers, perhaps even most reporters, barely recognize.

Conway did not enter the 2016 election cycle as a Trump backer. At the behest of her political paymasters, billionaire hedge fund manager Robert Mercer and his daughter Rebekah ("the First Lady of the alt-right"), Conway ran the Keep the Promise political action committee that championed the doomed candidacy of Texas senator Ted Cruz. Americans who were not familiar with Conway got to know her as the regular on CNN who ripped Trump as "fairly unpresidential" and who objected that the billionaire "built a lot of his business on the backs of the little guy." She called Trump "vulgar" and criticized him for failing to be "transparent" with his tax

returns. She even pointed out that he did not seem to understand the basic premises of the "pro-life movement," which the once pro-choice Trump embraced with increasing passion as the 2016 race evolved.

After Trump burned through a pair of caricature campaign managers (the thuggish Corey Lewandowski and the oligarch-obsessed Paul Manafort), the candidate was left with the Republican nomination but no real campaign infrastructure. The Mercers, who had transformed Conway's pro-Cruz Keep the Promise super PAC into a pro-Trump Make America Number One super PAC, began pulling strings for the woman who says: "Rebekah's a very close friend of mine, personally."

As the *New Yorker* explained: "In August, the Mercers recommended that Trump bring in Bannon to lead a reorganized effort. 'I've never run a campaign,' Bannon told Trump. 'I'd only do this if Kellyanne came in as my partner.' Conway said that Trump offered her the job of campaign manager on August 12th, in a private meeting in his office. 'We're losing,' she told him. 'No—look at the polls,' Trump replied. 'I looked at the polls. We're losing,' she said. 'But we don't have to lose. There's still a pathway back.'"

It was a torturous pathway, to be sure. But the Mercers got the campaign manager they wanted, and the president they had not wanted but were more than willing to work with. And Conway, as the ill-defined but ubiquitous "counselor" to the new president, got to redefine spin in her own image.

She achieved the task fully just two days into Trump's presidency, with an appearance on NBC's *Meet the Press* that literally rewrote the language, and obliterated the boundaries, of American politics. Moderator Chuck Todd was pressing Conway on a point of fact. White House press secretary Sean Spicer had claimed, in stark contrast with the physical and historical record, that Trump had attracted "the largest audience to ever witness an inauguration."

After several attempts to get a clear explanation from Conway, a frustrated Todd said: "You did not answer the question of why the president asked the White House press secretary to come out in front of the podium for the first time and utter a falsehood. Why did he do that? It undermines the credibility of the entire White House press office on day one."

"No it doesn't," snapped Conway. "Don't be so overly dramatic about it, Chuck. You're saying it's a falsehood." But it wasn't, Conway asserted. "Sean Spicer, our press secretary, gave alternative facts to that. But the point remains—"

Todd had had enough.

"Wait a minute—alternative facts? Alternative facts? Four of the five facts he uttered . . . were just not true. Look, alternative facts are not facts. They're falsehoods."

Chuck Todd was absolutely right. Kellyanne Conway did not care.

When Todd made one last game attempt to get Conway to acknowledge reality, she threw a word salad at him: "Maybe this is me as a pollster, Chuck," "You know data well," "Prove those numbers," "No way to really quantify crowds."

Todd was dumbfounded and he smiled as the dumbfounded do.

"You can laugh at me all you want," snapped Conway.

"I'm not laughing," Todd said, "I'm just . . . befuddled." So were the viewers. Conway smiled. Her work here was done.

—4—

HE WHO WILL NOT BE QUESTIONED

Stephen Miller

Senior Advisor to the President

The makers of films such as *1984* and *V for Vendetta* have given us some eerie embodiments of Big Brother. But they never created a Big Brother character as ominous as Stephen Miller, the squinting thirty-one-year-old Trump true believer who appeared on CBS's *Face the Nation* on the morning of February 12, 2017.

It was an important appearance. Top Trump communications aides Sean Spicer and Kellyanne Conway had fumbled badly in recent appearances. They were being mocked on comedy shows. Their names were becoming synonymous with "fake news" and "alternative facts." Even conservative commentators were suggesting that "the communications team" was harming rather than helping the Trump agenda. After "a week of chaos and interruptions, none bigger than an appeals court decision upholding the block on the president's travel ban," host John Dickerson noted that an "undeterred . . . Mr. Trump promised to fight, but also maybe to start over."

Perhaps a new face could begin the reset.

"We go now to the White House briefing room and President Trump's senior policy advisor, Stephen Miller," announced Dickerson. And there, glaring at the camera, was the man the Trump administration was counting on to reassure America.

It soon became clear that cold comfort was on the agenda. Asked about reports of North Korean weapons testing, Miller replied that Trump would supercharge Department of Defense spending so that "we will have unquestioned military strength beyond anything anybody can imagine." For good measure, he added that Trump's appearance the evening before with the prime minister of Japan had been "a show of strength . . . to all of planet Earth."

Miller certainly had a way with words. And he upped the volume when he was asked about the decisions by federal judges across the United States to block the president's executive order banning travel from seven predominantly Muslim countries.

"[We're] considering new and further executive actions that will enhance the security posture of the United States," he declared, while asserting that "the point, John, is that the president has enormous powers, both delegated to him by Congress and under the Constitution, his Article 2 foreign affairs power, to control the entry of aliens into our country and he's going to use that authority to keep us safe."

There would be no backing off, no backing down for Stephen Miller, as he robotically advanced ever more outlandish assertions. Dickerson asked, gingerly, whether the White House might have learned anything from the rollout of the executive order that was broadly acknowledged to have been a fiasco.

"Well," said Miller, "I think that it's been an important reminder to all Americans that we have a judiciary that has taken far too much power and become in many cases a supreme branch of government. One unelected judge in Seattle cannot remake laws for the entire country. I mean this is just crazy, John, the idea that you have a judge in Seattle say that a foreign national living in Libya has an effective right to enter the United States is—is—is beyond anything we've ever seen before."

Actually, the federal judge's order in Seattle wasn't "crazy" or "beyond anything we've ever seen before." The respected jurist's ruling had been upheld by a three-judge panel from the U.S. Court of Appeals for the Ninth Circuit, which determined that "the government has pointed to no evidence that any alien from any of the countries named in the order has perpetrated a terrorist attack in the United States." Of particular note was the panel's absolute rejection of the Trump administration's expansive claim of executive power—a claim so vast that it suggested the courts should defer to

 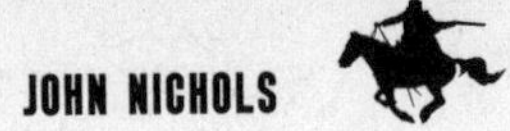

the executive branch rather than review the case. The appeals court explained that "there is no precedent to support this claimed unreviewability, which runs contrary to the fundamental structure of our constitutional democracy."

The senior advisor to the president was having none of this.

"The end result of this," Miller said with regard to all the protests and legal rulings against the president's order, "is that our opponents, the media and the whole world will soon see as we begin to take further actions, that the powers of the president to protect our country are very substantial and will not be questioned."

"Well, I guess, let me step back," said a startled Dickerson. "The question, as I talked to Republicans on the Hill, is what you're learning inside the White House about the way you do things. It's been pretty busy up there. Just stepping back, do you feel like you and your staff there, that you're in control of events at the White House?"

"I think to say that we're in control would be a substantial understatement," declared Miller, who asserted that "the president of the United States has accomplished more in just a few weeks than many presidents accomplish in an entire administration. On issue after issue we're taking forceful action to deliver on the president's campaign promises on a breathtaking scale."

Miller did not stop with *Face the Nation*. That same morning, he announced on *Fox News Sunday* that "in the end, the powers of the president of the United States will be reaffirmed." He told NBC's *Meet the Press* that the courts could not be permitted to "take power for themselves that belongs squarely in the hands of the president of the United States." On ABC's *This Week*, he said: "The bottom line is the president's powers, in this area, represent the apex of executive authority." Then he veered off into even more uncharted territory, telling host George Stephanopoulos, in the sternest of terms, that the president's entirely debunked claim that he had lost the November popular vote because of massive voter fraud was not debunked at all. "George," said Miller, who spoke in a theatrically threatening cadence, "it is a fact and you . . . will . . . not . . . deny . . . it that there are massive numbers of noncitizens in this country who are registered to vote. That is a scandal; we should stop the presses and as a country we should be aghast about the fact that you have people that have no right to vote in this country registered to vote canceling out the franchise of lawful citizens of this country. That's the story we should be talking about and I am prepared to go on any show, anywhere, anytime and repeat it and say the president of the United States is correct one hundred percent."

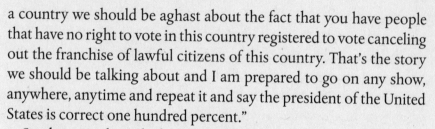

Stephanopoulos asked, repeatedly: "Do you have any evidence?" But Miller said it was not the time for facts and details, before spinning off new claims that were even more outlandish than those made by Trump. "Just for the record, you have provided absolutely no evidence," concluded Stephanopoulos, who finally grew so frustrated with Miller that he cut off a final tirade from the presidential advisor by saying, "You can start by providing evidence to back up your claims. Thanks for joining us this morning."

Donald Trump feigned enthusiasm for his aide's draconian appearances on the various networks ("Congratulations Stephen Miller—on representing me this morning on the various Sunday morning shows," read the presidential tweet. "Great job!"). But the fact was that Miller had scared people—and, worse yet from a political standpoint, his appearances had demanded mockery. Senator Chris Coons, a Delaware Democrat, observed that Miller's comments about presidential powers evidenced "a striking lack of understanding of the structure of our government." Former Republican congressman Joe Scarborough said the following morning on his MSNBC show that Miller's apologias for Trump were "the talk of a dictator." "That sounds like a spokesman for Vladimir Putin. It sounds like a spokesman out of Turkey." The *Washington Post* review of the *Face the Nation* outburst was headlined "Stephen Miller's authoritarian declaration: Trump's national security actions 'will not be questioned.'" A *Chicago Tribune* column found "Miller's strident defense of unlimited presidential power" to be frightening but assured readers that the White House aide was an actual human being who seemed to believe what he was saying: "Yes, he looked robotic and overconfident . . . But Miller wasn't reading a teleprompter. His well-articulated appetite for authoritarian rule leapt from his mind, not a machine." Referring to the "will not be questioned" line,

late-night comic Seth Meyers observed: "The only way that statement could be more terrifying is if he yelled it in German." "'Will not be questioned'?" asked Stephen Colbert. "Let me test that theory: What the [expletive] are you talking about?"

Colbert mocked Miller mercilessly. Recalling the promise "to go on any show, anywhere, anytime and repeat it and say the president of the United States is correct one hundred percent," the late-night comic invited the Trump apologist he referred to as "young Gargamel" to appear on his CBS show with a promise that "if you don't show up, I'm going to call you a liar. And if you do show up, I'm going to call you a liar to your face."

There is a favorite fantasy about White House work that goes something like this: just when a presidential administration seems to have crashed and burned, a young aide, fresh-faced and idealistic, untainted by the cynicism of Washington, more in touch with the country than the old-timers who have the president's ear, steps up and saves the day. It is a fantasy grounded in a little bit of reality and a lot of *West Wing* episodes. But when Stephen Miller stepped up, he did the opposite, revealing, as Joe Scarborough reflected during that Monday morning autopsy, that the crisis was severe. "Oh. My. God," marveled Scarborough. "It's much worse than I ever thought."

By just about any measure, Miller is the "much worse than I ever thought" Trumpkin, a true believer who says he was inspired to embrace conservatism by reading one of those hysterical Constitution-warping screeds by longtime National Rifle Association CEO Wayne LaPierre—*Guns, Crime and Freedom*—that even National Rifle Association members know to take with a grain of salt. (Miller didn't. He famously showed up at a freshman mixer in college and announced: "My name is Stephen Miller, I am from Los Angeles, and I like guns.")

At Santa Monica High School, Miller literally pestered Mexican American students with demands that they work on their English and, as the *Los Angeles Times* recounted, "bemoaned the school's Spanish-language announcements, the colorful festivals of minority cultures, and the decline, as he saw it, of a more traditional version of American education." His pro–Iraq invasion column for the school paper was titled "A Time to Kill." (Sample section: "We have all heard about how peaceful and benign the Islamic religion is, but no matter how many times you say that, it cannot change the fact that millions of radical Muslims would celebrate your death for the simple reason that you are Christian, Jewish or American.")

Miller showed up at school board meetings to criticize programs that served immigrants and delivered a speech that asked why students had to pick up their trash when janitors were paid to do the job. Miller says he "resolved to challenge the campus indoctrination machine," echoing the combative critique of David Horowitz, the right-wing critic of "political correctness" and "campus radicals."

Miller preached Horowitz's doctrines at Duke University, where he headed the campus chapter of his mentor's Students for Academic Freedom group, griped about liberal professors and appeared on national television programs to amplify those complaints. He got to know white nationalist Richard Spencer, then a Duke graduate student, through the Duke Conservative Union. Miller formed the Terrorism Awareness Project to make "students aware of the Islamic jihad and the terrorist threat, and to mobilize support for the defense of America and the civilization of the West" with events like Islamo-Fascism Awareness Week. He even found time to write a campus column that offered insights like this one: "[The] pay gap has virtually nothing to do with gender discrimination. Sorry, feminists. Hate to break this good news to you."

"He's the most sanctimonious student I think I ever encountered," John Burness, Duke's former senior vice president of public affairs and government relations, told the *Charlotte Observer*. "He seemed to be absolutely sure of his own views and the correctness of them, and seemed to assume that if you were in disagreement with him, there was something malevolent or stupid about your thinking." Burness termed Miller "incredibly intolerant."

That's been a common complaint. Oscar de la Torre, a Santa Monica school board member who grew up in the city's historically Latino and African American Pico neighborhood, recalled arguing with a teenaged Miller about the need to address funding inequities between schools in high-income and low-income parts of town.

"Early on in life, he was on a crusade against liberalism and liberals," de la Torre told the *Los Angeles Times*. "He just didn't buy it. He didn't believe the oppression existed. This guy is 17 years old, and it's like listening to someone who's 70 years old—in the 1930s."

That kind of thinking made Miller a natural fit with the man who would move him from the far-right fringe to the center of American politics in 2016. After a predictable stint working in the office of Minnesota congresswoman Michele Bachmann, Miller—with encouragement from Horowitz—joined the Jeff Sessions team, initially as a Judiciary Committee aide and then as a senior staffer in the Alabama senator's office. Sessions found an ideological soul mate in Miller, according to Stephen Boyd, the senator's former communications director. "Miller has demonstrated an ability to capture the voice of his boss in a way that is very important and also exceeds the ability of most Capitol Hill staff," Boyd told Alabama writer Howard Koplowitz. *Politico* referred to the Sessions-Miller connection as a "mind meld," especially when it came to opposing even modest immigration reforms and falsely labeling bipartisan proposals such as the DREAM Act as what Miller called "mass amnesty that would even include those who have committed serious criminal offenses."

"Whether the issue was trade or immigration or radical Islam, for many years before Donald Trump came on the scene, Senator Sessions was the leader of the movement and Stephen was his right-hand man," explained Stephen Bannon, who got to know the younger right-winger when Breitbart News provided vital support for a Sessions-led effort to scuttle the "Gang of Eight" effort of moderate Democrats and mainstream conservative Republicans to enact an immigration-reform bill. Miller gets high marks from Bannon for helping to forge the populist anti-immigrant, Muslim-bashing message that fueled the Trump campaign. "You could not get where we are today with this movement if it didn't have a center of gravity that was intellectually coherent," Bannon told *Politico* in 2016. "And I think a ton of that was done by Senator Sessions's staff, and Stephen Miller was at the cutting edge of that."

Miller returns the compliment.

"Steve and I got to know each other very well during the 2013 immigration debate," Miller told Rosie Gray of the *Atlantic*. "He and I and Sessions would spend an enormous amount of time developing plans and messaging and strategy; also him just covering what we were doing, pushing out narrative and copy. I got to know him, I got to know a lot of his staff, a lot of people who came in to the Breitbart embassy." (That's a reference to the Capitol Hill row house where Bannon and his allies set up shop several years before they set up shop in the White House.)

The Miller-Bannon-Sessions connection explains a lot about the Trump White House. Miller was attracted to the Trump campaign in 2015 and quickly got close to the candidate (eventually emerging as Trump's principal speechwriter and a fiery warm-up speaker at Trump rallies). He quickly drew Sessions into the fold, helping to secure an endorsement of Trump by the Alabaman that came months before other prominent Republicans fell in line. Both men then welcomed Bannon's arrival (after the exits of Lewandowski and Manafort) as the fall campaign's CEO and chief strategist. But the trio had worked together long before they were working with Trump. They were not always respected, let alone successful, in the early days of their acquaintance. But they rose together, based on a shared set of ideals that white nationalist Jared Taylor tried to sum up in a piece he wrote after Trump's inauguration. Though he warned that Trump was "not a racially conscious white man," Taylor allowed as how there were "men close to him—Steve Bannon, Jeff Sessions, Stephen Miller—who may have a clearer understanding of race, and their influence could grow."

That is not how Bannon, Sessions and Miller characterize themselves, or their mission. But they understand that they were until very recently outsiders. Miller's presence in the inner circle is in many ways the proof of the political transformation they have forced upon the Republican Party and official Washington by Trump's election. Even if the insider intrigues of the West Wing may alter the precise roles, and the precise influence, of men like Miller and Bannon, the fact that they are "at the table" when the president's inner circle gathers is a jarring reminder that this administration operates with a dramatic different set of standards than those that came before.

"The ascent of Mr. Miller from far-right gadfly with little policy experience to the president's senior policy adviser came as a shock to many of the staff members who knew him from his seven years in the Senate. A man whose emails were, until recently, considered spam by many of his Republican peers is now shaping the Trump administration's core domestic policies with his economic nationalism and hard-line positions on immigration," wrote Glenn Thrush and Jennifer Steinhauer in a *New York Times* profile of Miller. "But his unlikely rise is emblematic of a White House where unconventional résumés rule—where the chief strategist is Stephen K. Bannon, until recently the head of the flame-throwing right-wing website Breitbart News, and the president himself is a former reality television star who before winning the nation's highest office had never shown much interest in the arcana of governing."

The *Times* profile was published just hours before Miller made his fateful round of appearances on that Sunday morning in February. Miller's moment had come. He was an essential man in the Trump White House, working with Bannon to craft the president's incendiary inaugural address and the Muslim-ban executive order that unleashed so much chaos.

"Steve is a true believer in every sense of the word, not just in this message of economic populism but in President Trump as a leader," said Jason Miller, the unrelated Trump spokesman who worked closely with Stephen Miller throughout the campaign. "Steve's fiercely loyal and has a better understanding of the president's vision than almost anyone."

That is probably true. There is no reason to doubt that Miller was channeling Donald Trump when he announced on *Face the Nation* that the powers of the president "will not be questioned."

The problem is that presidents are almost always ill-served by true believers who do not know when to stop channeling the worst impulses of their bosses and when to start reassuring the American people that they have not elected an autocrat.

— 5 —

THE JIHAD WHISPERER WITH THE ANTI-SEMITISM BADGE

Sebastian Gorka

Deputy Assistant to the President

When the notorious anti-Semite vice-admiral Miklós Horthy de Nagybánya took control of Hungary in the aftermath of World War I, he dubbed himself "His Serene Highness the Regent of the Kingdom of Hungary" and established the Vitézi Rend, an institution of supposedly "chivalric character." Later, after Horthy aligned Hungary with Adolf Hitler's Axis during World War II and approved the enactment of Nazi-style anti-Jewish laws, Hungarian property that was forcibly taken from Jews was awarded to members of the Vitézi Rend and its collaborationist allies.

U.S. State Department officials would eventually include the Vitézi Rend on its list of World War II–era Nazi-allied and Nazi-directed organizations. Despite post-war efforts to dissolve the group, to this day it remains a presence in Hungary. And in the Hungarian expatriate community that includes one of Donald Trump's most influential aides. That aide was the subject of what was arguably the most remarkable exposé of the Trump administration's first hundred days. "Nazi-Allied Group Claims Top Trump Aide Sebastian Gorka As Sworn Member," read the headline of the *Forward* article by its correspondent in Budapest. "Sebastian Gorka, President Trump's top counter-terrorism adviser," the newspaper reported, "is a formal member of a Hungarian far-right group that is listed by the U.S. State Department as having been 'under the direction of the Nazi Government of Germany' during World War II, leaders of the organization have told the *Forward*."

Gorka did not respond to repeated efforts by the highly regarded paper, which began more than a century ago as the *Jewish Daily Forward*, to get his response to the news that Vitézi Rend leaders had said that the presidential advisor took a lifelong oath of loyalty to their group. After initially telling reporters to direct their questions about the March 16, 2017, report to the White House press office, Gorka contacted another publication, *Tablet* magazine, and asserted that he had "never been a member of the Vitez Rend" and had only occasionally worn "my father's (Vitézi Rend) medal and used the (Vitézi Rend symbol) 'v.' initial to honor his struggle against totalitarianism."

Then a Vitézi Rend faction to which the *Forward* had tied the Trump aide confirmed to *BuzzFeed* that Gorka was, indeed, a current member.

The dispute may seem obscure to some, but those with a sense of history (and those with fears that it might repeat itself) recognized the profound implications of the concerns that have been raised with regard to Gorka and his associates in the Trump White House. Whether Gorka is a "sworn member" or simply a young man with nostalgic sympathies, this is not the sort of organization with which presidential advisors ought to be linked.

"The group to which Gorka reportedly belongs is a reconstitution of the original group on the State Department list, which was banned in Hungary until the fall of Communism in 1989," explained the *Forward*. "There are now two organizations in Hungary that claim to be the heirs of the original Vitézi Rend, with Gorka, according to fellow members, belonging to the so-called 'Historical Vitézi Rend.' Though it is not known to engage in violence, the Historical Vitézi Rend upholds all the nationalist and oftentimes racial principles of the original group as established by Horthy."

Horthy's legacy is a complicated one. He was a nationalist who shifted loyalties between the Axis and the Allies and who claimed to have resisted some of Hitler's most brutal demands. Yet, there was never any question of his anti-Semitism. Horthy declared it in a blunt letter to Hungarian prime minister Pál Teleki. Written as Hungary was imposing Nazi-inspired "Jewish laws" that restricted Jewish involvement in government, commerce and the professions, prohibited

Jews from marrying non-Jews and identified non-Jews who had Jewish ancestors as "racially Jewish," Horthy's letter explained that "as regards the Jewish problem, I have been an anti-Semite throughout my life. I have never had contact with Jews. I have considered it intolerable that here in Hungary everything, every factory, bank, large fortune, business, theatre, press, commerce, etc. should be in Jewish hands, and that the Jew should be the image reflected of Hungary, especially abroad. Since, however, one of the most important tasks of the government is to raise the standard of living, i.e., we have to acquire wealth, it is impossible, in a year or two, to replace the Jews, who have everything in their hands, and to replace them with incompetent, unworthy, mostly big-mouthed elements, for we should become bankrupt. This requires a generation at least."

When the Nazis and their Hungarian supporters began the forced deportation of Jews to Auschwitz in 1944, at a rate of twelve thousand a day, Horthy complained about "the handling of the Jewish question in a manner that does not correspond to the Hungarian mentality" but explained that "in these matters I was forced into passivity."

Only after Franklin Roosevelt carried through on his threat to begin massive aerial bombing of Hungary did Horthy overcome his passivity and order a halt to the deportations. By that time, however, historians tell us that at least 437,000 Jews had been sent to Hitler's concentration camps, where all but a handful perished.

Yet, today, notes the *Forward*, "the Vitézi Rend has not left its legacy of racism behind. Horthy is revered among the organization's members." The former leader's speeches about the need for Hungarians to practice "love of their race" are widely quoted at a time when Hungary has experienced a resurgence of right-wing extremism and overt anti-Semitism.

As for Gorka, while he and other Trump administration officials refused to discuss Vitézi Rend or Hungarian nationalism, evidence mounted that he wore his connection to the haunted past of his ancestral homeland with pride. The London-born Gorka was for a number of years active on the right wing of Hungarian politics (he's a man "with close ties then to Hungarian far-right circles, and has in

the past chosen to work with openly racist and anti-Semitic groups and public figures," according to the *Forward*) before becoming a naturalized U.S. citizen in 2012. And he wore a Vitézi Rend medal when he attended a Trump inaugural ball as a newly minted deputy assistant to the president.

Gorka defended his sartorial choice (wearing not only the badge but a tunic and ring associated with Vitézi Rend) as an homage to his father's anti-communist activism in post-war Hungary. It was not the first time Gorka had rejected complaints about the use of symbols with anti-Semitic or fascist connections. In 2006, when Hungarian right-wingers were making a priority of displaying the Arpád flag, a historic red-and-white banner that was favored by the Hungarian Arrow Cross Party at the time when its followers were murdering thousands of Budapest Jews, Gorka (then the executive director of a conservative think tank in Budapest) told the Jewish Telegraphic Agency: "If you say eight centuries of history can be eradicated by 18 months of fascist distortion of symbols, you're losing historic perspective."

That comment anticipated the rejection of historical memory, and sensitivity, by Donald Trump and his supporters as "political correctness run amok." When the *Times of Israel* noted in February 2017 that "Top Trump aide wears medal of Hungarian Nazi collaborators" and when *Talking Points Memo* asked: "Did Gorka really wear a medal linked to Nazi ally to Trump inaugural ball?" they were attacked with a vengeance by the editors of the Breitbart News site, who decried the "media attempt to smear Sebastian Gorka as a Nazi sympathizer" as "Fake News."

Gorka was simply misunderstood, Breitbart columns and headlines declared. They knew, because as the Breitbart News national security editor he had written articles that attacked former President Obama ("Obama's Reign of Error: How America Lost Its Way and Is Losing the War Against Jihad"), provided fodder for Donald Trump's attacks on Obama and on fellow Republicans ("The Real Threat: The JV Team in the White House" and "Rand Paul: It's America's Fault") and defended Trump's most controversial statements ("The Donald v. NATO: He's on the Money").

A close associate of Breitbart boss Steve Bannon, Gorka came to the White House with Bannon, was installed as a member of the Strategic Initiatives Group that Bannon and First Son-in-Law Jared Kushner set up, and was charged with providing the president with advice and counsel on "irregular warfare, counterinsurgency and counterterrorism." When the outcry over Gorka's presence in the White House rose, amid new revelations about his troublesome ties to extremist groups and dubious academic credentials, New York congressman Jerrold Nadler declared: "There should be zero tolerance for anyone working anywhere in the Administration who shares the offensive views propagated by the organizations to which Mr. Gorka has been associated," and there was talk in early May that Gorka would be removed from his role at the White House and assigned new duties elsewhere in the administration. But he got a reprieve. "Trump and Bannon 'Personally Intervened' to Save Seb Gorka," announced the *Daily Beast* on May 5. "Seb Gorka's job as a White House national security aide was on the line; lucky for him he has friends in the highest places."

While Bannon remained in position as the Trump White House's "chief strategist," Gorka was sticking around as the "irregular warfare" strategist, with a place at the table when the vital decisions are made about issues of war and peace, diplomacy and international relations.

Giving Gorka so powerful a position, explained the *Washington Post*'s Greg Jaffe, signaled "a radical break" with the stance of the Republican and Democratic administrations and foreign-policy experts of the George W. Bush and Barack Obama eras in Washington. Bush and Obama emphasized respect for Islam and recognized terrorism as an affront to the values of the vast majority of Muslims, while Trump and his associates veer toward a view that focuses on what they see as "the Islamic doctrinal and scholarly roots of jihadist terror."

Gorka has contributed mightily to the development of Trump's most extreme positions, with his book *Defeating Jihad* and with Breitbart essays that ripped Bush and Obama preachments that poverty, alienation and geopolitical factors must be taken into account by

 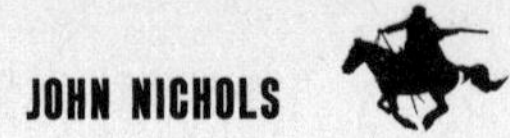

those who would combat terror. "That story is not one of America failing to provide jobs for the world's needy, or the lack of community outreach in America," wrote Gorka. "It is a story of Islam under attack by the West, a perpetual Holy War against the infidel until the House of Islam—Dar al Islaam—covers the world and all live under sharia in a new Caliphate." *Newsweek* says that Gorka's "views on the 'global jihadist movement,' as he calls it, align with a small cadre of right-wing observers who depict Islamist militants and extremists as being driven principally by passages from the Koran, rather than by government repression, or sectarian, tribal, political or economic factors."

Gorka's writing appealed to Trump, but has long unsettled experts on terrorism.

"He doesn't understand a fraction of what he pretends to know about Islam," explains Mia Bloom, a former fellow at Pennsylvania State's International Center for the Study of Terrorism who now teaches at Georgia State University and who has written extensively on ethnic killing, suicide bombings and terror. Adrian Weale, a former British Intelligence Corps officer, says Gorka "has never been an operational practitioner of counter-terrorism."

The man who has been referred to as Trump's "Jihad whisperer" "does not speak Arabic and has never lived in a Muslim-majority country," according to the *Washington Post.* Nor has he been a contributor to the leading peer-reviewed scholarly journal in the field, *Terrorism and Political Violence.* "Gorka has not submitted anything to the journal in the last five or so years, according to my records, and we have never used him as a reviewer," explained Lawrence P. Rubin, the associate editor. "We would not have used him as a reviewer because he is not considered a terrorism expert by the academic or policy community."

Asked about Gorka by the *Post,* Cindy Storer, a former CIA expert on the relationship between religious extremism and terrorism, said: "He thinks the government and intelligence agencies don't know anything about radicalization, but the government knows a lot and thinks he's nuts."

Nuts? Perhaps. After assuming his position in the Trump White House, the presidential advisor found the time to track down the phone number of an actual terrorism expert, who had criticized Gorka on Twitter, and berated the man for more than twenty minutes.

Powerful? Unquestionably. And that's what raises concerns not merely about Gorka's anti-Muslim ranting and raving but also about his linkages to groups such as Vitézi Rend, whose members the State Department's *Foreign Affairs Manual* explains "are presumed to be inadmissible" to the United States under the Immigration and Nationality Act.

Bruce Einhorn, the former Justice Department official who now teaches nationality law at Pepperdine University, explained to the *Forward* that Gorka's refusal to respond to its legitimate questions about his own past—and about his connections to groups that have been linked with Nazism—were indefensible.

"Gorka is part of an administration issuing travel bans against countries and people as a whole," says Einhorn, who served for a number of years as deputy chief for the Justice Department's Office of Special Investigations, which was charged with tracking down Nazis and Nazi allies who entered the United States illegally after World War II. "For someone who is part of this effort to not answer your question [about his membership in Vitézi Rend] and yet support what's going on in the West Wing where he works is the height of hypocrisy. The administration that makes so much of protecting us from extremists while looping the guilty in with the innocent should at least require its officials tell the truth."

— 6 —

THE LEOPARD THAT DID NOT CHANGE HIS SPOTS

Jefferson Beauregard Sessions III

Attorney General of the United States

What can be said about Jeff Sessions that has not already been said by Dr. David Duke?

When Donald Trump announced that Jefferson Beauregard Sessions III was his pick to serve as the eighty-fourth attorney general of the United States, the former Imperial Wizard of the Knights of the Ku Klux Klan and longtime head of the National Association for the Advancement of White People ("a Klan without robes") hailed the selection as "Great!" and expressed his hope that "Sessions as AG will stop the massive institutional race discrimination against whites!"

Trump's selections of Sessions, White House chief strategist Steve Bannon and now-former national security advisor Michael Flynn for top posts were, Duke said, "the first steps in the long and arduous project of taking America back."

"Sessions has been hated for years by the Jewish-dominated media for his opposition to massive immigration into America and for the fact that he has dared to publicly oppose the massive, institutionalized racial discrimination against white people called affirmative action," explained Duke, a former Republican state legislator, gubernatorial nominee and U.S. Senate candidate, who counseled Trump's pick for attorney general to use his confirmation hearing to "expose the blatant media and political blather of 'equal rights and opportunity' when white people face destructive anti-white affirmative action racist policies that dominate major corporations,

Federal, State, and city governments, colleges and educational institutions."

Duke then went back to his day-job work of defending his choice for president ("Jewish Supremacist, anti-White filth, Rob Reiner, viciously attacks and disrespects President Trump live on MSNBC," "American hating, Cultural Marxists pushing, rabble rousing slob, Michael Moore, once again goes on television to disrespect President Trump," "Can Donald Trump & Vladimir Putin together overthrow Zionist Globalist Hegemony?") and revisiting the staples of his advocacy: Holocaust denial, portraying immigrants as criminals and asking "Why isn't Hillary Clinton in jail yet?"

When Sessions was confirmed as the new head of the U.S. Department of Justice, however, it was time once more for Duke and his fellow "white nationalists" to celebrate. The former imperial wizard posted a huge photo of the new attorney general with the message "Law & Order, welcome back."

What made Duke so enthusiastic about Sessions? Why did white-nationalist websites like the Daily Stormer ("the newest up and comer in the heated competition to rule the hate web," according to the Southern Poverty Law Center, which notes that the online publication was "named for prominent Nazi Julius Streicher's virulently anti-Semitic weekly newspaper the *Stormer*") respond to Trump's nomination of Sessions by declaring "It's like Christmas" and hail Senate approval of Trump's top lawyer with the headline "Jeff Sessions Confirmed: We are One Step Closer to Complete Control"?

After all, Sessions says, "I detest the Klan." The former senator is quick to remind folks that he once co-sponsored a Senate bill to honor Rosa Parks. And in his answers to questions posed by the Senate Judiciary Committee regarding his nomination, he wrote that prosecuting an Alabama Klan leader for murder was one of the "ten most significant litigated matters" he had "personally handled" in his career. (A nice sentiment, even if *Atlantic* magazine senior editor Adam Serwer would note after an extensive review of the case that "in seeking to defend Sessions from charges of racism, Sessions's allies, and even Sessions himself, seem to have embellished

key details, and to have inflated his actual role in the case, presenting him not merely as a cooperative U.S. attorney who facilitated the prosecution of the two Klansmen, but the driving force behind the prosecution itself. The details of the case don't support that claim.") How to sort this out?

Let's turn to Coretta Scott King, the widow of slain civil rights leader Martin Luther King Jr., for some insight. When Sessions was nominated by Ronald Reagan to serve as a federal judge for the Southern District of Alabama in the mid-1980s, Mrs. King, a native Alabaman, penned a poignant letter to then–committee chairman Strom Thurmond, the South Carolina senator who ran for the presidency in 1948 as the head of the segregationist States' Rights Democratic Party ticket.

"I write to express my sincere opposition to the confirmation of Jefferson B. Sessions as a federal district court judge for the Southern District of Alabama," she began, before explaining that "Mr. Sessions has used the awesome powers of his office in a shabby attempt to intimidate and frighten elderly black voters. For this reprehensible conduct, he should not be rewarded with a federal judgeship. I regret that a long-standing commitment prevents me from appearing in person to testify against this nominee. However, I have attached a copy of my statement opposing Mr. Sessions' confirmation and I request that my statement as well as this letter be made a part of the hearing record."

What Coretta Scott King's statement explained was that "Mr. Sessions' conduct as U.S. Attorney, from his politically-motivated voting fraud prosecutions to his indifference toward criminal violations of civil rights laws, indicates that he lacks the temperament, fairness and judgment to be a federal judge."

In particular, she detailed one of those transgressions: a 1984 prosecution of allies of her late husband "for assisting elderly and illiterate blacks to exercise [the] franchise" that the Voting Rights Act was intended to protect. "The actions taken by Mr. Sessions in regard to the [1985] voting fraud prosecutions represent just one more technique used to intimidate Black voters and thus deny them this most precious franchise. The investigations into the absentee voting process were conducted only in the Black Belt counties where blacks had finally achieved political power in the local government. Whites had been using the absentee process to their advantage for years, without incident. Then, when Blacks, realizing [the absentee process's] strength, began to use it with success, criminal investigations were begun."

Mrs. King explained that "in these investigations, Mr. Sessions, as U.S. Attorney, exhibited an eagerness to bring to trial and convict three leaders of the Perry County Civic League including Albert Turner despite evidence clearly demonstrating their innocence of any wrongdoing. Furthermore, in initiating the case, Mr. Sessions ignored allegations of similar behavior by whites, choosing instead to chill the exercise of the franchise by blacks by his misguided investigation. In fact, Mr. Sessions sought to punish older black civil rights activists, advisers and colleagues of my husband, who had been key figures in the civil rights movement in the 1960's. These were persons who, realizing the potential of the absentee vote among Blacks, had learned to use the process within the bounds of legality and had taught others to do the same. The only sin they committed was being too successful in gaining votes.

"The scope and character of the investigations conducted by Mr. Sessions also warrant grave concern. Witnesses were selectively chosen in accordance with the favorability of their testimony to the government's case. Also, the prosecution illegally withheld from the defense critical statements made by witnesses. Witnesses who did testify were pressured and intimidated into submitting the 'correct' testimony. Many elderly blacks were visited multiple times by the FBI who then hauled them over 180 miles by bus to a grand jury in Mobile when they could more easily have testified at a grand jury twenty miles away in Selma. These voters, and others, have announced they are now never going to vote again."

That was a heartbreaking prospect for Albert Turner, who was known in southern Alabama as "Mr. Voter Registration."

When Turner died in 2000, at the age of sixty-four, a long *New York Times* obituary recognized him as "a civil rights leader and adviser to the Rev. Dr. Martin Luther King Jr." who "helped lead

the voting rights march from Selma to Montgomery, on March 7, 1965." Recalling the "on-the-frontlines" role that Turner played on that "Bloody Sunday," when "peaceful protesters . . . were beaten, chased and tear-gassed" by stick-wielding Alabama state troopers," Alabama civil rights lawyer J. L. Chestnut told the *Times*: "Whenever there was something of unusual danger, and nobody wanted to, you could count on the fact that Albert and John Lewis would lead it."

"I really do not know of a single individual in Alabama who has given more to the political progress of African-Americans in this state than Albert," Chestnut said of the civil rights champion who had served as Dr. King's field director in Alabama.

Only deep in the story, almost as an aside, was mention made of the prosecution of Turner by Sessions.

"With his wife, Evelyn, Mr. Turner was cleared of voter fraud in the 1980's, when prosecutors charged them with altering absentee ballots collected from rural blacks," read the obituary, which also noted that afterward the Sessions prosecution collapsed when a biracial jury quickly returned a not-guilty verdict. The takeaway message came from Turner, who said at the time of his acquittal: "The indictments come because blacks have gotten too well organized for political empowerment in the Black Belt of Alabama. They didn't spend a million dollars because they think a few old folks' ballots were changed."

This was what Coretta Scott King wanted senators to recognize about Jeff Sessions. "I urge you to consider carefully Mr. Sessions' conduct in these matters," she wrote back in 1986. "Such a review, I believe, raises serious questions about his commitment to the protection of the voting rights of all American citizens and consequently his fair and unbiased judgment regarding this fundamental right."

Observing that giving Jeff Sessions authority over cases involving civil rights would "irreparably damage the work" of the Reverend Dr. Martin Luther King Jr. proved to be a damning indictment in 1986. Recollections of the Turner case—and testimony from an African American assistant U.S. attorney that Sessions had called him "boy," made racist remarks, referred to the American Civil Liberties Union, the NAACP Defense Fund and the National Council of Churches as "un-American" and joked that he thought Klan members "were O.K. until I found out they smoked pot"—caused even GOP members of the Republican-controlled Senate Judiciary Committee to distance themselves from the nominee. Faced with united opposition from the NAACP, the Urban League, the American Jewish Congress, the National Council of Churches and the 185 coalition members of the Leadership Conference on Civil Rights, the committee voted 10–8 to reject Sessions, and he withdrew his nomination. "This sends notice to the Justice Department and others making recommendations for Federal judges that the Senate and the committee is taking its constitutional responsibility seriously," said Elaine Jones of the NAACP Legal Defense and Educational Fund Inc. "It is not a rubber stamp."

In that moment, yes, but not necessarily forever.

After the 1986 debacle—in which his own testimony appeared, at many turns, to do him as much harm as that of others (attempting to deny accusations that he had said the "NAACP hates white people" and called the civil rights organization a "commie group and pinko organization," he told the committee: "I am loose with my tongue on occasion and I may have said something similar to that or could be interpreted to that . . .")—Sessions got himself elected as attorney general of Alabama in the "Republican wave" election year of 1994. Two years later, he won the U.S. Senate seat of retiring Senator Howell Heflin, who as a member of the Judiciary Committee in 1986 had cast an agonized vote against the Sessions nomination. Explaining the rare opposition of a senator to a home-state nominee, Heflin said that he had "read and reread the transcript" of the confirmation hearing and finally determined that "a person should not be confirmed for a lifetime appointment if there are reasonable doubts about his ability to be fair and impartial."

After his election to the Senate, Sessions joined the very Judiciary Committee that had once rejected him and served as a very right-wing member—criticizing not just "amnesty" for undocumented immigrants but legal immigration, promoting the construction of a wall along the U.S.-Mexican border, proposing a constitutional amendment banning same-sex marriage and opposing repeal of the "Don't Ask, Don't Tell" rule and efforts to end discrimination in the

military, and seeking at every turn to undermine a woman's right to choose. (As a senator, Sessions sponsored legislation to "defund" Planned Parenthood and demanded that the Department of Justice (DOJ) launch investigations into the health care provider. When Sessions was nominated for attorney general, Planned Parenthood and seventy groups that defend access to reproductive health and abortion rights objected; their letter said the Sessions nomination raised "reason for concern for all who value the safety of women's health providers and their patients.") Sessions probably did not note the irony in the fact that, as someone who continues to bemoan the scrutiny he faced as a judicial nominee, he emerged as one of the Senate's most ardent critics of the judicial nominees of Democratic presidents. He led the opposition to the Supreme Court nominations by Barack Obama of Justices Sonia Sotomayor (complaining that Sotomayor had engaged in thoughtful discussions of how the perspective of the judiciary could be broadened by "the presence of women and people of color on the bench") and Elena Kagan (employing what *Politico* referred to as "jarring comments" to question whether the former Harvard Law School dean "had the intellectual honesty, the clarity of mind, that you would expect on the Supreme Court of the United States"). And when Supreme Court justice Antonin Scalia died in February 2016, Sessions did not just oppose President Obama's nomination of Judge Merrick Garland as a replacement; the senator's office announced that "no nominee will receive a hearing."

Despite his "southern gentleman" manner, Sessions served in the Senate as a fierce partisan, a rigid ideologue, an unapologetic obstructionist and a cutthroat partisan operative. To a greater extent than any other senator, he cleared the way within the Republican Party for the politics of Donald Trump.

Still, even Republican insiders were a bit surprised early in 2016 when Sessions became the first senator to endorse Trump for president and quickly emerged as the most prominent defender of the candidate's outrageous words and deeds. Even as other top Republicans avoided entanglement with a presidential contender who seemed always to be on the verge of a public meltdown, Sessions embraced the opportunity to deliver the speech nominating the billionaire for the presidency at that summer's Republican National Convention. In the fall, Sessions integrated himself and his staff into the Trump campaign. That integration would come to haunt Sessions when it was revealed that he had failed to divulge his contacts with the Russian ambassador during the summer and fall of 2016, even after he was asked straightforward questions about those contacts by Vermont senator Patrick Leahy, the ranking Democrat on the Judiciary Committee, and Minnesota senator Al Franken. Those deceptions would eventually lead to calls, from Republicans as well as Democrats, for Sessions to recuse himself from inquiries into connections between Trump's inner circle and the Russians. His decision to answer those calls and distance himself from the investigation calmed critics but infuriated Trump.

Sessions was not close to Trump before the 2016 campaign began. His support for the billionaire was rooted in ideology and enthusiasm for eventual Trump campaign CEO Bannon. Sessions was a big fan of Bannon's bombastic approach at Breitbart; when reporter Reid Cherlin encountered the senator from Alabama at a 2014 dinner with Bannon, Cherlin recalls:

"I asked Sessions some questions about his relationship to Breitbart, mostly to be polite to my hosts. He surprised me by giving Breitbart credit for fatally poisoning a congressional immigration-reform deal that he himself had crusaded against. 'You might not think it could' kill the bill, Sessions said, 'but it did.' He told me that he read the site almost daily and that his constituents regularly quoted Breitbart articles to him by author name. 'From my perspective, Breitbart is putting out cutting-edge information that's independent, geared to the average working American, that's honest and needs to get out.'"

When Trump prevailed on November 8, 2016, Sessions was in the thick of the president-elect's transition process and, within weeks of the election, the president-elect nominated his most ardent congressional backer to lead the Department of Justice.

"Jeff Sessions, as Attorney General, Could Overhaul Department He's Skewered," read the banner headline in the *New York Times*, which noted that "Mr. Sessions has a growing list of gripes about

how the Obama administration has run his old department, from its 'breathtaking' stance on immigration to its 'shameful' refusal to defend a federal ban on gay marriage." No one doubted that George Washington University law professor Jonathan Turley was right when he said: "The Justice Department is likely to be one of the most transformed departments in the cabinet in a Trump administration." Change was in the air. But had Jeff Sessions changed?

Republicans stumbled over themselves to vouch for the nominee, while media outlets noted the seventy-year-old senator's "courtly" manner. Trump claimed that "Jeff is greatly admired by legal scholars and virtually everyone who knows him." But that simply was not the case, as Alabamans tried to make clear to the nation. Albert Turner had passed, but his widow just laughed when she was asked whether the man who had prosecuted her was ready to serve as attorney general. "While my husband and I were trying to help black people vote in Alabama, Jeff Sessions was trying to put us in jail," Evelyn Turner explained. She recounted the story of her acquittal on charges pursued by Sessions, but she did not stop there. Turner noted that "as a senator, Jeff Sessions has voted against affirmative action and federal hate crimes laws and supported voter suppression laws. He has been a leading opponent of criminal justice and sentencing reforms. He has whitewashed his real history on race, exaggerating his past to paint himself as a champion of school desegregation and as a righteous prosecutor of the Ku Klux Klan." She was not alone in arguing that Sessions had not changed. Those who had watched him most closely were most dubious.

"Despite 30 years of our nation moving forward on inclusion and against hate, Jeff Sessions has failed to change his ways," said Benard Simelton, the president of the Alabama State Conference of the NAACP. "[Sessions has] been a threat to desegregation and the Voting Rights Act and remains a threat to all of our civil rights, including the right to live without the fear of police brutality." Alabama NAACP members were so opposed to the Sessions nomination that they occupied the senator's Mobile office and were arrested for civil disobedience. "This is too important for us to sit idly by and let our country turn back time," explained Simelton.

Voices of opposition and concern rose from across Alabama. John Saxon, an Alabama attorney, who once served on a federal appointments committee that recommended nominees for Alabama federal judgeships, warned that "the senator has a problem putting African Americans on the federal bench in Alabama." When President Obama nominated an African American jurist, Abdul Karim Kallon, to serve on the U.S. Court of Appeals for the Eleventh Circuit in 2016, Alabama legal observers were hopeful because Sessions had not blocked Kallon's selection to serve on a lower court bench and because seemingly everyone agreed that Obama was right when he said that "Judge Kallon has a long and impressive record of service and a history of handing down fair and judicious decisions." The American Bar Association rated Kallon "Unanimously Well Qualified." Yet, the nomination languished for 327 days in the judiciary committee where an Alabaman, Sessions, served, and had all the stature and connections that were necessary to advance it. After the 114th Congress finished its business on January 3, 2017, the Kallon nomination was returned to Obama. "When Obama nominated Kallon to the vacant 11th Circuit seat in February 2016, Sessions opposed his confirmation," noted *Mother Jones* magazine, which explained that "one-quarter of the residents of the 11th Circuit, which represents Alabama, Georgia, and Florida, are black—the highest percentage of any federal appeals court in the country—but only one of the court's 11 judges is African American. The seat on the court reserved for an Alabaman has never been held by a black judge." Alabama state senator Hank Johnson told the magazine that when efforts were made to diversify the federal bench, "it was definitely Jeff Sessions that was preventing the appointment of an African American."

That wasn't the only problem that Alabamans had with Sessions. "We have known Senator Sessions for many years," explained Richard Cohen, the president of the Alabama-based Southern Poverty Law Center. "But we cannot support his nomination to be the country's next attorney general. Senator Sessions not only has been a leading opponent of sensible, comprehensive immigration reform, he has associated with anti-immigrant groups we consider to be

deeply racist, including the Federation for American Immigration Reform and the Center for Security Policy. If our country is to move forward, we must put all forms of racism behind us."

This broader concern about Sessions's commitment to oppose all forms of racism was raised by national civil rights groups. "Do not allow Senator Jeff Sessions to become the U.S. Attorney General," read a petition that was signed by more than one million Americans and submitted to the Senate in early February by a coalition that included the Leadership Conference on Civil and Human Rights, People For the American Way, UltraViolet, Color Of Change, Common Cause, Friends of the Earth, NARAL Pro-Choice America, Rock the Vote, Faith in Public Life, Voto Latino, Free Press, Asian Americans Advancing Justice and the Bill of Rights Defense Committee, among others. "He has fought the U.S. government's (including the Department of Justice's) efforts to protect the rights of marginalized people, including women, people of color, LGBTQ people, Muslims, and immigrants. Trump's appointment of him as U.S. Attorney General is a blatant affront to these people," the petition declared. "It would be outrageous to let him lead the Department of Justice."

Leadership Conference on Civil and Human Rights president Wade Henderson explained that the signers "believe that Senator Sessions would be a disaster for civil rights, for the rule of law, and for an independent Justice Department. Senator Sessions has built his career on demonizing people of color, women, the LGBT community, people with disabilities, immigrants and refugees." Sessions, said Henderson, was "entirely unfit to be the Attorney General." Rashad Robinson, the executive director of the group Color Of Change, was even more forthright. "Our question for members of the Senate is simple: do they support racism, or do they not?" asked Robinson. "In 1986, the Republican-controlled Judiciary Committee refused to confirm Sessions to the federal bench. In 2017, the Senate should be just as unequivocal: 'no' to racism means 'no' to Jeff Sessions."

Not a single Republican would do what Republicans had done thirty years earlier. While those who knew Sessions said he had not changed, the Republican Party, the party of Lincoln, had changed a great deal. Even supposedly "moderate" GOP senators embraced the nomination. The Judiciary Committee and then the Senate split along party lines and narrowly approved Jeff Sessions to serve as attorney general. "I have never witnessed anything to suggest that Senator Sessions is anything other than a dedicated public servant and a decent man," Susan Collins, the Republican senator from Maine, told committee members, before repeating a talking-points claim that Sessions "is not motivated by racial animus."

But Evelyn Turner, who had kept a close eye on Sessions over the years, was not buying it. "Sessions has not changed. Have you ever known a leopard to change his spots? I haven't," she said. "Sessions is still a racist." The survivor of the zealous prosecution by Jeff Sessions of voting rights activists expressed her fear "that Sessions would fail to emphasize or enforce civil rights laws and protections."

"I am fearful," she concluded, that "Sessions would support policies that would make it more difficult for black citizens to vote."

Within days of Sessions's swearing in as attorney general, the Department of Justice rescinded orders protecting transgender students and to phase out the use of private prisons by the federal government, undoing years of work by coalitions of civil rights and social justice groups. Then, on February 27, 2017, the Department of Justice announced that it would literally switch sides on the issue of voting rights in Texas. One day before a legal team that was challenging the Lone Star State's overly restrictive voter-ID law, which critics asserted was developed by Republican lawmakers to discriminate against African American and Latino voters, the Sessions DOJ withdrew from the six-year-long voting rights initiative. It was, *Salon* noted, "the first major voting rights case the DOJ faced under Sessions, who called the Supreme Court's [2013] gutting of the Voting Rights Act's pre-clearance provision 'good news, I think, for the South.'"

For voting rights advocates, however, it was something else altogether: confirmation that Evelyn Turner was right to be fearful that the man the white nationalists could not wait to get installed as attorney general, Jefferson Beauregard Sessions III, "would support policies that would make it more difficult for black citizens to vote."

— 7 —

THE LAWMAN WHO FORGOT WHICH SIDE HE WAS ON

Rod Rosenstein

Deputy Attorney General

Rod Rosenstein is a very powerful man, with immense authority and an even more immense duty to the republic he has sworn to serve as a U.S. Department of Justice lifer who literally started fresh out of Harvard Law School, in the Attorney General's Honors Program that steers ambitious young barristers into public service, and has now risen to the office next to the corner office. If Attorney General Jeff Sessions is the chief executive officer of the U.S. Department of Justice, then Deputy Attorney General Rosenstein is the chief operating officer. Rosenstein has his hand in everything, at least in part because there are so many things that the scandal-plagued Sessions is not supposed to be handling.

Unfortunately, Sessions cannot keep his scandals to himself. So it was that, just days after assuming his position, the man who had been sold to the U.S. Senate and the nation as a proper minder was drawn into the crisis of confidence that is Jeff Sessions.

In early March 2017, the *Washington Post* revealed that during the 2016 presidential campaign, when Sessions was a close counselor and top surrogate for Donald Trump, he spoke twice with Russia's ambassador to the United States. Sessions acknowledged the meetings following the *Post* report. That created a problem for the newly installed attorney general. When Sessions appeared before the Senate Judiciary Committee as Trump's nominee to fill the nation's chief law enforcement position the previous January, he announced: "I did not have communications with the Russians." In response to a written question from Senator Patrick Leahy, D-Vermont, about whether he had been "in contact with anyone connected to any part of the Russian government about the 2016 election, either before or after Election Day," Sessions responded with one word: "No."

The *Washington Post* report put a spotlight on Sessions, and it was not flattering. House minority leader Nancy Pelosi said: "Jeff Sessions lied under oath." It was hard to argue with the conclusion. Unless we imagine that Sessions is far too absentminded to continue to serve as attorney general (a circumstance no one who knows the guy seriously entertains), then there can be no question that this man engaged in a blatant attempt to deceive the very Senate that was charged with determining whether he would take charge of the Department of Justice.

The new attorney general had to think fast. Sessions determined that he could avoid accountability by announcing that he was recusing himself from any examination of Russian involvement with President Trump's campaign. It worked. The heat was off—for two months.

But the inquiry into Russian ties to the Trump campaign was only beginning. And the headlines grew more and more unsettling:

Washington Post: "FBI Director Comey confirms probe of possible coordination between Kremlin and Trump campaign" (March 20, 2017)

Wall Street Journal: "Trump Team's Ties to Russia: Who's Who" (March 31, 2017)

New York Daily News: "FBI used controversial dossier on Russia-Trump ties to obtain warrant to spy on ex-campaign aide Carter Page" (April 18, 2017)

New York Times: "Trump Adviser's Visit to Moscow Got the FBI's Attention" (Apr 19, 2017)

CNN: "Sources: Russia tried to use Trump advisers to infiltrate campaign" (April 21, 2017)

NPR: "Yates, Clapper To Testify In Senate Hearing On Russian Election Meddling" (April 25, 2017)

Voice of America: "FBI Chief to Face More Questions on Russia's Activities During Election" (May 4, 2017)

New York Times: "Private Hearing With Intelligence Chiefs Revives House Inquiry on Russia" (May 4, 2017)

The heat was not just still on. Indeed, the temperature was rising. And Trump was getting agitated. Really, really agitated. *Politico* reported that Trump "had grown enraged by the Russia investigation," and that the president "repeatedly asked aides why the Russia investigation wouldn't disappear." Shortly, Federal Bureau of Investigation director James Comey, who by many accounts was focusing more attention and resources on the Russia inquiry, was expected to testify before the Senate Intelligence Committee on May 11, 2017. Trump moved from agitation to action. Comey was going to be fired. Paperwork was needed to justify the termination. But it would not do to have Sessions write it, as he had supposedly recused himself. So it fell to Rod Rosenstein to pull together a memo making a case against Comey.

Rosenstein delivered a credible bill of particulars, as might be expected from a permanent fixture in and around the U.S. Department of Justice for almost three decades, who had served since the early 1990s in the public integrity section of the Criminal Division, a special assistant to the Criminal Division assistant attorney general, an associate independent counsel, a principal deputy assistant attorney general for the Tax Division, an assistant U.S. attorney, the U.S. attorney for the U.S. district court for the District of Maryland, a member of the attorney general's Anti-Gang Coordination Committee and a member of the Advisory Committee of U.S. Attorneys and Subcommittees on Violent and Organized Crime, White Collar Crime, Sentencing Issues and Cyber/Intellectual Property Crime. The guy certainly knew how to write a legal memo, and he also knew his way around controversial inquiries: he was a key player on the team of prosecutors that independent counsel Ken Starr used to put together allegations of wrongdoing by President Bill Clinton.

Rosenstein titled his Comey memo "Restoring Public Confidence in the FBI." It was rough on Comey, to be sure. But, notably, it did not make a specific recommendation that the director be fired. That came in a separate, recusal-be-damned letter penned by Sessions.

Trump removed Comey on May 9, 2017, releasing a statement from the president, the recommendation letter from Sessions and the memo from Rosenstein. Then all hell broke loose as Congressman Jerrold Nadler, the former chair and ranking Democratic member of the House Judiciary Subcommittee on the Constitution, said the United States was "careening towards a constitutional crisis." Nadler warned that "the Administration [is] systematically attacking all of the institutions that are meant to put a check on the power of the President." Republicans joined Democrats in expressing their frustration and concern with the president and the Department of Justice. "Why? Why at this time? Investigations are going on about the Trump campaign and, you know, undertaken by the FBI headed by James Comey. And when that person is fired by the president, then obviously there are going to be questions," Arizona senator Jeff Flake told NPR. Speaking specifically about the Comey firing, Flake said that "when that action is taken while an active investigation is going on and reasons are given that may not hold up to scrutiny, then I think it's our responsibility as members of Congress to question that. And that's what I'm trying to do."

The White House claimed that the Rosenstein memo and the Sessions recommendation letter led Trump to make a draconian decision that was executed in such a bumbling manner that Comey initially thought someone was playing a joke on him. The deputy attorney general's memo became a subject of controversy; Massachusetts senator Elizabeth Warren complained that "it reads like a

 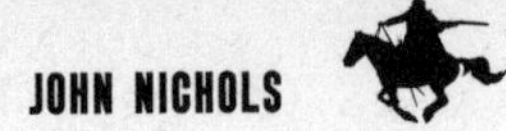

press release, not a measured explanation of why someone has been fired. It's a deeply political document. It's totally outside the context of what the Department of Justice should do."

NBC News asked: "Who Is Rod Rosenstein, the Man Who Swung the Ax on Comey?" Trump quickly contradicted them, which only made matters worse.

Comparisons with the Watergate scandal of the early 1970s were inevitable, yet still chilling.

"Today's action by President Trump completely obliterates any semblance of an independent investigation into Russian efforts to influence our election, and places our nation on the verge of a constitutional crisis," said former House Judiciary Committee chairman John Conyers, D-Michigan, on the evening that Comey was fired.

The senior member of the House of Representatives, and the only remaining member of the committee that approved articles of impeachment against President Nixon in 1974, did not hesitate to draw a comparison between Trump's decision to remove Comey and Nixon's Watergate-era machinations to force the removal of the special prosecutor who was investigating Nixon's high crimes and misdemeanors. "There is little doubt that the president's actions harken our nation back to Watergate and the 'Saturday Night Massacre,'" asserted Conyers. "This decision makes it clear that we must have an independent, nonpartisan commission to investigate both Russian interference in the U.S. election and allegations of collusion between the government of Vladimir Putin and the Trump campaign. Today's actions reek of a cover up and appear to be part of an ongoing effort by the Trump White House to impede the investigation into Russian ties and interference in our elections."

True enough. But there was one big difference.

On the evening of October 20, 1973, a scandal-plagued Richard Nixon was determined to fire independent special prosecutor Archibald Cox, who was investigating presidential wrongdoing as part of a broader inquiry into issues raised by the Watergate scandal. Attorney General Elliot Richardson and Deputy Attorney General William Ruckelshaus resigned rather than follow Nixon's orders. Finally, Robert Bork took over as acting attorney general and did the deed. The chaotic developments of that evening came to be known as the "Saturday Night Massacre."

No one expected Jeff Sessions to be an Elliott Richardson.

But Rosenstein, a veteran U.S. attorney who had a reputation as an experienced and responsible man of the law, could and should have been a William Ruckelshaus. Rosenstein's decision was at least a little bit surprising. Yes, he was a political appointee and, yes, he had a record that included several controversial moves. As the *Baltimore Sun* noted: "Rosenstein is no stranger to complicated investigations that are intertwined with politics. He was associate independent counsel under Kenneth W. Starr, who oversaw the Whitewater investigation into real estate dealings involving Bill and Hillary Clinton." But the Harvard-educated lawyer generally got high marks from Republicans and Democrats. "If it comes down to a Nixonian scenario, I believe he will do the right thing," said Gregg Bernstein, a former state's attorney in Maryland, where Rosenstein served as U.S. attorney.

Bernstein certainly seemed to suggest that Rosenstein was a Ruckelshaus for our own times.

When the Nixonian scenario played out, however, Rosenstein did not resign. He may have thought about it. ABC News reported: "Deputy Attorney General Rod Rosenstein was so upset with the White House for pinning the firing of FBI Director James Comey on him Wednesday that he was on the verge of resigning." But when he was confronted, Rosenstein announced: "No, I'm not quitting."

When Rosenstein appeared before the Senate Judiciary Committee in March 2017 to make the case for his confirmation as deputy attorney general, he was asked how he would handle the Russia inquiry from which Sessions had recused himself. Rosenstein offered a bold and patriotic response. "I don't know the details of what, if any, investigation is ongoing," the nominee said, "but I can certainly assure you if it's America against Russia, or America against any other country, I think everyone in this room knows which side I'm on."

The committee recommended his confirmation and in late April the Senate voted 94–6 to make him deputy attorney general. One of

the six "no" votes came from Senator Richard Blumenthal, D-Connecticut, who said he opposed the nomination because Rosenstein would not appoint a special counsel to oversee an inquiry into Moscow's meddling in the 2016 campaign and potential connections between Trump aides and the Russians. "Mr. Rosenstein has said that he wants to be approved by the Senate before he decides whether to appoint a special prosecutor," warned Blumenthal, "but that delay will mean that a man who was hired and can be fired by President Trump will decide whether the Trump administration will face a thorough and complete investigation."

Senator Warren cast another "no" vote. Asked why she was one of the few senators to reject Rosenstein, she said she was frustrated that the nominee "would not give a straight answer" to questions about standing up to Trump and appointing a special investigator.

Warren was right to worry. Rosenstein got very high marks on May 17, 2017, when he announced the appointment of Robert S. Mueller III, a highly regarded former prosecutor and FBI director, who would serve as a special counsel charged with investigating the prospect of coordination between Trump's associates and the Russians. There were many who commended Rosenstein for preserving his authority and using it to bring in a proper investigator. Yet, when he appeared before the Senate Intelligence Committee on June 7, he failed to make a clear commitment to defend the independence of the Mueller inquiry.

That was unsettling, but not surprising. The fact remains that, at the critical moment when Trump and Sessions were abusing *their* authority by scheming to "legitimize" the firing of Comey, the deputy attorney general was drawn into the wicked game that the president and the attorney general were playing. Rosenstein may well have been deceived and ill-treated by his superiors. But once he recognized that he was entangled in their deceits, he should have extracted himself as Richardson and Ruckleshaus did, by refusing to facilitate a president who was steering the country toward a constitutional crisis.

—8—

"THE KING OF VOTER SUPPRESSION"

Kris Kobach

Vice Chair of the Presidential Advisory Commission on Election Integrity

In 2012, the ALEC Exposed project revealed the shadowy circle of right-wing operatives who worked with the corporate-funded American Legislative Exchange Council to craft so-called model legislation for conservative state legislators to propose on issues ranging from wages to education and voting rights. The *Nation* magazine published a series of articles by reporters, academics and activists that highlighted the Center for Media and Democracy's ongoing examination of the conservative "bill mill." In a section on ALEC initiatives to refocus debates about election law, I wrote on how the Corporate Executive Committee for ALEC's Public Safety and Elections Task Force "began highlighting voter ID efforts in 2006, shortly after Karl Rove encouraged conservatives to take up voter fraud as an issue."

The article explained that "Kansas Republican Kris Kobach, who along with ALEC itself helped draft Arizona's anti-immigration law, has warned of 'illegally registered aliens.' . . . And when midterm elections put Republicans in charge of both chambers of the legislature in twenty-six states (up from fifteen), GOP legislators began moving bills resembling ALEC's model," the piece explained, before concluding that "restricting voting and direct democracy while ensuring that corporations can spend freely on campaigning makes advancing the conservative agenda a whole lot easier. 'Once they set the rules for elections and campaigns,' says Wisconsin State Representative Mark Pocan, a longtime ALEC critic, 'ALEC will pretty much call the shots.'"

 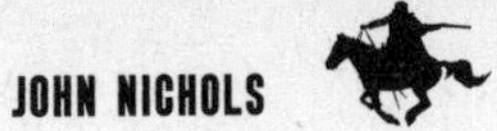

As it turned out, ALEC had to stand down in 2012, amid an outcry from civil rights groups over the organization's promotion of so-called stand-your-ground gun bills. As the Center for Media and Democracy noted: "ALEC temporarily disbanded its corporate-legislator task force that had approved extreme gun bills and voter restrictions, but ALEC did not take any steps to get those bills repealed where they had been enacted."

Though ALEC stood down, Kris Kobach kept right on campaigning. He got himself elected as the secretary of state of Kansas and emerged, in the words of the American Civil Liberties Union's Voting Rights Project, as "the king of voter suppression." That's a widely held view. Kristen Clarke, the president of the Lawyers' Committee for Civil Rights Under Law, says: "Kobach is public enemy number one when it comes to voter suppression in our country."

"During his tenure as Kansas' top election official, he has championed some of the strictest voting laws in the country, including the state's controversial proof-of-citizenship law, which requires people to provide birth certificates or passports in order to register to vote," noted a lengthy assessment of Kobach by the highly regarded DC bureau of the McClatchy newspaper group, which added that "judges who have ruled against Kobach in voting rights cases have accused him of engaging in 'wordplay meant to present a materially inaccurate picture of the documents' and dismissed his assertions about voter fraud because they were backed by 'scant evidence' or based on 'pure speculation.'"

Though Kobach's claims have been discredited and dismissed for years, he's got a fan in Donald Trump. The president repeatedly claimed that his 2016 presidential run was undermined by "serious voter fraud" and even suggested that he would have "won the popular vote if you deduct the millions of people who voted illegally." Trump's claims have been debunked by the Pulitzer Prize–winning PolitiFact project, which labels them "Pants on Fire" deceptions. So where does the president get his information? "While other secretaries of state, as well as government and academic studies, say occurrences of voter fraud are rare, Kellyanne Conway and other top Trump advisers cited Kobach as the source of the president's unsupported claim that millions of illegal ballots had tipped the popular vote in Democrat Hillary Clinton's favor," noted McClatchy. "So far, Kobach has provided no hard evidence of widespread voter fraud. The author of one study he cited, the Cooperative Congressional Elections Study, has said it actually shows a rate of noncitizen voting of about zero."

The president's reaction? On May 11, 2017, Trump named Vice President Mike Pence and Kris Kobach as the heads of his new Commission on Election Integrity. Senate minority leader Charles Schumer, D-New York, said that "putting an extremist like Mr. Kobach at the helm of this commission is akin to putting an arsonist in charge of the fire department." In a statement, Schumer decried the commission as "a clear front for constricting the access to vote." Ari Berman, the author of the book *Give Us the Ballot: The Modern Struggle for Voting Rights in America,* says that "if Trump followed Kobach's advice and pushed for policies like requiring documentary proof of citizenship for voter registration nationwide, it would have a massively suppressive impact on voting in America."

States write election laws. But no one knows better than Kris Kobach that conservative legislators have a penchant for embracing and enacting "model legislation" that made it harder for Americans to vote. Kobach told the *New York Daily News* on May 11, 2017, that "as a practical matter I'll be leading the commission" that has been positioned to make a major statement regarding elections and election laws in the United States. How major? Critics argue that the commission has been established not just to legitimize Donald Trump's false claims about massive voter fraud but to advance an agenda that could inspire radical rewrites of state election laws and massive voter suppression.

"It's not surprising that the Trump administration wants Kobach to lead this commission. Both Kobach and Trump have repeatedly dealt in lies about 'illegal voting.' We've seen this before—throughout our history, politicians have used propaganda about illegal voting to create unnecessary restrictions on the right to vote. And we know who this hurts—people of color, young people, first-time voters, low-income voters," argues the ACLU. "No matter how much

they lie, they can't change the facts. Voter suppression is the real threat to election integrity. But that's not a problem that any commission led by Kris Kobach is equipped to address."

PART 2

Generals and CEOs Searching for Monsters to Destroy

Freedom makes a huge requirement of every human being. With freedom comes responsibility. For the person who is unwilling to grow up, the person who does not want to carry his own weight, this is a frightening prospect.

—ELEANOR ROOSEVELT, 1960

[Technology] has brought forth terrifying weapons of destruction, which for the future of civilization, must be brought under control through a workable system of disarmament . . . This is, indeed, a moment for honest appraisal and historic decision. We can strive to master these problems for narrow national advantage or we can begin at once to undertake a period of constructive action which will subordinate selfish interest to the general well-being of the international community.

—PRESIDENT DWIGHT EISENHOWER, 1960

The most important speech on American foreign policy was not given by a president of the United States but by a future president who was then serving as secretary of state. John Quincy Adams was an experienced man of government when he stood before the U.S. House of Representatives on July 4, 1821 (four years before he was sworn in as the sixth president of the republic). But on this day he spoke with the authority of a worldly man, who as a precocious youth had joined his father John Adam's Revolutionary War–era diplomatic missions to France and the Netherlands, and who at the age of fourteen had traveled in the early 1780s with Francis Dana to initiate U.S. relations with the Russian Empire. A classicist, Adams was fluent in Latin and Greek and French and Dutch, and conversant in most of the languages of Europe. He had served as George Washington's minister to the Netherlands and Portugal, and is said to have contributed to Washington's farewell address as president. After his father succeeded Washington as president in 1797, John Quincy Adams represented the United States as minister to Prussia, where he renewed the essential Prussian-American Treaty of Amity and Commerce. He served as the first U.S. minister to Russia under James Madison, witnessed the Napoleonic Wars, negotiated the Treaty of Ghent to end the War of 1812 and renewed U.S. relations with Great Britain as the minister to the Court of St. James. As James Monroe's secretary of state, he negotiated treaties that defined the continental character of the United States, recognized and encouraged declarations of independence by new Latin American nations and helped to forge the Monroe Doctrine.

John Quincy Adams never served as a general, nor as the CEO of an oil company. But Adams knew a thing or two about the world, and about what was required for the United States to achieve peace and prosperity. So when he spoke to the Congress on that anniversary of American independence in 1821, at a time in American history when the country was still young enough to use July 4 as a moment for reflection rather than barbecue partying, the message that Adams brought to the Seventeenth Congress of the United States was taken seriously. As it should be to this day.

The United States, said Adams, entered the assembly of nations speaking "the language of equal liberty, of equal justice, and of equal rights. She has, in the lapse of nearly half a century, without a single exception, respected the independence of other nations while asserting and maintaining her own."

"Wherever the standard of freedom and independence has been or shall be unfurled, there will her heart, her benedictions and her prayers be," Adams said of the nation he had represented on the global stage for decades. "But she goes not abroad, in search of monsters to destroy."

The United States, Adams explained, was "the well-wisher to the freedom and independence of all" but "the champion and vindicator only of her own." The American duty was to lead by example, and to avoid the foreign entanglements about which Washington and Jefferson had warned.

To this day, there are those who read Adams's words and imagine they have discovered a lost isolationist appeal. But nothing could be further from the case. Adams was an internationalist, a man of science and scholarship who introduced to the United States the great ideas of the world and took to the world American ideas of equal greatness.

John Quincy Adams saw the United States as a member of the community of nations. But he warned that any attempt to aggressively command that community would diminish the ability of America to forge and maintain her own identity, and to address the inequalities and injustices that extended from a rough and imperfect founding. Adams, the fierce foe of slavery and ardent champion of education and scientific inquiry, had no desire to "make America great *again*." He wanted to make America greater. And he understood that greatness would extend from honest engagement with the world rather than demands placed upon it, from diplomacy rather than war.

Adams knew that a meddling and mangling interaction with the world would divert the attention of the United States from the task of perfecting itself, and of serving as a light unto the nations. Speaking of America on that July 4 in 1821, he said: "She well knows that by once enlisting under other banners than her own, were they even the banners of foreign independence, she would involve herself beyond the power of extrication, in all the wars of interest and intrigue, of individual avarice, envy, and ambition, which assume the colors and usurp the standard of freedom."

The world has changed a good deal since Adams uttered those words, and there are those who will tell you that it has become more complicated. In fact, the opposite is true. The world is more connected and more homogenous than at any time in history.

The only complication is that leaders and nations must now, from a position of knowledge and involvement, deal with issues that were once left to chance or simply neglected. The opportunities are immense, but so are the potential pitfalls for nations that go abroad searching for monsters to destroy.

Americans are told that their country has become the essential nation, and it is certainly true that the United States is a global economic and military powerhouse. But that does not mean that the United States must define the world at every turn. Even if the only purpose of the United States is to advance its economic and political influence, a sorry history of mercantilism and bumbled wars from Vietnam to Iraq tells us that attempts to impose the will of even the most powerful nation in the world often invite blowback and a loss of prestige.

Former secretary of state Colin Powell was said to have preached the "Pottery Barn Rule" ("you break it, you own it") when he tried to warn George W. Bush and Dick Cheney about the consequences of invading and occupying Iraq; he recalls that he told officials in the administration: "Once you break it, you are going to own it, and we're going to be responsible for 26 million people standing there looking at us. And it's going to suck up a good 40 to 50 percent of the Army for years. And it's going to take all the oxygen out of the political environment." That was a very John Quincy Adams observation, a very Dwight Eisenhower observation. But Powell got no buy-in from Bush or Cheney for his commonsense assessment. And there is no evidence to suggest that historical perspective and common sense will guide Donald Trump.

The election of Trump was a jarring event for not just the United States but for the world. This presidency will change U.S. foreign policy, and it will change the policies of other countries toward the United States. Unfortunately, Trump arrived in the White House with a convulsive and convoluted worldview that mixed the crude "Know-Nothing" dogmas of the 1840s with the empty-headed "America First" dogmas of the 1940s, and stirred in a military schoolboy's obsession with generals and bombs to blend the worst of isolationism with the worst of interventionism. Apocalyptic on one turn, usually after he's spent some time with Steve "American Carnage" Bannon, and naïve on the next, Trump speaks casually about the use of nuclear weapons ("Somebody hits us within ISIS—you wouldn't fight back with a nuke?" "The last person that wants to play the nuclear card believe me, is me; but you can never take cards off the table either," "I use the word unpredictable; you want to be unpredictable with nuclear weapons") and about nuclear proliferation ("Wouldn't you rather in a certain sense have Japan have nuclear weapons") and about exiting NATO ("obsolete") or not ("We strongly support NATO").

When Trump's worldview is not frightening, it is incoherent. He throws opposite camps together—anti-war isolationists and neoconservatives, multinational corporatists and opponents of free trade—and then cannot figure out why they won't coalesce. He answers the siren calls of charlatans like General Michael Flynn, his disgraced former national security advisor, puts people he barely knows and doesn't necessarily agree with (CIA director Mike Pompeo) in charge of powerful agencies and lets people he knows too well (Bannon) take seats at the tables where questions of war and peace are debated.

The one constant is Trump's adoration of generals. The New York Military Academy cadet captain cannot get enough of them, especially the ones who want to wage overwhelming, no-holds-barred wars. It is true that Trump studiously avoided actual military service during the Vietnam War. And it is true that he said during the 2016 campaign that "I know more about ISIS than the generals do, believe me." But after his election, Trump assembled what *Politico* called "the most military-heavy White House and civilian administration since at least World War II." As retired U.S. Army colonel Andrew Bacevich, the great historian of American diplomatic and military history, says: "Suddenly we have a romance, an infatuation, with generals."

"Trump has a particular fascination with swashbuckling World War II Gens. Douglas MacArthur and George Patton. Four sources close to Trump said that 'Patton,' the 1970 film starring George C. Scott that depicted Gen. Patton, is among the president-elect's favorite films—one he has watched repeatedly over the years. 'Trump,'

one of the people close to him said, 'loves this movie,'" wrote veteran DC reporter Shane Goldmacher in an essay titled "Why Trump Is So Obsessed with Generals."

"Frankly, he's way too impressed in the generals," a Trump confidante told Goldmacher. "The more braid you have on your shoulders and the more laurels that you have on your visor, the more impressed he is."

Some bright-siders, like David Graham of the *Atlantic*, imagine that the more sober of the generals (perhaps Defense Secretary Jim Mattis, perhaps National Security Advisor General H. R. McMaster) might temper Trump—or, at the very least, avert catastrophe. "Democrats, a beleaguered minority, have little means to slow the White House down. With some notable exceptions, most Republicans in Congress are unwilling or unable to mount any serious opposition to Trump's policies, both because they have other areas where they hope to work with Trump and also because the White House is reportedly drafting congressional staffers into service without their bosses' knowledge," wrote Graham as the new administration entered its second crazy week. "That leaves few people in a better position to push back than Trump's generals. They're within the administration, and they were chosen in part to give the president some credibility: Their military experience made them respectable, and imparted competence that Trump needed to borrow. And while Trump's critics worried that they would either lean toward an authoritarian model or else follow commands in the military manner, a series of reports suggests that they're already frustrated with the president and feuding with his aides."

The problem, of course, is summed up by that last line. As Bacevich notes, even the most sound of the generals are competing with other circles of Trump influencers inside the White House, including the one led by Bannon, who, as a former surface warfare officer in the Pacific Fleet and onetime special assistant to the chief of naval operations at the Pentagon, is quite confident elbowing aside the generals in a White House where he is the superior officer. "Of course, with Trump, we have the additional question, and that is: Can anybody really influence him?" notes Bacevich. "To what degree is he a person who will be amenable to taking counsel of advisers? We were pretty sure previous presidents were willing to do that. We can't be certain about this president."

As the Trump presidency gathered steam in March, Fred Kaplan, a savvy observer of the White House and international relations, was already commenting on the powerlessness of Mattis, McMaster and Secretary of State Rex Tillerson, writing in *Slate*: "The few grown-ups in Trump's Cabinet are getting sidelined, their expertise goes ignored, and the pledge that they could choose their own teams—an assurance they were given upon taking their jobs—lies in tatters."

But there is one area where these men and Trump can find common ground, and that is with regard to the military-industrial complex about which Dwight Eisenhower warned almost six decades ago. Trump's generals, and the civilians aligned with them, share the current president's passion for massive military spending, for a pumped-up Pentagon, for war preparation on an unprecedented level and for the waging of wars with a no-holds-barred aggressiveness that could unsettle Dick Cheney. As for diplomacy, they're barely respectful. It is perhaps true that Trump's generals are more worldly in their views than the president and Vice President Mike Pence. But you will not find the contemporary equivalent of the risk-taking yet often successful diplomats of the past, a George Kennan or even a Jim Baker, in this crowd.

This creates a dangerous calculus. Trump is surrounded by men who might actually offer him some good advice but whose vision for engaging with the world draws more from George Patton or George Bush than from John Quincy Adams or Dwight Eisenhower. "At some point," says Phillip Carter, an Iraq War veteran who is now the director of the Military, Veterans, and Society Program at the Center for a New American Security, "you worry about it being an echo chamber in the [situation] room."

"No doubt these men bring tremendous experience. But we should be wary about an overreliance on military figures," argues Carter, who has written with former Pentagon and National Security Council official Loren DeJonge Schulman about the dangers of a general-heavy administration. "Great generals don't always make

great Cabinet officials. And if appointed in significant numbers, they could undermine another strong American tradition: civilian control of an apolitical military."

America has always been at its best when it has a clear vision of how it will engage with the world, and when that vision has been based on an awareness that the military is a tool rather than a driving force in American foreign policy. "What we've learned over the last 15 years is that the U.S. military, as capable as it is, is not great at bringing political reconciliation to other parts of the world," explains Senator Chris Murphy, the Connecticut Democrat who serves on the Senate Foreign Relations Committee. "I generally worry about a foreign policy that is heavily dependent on U.S. military when we have so many other tools at our disposal."

The wisest of our forebears proposed to assemble administrations that would guard against foreign entanglements and against the corruptions of empire at home and abroad. They wanted to err instead toward "the light of reason in the human mind." In the Trump administration, unfortunately, that light is extinguished.

—9—

THE "MAD DOG"

General James Mattis (ret.)

Secretary of Defense

"Even when there is a necessity of military power, within the land," wrote Samuel Adams in 1768, "a wise and prudent people will always have a watchful and jealous eye over it."

Eight years later, Adams signed his name to a declaration of independence that included among its complaints against King George III a notation that "he has affected to render the Military independent of and superior to the Civil power."

The founders of the American experiment well understood the danger of ceding control over the military to generals. When they wrote a constitution in 1787, they sought to chain the dogs of war by requiring that Congress declare the intent of the United States to engage in military conflicts and by empowering an elected president to serve as commander in chief.

Americans have understood, as a basic value of their national experience, the equation detailed by University of North Carolina at Chapel Hill professor Richard Kohn when he wrote that "for democracy, civilian control—that is, control of the military by civilian officials elected by the people—is fundamental. Civilian control allows a nation to base its values and purposes, its institutions and practices, on the popular will rather than on the choices of military leaders, whose outlook by definition focuses on the need for internal order and external security."

That's not an anti-military construction. It is an articulation of the essential balance that is as old as the American experiment. Phyllis Bennis of the Institute for Policy Studies says of civilian oversight of the nation's armed forces: "That's a principle, not just a suggestion."

This understanding of the need to maintain civilian control has extended and deepened over time, with the enactment (as part of the 1947 law creating the Department of Defense) of a requirement that a military officer must be out of uniform for ten years before assuming the pivotal position of secretary of defense. The waiting period was eventually reduced to seven years in 2008, but the principle remained.

For retired marine general James Mattis, however, that principle was a problem. Having only retired in 2013 as commander of the U.S. Central Command, Mattis needed a congressional waiver to get around the law that was written to keep civilians in charge of the Pentagon.

Most members of the Senate and House rushed to provide it, as Mattis was widely regarded within the military and within the corridors of power in Washington as an able commander with an intellectual bent. "He knows the Middle East, South Asia, NATO and other areas and has evinced both a nuanced approach to the wars we're in and an appreciation for the importance of allies," explained Richard Fontaine, the president of the Center for a New American Security.

This was not, of course, what drew the new president to General Mattis.

What Trump seemed to really like about the general was his nickname, "Mad Dog."

"We are going to appoint Mad Dog Mattis as our Secretary of Defense," Trump announced dramatically to a campaign-style rally in Cincinnati a month after his election. "But we're not announcing it 'til Monday, so don't tell anyone—Mad Dog. He's great. He is great."

The nickname was never a favorite of the general, who fashions himself as something of a "warrior monk," encourages recruits to read widely and deeply about military strategy and once told a group of marines: "The most important six inches on the battlefield is between your ears." Mattis preferred to be remembered as the strategist who told troops in Iraq, where he was a key commander: "Engage your brain before you engage your weapon."

But he was also remembered for telling marines: "Be polite, be professional, but have a plan to kill everybody you meet." And for his message to Iraqi leaders in a region occupied by his troops: "I come in peace. I didn't bring artillery. But I'm pleading with you, with tears in my eyes: If you fuck with me, I'll kill you all." Mattis earned the "Mad Dog" moniker with warnings like these and with an infamous appearance at a 2005 San Diego forum where he said: "You go into Afghanistan, you got guys who slap women around for five years because they didn't wear a veil. You know, guys like that ain't got no manhood left anyway. So it's a hell of a lot of fun to shoot them. Actually it's quite fun to fight them, you know. It's a hell of a hoot. It's fun to shoot some people. I'll be right up there with you. I like brawling."

That swagger appealed to Trump. It had also earned Mattis occasional encouragement to watch his words during a marine career that saw him command the First Battalion, Seventh Marines, during the Persian Gulf War, command the Seventh Marine Regiment during the Afghanistan War and command the First Marine Division during the 2003 invasion of Iraq. Even if he did sound off now and again, however, Mattis was generally seen as "a general's general." And the fact that Mattis rejected torture, decried anti-Muslim rhetoric, sought to appoint women to key positions and respected the reality of climate change distinguished him as a general's general who was far more thoughtful than the Fox News "military analysts" who had won Trump's favor in the past.

It was harder, however, to make the case that Mattis, a career military man not long out of uniform, was a civilian's civilian.

That worried a handful of legislators who still embraced the wisdom of the founders. The members of the House and Senate who challenged the Mattis appointment did not do so out of disdain for Mattis, who they freely acknowledged would be one of the more reasonable members of Trump's cabinet. They did so out of respect for historic American values, and out of concern, as Connecticut senator Richard Blumenthal noted, about "the precedent that [a recently retired general] assuming this office would set."

 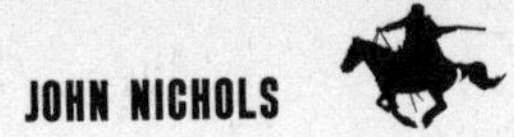

Ultimately, the Senate voted 81–17 on January 12 to grant the Mattis waiver. Greater opposition was seen in the 235–188 vote for the waiver by the House. Many House members expressed frustration after Trump's transition team canceled a planned appearance before the House Armed Services Committee in which Mattis was to address the waiver issue and to speak about civilian-control concerns. That cancellation drew rebukes from not just Democrats but also from House Armed Services chairman Mac Thornberry, a Texas Republican, who correctly complained that "there are major principles of government involved with this exception, which has been requested for the first time in 67 years. Unfortunately, shortsightedness prevailed."

Shortsightedness would continue to prevail on January 20, the day of Trump's inauguration when, with scant debate, the Senate voted 98–1 to confirm Mattis.

The sole dissenting vote came from New York Democrat Kirsten Gillibrand, the ranking member on the Senate Armed Services Committee's Subcommittee on Personnel, who had responded to Trump's December selection of Mattis with an immediate announcement that "while I deeply respect General Mattis's service, I will oppose a waiver. Civilian control of our military is a fundamental principle of American democracy, and I will not vote for an exception to this rule." Gillibrand stuck with that principle. After meeting in early January 2017 with Mattis, the senator said: "He has served our country admirably. He is well-regarded as an extraordinary general, and I am very grateful for that service, and I'm very grateful that he's willing to continue his service for the president-elect. But I still believe that civilian control of our military is fundamental to the American democracy."

Gillibrand's stance was a lonely one. But it will be remembered as one of the most important dissents of the transition to Trump's presidency. It is easy to rewrite the rules in the moment, to entertain exceptions on the theory that particular requests truly are exceptional. Most Democrats embraced that compromise, as they embraced Mattis. But the senator from New York did not just refuse. She raised the issue again and again. Asked before the final vote to comment on other members of the Senate, including Democrats, who had not joined her in declaring early and consistent opposition to the waiver, Gillibrand replied: "You'll have to ask them. I just think it's fundamental to the Constitution."

— 10 —

THE DEPUTY SECRETARY FOR BOEING

Patrick Shanahan

Deputy Secretary of Defense Designee

Secretary of Defense James Mattis knew who he wanted to have as his second-in-command at the Pentagon: Michèle Flournoy, the former under secretary of defense for policy who served as a principal advisor to Secretaries of Defense Robert Gates and Leon Panetta during President Obama's first term. A senior fellow at Harvard's Belfer Center for Science and International Affairs who serves as CEO of the Center for a New American Security—and whose resume includes work with the Defense Policy Board, the Project on National Security Reform and the Defense Science Board Task Force on Transformation—she was on the cutting edge when it came to thinking about everything from national security to defense spending to the delicate balances that must be achieved to keep the peace and extend it. Had Hillary Clinton been elected president in 2016, Flournoy might herself have become secretary of defense. She had praised Trump's selection of Mattis (calling him "a much respected military thinker") for the top post and Mattis very much wanted her on his team. So it was all good.

Or maybe not.

"Flournoy had preliminary conversations with Mattis and went to New York to brief people on the Trump team on her work on defense and National Security Council reform but withdrew her name from any consideration in mid-December," reported CNN. Why? The key appears to have been that trip to New York to meet with the Trump team. As much as she respected Mattis, Flournoy said, she determined that "he needed a deputy who wouldn't be struggling every other day about whether they could be part of some of the policies that were likely to take shape." Translation: she could not see a way to fit into an administration with Donald Trump as the commander in chief.

It was clear that expectations would have to be lowered.

A few weeks later, President Trump named his pick for deputy secretary of defense: Patrick Shanahan, the senior vice president for Supply Chain & Operations at Boeing.

Yes, Boeing, the second-largest U.S. defense contractor after Lockheed Martin Corporation.

Shanahan was tapped to oversee defense policy, the budget and, um, the acquisition teams at the Pentagon. "Shanahan, 54, has no military or political experience," noted the *Seattle Times* when the selection was announced in March. "He is, however, familiar with defense procurement from the business side." Very familiar.

Shanahan worked for many years as the vice president and general manager of Boeing Missile Defense Systems, and before that he was general manager for Rotorcraft Systems and U.S. Army Aviation programs.

In other words, if there was a living, breathing embodiment of the military-industrial complex, it was Patrick Shanahan, a thirty-one-year Boeing employee, member of the Boeing executive council and now the guy who will be helping the Pentagon with procurement issues. Shanahan's defenders pointed out that he was no more of a Republican than was Flournoy; in fact, he had donated to the campaigns of Democrats in the past. And they also noted that ethics rules would require Shanahan to recuse himself from specific involvement with Boeing buys for two years.

But two years out of Boeing does not take the Boeing out of the Boeing exec.

And that was fine by Donald Trump. The president knew exactly what he was doing when he picked Shanahan.

"After a rocky start between the new administration and aerospace giant Boeing," reported the *Seattle Times*, "President Donald Trump's nomination Thursday of senior company executive Pat Shanahan as deputy secretary of defense is the latest sign of an increasingly cozy relationship." The president had griped back in November 2016

 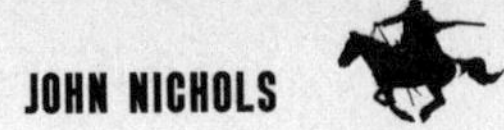

about the cost of the next Air Force One being produced by Boeing. But Boeing chief executive officer Dennis Muilenburg had already flown to Washington and down to Trump's Mar-a-Lago resort in Florida to work on the relationship.

As the president was announcing the Shanahan nomination, the White House was also announcing a budget blueprint with $13.5 billion in funding proposed for procuring new military aircraft, including $4 billion for Boeing's F/A-18 fighter jets.

The *Washington Post* noted that Shanahan's time with Boeing "might highlight Trump's propensity to lean on the revolving door of the defense industry and the U.S. military" in making appointments to Pentagon posts. Well, yes, that it might.

— 11 —

DIRECTOR OF THE OFFICE OF THE MILITARY-INDUSTRIAL COMPLEX

Mick Mulvaney

Director of the Office of Management and Budget

Donald Trump used his first joint address to the Congress of the United States on February 28, 2017, to engage in an unprecedented flight of fiscal fantasy. Specifically, the president imagined that the United States could cut taxes for wealthy Americans and corporations, rip tens of billions of dollars out of domestic programs (and from diplomacy and climate-change initiatives), hand that money over to the military-industrial complex and somehow remain a functional and genuinely strong nation.

Trump did not articulate this agenda quite so bluntly. The president's hour-long speech was far more traditional and temperate in character than his ballistic inaugural address. The themes were, for the most part, predictable: "construction of a great wall along our southern border," "vetting procedures," "construction of the Keystone and Dakota Access Pipelines," "for every one new regulation, two old regulations must be eliminated," "school choice." The rhetoric was, by the standards of this presidency, disciplined. But the specifics were few. Only toward the end did the president get precise, saying: "I am sending the Congress a budget that rebuilds the military, eliminates the Defense sequester, and calls for one of the largest increases in national defense spending in American history."

Trump made little effort to explain how he would pay for that increase, aside from mentioning the fact that he had "placed a hiring freeze on non-military and non-essential Federal workers." The president let John Michael "Mick" Mulvaney, a wealthy political careerist

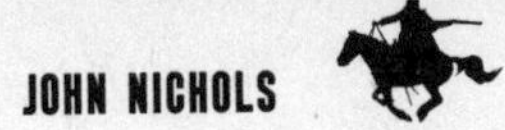

from South Carolina (elected to the state house in 2006, elected to the state senate in 2008, elected to the U.S. House in 2000, tapped to join Trump's cabinet as director of the Office of Management and Budget shortly after the 2016 election), do the heavy lifting.

An unblinking, and often unthinking, advocate for domestic austerity budgets even in times of plenty, Mulvaney made a name for himself as a debt-and-deficits-obsessed congressman who was always on the hunt for an excuse to shut down the federal government. The *New York Times* noted that Mulvaney took such a hard line against raising the nation's debt limit that he and his allies embraced "the term 'Shutdown Caucus' because of their willingness to shut the government down" instead of passing the routine resolutions that had been approved by past Congresses with nary a notice. If Mulvaney could not find a fiscal argument for a shutdown during Barack Obama's tenure, he would come up with something else: like that time in 2015 when he opposed a compromise plan to keep the government up and running because it included funding for Planned Parenthood.

Mulvaney was so far out on the fiscal fringe that he backed libertarian-leaning Kentucky Senator Rand Paul for the Republican presidential nomination in 2016, which fed the concerns of hawkish senators like Arizona Republican John McCain that Mulvaney might be a bit too open to imposing mild restraints on Department of Defense spending. (McCain needn't have worried, as would soon become evident.)

After Paul's campaign fizzled, Mulvaney jumped on board the Trump train. Trump and Mulvaney had some things in common; for instance, Mulvaney had tried his hand at real-estate development. And, as with Trump, it had not always gone well. During his first campaign for Congress, local papers were filled with reports of how "Republican U.S. House candidate Mick Mulvaney is fending off questions over his role in a housing development plagued by financial and environmental problems."

A television ad from the campaign of the man Mulvaney was challenging, then–House Budget Committee chairman John Spratt, summed up the complaint: "Mick Mulvaney convinced Lancaster

County to approve $30 million in bonds to improve this property. Then Mulvaney flipped the property for a $7 million profit to another developer who had defaulted on a $78 million loan." Mulvaney called the charges "outrageous" and claimed, with a Trumpian twist, that Democratic policies were to blame for anything that went awry with the deal. Then Stanley Smith, a Lancaster County council representative, recounted details of the so-called Edenmoor deal in the local papers, declaring that "we trusted Mick, and we shouldn't have. Now that Edenmoor is an 800-acre polluted wasteland with over $5 million in unpaid property taxes, Mick Mulvaney says it's not his problem. He has walked away and says that people need to understand that that's how business is done. I am a Republican, but I cannot bring myself to vote for a man like Senator Mulvaney who thinks it's okay to take advantage of people and use government for his own personal gain."

That might have put a roadblock in the way of Mulvaney's ambitions in some election years. But in the Republican-wave year of 2010, he prevailed with relative ease and made his way to Congress. Mulvaney quickly made a name for himself as one of the fiercest of the right-wing Freedom Caucus's fiscal hawks. He posted on Facebook about "the best question: do we really need government-funded research at all?" and anticipated the "alternative facts" era by responding to numbers he did not like by claiming that the Department of Labor manipulated unemployment statistics. (As a member of the Trump administration, he was back at it, griping that the nonpartisan Congressional Budget Office might not be up to assessing large pieces of legislation like the Republican "repeal and replace" answer to the Affordable Care Act.)

When Trump tapped Mulvaney for the Office of Management and Budget (OMB), there were still a few romantics who imagined that the new president might keep some of his big-spending campaign promises. For them, the Mulvaney pick made no sense. Headlines warned that "Trump promised to save entitlements. His budget director pick wants him to break his vow." In fact, Trump's selection of Mulvaney was a signal that the president was not going to be keeping a lot of promises. The Mulvaney pick tipped the balance toward the

Steve Bannon wing of the White House, which combined a determination to pursue both the "deconstruction of the administrative state" and the construction of unprecedented military power for the real and imagined wars to come. Trump in transition became what Trump as a candidate had rarely been: a fiscal "hawk" who fretted that "we are nearly $20 trillion in debt" while pointing to Mulvaney as "a very high-energy leader with deep convictions for how to responsibly manage our nation's finances and save our country from drowning in red ink."

Trump promised his administration would make "smart choices" with Mulvaney helming the OMB. In fact, Trump and the people around him knew that Mulvaney, the career ladder–climbing candidate from South Carolina, would make political choices.

That was hinted at in Trump's speech to Congress and confirmed a few weeks later, when Mulvaney released a budget blueprint proposal that asked Congress for a $54 billion increase in Pentagon spending—a 10 percent hike over the previous fiscal year's budget—and a 6 percent increase for the Mexican border wall–building Department of Homeland Security. At the same time, the budget projected no increase in the deficit, making it appealing to at least some of Mulvaney's old friends from the House Freedom Caucus. How was this fiscal fête achieved? By pretty much gutting everything else. Seriously—CNN ran a list of the cuts:

- Health and Human Services, the department responsible for implementing Obamacare and its proposed repeal, would face a $12.6 billion cut—a 16.2% decrease.
- Environmental Protection Agency: $2.6 billion, or 31.4%.
- State Department: $11 billion, or 28.7%.
- Labor Department: $2.5 billion, or 20.7%.
- Agriculture Department: $5 billion, or 20.7%.
- US Army Corps of Engineers: $1 billion, a 16.3% cut.
- Cuts National Institutes of Health spending by $5.8 billion, a nearly 20% cut. Also overhauls NIH to focus on "highest priority" efforts and eliminates the Fogarty International Center.

- Other double-digit cuts include Commerce at 15.7%; Education at 13.5%; Housing and Urban Development at 13.2%; Transportation at 12.7%, and Interior at 11.7%.

Targeted for elimination were Community Service Block Grants that fund programs such as Meals on Wheels, the Corporation for Public Broadcasting, the Global Climate Change Initiative, the Legal Services Corporation, the Low Income Home Energy Assistance Program, the National Endowment for the Arts, the National Endowment for the Humanities and dozens of Environmental Protection Agency and Department of Education programs and initiatives. Funding for Amtrak was cut, as was funding for the Clean Power Plan and for payments to fund United Nations climate change initiatives. "I think the President was fairly straightforward—we're not spending money on that anymore; we consider that to be a waste of your money to go out and do that," announced Mulvaney, when asked about programs to address climate change.

The OMB director explained, with a straight face, that cuts to Meals on Wheels and Head Start programs weren't hard-hearted at all. "I think it's probably one of the most compassionate things we can do," said Mulvaney, who argued that it was "fairly compassionate" to refuse to fund programs "unless we can guarantee to you that that money is actually being used in a proper function."

"Meals on Wheels sounds great," Mulvaney told the White House press corps. But, he said, "we're not going to spend [money] on programs that cannot show that they actually deliver the promises that we've made to people."

Actually, it is Meals on Wheels that delivers on promises, in the form of hot meals and a friendly check-in for millions of elderly Americans in small towns and big cities across the United States. "Cuts of any kind to these highly successful and leveraged programs would be a devastating blow to our ability to provide much-needed care for millions of vulnerable seniors in America, which in turn saves billions of dollars in reduced healthcare expenses," explained Ellie Hollander, president and CEO of Meals on Wheels America.

Virtually all of the cuts proposed by Trump and Mulvaney assault the social fabric of America. So over-the-top was the plan that, when the president in early May signed a $1 trillion spending bill to keep the government operating through September, few of the proposals for draconian domestic cuts were included. But the "compromise" did include a dramatic increase in the allocation for the Pentagon, up $15 billion. So it wasn't like Trump had abandoned the initial plan. He had merely delayed some of the uglier slashing and burning at home in order to avert an embarrassing government shutdown at the close of his first hundred days in office. Mulvaney was still on the case, peddling what serious legislators identified as an immoral agenda.

"It's said that a budget is a statement of values," explained Oregon senator Jeff Merkley when describing the spending priorities that Trump and Mulvaney outlined initially and that the OMB director continued to promote as the year went on. "If so, this budget makes it perfectly clear that the Trump Administration values special interests and defense contractors over American middle-class families."

Merkley identifies Mulvaney's plan as "an attack on our families' most essential needs, from the clean air and water we breathe and drink, to the schools our kids attend, to the very investments that create American jobs."

Describing the budget blueprint as "morally bankrupt," California congresswoman Barbara Lee says: "This budget would offer massive handouts to defense contractors while gutting lifesaving programs for the poor and middle class. Despite the rampant waste, fraud and abuse at the Pentagon, this budget funnels even more taxpayer money into the pockets of defense contractors. Rather than make us safer, this budget outline is a recipe for greater instability, hunger and hopelessness around the world. By cutting the Department of State and USAID by more than $10 billion, the Trump Administration is undermining our global leadership and sentencing families around the world to poverty and illness."

Lee has fought these battles before. But never like this.

This argument in favor of austerity for working families and munificence for military contractors is not exactly new. It has been a conservative mantra since the Grand Old Party purged itself of the "Modern Republicans" who clung to the vision of former president Dwight Eisenhower and made theirs a party of reaction rather than reason. But even Ronald Reagan and George W. Bush eschewed the budgetary extremism that Trump, via Mulvaney, embraced with a fervor that arrested any fantasy that a "billionaire populist" president might steer his adopted party back from the brink.

The budget proposal that Trump took to Congress, and that Mulvaney continues to peddle is not the final statement on fiscal priorities. It is, as they say, a blueprint. And final budgets are never built to spec.

But the indications are clear. Trump's Office of Management and Budget does not intend to plot a course to "make America great again." Rather, it proposes to tip the balance against greatness by making what the first Republican president, Abraham Lincoln, referred to as "the last best hope of earth" into an ever more heavily militarized state that will not care for its own.

This is by design. It is not a grand design, however. Rather, it is an approach that Trump has adopted as he has moved from the capricious politics of his initial candidacy to the reality of a rigidly right-wing presidency.

Mulvaney said on the eve of the president's "Budget Blueprint" speech: "The president is doing what he said he'd do when he ran." But Trump said a lot of things when he was bidding for the presidency in 2016. He made big promises about jobs and infrastructure, delivering more and better health care, protecting Social Security and Medicare. He portrayed himself as a critic of the war in Iraq, a skeptic about new military adventures and a foe of "the fraud and abuse and everything else" in bloated Department of Defense budgets. "I'm gonna build a military that's gonna be much stronger than it is right now," he announced on NBC's *Meet the Press* in 2015. "It's gonna be so strong, nobody's gonna mess with us," he promised. "But you know what? We can do it for a lot less."

That seemed reasonably definitive.

But, as everyone who has been paying attention knows, Trump bounced all over the ideological landscape during the 2016 campaign, and his presidency hasn't exactly been a model of consistency. Unless you listen to Mulvaney. The OMB director claims, against all evidence to the contrary, that bloating up the Pentagon budget was always a high priority of the Trump campaign. "What you see in this budget," the budget director explained in February 2017, "is exactly what the president ran on. He ran on increasing spending on the military."

Mulvaney was unsettlingly vague when asked about keeping Trump's promise to guard against Social Security cuts. But he was clear about the general thrust of the administration's approach to budgeting. "[We] took $54 billion out of non-defense discretionary spending in order to increase defense spending—entirely consistent with what the president said that he would do," Mulvaney said. "So what's the president done? He's protected the nation, but not added any additional money to the 2018 deficit. This is a winning argument for my friends in the House and a winning argument for a lot of folks all over the country. The president does what he says but doesn't add to the budget [deficit]. That's a win."

Mulvaney is wrong. That's not a win.

That does not protect America, at least not in the sense that Democratic and Republican presidents have historically understood the preservation of the republic. Budgeting is always a matter of striking balances. When the balance is right, the American experiment advances. When there is an imbalance, it is threatened.

Dwight Eisenhower explained this when he appeared barely two months into his presidency before the American Society of Newspaper Editors. The speech was much anticipated. Eisenhower was the first Republican commander in chief in two decades, and he was still placing his imprint on the Oval Office, the country and a world that was in the grips of a "Cold War." The new president could have chosen any topic for his first major address to the assembled media luminaries. He chose as his topic the proper balancing of budget priorities.

Eisenhower recognized the threats that existed. He spoke, at length, about difficult relations between the United States and the Soviet Union and he addressed the threat of annihilation posed by the spread of atomic weaponry. But the career military man—the supreme commander of the Allied Expeditionary Forces in Europe during World War II, the chief of staff of the army during the post-war era when tensions with Moscow rose—did not come to suggest that increased defense spending was a singular priority. In fact, his purpose was the opposite. He spoke of the "dread road" of constant military escalation and warned about "a burden of arms draining the wealth and the labor of all peoples; a wasting of strength that defies the American system or the Soviet system or any system to achieve true abundance and happiness for the peoples of this earth."

"Every gun that is made, every warship launched, every rocket fired signifies, in the final sense, a theft from those who hunger and are not fed, those who are cold and are not clothed," said Eisenhower, who explained:

> This world in arms is not spending money alone.
>
> It is spending the sweat of its laborers, the genius of its scientists, the hopes of its children.
>
> The cost of one modern heavy bomber is this: a modern brick school in more than 30 cities.
>
> It is two electric power plants, each serving a town of 60,000 population.
>
> It is two fine, fully equipped hospitals.
>
> It is some fifty miles of concrete highway.
>
> We pay for a single fighter with a half million bushels of wheat.
>
> We pay for a single destroyer with new homes that could have housed more than 8,000 people.
>
> This, I repeat, is the best way of life to be found on the road the world has been taking.
>
> This is not a way of life at all, in any true sense. Under the cloud of threatening war, it is humanity hanging from a cross of iron.

Eisenhower did not propose surrender or immediate or casual disarmament. But he did propose diplomacy ("We welcome every honest act of peace") and the sincere pursuit of a world with fewer weapons and fewer excuses for war making ("This we do know: a

world that begins to witness the rebirth of trust among nations can find its way to a peace that is neither partial nor punitive").

"The monuments to this new kind of war would be these: roads and schools, hospitals and homes, food and health," Eisenhower concluded. "We are ready, in short, to dedicate our strength to serving the needs, rather than the fears, of the world."

These are different times. The world has changed, and so has the United States. But what has changed the most is the understanding, once shared by Republicans and Democrats, that providing for the common defense does not preclude the promotion of the general welfare.

Conservatives like to say, "There is no free lunch," and that is certainly true when it comes to budgeting. It is not possible to move tens of billions of dollars out of domestic programs that have already in many cases been squeezed to austerity levels and into a military budget so vast, the National Priorities Project reports that "U.S. military expenditures are roughly the size of the next seven largest military budgets around the world, combined."

On a planet where Americans account for 4.34 percent of the population, U.S. military spending accounts for 37 percent of the global total. And Trump, with Mulvaney's assistance, appears to be determined to push the latter percentage way upward.

That is a problematic imbalance in itself. But what makes it even more problematic is Mulvaney's signal that, under Trump, the imbalance will be maintained not by collecting new revenues but by redistributing money that could have been spent on health care and housing and education at home—and on the international diplomacy and foreign aid that might actually reduce the need for military expenditures. "While Trump claims he's serious about great negotiation, his plan to pillage funds from the State Department and foreign aid to feed the insatiable Pentagon budget says otherwise," notes Peace Action executive director Jon Rainwater. Instead of putting Americans first, Trump's "plans to line the arms industry's pockets by cutting programs like health care that provide real security to American families [say] otherwise."

This is the contemporary realization of the fear that President Thomas Jefferson expressed on December 2, 1806, in his sixth annual address to the new United States. "Our duty is, therefore, to act upon things as they are and to make a reasonable provision for whatever they may be. Were armies to be raised whenever a speck of war is visible in our horizon, we never should have been without them," warned Jefferson. "Our resources would have been exhausted on dangers which have never happened instead of being reserved for what is really to take place."

— 12 —

THE ABSOLUTIST

Lieutenant General H. R. McMaster

National Security Advisor

One month into Donald Trump's presidency, the White House was such a mess that the president had to devote a holiday weekend to the desperate search for a new national security advisor. His initial choice, retired general Michael Flynn, had been fired for withholding information from Vice President Mike Pence about contacts with Russia's ambassador to the United States.

The storyline read like chapter 2 of a Tom Clancy novel that would not end well for the commander in chief. So it was perhaps appropriate that Trump's pick to fill the void opened by Flynn's exit was the best-selling author of a book that delves into the White House intrigues and military missteps of another time. The notable distinction, however, is that Lieutenant General H. R. McMaster is a nonfiction writer.

A scholar and a soldier who earned a doctorate in military history from the University of North Carolina at Chapel Hill and a Silver Star for commanding a unit in a 1991 Persian Gulf War battle with Iraq's Republican Guard (along with broad recognition for his leadership of the Third Armored Cavalry Regiment during George W. Bush's second Iraq War), in 1997, General McMaster wrote the best-selling book *Dereliction of Duty: Johnson, McNamara, the Joint Chiefs of Staff, and the Lies That Led to Vietnam.*

General McMaster is a smart and confident man, with an independent streak. That explains why he was not Trump's first choice for the job, and why, since his selection, there have been a number of reports of clashes between the general and the president. It also explains why Trump doubters celebrated the selection of General McMaster.

Arizona senator John McCain, who had emerged as a frequently pointed critic of the president in a Republican Congress where most members of the House and Senate served as little more than rubber stamps, hailed the naming of the general as "outstanding."

Defense Secretary Jim Mattis, broadly (if not entirely accurately) seen as a cabinet-level check and balance on Trump, encouraged his former colleague to take the job. And former Obama Defense Department official Andrew Exum described General McMaster as "one of the most talented men I know. A great officer and thinker. Huge upgrade."

No one was going to debate that General McMaster was a huge upgrade from the scandal-plagued Flynn. But that does not necessarily mean that General McMaster was the right choice for one of the most important jobs in the White House—as the general's embarrassing defense of Trump's firing of FBI director James Comey soon confirmed.

The national security advisor post, which was established during the Cold War, has traditionally been occupied by civilians, usually with military experience, as opposed to active-duty military men such as General McMaster. While generals have held the position before (including then–lieutenant general Colin Powell, who held the post during Ronald Reagan's second term), the national security advisor job is not a military posting. Rather, it is a senior slot in the executive office of the president, whose commander-in-chief status maintains civilian control over the military.

"President Trump's placement of career military personnel in positions usually filled by civilians is troubling," said Paul Kawika Martin, senior director for policy with Peace Action, the nation's largest grassroots peace organization. Noting that the United States already devoted over half its discretionary spending to the Pentagon, weapons and past wars, Martin explained that "as they say, if you only have a hammer, everything looks like a nail. The world is too complex for only one tool. The threats of climate change, terrorism and nuclear weapons require long-term solutions around energy policy, alleviating poverty, increased education and negotiating nuclear weapons agreements. Naming another general as national

 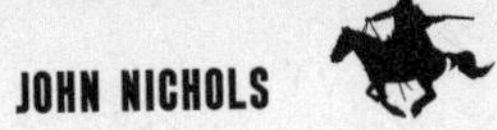

security advisor is a mistake, instead the White House needs more diplomatic skills in its tool box."

That's an old-fashioned American conception.

The founders of the American experiment, having only recently unshackled thirteen colonies from the British Empire, were wary of monarchs and the armies they had used to maintain "the divine right of kings." "Among the Romans it was a standing maxim to excite a war, whenever a revolt was apprehended. Throughout all Europe, the armies kept up under the pretext of defending, have enslaved the people," explained James Madison, the essential author of the Constitution, who warned that "in time of actual war, great discretionary powers are constantly given to the Executive Magistrate. Constant apprehension of War, has the same tendency to render the head too large for the body. A standing military force, with an overgrown Executive, will not long be safe companions to liberty. The means of defense against foreign danger, have been always the instruments of tyranny at home."

Long before President Dwight Eisenhower counseled wariness with regard to a "military-industrial complex," Elbridge Gerry, a delegate to the Constitutional Convention, observed that "standing armies in time of peace are inconsistent with the principles of republican Governments, dangerous to the liberties of a free people, and generally converted into destructive engines for establishing despotism."

Today, the United States has a standing army. It is huge and expensive. Trump seems to be intent on making it huger, and more expensive—so big and so costly that his approach calls into question whether he even begins to comprehend what Eisenhower was talking about when he warned that "this conjunction of an immense military establishment and a large arms industry is new in the American experience. The total influence—economic, political, even spiritual—is felt in every city, every statehouse, every office of the federal government. We recognize the imperative need for this development. Yet we must not fail to comprehend its grave implications. Our toil, resources and livelihood are all involved; so is the very structure of our society."

"In the councils of government," Eisenhower argued, "we must guard against the acquisition of unwarranted influence, whether sought or unsought, by the military-industrial complex. The potential for the disastrous rise of misplaced power exists, and will persist. We must never let the weight of this combination endanger our liberties or democratic processes. We should take nothing for granted. Only an alert and knowledgeable citizenry can compel the proper meshing of the huge industrial and military machinery of defense with our peaceful methods and goals so that security and liberty may prosper together."

General McMaster understands this concept. At the University of North Carolina at Chapel Hill he studied with Richard Kohn, the brilliant historian of peace, war and defense arrangements who famously explained that "the point of civilian control is to make security subordinate to the larger purposes of a nation, rather than the other way around. The purpose of the military is to defend society, not to define it. While a country may have civilian control of the military without democracy, it cannot have democracy without civilian control."

General McMaster's book, *Dereliction of Duty*, examines the challenges that arose when civilian leaders and the Joint Chiefs of Staff worked with one another during the Vietnam War. (A favorable *New York Times* review referred to it as "a comprehensive, balanced and relentless exploration of the specific role of the Joint Chiefs of Staff.") General McMaster dismisses the simplistic contentions of partisans and pundits—at the time and today. "The war in Vietnam was not lost in the field, nor was it lost on the front pages of *The New York Times*, or on the college campuses," he explains. "It was lost in Washington, D.C., even before Americans assumed sole responsibility for the fighting in 1965 and before they realized the country was at war." It was, he writes, "a uniquely human failure, the responsibility for which was shared by President Johnson and his principal military and civilian advisors."

General McMaster's "solution" is to argue that military commanders must be more assertive in defining strategic objections and making a case for decisive military action. That's a popular notion

with military commanders. But, as Dr. Steven Metz, the Henry L. Stimson Professor of Military Studies, U.S. Army War College, noted in a 1997 review of the book, it's problematic.

"While *Dereliction of Duty* might set new standards for stridency in its criticism of America's entry into Vietnam, it does not offer radically new ideas, evidence, or concepts," wrote Metz. "It is, rather, a powerful case study of the approach to national security that predominates in the US officer corps and other conservative segments of the American public. In a sense, McMaster has taken precisely the tack on Vietnam that one would expect of a very bright, passionate, and articulate US Army officer. For instance, McMaster implies that national security should be above or at least quarantined from 'normal' politics. He clearly sympathizes with those service Chiefs who were unable or unwilling to link Vietnam policy with other concerns such as Johnson's reelection and the passage of the Great Society legislation. He condemns military leaders like Maxwell Taylor who did think in such terms. In this, McMaster runs counter to the post-Vietnam tendency within the American military which teaches strategic leaders to consider the wider political context in which military decisions are made (even though not necessarily framing strategic advice in terms of domestic politics)."

Another concerning aspect of General McMaster's approach, explained Metz "is what might be called an 'absolutist' perspective on the use of force which posits a clear distinction between peace and war. This too has a long and deep tradition in the American ethos. For an absolutist, the objective in war is to use overwhelming force to impose your will on the enemy."

That sort of thinking is likely to go over well in a Trump White House. But it is at odds with what Metz has described as the "realist" understanding "that in a bipolar, nuclear-armed world, force and statecraft must be inextricable."

Of course, General McMaster wrote his book, and Metz reviewed it, twenty years before Trump named the general as the country's twenty-sixth national security advisor. The Iraq War proved that many of the lessons learned from the Vietnam experience were unlearned too quickly. And the struggle with ISIS brings new urgency to an old question articulated by Metz about "whether the United States could again stumble into a form of armed conflict that it does not understand."

The answer in the Trump era, when an ill-prepared and egotistical president is the commander in chief, is at once the great unknown and the great fear. There are no guarantees that Trump, or Steve Bannon, will listen to General McMaster on every issue. In fact, given the general's stated view that the label "radical Islamic terrorism" is not helpful because terrorists are "un-Islamic," it is quite likely that they will dismiss much of what their advisor says.

The likely, and troubling, prospect is that Trump and Bannon will hear what they want to hear from General McMaster. And what they will hear, in particular, are arguments for a dramatically extended military-industrial complex.

"Like Trump, McMaster's positions on American grand strategy remain to be seen," Metz wrote in a thoughtful February 2017 assessment for *World Politics Review*. "[McMaster] has, though, taken strong positions on the application of armed force. This means that his writing and speeches may indicate how the Trump administration in general will think about the use of the U.S. military."

In particular, Metz suggests, General McMaster is likely to counsel a "go big or stay home" approach that may be cautious about launching wars but that is committed to winning them: "no half-measures or incremental escalation designed to send subtle messages." The point is to be definitional and overwhelming. And, of course, that demands a very big, ever-at-the-ready military. Coupled with General McMaster's advocacy for dramatically expanding the size of the U.S. Army—in 2016 he told a Senate Armed Services subcommittee that the army "risks being too small to secure the nation"—the "go big or stay home" strategy is a recipe for precisely the sort of dramatic increases in Pentagon spending that have been outlined in the White House budget plans advanced by OMB director Mick Mulvaney.

The wise counsel that says defense spending levels do not need to rise in order to keep America secure is not going to come from this national security advisor. It may be that Trump would never

 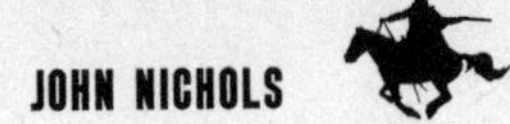

have put anyone in the position who would provide that counsel. But this does not change the fact that General McMaster seems to be determined to build up the military at the expense of every other prospect.

That's dangerous not just in this moment but for the long-term prospects of a nation that must do more than simply prepare for the next war.

The historian Andrew Bacevich argues that the national security advisor should focus on "grand strategy." "In this rarified atmosphere, preparing for and conducting war coexists with, and arguably should even take a backseat to, other considerations. To advance the fundamental interests of the state, the successful grand strategist orchestrates all the various elements of power. While not shrinking from the use of armed force, he or she sees war as a last resort, to be undertaken only after having exhausted all other alternatives." Bacevich asks rhetorically: "Can General McMaster restore the distinction between grand strategy and military strategy and resubordinate the latter to the former?" The historian's answer is a sad one. "Little reason exists to suggest that he will do so—indeed, whether he is even inclined to make the effort."

— 13 —

THE KOCH BROTHER

Mike Pompeo

Director of the Central Intelligence Agency

In the "Republican wave" election of 2010, when brothers Charles and David Koch emerged as defining figures in American politics, the greatest beneficiary of Koch Industries largess was newly elected congressman Mike Pompeo. Since his election, Pompeo has been referred to as the "Koch Brothers' Congressman" and "the congressman from Koch."

Now, under President Trump, Pompeo is the director of the Central Intelligence Agency.

A foreign policy hawk who has fiercely opposed the Iran nuclear deal, stoked fears of Muslims in the United States and abroad and opposed closing the Guantánamo Bay detention camp, Pompeo has defended the National Security Agency's (NSA) unconstitutional surveillance programs as "good and important work." An advocate for the sort of secrecy that allows the government to act in our name but without our informed consent, Pompeo has even gone so far as to say that NSA whistle-blower Edward Snowden "should be brought back from Russia and given due process, and I think the proper outcome would be that he would be given a death sentence."

Pompeo is a hardliner, so much so that Human Rights Watch urgently opposed his confirmation as CIA director. "Pompeo's responses to questions about torture and mass surveillance are dangerously ambiguous about whether he would endorse abusive practices and seek to subvert existing legal protections," said Maria McFarland Sánchez-Moreno, the group's U.S. program co-director. "Pompeo's failure to unequivocally disavow torture and mass surveillance, coupled with his record of advocacy for surveillance of

Americans and past endorsement of the shuttered CIA torture program, make clear that he should not be running the CIA."

Pompeo's open disregard for privacy rights in particular and civil liberties in general, as well as his penchant for extreme language and more extreme policies, marked him as an exceptionally troublesome pick to serve as the head of a powerful intelligence agency. But the Republican-controlled Senate didn't see things that way. Pompeo was confirmed by a wider margin than most Trump picks, 66–32, when the Senate considered his nomination in January 2017. The Senate's failure to provide proper oversight with regard to the Pompeo nomination was problematic because of his aggressive disregard for civil liberties in general and privacy rights in particular. But it was perhaps even more disturbing because the new CIA director comes with strings attached. Pompeo has assumed a position of great sensitivity as one of the most strikingly conflicted political figures in the frequently conflicted city of Washington, thanks to his ties to the privately held and frequently secretive global business empire that has played a pivotal role in advancing his political career. He is not the only Koch-tied politician in the Trump administration. UN ambassador Nikki Haley is another. OMB director Mick Mulvaney is another. EPA administrator Scott Pruitt is still another. But it is fair to say that Pompeo is the most Koched up of the bunch, and that's a big deal, as the experience of bending to the Koch brothers does not prepare politicians to serve honorably in positions of public trust.

The Kochs were not big fans of Trump in 2016, and Trump was not a big fan of the Kochs. But as he staffed up his cabinet, Trump was looking for pliable politicians. And Koch politicians are definitionally pliable.

They are reliably pro-corporate, and reliably friendly to the sort of crony capitalism that keeps contractors not just for the military but for the intelligence services rolling in tax dollars. The Kochs like to say they are against crony capitalism. So does Trump. But, just as Trump has not drained the Washington swamp, so Koch-tied appointees like Pompeo are not going to oppose the contracting schemes that barter off intelligence gathering and monitoring almost as aggressively as the Pentagon barters off what was once military work to the highest bidders of the military-industrial complex.

As Trump slashes funding for the State Department, watch for him to make more use of the CIA—once he is satisfied that the agency is sufficiently loyal to him. Watch for Pompeo to display that loyalty to Trump, his new boss, just as he was steadily loyal to his old bosses the Kochs.

The Pompeo-Koch connection runs deep.

Pompeo came out of the same Wichita, Kansas, business community where the Koch family's oil and gas conglomerate is headquartered. Indeed, Pompeo built his own company with seed money from Koch Venture Capital.

More important, from a political standpoint, is the fact that Pompeo made the leap from business to government with a huge boost from the Koch brothers and their employees. "I'm sure he would vigorously dispute this, but it's hard not to characterize him as the congressman from Koch," said University of Kansas political science professor Burdett Loomis.

In fact, that's a strikingly appropriate characterization for the man who Donald Trump chose for a position in which Pompeo is required to "serve as head of the United States intelligence community; act as the principal adviser to the President for intelligence matters related to the national security; and serve as head of the Central Intelligence Agency." As the Center for Food Safety, which once wrangled with Pompeo on food-labeling issues that are of tremendous interest to the global agribusiness and grocery industries, noted in 2014: "Congressman Mike Pompeo was the single largest recipient of campaign funds from the Koch Brothers in 2010. After winning election with Koch money, Congressman Pompeo hired a Koch Industries lawyer to run his office. According to *The Washington Post,* Congressman Pompeo then introduced bills friendly to Koch Industries while Koch hired outside lobbyists to support them."

Recalling the 2010 election, the Center for Responsive Politics explained that "Koch Industries had never spent as much on a candidate in a single cycle as it did on Pompeo that time around,

giving him a total [of] $80,000. Koch outdid itself again in the 2012 cycle by ponying up $110,000 for Pompeo's campaign."

When Pompeo ran for reelection in 2014, he faced a tight primary contest with another local Republican who had Koch ties. One of the biggest turning points in that race came when the Kochs sided with Pompeo. "KOCHPAC is proud to support Mike Pompeo for Congress based on his strong support for market-based policies and economic freedom, which benefits society as a whole," Mark Nichols, the vice president of government and public affairs for Koch Industries, told *Politico*.

Just as the Kochs have been loyal to Pompeo, so Pompeo has been loyal to the Kochs. He's a regular at their behind-closed-doors gatherings and he's outspoken in their defense, claiming that President Obama and "Nixonian" Democrats have unfairly "vilified" Charles and David Koch.

But, of course, the supposed vilification has simply involved a questioning of the influence wielded by billionaires in general and the Kochs in particular over American politics and governance. That's hardly an unreasonable concern, considering that, as one of the most prominent Koch-backed politicians in the country, Pompeo was called out just weeks after taking office for proposing legislative initiatives that "could benefit many of [the Kochs'] business interests."

"The measures include amendments approved in the House budget bill to eliminate funding for two major Obama administration programs: a database cataloguing consumer complaints about unsafe products and an Environmental Protection Agency registry of greenhouse-gas polluters," reported the *Washington Post* back in 2011. "Both have been listed as top legislative priorities for Koch Industries, which has spent more than $37 million on Washington lobbying since 2008, according to disclosure records."

"It's the same old story—a member of Congress carrying water for his biggest campaign contributor," Common Cause's Mary Boyle complained at the time.

Now, however, it's a different story, because "the congressman from Koch" is carrying water for Donald Trump as the director of one of the most powerful intelligence-gathering agencies in the world.

— 14 —

THE U.S. AMBASSADOR TO THE AMERICAN ANTI-CHOICE MOVEMENT

Nikki Haley

U.S. Permanent Representative to the United Nations

On January 17, 2017, Samantha Power, the founding executive director of the Carr Center for Human Rights Policy at the Harvard Kennedy School of Government, Anna Lindh Professor of Practice of Global Leadership and Public Policy at that school, author of the Pulitzer Prize–winning book *A Problem from Hell: America and the Age of Genocide*, member of the Obama State Department transition team, former special assistant to the president and senior director for Multilateral Affairs and Human Rights on the National Security Council and chair of the White House Atrocities Prevention Board, delivered the last speech of her long tenure as U.S. Permanent Representative to the United Nations. It was a tour de force foreign policy address, ably delivered, bluntly honest and scathing in its denunciation of those who dared neglect the essential issues facing the world.

Ambassador Power made news, with her detailed explanation of how "the Russian Government under President Putin is taking steps that are weakening the rules-based order that we have benefitted from for seven decades. Our values, our security, our prosperity, and our very way of life are tied to this order. And we—and by 'we,' I mean the United States and our closest partners—must come together to prevent Russia from succeeding." It was a damning assessment, described as "scathing," "blistering," "brilliant."

Everyone with even a passing interest in foreign affairs, diplomacy and the United Nations was talking about "the speech."

So it made sense that U.S. senator Chris Coons, a Delaware Democrat who had distinguished himself as one of Washington's savviest and most engaged observers of security threats facing the United States, would ask about the Powers speech when South Carolina governor Nikki Haley appeared the following day before the Senate Foreign Relations Committee. After all, Haley was making the case for her confirmation as Donald Trump's replacement to Samantha Powers.

"I have real trouble with [Trump's] idea that, in any way, we should trust Vladimir Putin and his Russia at an equal level as Angela Merkel and Germany, and all of our NATO allies," Coons began. "[Trump's] ongoing, steady diminution of the value of NATO, when NATO has been the strongest, most enduring alliance we've dealt with and been a part of. Ambassador Power gave a very pointed farewell speech yesterday, where she laid out the case that Russia is the single greatest threat to the world order today—the world order we've built, the so-called liberal rules-based world order that the U.N. is one of the highest examples of. Did you read or follow that speech?"

"I did not," replied Haley, who allowed that she would try to do so. But Haley was obviously upset by the line of questioning.

"Senator..." she griped, "I know that your concerns over the comments of the President-elect are probably best suited to ask him, as opposed to me."

"He is not in front of me, you are, so forgive me . . ." Coons explained.

"And you're not getting an answer from me on that," snapped Haley, interrupting the senator who was charged by the Constitution with getting just such answers before affirming nominees to sensitive posts. "I'm just telling you again in the importance of time."

Haley never claimed to know much about the job of UN ambassador. She did not put much effort into preparing for it, as was made obvious by her neglect of her predecessor's headline-grabbing final speech. And she shut down dialogue about the elephant in the room: a series of bizarre statements and troubling actions by the

 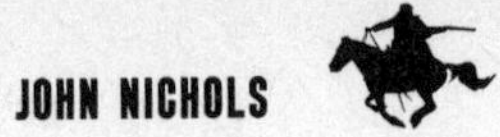

president-elect who had appointed her about the issues she would have to address at the United Nations.

Coons did not vote to confirm Haley, when her nomination was overwhelmingly approved by a Senate that was, frankly, overwhelmed by the atrociousness of so many Trump picks that it failed to do due diligence regarding Trump nominees, especially nominees who were as politically skilled as Haley. Only a handful of Democratic senators took the Haley nomination seriously enough to examine her record. But those who did determined that she simply was not qualified to represent the United States at the United Nations. Noting that "Governor Haley's lack of foreign policy experience combined with a President who promotes isolationism and has been near outright hostile to the institution," New Mexico senator Martin Heinrich said that "after careful review of Governor Haley's testimony and written statements, and the number of difficult issues that we can expect the UN to encounter in the years ahead, I'm skeptical that the President and our Ambassador will play a constructive role in addressing the refugee crisis, climate change, nuclear nonproliferation, or the fundamental operations of the United Nations." His colleague Tom Udall (another of the group of four "no" voters that included three Democrats and Vermont independent Bernie Sanders) complained about Haley's lack of "requisite experience." He also explained that she also lacked "the right positions on key questions of American foreign policy."

Udall said he appreciated Haley's willingness to say a few tough things about Russia, as did much of the U.S. media several weeks later, when Haley added a condemnation of "the dire situation in eastern Ukraine" to an initial UN address where she said: "We do want to better our relations with Russia." But Udall said in explaining his vote against Haley's nomination that "I am troubled by her positions on several central issues, which ultimately convinced me that I could not support her confirmation. For example, she has indicated that she opposes the historic nuclear agreement with Iran, a deal which Defense Secretary Mattis has stated we must uphold. On Cuba, Governor Haley suggested that she would double down on decades of failed policy that have done nothing to bring freedom and openness to the Cuban people. She was noncommittal when I asked her to pledge to remain in the Paris Climate Agreement, and indicated that she does not envision the United States as the global leader in combating climate change. Governor Haley has not demonstrated any commitment to advocating for a livable wage in foreign countries where there is a record of mistreatment of workers. And, she would not pledge to support longstanding, bipartisan U.S. policy stating that settlement expansion is a barrier to peace in the Middle East."

In addition to those issues, there was another one that put Haley dramatically at odds with what was once bipartisan U.S. policy. In a remarkable "Cabinet Exit Memo for the U.S. Mission to the United Nations" filed by Ambassador Power three weeks before she left her position, she noted the accomplishments of her tenure. Among them: "We have . . . repealed the 'global gag rule,' which prevented women from gaining access to essential information and healthcare services."

That initiative was not listed at the beginning of the memo Power submitted. It came toward the end. But there were some Americans who put the issue at the top of their agendas: members of the anti-choice movement that provided critical, arguably definitional, support for Donald Trump's presidential campaign.

Trump and Mike Pence ran in 2016 on a Republican platform that decried U.S. support of the UN's Population Fund and decried the institution in general for the respect it had displayed for a woman's right to choose. The platform hailed former president Ronald Reagan for making the U.S. debate about abortion rights part of U.S. foreign policy, by setting up what the platform described as "a wall of separation—his Mexico City policy, which prohibits the granting of federal monies to non-governmental organizations that provide or promote abortion." Deferring, as Republican platforms so frequently do, to the idolized Reagan, the manifesto declared that "we affirm his position and, in light of plummeting birth rates around the world, suggest a reevaluation of the U.N.'s record on economic progress."

It may surprise international observers, and most American voters, that this particular issue is such a very big deal for Republican voters, many of whom, especially in the Trump era, tend toward an isolationist worldview. But opposition to the "global gag rule," which bars the allocation of U.S. global family planning assistance money to international nongovernmental organizations (NGOs) unless they certify that they will not "perform or actively promote abortion as a method of family planning," is a huge issue for American anti-abortion rights activists or, as they prefer, "pro-life champions."

Restricting access to abortion is such a big deal for these activists, in fact, that social conservatives have over the years resisted, challenged and opposed human rights initiatives for women and girls that might lead to the expansion of reproductive health and family planning services. That's especially important now because, as the International Women's Health Coalition notes: "Advocates worldwide have (in recent years) looked to the US to play a lead role in championing reproductive rights at the United Nations. The Obama Administration's leadership at the United Nations was critical toward ensuring the inclusion of universal access to sexual and reproductive health and reproductive rights in the Sustainable Development Goals (SDGs)—a bold set of global goals aimed at ending poverty and reducing inequality and injustice by 2030."

As of now, analysts with the coalition explain: "The US has committed to achieving each of the 17 goals and targets outlined by the SDGs domestically and through its foreign policy. These include ending all forms of discrimination and violence against women and girls, and ensuring universal access to sexual and reproductive health services." But, they conclude, "nothing about the current composition of the Trump Administration, with Governor Haley playing a key role in multilateral negotiations and commitments, indicates that the US could meet its obligations to the SDGs."

That 2016 Republican platform left little doubt that, in a Trump-Pence administration, working with the United Nations to advance human rights for women and girls was off the agenda. "Precisely because we take our country's treaty obligations seriously," the document declared, "we oppose ratification of international agreements whose long-range implications are ominous or unclear. We do not support the U.N. Convention on Women's Rights, the Convention on the Rights of the Child, the Convention on the Rights of Persons with Disabilities, and the U.N. Arms Trade Treaty, as well as various declarations from the U.N. Conference on Environment and Development."

Even if Nikki Haley was never the biggest fan of Donald Trump when he was running for the presidency, she announced that she would vote for him in October 2016 because "what it is about is policy." And if there is one policy Nikki Haley has always abided by, it is the one that says every option, every angle, every position should be exploited to restrict the ability of women to make choices about their own bodies.

Haley, like most Republican political careerists in recent decades, clearly and unequivocally aligns herself with the anti-choice movement in the United States. She is best known to most Americans as the first woman governor of South Carolina, as the daughter of Sikh Indian immigrants and as the rare southern Republican who hauled down a Confederate battle flag, having finally come to the conclusion—as the forty-three-year-old chief executive of a state that had experienced unspeakable violence at the hands of a gun-toting white supremacist who murdered nine African American worshipers in a Charleston church—that the symbol of the rebellion waged by the defenders of human bondage "should have never been there." All of that may have counted for something with Donald Trump when, at a point when he was taking heat for naming too few women and people of color to key posts in his administration, he decided Haley belonged at the United Nations. But what counted with Trump's political team was the fact that Haley had a proven track record of opposition to abortion rights, as the social-conservative voters who elected Trump demanded of his pick for the ambassadorship.

"President-Elect Donald Trump Names Pro-Life Gov. Nikki Haley as UN Ambassador," announced the front page of the LifeNews.com website that has been "harnessing the power of the Internet since 1992 to bring pro-life news to the pro-life community." LifeSiteNews took time out from warning about "secularists attempting to eliminate Christian morality and natural law principles which are seen as the primary obstacles to implementing their new world order" to

announce that "Pro-life Nikki Haley's confirmation as ambassador could lead to UN reining in abortion promotion."

"She is going to have a tough job, especially since she is unfamiliar with how the UN bureaucracy operates," explained Stefano Gennarini, a lawyer whose work includes "advising UN delegations and liaising with pro-family organizations around the world."

"But," added Gennarini, "we are confident that Nikki Haley will be able to push back against the global abortion lobby." Other Trump picks might not "wake up in the morning thinking about abortion rights," suggested Susan Yoshihara, the senior vice president for research at the conservative Center for Family and Human Rights, which serves as an anti-abortion lobby at the UN. "But Nikki Haley has a solid pro-life background, and we are hopeful." The National Right-to-Life Coalition echoed that assessment: "The appointment and confirmation of pro-life Ambassador Haley to the United Nations brings hope to all who seek to protect women and children from the violence of abortion globally and who struggle against UN elitists who feverishly promote abortion."

What gave them such confidence? It wasn't just Haley's record as a militantly anti-choice state representative and as a governor who capped her tenure by signing South Carolina legislation that made it illegal for a woman to obtain an abortion after her pregnancy reaches twenty weeks—with no exceptions for rape or incest and a provision for jailing physicians who violate the law for up to three years. It wasn't just that NARAL Pro-Choice America gave Haley a zero rating as a defender of reproductive rights. It wasn't just that Haley had a history of making wild assertions, like her announcement on ABC's *The View* that "women don't care about contraception; they care about jobs and the economy and raising their families and all those things." It wasn't just that Haley's late-in-the-2016-race endorsement of Trump—after she had called him "everything a governor doesn't want in a president"—highlighted the prospect that he could name one or more Supreme Court justices: a decision-point issue for religious-right voters. It was that Haley made no concessions to diplomacy as she moved to assume the nation's most high-profile and influential ambassadorial assignment.

When Haley appeared before the Senate Foreign Relations Committee, New Hampshire senator Jeanne Shaheen explained the vital role that the United Nations Population Fund and related programs play internationally, placing particular emphasis on the importance of family planning services for millions of women around the world. Haley responded by making her position plain: "I am strongly pro-life, so anything we can do to keep from having abortions, or to keep them from not knowing what is available, I will support." The nominee accepted the notion that women can have access to some information about family planning methods. But when Shaheen pressed Haley on the issue, Trump's choice to represent the United States at the United Nations repeated her absolute commitment to "pro-life principles." New Jersey senator Cory Booker tried another angle but got the same answer: "Well, and as we discussed," said Haley, "I am strongly pro life and will always be pro life."

Nikki Haley's representation of the United States at the UN will define the direction of global policymaking on thousands of issues—from war and peace to climate change, from extreme poverty to failed states, from human rights to humanitarian aid, from the status of refugees to disputes over Antarctica. As such, *Slate* noted, she is "an odd choice" for the position once occupied by Henry Cabot Lodge Jr., Adlai Stevenson, George H. W. Bush, Daniel Patrick Moynihan, Andrew Young, Thomas Pickering, Madeleine Albright and Samantha Power. "Other than participating in some trade delegations as governor," noted the news site, "she has basically no foreign policy experience."

This odd choice was not, however, an "outside the box" masterstroke by a president committed to opening up fresh global vistas. Haley was not named to the ambassadorship to provide new leadership or new vision at what remains an essential forum for international negotiations and an essential force for human progress. She was not even chosen to advance reform of a global body that has at times struggled to adjust to the demands of the twenty-first century. She was chosen because she is a domestically focused social conservative. "To Trump, the U.N. is just a talking shop," explains Charles Tiefer, a former solicitor of the U.S. House of Representatives and

member of the federal Commission on Wartime Contracting in Iraq and Afghanistan, who argues that Trump selected Haley "to show his contempt for conducting foreign affairs through the U.N. in particular and multilateral organizations in general. He is giving the post to someone with no foreign affairs credentials (or any other national security credentials, for that matter)."

The Haley pick is, argues Tiefer, "a throw-away" for Trump that might score him a few points for adding a woman and an Asian American to his Cabinet. But it also scores him a lot of points with social conservatives for whom restricting reproductive rights in general and access to abortion in particular is an obsession.

Unfortunately, this is one area where, no matter how disconnected and disempowered Haley may be within the Trump administration, she can do immense harm.

"Reproductive rights have been embedded in UN agreements for more than two decades, since the landmark International Conference on Population and Development in 1994. Feminist advocates from Africa to Latin America and beyond have leveraged landmark treaties to secure laws and policies in their home countries that promote healthy lives and benefit millions of women and girls. A rollback of these commitments could dramatically set back decades of progress," explained the International Women's Health Coalition's review of President Trump's appointment. "Her hostility toward the United Nations, lack of credible foreign policy experience, and history of opposing women's rights make her poorly suited to the task."

— 15 —

"PART AND PARCEL OF AN ORGANIZED ARMY OF HATRED"

David Friedman

U.S. Ambassador to Israel

David Friedman, the New York bankruptcy lawyer who helped Donald Trump save his empire when the supposed billionaire's hotels failed in Atlantic City, was the featured speaker at a "Trump for president" rally just weeks before the 2016 election. In some ways, it was a typical Trump rally. References to Democratic presidential nominee Hillary Clinton were greeted with chants of "Lock her up!" Conspiracy theories were indulged. But this was not quite like the Trump rallies in Fayetteville, Georgia, or Fayetteville, Louisiana, or in Cedar Rapids, Iowa, or Grand Rapids, Michigan.

For one thing, the "Make America Great Again" signs were in Hebrew.

For another thing, the turnout was disappointing, as the organizers of Donald Trump's "get out the vote" rally in Jerusalem had trouble attracting an "A" list speaker.

Only about 250 people showed up for the gathering on a rooftop overlooking Jerusalem's Old City. Scheduled by Republicans Abroad Israel as an effort to remind Americans living in West Bank settlements to cast their absentee ballots for Trump, the rally's organizers had hoped to attract a big-name Trump backer like former New York mayor Rudy Giuliani or bombastic former U.S. ambassador to the United Nations John Bolton. Instead, they got videos from Trump and Republican vice presidential nominee Mike Pence, as well as Friedman, who was in Israel anyway and agreed to drop by.

Once he got started, however, Friedman had a lot to say. "It's very simple. The simple act that Americans living in Israel need to do to protect the eternal city of Jerusalem, and the sanctity and the safety and the security of the state of Israel, is very simple: just vote," he began. "Just vote. And I think we all know who you ought to vote for."

Then things got interesting. "Let me tell you a little about what a Trump administration is going to look like," said the bankruptcy lawyer. "Under a Trump administration, there's going to be no daylight, none, no daylight between the United States and the state of Israel. If there are disagreements—and none are anticipated—but if there are disagreements they're handled in private as would befit the closest of friends."

How private did Friedman envision? It certainly did not sound like he was planning to invite any career diplomats from the U.S. Department of State.

"Every president gets elected and he says to the State Department—what about this law, should we move the embassy from Tel Aviv to Jerusalem, and they say 'absolutely not, absolutely not,'" griped Friedman. That was a reference to the decades-old debate about where to locate the U.S. embassy for Israel—in the modern oceanfront city of Tel Aviv, where it has been headquartered for decades at 71 HaYarkon Street, or in Jerusalem, the holy city for the three major Abrahamic religions of Judaism, Christianity and Islam that is claimed as a capital by citizens of both Israel and Palestine.

The embassy debate is one of the bitterest areas of dispute between Israelis and Palestinians. It is infused with historical, political, religious and economic passion. It is complicated by the complex claims that competing states and competing peoples make on specific neighborhoods, specific streets, specific homes. And it is charged by all the external stresses and strains that inflame so many issues in the Middle East. But, never mind, as far as David Friedman was concerned, this was not a complicated issue at all.

Why hadn't the embassy been moved when the U.S. Congress said the shift could be made in 1995? "Because the law provides that the requirement for the embassy to be moved can be waived at the desire of the State Department. The same State Department that has been anti-Semitic and anti-Israel for the past 70 years," Friedman explained.

That might have come as something of a surprise to former secretaries of state Henry Kissinger (who as a Jewish child fled Nazi persecution in Germany), Madeleine Albright (the daughter of Czechoslovakian Jewish converts to Catholicism who also fled European fascism) or John Kerry (whose paternal grandparents were Austro-Hungarian Jewish immigrants to the United States) and to the hundreds of Jewish Americans who have served alongside Arab Americans and Americans of all backgrounds in vital State Department positions over the decades, including the staff of the Office to Monitor and Combat Anti-Semitism and the department's former special envoys to monitor and combat anti-Semitism, such as Hannah Rosenthal and Ira Forman.

No matter. Friedman was on a roll.

"The lifers in the State Department are absolutely, positively committed to never moving the embassy to Jerusalem. What's different about Donald Trump? You all know Donald Trump. If there is anybody in world politics who could stand up to the State Department it is Donald Trump," declared Friedman. "When Donald Trump has his first meeting with the lifers in the State Department and they say, 'Mr. Trump, with all due respect, you have only been president for a couple of days, we've been living here for the last 20 years, we don't do it that way, we do it this way—we don't move the embassy, that's been State department policy for 20 years,' the reaction from Donald Trump is going to be, 'You know what guys, you're all FIRED!'"

Once Friedman had that issue sorted, he moved on to the main event of the evening: warning Israelis not to even think of placing their trust in Hillary Clinton.

"Who does Hillary Clinton get her advice from?" Friedman asked rhetorically.

"*Huma Abedin!*" someone shouted.

Friedman moved into attack mode.

Referring to the longtime Clinton aide, who assisted with the 2000 Camp David summit between Israeli prime minister Ehud

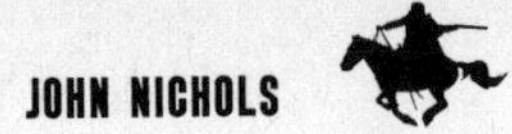

Barak and Palestinian leader Yasser Arafat, and who has since worked closely with former secretary of state Clinton on a host of Israeli-Palestinian, Middle Eastern and global issues, the lawyer replied: "Huma Abedin. Grew up in Saudi Arabia, close connections to the Muslim Brotherhood." Someone in the crowd shouted, "And al-Qaeda." "And al-Qaeda, right," responded Friedman.

Abedin is Muslim, but she was born in Kalamazoo, Michigan, and, while the academic careers of her parents took the family to Saudi Arabia, she was educated in British international schools and at George Washington University. Long before Friedman appeared at the Trump rally in Jerusalem, the *Washington Post* Fact Checker gave claims that Abedin was connected with the Muslim Brotherhood four Pinocchio's, its lowest-possible rating on the truthfulness scale. When Trump-supporting Wisconsin congressman Sean Duffy tried in August 2016 to make a case about "Huma and her ties to the Muslim Brotherhood," the PolitiFact website concluded its review of the claim: "We rate his statement False." As for the even more incendiary suggestion of an al-Qaeda tie, Friedman admitted later that he had no evidence to sustain the claim. But he still didn't back off entirely, telling an interviewer: "I don't know one way or another if that's true."

Republicans who actually know a thing or two about foreign affairs in general and the Middle East in particular had repeatedly dismissed the attacks on Abedin as absurd. "That kind of assertion certainly doesn't comport with the Intelligence Committee, and I can say that on the record," said former House Intelligence Committee chair Mike Rogers. "I have no information in my committee that would indicate that Huma is anything other than an American patriot." Arizona senator John McCain dismissed the allegations against Abedin as "nothing less than an unwarranted and unfounded attack on an honorable citizen, a dedicated American, and a loyal public servant."

Donald Trump surrounded himself with a number of fringe figures who peddled fake news and outright fantasy during the 2016 campaign, but David Friedman carved out a special niche for himself. Few members of Trump's inner circle made so many warrantless claims so aggressively, and so frequently, as Friedman. So when Trump named Friedman as his pick for ambassador to Israel, supporters of Middle East peace and basic common sense in foreign relations were shocked. "Meet David Friedman—Trump's Most Alarming Nominee?" read the headline of a response from J Street, the Jewish American advocacy group that Israeli author Amos Oz hails for its "pragmatic, humanistic and peace-loving ideas." Six hundred rabbis and cantors wrote to the Senate Foreign Relations Committee, explaining that "the Rabbis of the Talmud are adamant that we are to speak to and about other people—particularly those with whom we disagree—with love and respect. We are taught that shaming a person is tantamount to shedding their blood. Yet Mr. Friedman seems to have no qualms about insulting people with whom he disagrees." Dozens of Holocaust survivors signed a letter to the committee's ranking members, in which they expressed "our deep outrage at the cheapening of the worst catastrophe in Jewish history by President Donald Trump's nominee to be U.S. ambassador to Israel, David Friedman." In particular, they objected to Friedman's assertion that Jewish supporters of a negotiated peace settlement between Israel and Palestine, and of a two-state solution to the region's challenges, were "far worse than kapos."

"Kapos" was the term used for Jews who aided the Nazis during the Holocaust. "To brand one's political opponents, engaged in legitimate debate in our democracy, as kapos is incredibly offensive. To compare them with Jews who collaborated with Nazis, to suggest that they are in effect willingly and knowingly aiding in the mass extermination of the Jewish people, is slanderous, insulting, irresponsible, cynical and immensely damaging to our people," explained the letter. "Using this term to describe one's political opponents actually aids the evil work of Holocaust deniers because it suggests that kapos are an everyday phenomenon that arise in every generation—and not a tragic group of people caught in a uniquely awful dilemma [that occurred in] the extreme borderline conditions in which people, robbed of humanity, were essentially dead while still alive."

"Friedman's adoption of this awful term shows he is part and parcel of an organized army of hatred sowing divisions within the

Jewish community and within our nation," wrote the survivors, who finished their letter by bluntly declaring that "he is unfit to represent the United States as our ambassador to Israel."

Many Israelis were equally unsettled by Trump's choice to represent the United States in their country. An analysis by a senior writer for the Israeli newspaper *Haaretz* featured the headline "It's a good thing ambassador-designate David Friedman will have diplomatic immunity; otherwise he might get arrested for incitement."

"By Israeli standards, Donald Trump's designated Ambassador to Israel, David Friedman, is an extreme right-winger," the article began. "He might find a place in the settler movement or with [hardliner] Naftali Bennett's Habayit Hayehudi Party, but only on its right-wing fringes. He makes [Israeli prime minister] Benjamin Netanyahu seem like a left-wing defeatist. From where Friedman stands, most Israelis, never mind most American Jews, are more or less traitors." Another *Haaretz* writer noted that "David Friedman, who has been named America's next ambassador to Israel, heads a fundraising organization that has raised tens of millions of dollars for one of the most radical settlements in the West Bank."

The support for those settlements was particularly troubling to Palestinian officials on the West Bank, and to Palestinian Americans. "Friedman is very open about his pro-settlement stance and his willingness to support the annexation of these settlements into Israel," explained Kareem El-Hosseiny of the group American Muslims for Palestine, which notes that "Friedman has no diplomatic experience and holds biased views on the Middle East that favor the extremist settler movement."

The *New York Times* editorial board said Friedman would be "far more likely to provoke conflict in Israel and the occupied territories, heighten regional tensions and undermine American leadership."

Five former U.S. ambassadors to Israel who had served under Republican and Democratic presidents—Thomas Pickering (Ronald Reagan), William Harrop (George H. W. Bush), Edward Walker (Bill Clinton), Daniel Kurtzer (George W. Bush) and James Cunningham (George W. Bush and Barack Obama)—writing as Americans "who care deeply about Israel: an American ally, a stronghold of democracy in the Middle East and homeland for the Jewish people," argued that Friedman was "unqualified for the position."

"The American ambassador must be dedicated to advancing our country's longstanding bipartisan goals in the region: strengthening the security of the United States and our ally Israel, and advancing the prospects for peace between Israel and its neighbors, in particular the Palestinians. If Israel is to carry on as a democratic, Jewish nation, respected internationally, we see no alternative to a two-state solution," they explained. "We are concerned that David Friedman, nominated to serve as U.S. ambassador to Israel, strongly disagrees," noting Friedman's past statements dismissing a two-state solution as "an illusory solution in search of a nonexistent problem," the fact that he has been "active in supporting and financing the settler movement" to build Israeli communities on Palestinian land and his suggestion that it might be acceptable for Israel to occupy the West Bank.

When he appeared before the Foreign Relations Committee, Friedman tried to distance himself from a record of extremism and his own outrageous statements, suggesting that "they're not reflective of my nature and character." But, as Yael Patir, the director of the Israeli office of J Street (a group specifically targeted by Friedman), correctly noted on Israeli radio: "He did not apologize. He said 'I used words I shouldn't have.' There's a difference."

The most unnerving thing that Friedman said at his Senate hearing was that serving as ambassador to Israel would be "the fulfillment of my life's work," as his life's work certainly did not seem to be focused on promoting peace, tolerance and cooperation. The day after Friedman testified, the Union for Reform Judaism and more than twenty groups associated with the Reform movement declared: "We have never before opposed the nomination of a U.S. Ambassador. We do so now because of our firm belief that Mr. Friedman is the wrong person for this essential job at this critical time." The letter from the groups stated that, in addition to lacking the basic qualifications for the position, "Mr. Friedman's views on key issues suggest he will not be able to play a constructive role. The U.S. Ambassador to Israel has the important responsibility of advising, shaping, and

helping implement the President's foreign policy goals. Indeed, it appears that Mr. Friedman's extreme views on key issues related to the two-state solution, Israel's borders, settlements, and the location of the U.S. Embassy are already reflected in the White House."

The last thing that the United States, Israel, Palestine or the world needs in a Trump administration is an ambassador who reinforces what author and commentator Fareed Zakaria describes as Trump's "surreal" and "embarrassing" lack of preparation to deal with the Middle East. But instead of embracing insight and guidance from experienced hands at the State Department and in the diplomatic community, this inexperienced president will now be encouraged to handle the most complex and challenging issues "in private as would befit the closest of friends" by a bankruptcy lawyer who, as J Street notes, "has consistently aligned himself with some of the most irresponsible charges and conspiracy theories of the far-right, Islamophobic fringe in this country."

— 16 —

WITH THE RUSSIANS, TOO?

Wilbur Ross

Secretary of Commerce

"I went home with a waitress the way I always do," sang Warren Zevon at the opening of his song about international espionage and bad craziness, "Lawyers, Guns and Money." "How was I to know she was with the Russians, too?"

What a group of persistent senators wanted to know before they voted on whether to confirm Donald Trump's nominee to serve as secretary of commerce was whether Wilbur Ross was with the Russians, too.

A billionaire investor, number 232 on the 2016 Forbes 400, Ross became known during a long career of purchasing so-called distressed assets as the "King of Bankruptcy." The vulture capitalist swooped in, scooped up the remains of great manufacturing concerns, made them leaner and sometimes quite a bit meaner (by squeezing health care and pension plans for desperate workers) and then sold them off at a nice profit. It wasn't pretty. A messy merger Ross organized between two companies he owned, Safety Components International Inc. and International Textile Group Inc., led to a 2014 shareholder lawsuit that claimed Ross breached his fiduciary duty; he ended up paying out $86 million. In 2016, his WL Ross & Co. combine paid a fine of $2.3 million and reimbursed investors almost $12 million in order to clean up a Securities and Exchange Commission probe into charges that his firm failed to disclose transaction costs that were charged to investor funds. After the 2006 explosion at a Sago, West Virginia, mine owned by a firm Ross's International Coal Group had purchased before the disaster, a former executive of the coal company told the *New York Post* that "Wilbur had had

his executives in there, reporting back to him on a daily basis . . . He knew the mine was troubled." The newspaper reported that the executive said: "Ross knew the Sago mine had been shut down for safety violations—but he wouldn't tolerate long disruptions in production." Twelve miners died.

Those setbacks did scant damage to Ross's portfolio. His net worth was $2.9 billion when Trump—whose troubled Atlantic City casino operations had been saved from foreclosure in the 1980s by the aggressive intervention of Ross (then a Rothschild Inc. banker) and Carl Icahn (the investor who Trump named as his "special adviser" on regulatory reform)—tapped the seventy-nine-year-old Ross to serve as the thirty-ninth secretary of commerce of the United States. A Democratic-leaning businessman who had been critical of the free-trade policies that had fallen out of favor with many Democrats and Republicans, Ross was, despite his controversial history and continuing confusion over the many lawsuits he had faced or was facing, not ranked with the most troublesome of Trump picks. And he got high marks for promising that the National Oceanic and Atmospheric Administration would under his watch continue to maintain proper standards. "I see no valid reason to keep peer reviewed research from the public. To be clear, by peer review I mean scientific review and not a political filter," he wrote senators. On January 18, Ross sailed through his Senate's Committee on Commerce, Science, and Transportation confirmation hearing with relative ease, and a little over a week later the committee sent the nomination to the full Senate.

As concerns over Trump administration ties to Russian officials and oligarchs blew up with revelations regarding disgraced National Security advisor Michael Flynn, however, attention turned to a December 2016 McClatchy News Service report that "Billionaire investor Wilbur Ross, tapped by President-elect Donald Trump to serve as his commerce secretary, has been the top shareholder in a Cypriot bank with deep Russian ties and investors who made their fortunes under Russian President Vladimir Putin."

"Cyprus is often used by Russia's politically connected businessmen. In a March 2013 report, McClatchy detailed how Russians had come to dominate Cyprus as both customers and providers of financial services. Russian depositors and investors took losses that year in Cyprus when the European debt crisis nearly crumbled major banks," explained McClatchy, which noted that "Ross led a September 2014 rescue of Bank of Cyprus, the largest and most important bank in that island nation off the coast of Turkey. Ross' investment group took an 18 percent stake in the bank, and he remained the bank's vice chairman after his nomination by Trump."

That investment in the Bank of Cyprus put Ross in the orbit of the head of the second-largest investor in the bank: Russian billionaire Viktor Vekselberg, a close associate of Vladimir Putin, and in the dark vortex of Cypriot banking. "Because of its dependence on Russian clients, the banking system in Cyprus remains a money-laundering concern for the U.S. State Department," noted McClatchy, which highlighted a 2015 State Department report that said bank regulations on the island were "not sufficiently enforced to prevent money laundering."

McClatchy did not suggest that Ross was involved in money laundering, or other forms of wrongdoing. But the report caught the interest of a group of Democratic senators, as did the news that "as the lead investor in Bank of Cyprus, Ross helped put together the board of directors and tapped as its chairman Josef Ackermann, the retired CEO of Germany's Deutsche Bank. It was under Ackermann that Deutsche Bank repeatedly ran afoul of U.S. and European regulators." It was also under Ackermann that Deutsche Bank became a frequent and controversial financial lifeline for Donald Trump's expanding global empire.

A February 16, 2017, letter from six Democratic members of the Commerce Committee—Richard Blumenthal of Connecticut, Bill Nelson of Florida, Ed Markey of Massachusetts, Cory Booker of New Jersey, Tom Udall of New Mexico, and Tammy Baldwin of Wisconsin—asked Ross to answer questions about the Bank of Cyprus and the influence of Russian oligarchs. They wanted to know "whether there were any ties between current or former bank officials and the Trump Organization or Trump campaign," "whether anyone with ownership interest in the bank sought to directly or

indirectly influence the U.S. election of American policy positions" and whether Ross was "aware of any loans made by the Bank of Cyprus to the Trump Organization, directly or through another financial institution, its directors or officers, or any affiliated individuals or entities."

These were basic questions that could be easily answered.

Yet, a week passed and the senators got no response.

As the February 27 confirmation vote for Ross approached, Booker wrote an urgent follow-up letter to the nominee on February 24, explaining that "the Senate has a constitutional duty to give the president our advice and consent on his nominations to the Cabinet. Consistent with that constitutional duty, and prior to your confirmation, the United States Senate and the American public deserve to know the full extent of your connections with Russia and your knowledge of any ties between the Trump Administration, Trump Campaign, or Trump Organization and the Bank of Cyprus. Americans must have confidence that high-level officials in the United States government are not influenced by, or beholden to, any foreign power."

Booker's argument was buttressed by the fact that the Commerce Department is a global agency that oversees international trade and trade sanctions and, through its Bureau of Industry and Security, manages a wide range of issues that arise at the intersections of national security and high technology.

Watchdog groups weighed in as the confirmation vote approached. "Until Ross provides public answers about his ties to Putin's friends, it is clear Senators lack enough information about Ross' known ties to Russian oligarchs to provide informed 'consent,'" warned Jeff Hauser, who heads the Revolving Door Project, a Center for Economic and Policy Research initiative to increase scrutiny on executive branch appointments.

Yet, on the appointed day, the Senate convened and rushed through the process of approving Ross. Florida senator Nelson said he had gotten some verbal reassurances from Ross, but Senate minority leader Charles Schumer warned that the failure of the Trump White House to provide written answers to the questions posed by senators was "another example of this administration abandoning transparency and trying to jam their nominees through without making all the relevant information public and available."

Despite Schumer's appeal, the chamber voted overwhelmingly to approve Ross, with fifty-one Republican senators joined by twenty Democrats and independent senator Angus King of Maine voting "yes." Only twenty-five Democrats and independent Bernie Sanders refused their consent.

Yet, the questions lingered. As more and more details regarding Ross and the Bank of Cyprus, Ross and the Russians, and Trump and the Russians emerged, as national television commentators such as MSNBC's Rachel Maddow devoted programs to the evolving story, concerns multiplied. This was not a case of idle speculation about foreign intrigues. This was a case of the executive branch failing to cooperate with the legislative branch, and of too many members of the legislative branch acquiescing to a muted oversight role.

To their credit, a few senators refused to accept that diminished role. On March 10, 2017, Booker, Baldwin, Blumenthal and Markey wrote again to demand responses to the unanswered questions.

"As previously undisclosed contacts between the Trump presidential campaign and Russian officials have been revealed, we believe it is important for the public to know the full extent of relationships that may exist between the Russian Federation and members of the President's Cabinet," they declared. "The continued absence of a written response to our questions is alarming and raises new questions about the links between the Russian government, the Bank of Cyprus, and the Trump business and political apparatus."

The authors of the letter explained that "as members of the U.S. Senate, we have a constitutional responsibility to exercise proper oversight." That was clearly the case. Yet, because so many senators failed to accept that responsibility, and because the Trump administration took advantage of the opening created by that failure, the questions about what exactly Wilbur Ross was doing in Cyprus, about what he knew and when he knew it, remained unanswered.

—17—

THE FOSSIL-FUEL-POWERED DOLLAR DIPLOMAT

Rex Tillerson

Secretary of State

"I feel," Nebraska senator George Norris warned a century ago, "that we are about to put the dollar sign on the American flag." Decrying the advocacy by munitions merchants, speculators and stockbrokers for legislation that would further involve the United States in the European conflict that would come to be known as World War I, Norris thundered: "We are going into war upon the command of gold."

Along with a handful of allies that included Wisconsin senator Robert M. La Follette, Norris argued that the United States need not entangle itself in a distant war between the armies of kings and kaisers. The Nebraskan suggested that cynical appeals to patriotic sentiment by advocates for war cloaked the self-serving economic agenda of wealthy elites. "We are about to do the bidding of wealth's terrible mandate," Norris said of congressional action that steered the country toward war. "By our act we will make millions of our countrymen suffer, and the consequences of it may well be that millions of our brethren must shed their lifeblood, millions of brokenhearted women must weep, millions of children must suffer with cold, and millions of babes must die from hunger, and all because we want to preserve the commercial right of American citizens to deliver munitions of war to belligerent nations."

Norris, La Follette and the courageous foes of U.S. involvement in World War I, most of them Midwestern progressive populists, recognized the profound danger that arose when U.S. foreign policy became intertwined with the pecuniary demands of plutocrats and profiteers.

It is not just in matters of war and peace that those dangers arise, of course. When CEOs are calling the shots, everything from trade policy to energy policy and responses to climate change are warped by unenlightened self-interest. The potential for the corruption of America's foreign policy expands dramatically when businessmen with international interests assume positions of power. This is one of the reasons why, during the post-election transition period, almost two dozen senators urged President-elect Donald Trump to follow the advice of the nonpartisan Office of Government Ethics and divest from his business holdings before taking office.

"As a businessman with interests in the United States and around the world, your holdings have the potential for serious conflicts between the national interest and your personal financial interests," wrote Massachusetts senator Elizabeth Warren and twenty-two of her colleagues in a December 13, 2016, letter that argued: "Whether the president of the United States makes decisions about potential trade agreements or sending troops into war, the American people need to know that the president is acting in their best interest."

This was a sound argument for how Trump, whose candidacy was opposed by the majority of Americans, might bring a measure of legitimacy to his presidency. It was also a sound standard for examining Trump's nominees for key cabinet posts, particularly Rex Tillerson, the CEO of ExxonMobil who Trump had tapped to serve as secretary of state.

Before the Senate Foreign Relations Committee considered Tillerson's nomination, Wisconsin congressman Mark Pocan, the Wisconsin Democrat who serves as first vice chair of the Congressional Progressive Caucus [CPC], had offered a framework for applying the standard. "President-elect Trump's nomination of ExxonMobil CEO Rex Tillerson, as secretary of state, signals that U.S. diplomacy is now in the pockets of big oil. Tillerson has spent his entire career putting the profits of Exxon over our country's national interests," said Pocan in a December 13, 2016, statement issued by the CPC. "Not only does Tillerson have billions of dollars at stake with sanctions

 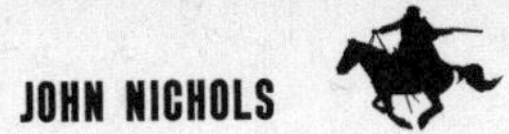

on Russia, his company has been under a formal investigation by the Securities and Exchange Commission for inaccurate accounting practices that affect global climate regulations," Pocan explained. "Our country needs a secretary of state who will guide U.S. foreign policy with a steady hand, not place profit margins ahead of diplomacy."

Pocan was right. The nomination of Tillerson to serve as secretary of state put a dollar sign on the American flag. To propose that this plunderer be allowed to represent the United States on the global stage was to assert that, under Donald Trump, America's first and only foreign policy would be crony capitalism. That was an insult to our best history, and a dangerous threat to our future.

Mark Pocan holds the U.S. House seat once occupied by "Fighting Bob" La Follette, who joined with George Norris in the great debates of a century ago. La Follette decried what he and others referred to as "dollar diplomacy." La Follette's weekly magazine defined dollar diplomacy as "the policy of using the Department of State and the presidential office in promoting the interests of American bankers in other countries." "Dollar diplomacy," La Follette argued, "is altogether too suggestive of the kind of business that has for its command: Your money or your life!"

The senator, who earned "profile in courage" marks from a young John Kennedy, was right to be concerned. Lives were at stake then. Ultimately, lives were lost because policies based on greed and self-interest trumped common sense and humanity. The dollar diplomacy of Donald Trump and Rex Tillerson again threatened lives—American lives and the lives of innocents around the world. Trump's nomination of Tillerson demanded scrutiny as the looming menace that it represented.

When the scrutiny came, Rex Tillerson failed the test.

Startlingly.

Tillerson's witless, contradictory and obfuscatory testimony before the Foreign Relations Committee in early January 2017 confirmed fears that the ExxonMobil CEO was, and is, too conflicted, too ill-prepared and too disengaged from accepted understandings with regard to diplomacy, sustainable development and human rights to be seriously considered for the position of secretary of state.

The most unsettling exchange took place after an initial round of questioning by New Jersey senator Robert Menendez. The veteran member of the Foreign Relations Committee asked what should have been a simple concluding question: "For all of these answers you've given me, does the president-elect agree with you?"

Rex Tillerson replied: "The president-elect and I have not had the opportunity to discuss this specific issue or this specific area."

Again, Senator Menendez: "Well, in your statement on page three, you say, 'In his campaign, president-elect Trump proposed a bold new commitment to advancing American interests in our foreign policy. I hope to explain what this approach means and how I'd implement that policy if I am confirmed as Secretary of State.' I assumed to some degree you've had some discussion about what it is that that world view is going to be in order to understand whether you are willing to execute that on behalf of the person you're going to work for?"

"In a broad construct and in terms of the principles that are going to guide that, yes, sir."

"I would have thought Russia would be at the very top of that, considering all that's taken place. Did that not happen?"

"That has not occurred yet, Senator."

"That's pretty amazing."

In an interview following the exchange during the January 11, 2017, hearing, Senator Menendez said it was "beyond my imagination" that Tillerson had not engaged in serious discussions about major foreign policy issues and concerns with President-elect Donald Trump.

No matter what Americans think of Trump or Tillerson, no matter what they think about U.S. relations with Russia and the issues that have arisen with regard to those relations, the notion that a corporate CEO would accept a nomination to serve as secretary of state without engaging in extended and serious discussions about major issues should be greeted with shock and dismay.

It is not as if Donald Trump's selection of his choice for secretary of state was a snap decision.

Trump's high-profile search for a nominee to take charge of the State Department took weeks. He rejected prominent prospects, such as 2012 Republican presidential nominee Mitt Romney and former U.S. ambassador to the United Nations John Bolton, during the most closely examined and consequential period of the cabinet-selection process.

Trump finally settled on a candidate who NBC News introduced to Americans as a "64-year-old veteran oil executive [who] has no government or diplomatic experience."

Yet Tillerson told the Senate that he and Trump did not engage in substantive discussions regarding hot-button issues that could complicate the working relationship between an incoming commander in chief and a nominee who would be charged with explaining and implementing what many expected would be a radical restructuring of foreign relations.

Reflecting on Tillerson's characterization of his conversations with the president-elect, Senator Menendez said: "I don't know how he's going to get to speak for [Trump] unless he knows what positions and views he has."

If Tillerson's conversations with Trump were as cursory as the nominee suggests, then it was clear that he had failed to display the basic curiosity and due diligence that would be expected of even the lowest-level diplomat. Indeed, Rex Tillerson's testimony indicated that he did not begin to recognize the responsibilities that go with the position he was seeking, let alone the unique challenges that would be associated with serving as Donald Trump's secretary of state. That was more than concerning. That was disqualifying.

Yet, the committee, and ultimately the Senate, approved Tillerson, who embarked on his new job with a lackadaisical, unfocused and ineffectual approach that seemed to suggest that his primary mission would be to implement Trump's radical downsizing of the State Department in order to pay for dramatically increased Pentagon spending. Less than months into Tillerson's tenure, the White

House proposed to cut the budget for the State Department and the Agency for International Development by 28 percent.

Diplomacy was being ditched. International human rights advocate Michael Abramowitz warned that the cuts "would make the world a more dangerous place." The president of Freedom House reminded Americans in a March 16, 2017, statement that "foreign assistance and diplomacy are critical to defend democratic values and U.S. interests at a time when both are increasingly under threat. When the United States pulls back, authoritarian powers that oppose our values, and interests will step in." But Tillerson welcomed the cuts.

"The level of spending that the State Department has been undertaking in the past—and particularly in this past year—is simply not sustainable," the secretary of state said in remarks delivered in Tokyo on March 16, 2017, during an Asian tour where he often sounded more like a Pentagon chief talking up war prospects with North Korea than the nation's chief diplomat.

Tillerson prattled on, Trump-like in his defense of the indefensible. He promised that a downsized and diminished Department of State would "be able to do a lot with fewer dollars." He was wrong. The only thing the State Department will do with Rex Tillerson at the helm is attach the dollar sign to the American flag.

PART 3

The Hacks

In the tired hand of a dying man, Theodore Senior had written: "The 'Machine politicians' have shown their colors . . . I feel sorry for the country however as it shows the power of partisan politicians who think of nothing higher than their own interests, and I feel for your future. We cannot stand so corrupt a government for any great length of time."

—EDMUND MORRIS, *The Rise of Theodore Roosevelt*

If I stayed in Washington, I might end up a government hack.

—ELLIOT RICHARDSON,
recipient of the Presidential Medal of Freedom

The Republican Party was, for a vital century, the major American political party that most frequently aligned with the cause of human rights, conservation, honest governance, regard for science and enlightened internationalism. The necessarily realistic Frederick Douglass wrote in the late nineteenth century: "I knew that however bad the Republican Party was, the Democratic Party was much worse. The elements of which the Republican Party was composed gave better ground for the ultimate hope of the success of the colored man's cause than those of the Democratic Party."

Douglass did not speak those words as an abolitionist alone. The absconder from human bondage who taught men like Abraham Lincoln to despise slavery is remembered in the shorthand of history for that blessed work. But he was, as well, a champion of women's rights and popular sovereignty, a diplomat and an international traveler who recognized the necessity of solidarity with oppressed peoples in distant lands, and the publisher of a *North Star* newspaper

that took as its motto "Right is of no Sex—Truth is of no Color—God is the Father of us all, and we are all brethren."

In speeches, books, letters and conversations, Douglass referred to the Republican Party as "the sheet anchor," "the ark," a party of "moral power . . . from first to last, on the side of justice" that "has only been baffled, in its efforts to protect the negro in his vote, by the Democratic Party."

One Douglass biographer quoted the great man as declaring that "the Republican Party is the ship and all else is the sea around us."

Yet, when Donald Trump referenced Frederick Douglass at a Black History Month event on February 1, 2017, he announced that "Frederick Douglass is an example of somebody who's done an amazing job and is getting recognized more and more, I notice." The bizarre mixing of tenses led the author and social commentator Touré to comment: "I doubt he knows who Frederick Douglass was." The *Washington Post* speculated on the even more unsettling prospect that the president "simply had no idea that the famous black abolitionist Frederick Douglass was, in fact, dead."

The mystery was not resolved when a reporter asked White House spokesman Sean Spicer to explain. "Today [the president] made the comment about Frederick Douglass being recognized more and more, do you have any idea what specifically he was referring to?"

"Well I think there [were] contributions," Spicer replied. "I think he wants to highlight the contributions that he has made and I think that through a lot of the actions and statements that he is going to make, I think that the contributions of Frederick Douglass will become more and more."

Late Night's Seth Meyers played the Spicer comment that evening.

"Who among us wouldn't panic if asked to recite stuff you learned in high school, but how did you not have time between the President's remarks and your press briefing to Google Frederick Douglass?" asked the comedian. "And not his full biography, just simple stuff. Like 'Is Frederick Douglass alive?'" That was a legitimate question.

But not the right question.

The right question is, "Has the Republican Party of Abraham Lincoln and his comrade Frederick Douglass died?" And the right answer to that question is yes.

The issue here is not one of partisanship or ideology. It is a matter of basic premises. And basic principles.

Well into the twentieth century, many leading Republicans took seriously their "Party of Lincoln" sobriquet and the responsibility that went with it. They worked to earn the votes of African Americans and all supporters of equal justice under the law, declaring in the party's 1960 platform that "this nation was created to give expression, validity and purpose to our spiritual heritage—the supreme worth of the individual. In such a nation—a nation dedicated to the proposition that all men are created equal—racial discrimination has no place. It can hardly be reconciled with a Constitution that guarantees equal protection under law to all persons. In a deeper sense, too, it is immoral and unjust. As to those matters within reach of political action and leadership, we pledge ourselves unreservedly to its eradication."

While Democrats struggled with their party's internal contradictions on the civil rights issues of the early 1960s—deferring far too frequently to the demands of southern segregationists who held powerful committee chairs in the House and Senate, and who commanded machines that delivered needed electoral votes—Republicans demanded action. "When President John F. Kennedy failed to submit a promised civil rights bill, three Republicans (Representatives William McCulloch of Ohio, John Lindsay of New York and Charles Mathias of Maryland) introduced one of their own," noted the *New York Times* in recalling the great struggles of the era. "This inspired Mr. Kennedy to deliver on his promise, and it built Republican support for what became the Civil Rights Act of 1964."

When the key votes in the House and the Senate came, Republicans of varying ideological tendencies (and, in those days, the party had liberal, moderate and conservative wings) were significantly more supportive of the Civil Rights Act than were Democrats. The measure passed the House on a 290–130 vote, with support from 61

percent of House Democrats (152 in favor, 96 opposed). But Republican lawmakers gave it 80 percent backing (138 in support, just 34 against).

The critical test came in the Senate in June 1964. Republicans aligned with northern Democrats to break the segregationist filibuster. Then, 82 percent of Republican senators backed the final passage of the measure, as opposed to two-thirds of Senate Democrats.

When President Lyndon Johnson signed the Civil Rights Act into law on July 2, 1964, he is said to have told an aide: "We [Democrats] have lost the South for a generation." But that statement did not just apply to the Democrats. Republicans represented the other part of the change equation. The question: Would Republicans remain the party of Lincoln or would they make a play for disenchanted Democrats in the south?

Two months later, the answer came. A key Democratic foe of civil rights, South Carolina senator Strom Thurmond, switched his party affiliation. Instead of refusing Thurmond, a crude segregationist who had sought the presidency as a defender of the "states rights" doctrines invoked by dead-enders from pre–Civil War days to the present, Republicans such as Richard Nixon and Ronald Reagan welcomed the man into their Grand Old Party (GOP) who literally a year before had been smearing the name of the Reverend Martin Luther King Jr.

Thurmond began working to remake the Republican Party so that it could appeal to the southern white voters who, as Johnson predicted, quickly lost faith in their Democratic Party. Thurmond's influence on Nixon, who developed a so-called southern strategy to realize the South Carolina senator's vision of a transformed political map, was immense. It extended deep into the thirty-sixth president's decision-making process for the selections of cabinet members and Supreme Court nominees. And it was embraced for one reason and one reason only: it worked.

There were Republicans who objected to tossing aside their party's sheet anchor and abandoning the ark of justice that Frederick Douglass described. But they were hounded from its fold by a new breed of hyper-partisan professionals—some elected, others operating behind the scenes—who had no interest in "moral force" politics. They pursued victory at any cost; they relished nothing so much as the personal power that extends from being on the winning side.

Those who embraced a genuine "Party of Lincoln" ethic were removed from positions of authority, and their elected posts. House minority leader Charles Halleck, the Indiana Republican who worked closely with the Johnson administration to pass muscular civil rights protections, was deposed the following January by his own caucus. John Lindsay, who was rejected in his own party's 1969 New York City mayoral primary (winning instead on the Liberal Party line), became a Democrat in 1971. Lindsay's ally in the 1963 civil rights push, Charles "Mac" Mathias, was so unsettled by the GOP's move to the right that he threatened to run for the presidency in 1976 as a progressive independent. Other champions of civil rights, such as California senator Thomas Kuchel (the Republican floor manager in the fights to pass the Civil Rights Act of 1964 and the Voting Rights Act of 1965), New Jersey senator Clifford Case and New York senator Jacob Javits, would eventually lose primaries to challengers who accepted the Republican Party's new politics.

The senators who were rejected did not lose merely because of their civil rights advocacy but because of their Lincolnesque vision of a progressive Republican Party that, in Kuchel's words, "brought to politics the philosophy of governing for the many."

That philosophy was replaced by a more rigid and divisive politics, which exploited not just racial resentment but the whole host of furies and angers that has come to define a "conservatism" that has little to do with ideology and much to do with manufactured bitterness and electoral exploitation. "The Republican Party that had been ceased to be sometime in the 1980s, and the modern party—the radical conservative party—not only has little or no interest in honoring its history, it is actively hostile to it," explained Geoffrey Kabaservice, the author of the brilliant 2012 book *Rule and Ruin: The Downfall of Moderation and the Destruction of the Republican Party from Eisenhower to the Tea Party*.

For a time in the 1950s and 1960s, enlightened Democrats and Republicans competed to be the party of civil rights. And the Republicans were in the lead through much of the period, inspiring Massachusetts senator Edward Brooke, the first African American elected to the Senate in the modern era, to observe that the Republican Party "was, I believe, much more progressive than the Democratic Party."

The tragedy of the Democratic Party through much of its history was an unwillingness to stand strong against its southern wing and to clearly align itself with the cause of social and economic progress. It rejected principles in favor of a dumb-beast partisanship that said winning elections, and accumulating the power that extends from those victories, mattered more than morality.

The tragedy of the Republican Party is that, when Democrats began finally to do the right thing, key figures in the GOP welcomed Thurmond and other segregationist Democrats into its fold and began to do the wrong thing. They crafted not just a "southern strategy" but a politics of reaction. There were plenty of Republicans who resisted the trend at the time, and there have been plenty of Republicans since (notably former congressman Jack Kemp and former secretary of state Colin Powell) who have sought to broaden the party's focus and appeal.

But as one of the great Republican advocates of civil rights, John Lindsay, noted when he left the GOP in 1971: "Today the Republican Party has moved so far from what I perceive as necessary policies . . . that I can no longer try to work within it."

There are no John Lindsays or Edward Brookes left in today's Republican Party because, as the Reverend Jesse Jackson has noted: "Republicans—beginning with Richard Nixon's southern strategy and continuing with Ronald Reagan and beyond—used racial dog-whistle politics to consolidate their party in the white South. The Grand Old Party (GOP) became the party of Jefferson Davis."

John Avlon, the longtime speechwriter for New York mayor Rudy Giuliani, who has since become a prominent advocate for centrist projects such as the "No Labels" movement, observed several years ago that "the Republican Party was right on civil rights for the first one-hundred years of its existence. It was right when the Democratic Party was wrong. Its future strength and survival will depend on rediscovering that legacy of individual freedom amid America's essential diversity. To win in the 21st century, the Party of Lincoln needs to start looking like the Party of Lincoln again."

But that is not going to happen anytime soon.

The Republican Party is now the "Party of Trump," not Lincoln. And certainly not Frederick Douglass—the man whose rich legacy is so neglected by the party that he defended to his death in 1895 now generates headlines like the one on a February 2017 Dana Milbank column for the *Washington Post*: "In which Trump discovers some guy named Frederick Douglass."

There are surely racists in the contemporary Republican Party: alt-right extremists, neoconfederates and old segregationists who climbed into the shell of the GOP with Thurmond. But there are many more practitioners of an insidiously warped version of the "benign neglect" Daniel Patrick Moynihan discussed during the period when the southern strategies of Thurmond and Nixon and Reagan were taking hold. They mouth pieties and attend their "Lincoln Day Dinners," they may even show up for Martin Luther King Day celebrations. But they practice a politics that denies and dissembles everything that was ever noble or necessary about the Republican Party.

They are not Republicans in any historical sense. They are the contemporary embodiments of the dictionary.com definition of political hacks: "a professional who renounces or surrenders individual independence, integrity, belief, etc. in return for money or other reward in the performance of a task normally thought of as involving a strong personal commitment." They are the political tricksters and fraudulent partisans "whose mad ambition," Frederick Douglass warned in his day, "would imperil the success of the Republican party."

These political hacks have no qualms about abandoning the "Party of Lincoln" for the "Party of Trump." In so doing, they have made possible not just a Trump presidency but Trumpism, and all the threats to the republic that extend from a moment when principles are abandoned.

These political parasites attached themselves to the Grand Old Party because it was their meal ticket. They are no different from the crudest ward heelers of the old urban machines that once sustained the Democratic Party. Just as Chicago mayor Richard Daley's most harmful henchmen may once have reflected kindly on the liberal ideals of a Franklin Roosevelt or a Harry Truman, so contemporary Republican hacks profess admiration for the cultured conservatism of a William F. Buckley or a Jack Kemp. But the contemporary conservatism of the Republican Party is a thing of theory rather than practice. It is rightly noted that even a Barry Goldwater or a Ronald Reagan would be unacceptable to the Republicans of today. Despite their own unfortunate compromises against historic Republican principles, Goldwater and Reagan would be too traditional in their inclinations for today's lot.

What matters to the Republican establishment of this time is not even conservatism, as was made evident by the 2016 campaign, in which party leaders embraced Trump's all-over-the-place politics. It is the power that is afforded those who identify with the once good name of the Republican Party, no matter how onerous its leadership may become, no matter how unsettling current manifestations of Republicanism may grow. That power is amplified by media outlets that celebrate hackery as evidence of a seriousness of purpose and pragmatic intent, while dismissing idealism and steadfast commitment as nonsense that has no place in our politics. It is further amplified by a donor class that sees every campaign contribution as an "investment."

It was the willingness of the Republican Party that once was to reject a compromised politics—saying no to the sins of human bondage, no to the moral compromises of the slave economy, no to anti-immigrant hysteria, no to an uneven distribution of the land that discriminated against the urban poor—that made Frederick Douglass a Republican.

In April of 1889, an aging Douglass addressed an audience in Washington, DC, shortly after Republican Benjamin Harrison had assumed the presidency following four years of governance by Democrat Grover Cleveland. "Well, now," the great orator declared, "the American people have returned the Republican Party to power; and the question is, what will it do?"

Douglass titled his address "The Nation's Problem." It was a prescient description for our times, as the nation's problem today is not merely a President Donald Trump but a Republican Party that is made up of the hacks who enable Trump in the name of their own mad ambition and the empty promise of a Republican Party that is no more. It is clear that Trump knows nothing about who Frederick Douglass was. It is equally clear that Trump's fellow Republicans know nothing about what Frederick Douglass, or Abraham Lincoln, or Teddy Roosevelt, or Dwight Eisenhower stood for.

— *18* —

SECRETARIAT STUMBLING

Reince Priebus

White House Chief of Staff

Reince Priebus was choking. Literally and figuratively. He was swallowing hard, again and again, trying to cough up the words that would explain away the firing of a national security advisor for lying to the vice president about cozying up to the Russians who had reportedly engaged in a massive attempt to deliver the 2016 election to his boss. But what really had him gagging was the task of justifying a presidential rant about how the practitioners of the constitutionally defined exercise of journalism were "enemies of the people."

It was February 19, 2017, and the permanent fixture in contemporary Republican politics was appearing on the favorite cable news channel of Republican elites, Rupert Murdoch's Fox News Network. He was talking to a host he had appeared with many, many times before. This was supposed to be easy.

But it wasn't working for the man who traded his title as chairman of the Republican National Committee (RNC) to take over as the chief of staff for a Republican president. What should have been a comfortable conversation was degenerating into another discussion of what Priebus referred to as "basically, you know, some treasonous type of accusations" that transpired on a daily basis after Donald J. Trump assumed the presidency. For a political hack who just wanted to be where the action was, this was a nightmare scenario.

"Joining us now from Mr. Trump's Mar-a-Lago Club in Palm Beach is White House Chief of Staff Reince Priebus," Chris Wallace began. "Reince, I want to start with President Trump's tweet on Friday afternoon. This is what he wrote: 'The FAKE NEWS media (failing

New York Times, NBC News, ABC, CBS, CNN) is not my enemy, it is the enemy of the American people.' Reince, the president believes that a free and independent press is a threat to the country?"

Priebus was rattled. His initial response skirted along the thin ice of incoherence. "No, I think—I think for the most part—and I understand where he's coming from—is that there are certain things that are happening in the news that just aren't honest. And we're not talking about everyone, Chris. We're not talking about all news, but we're talking about something that I guess he's termed as fake news." Then Priebus finally remembered his talking points.

The liberal *New York Times* was "inaccurate." "Grossly overstated." "Wrong." "Nothing to it." The conservative *Wall Street Journal* was "untrue." "Totally inaccurate." Reince was raving now. Everything the press was saying about his new boss's apologies for the sort of Russian autocrats who Republicans once abhorred, about Russian ties to disgraced Trump aides, about the linkages and relationships that Priebus would have decried as treasonous in a Democratic administration, everything that was being said about the Trump team was just, you know, "complete garbage."

But Wallace wasn't buying the spin this time.

"Here's the problem. Reince, wait a minute, here's the problem," the Fox man interrupted. "I don't have any problem with you complaining about an individual story. We sometimes got it wrong, you guys sometimes got it wrong. I don't have any problem with you complaining about bias. But you went a lot further than that, or the president went a lot further than that. He said that the fake media, not certain stories, the fake media are an enemy to the country. We don't have a state-run media in the country. That's what they have in dictatorships."

Priebus sputtered that "it's not just two stories. Then, it's followed up by twenty-four hours a day, seven days a week, of other cable stations, not necessarily Fox, that all day long, on every chyron, every seven minutes, they're talking about Russian spies, talking about the intelligence community, talking about how me and Steve Bannon don't like each other, and what's Kellyanne doing? All this is just total garbage."

Wallace did his best to prevent the great unraveling. "Here's the problem, when the president says we're the enemy of the American people, it makes it sound like if you are going against him, you are going against the country," explained the host.

"Here is the problem, Chris," the White House chief of staff announced, "the problem is you're right." Priebus was just going to keep unraveling, to keep losing it, right there, on Sunday morning, on national television. He was going to keep swallowing hard claiming that there was some kind of plan buried amid the chaos, a plan that was constantly obscured by a pattern of media coverage that failed to recognize how great things were going. Yes, yes, the networks might cover an awkward handshake with the Japanese prime minister, or an awkward handshake with the Canadian prime minister, or an awkward call with the Australian prime minister, or an awkward call with the Mexican president. "But then as soon as it was over," Priebus griped, "the next 20 hours is all about Russian spies."

"But you don't get to tell us what to do, Reince," said the host of the morning talk show on the network that was supposed to "get" the whole Trump thing.

"Nothing is happening," growled Reince. "Give me a break!"

Finally, everyone took a deep breath.

Priebus regained his composure.

"All right," said Wallace. "I need to ask you another question about Russia."

Reince Priebus, who during the 2016 campaign had so frequently hailed Fox as "fair" while ripping its competitors, was swallowing hard again, and grumbling and griping and groping for words—any words—that might get him through the ordeal.

"I don't know why you are so—I mean, it's fine that you're so going bananas here, Chris."

But it was Priebus who was going bananas.

In a media appearance that was supposed to position him as "the adult in the room" at the White House, or Mar-a-Lago, or wherever else the Trump circus was performing, Priebus came off as the bumbling clown who tries without success to distract attention from the wreck that everyone just witnessed.

When Donald Trump claimed the presidency early on the morning of November 9, at a chaotic and seemingly unplanned victory party, the president-elect of the United States called Reince Priebus to the stage at the New York Hilton. "Let me tell you about Reince . . . Reince is a superstar," said Trump. "But, I said, they can't call you a superstar, Reince, unless we win. Because you can't be called a superstar, like Secretariat. If Secretariat came in second, Secretariat wouldn't have that big beautiful bronze bust at the track . . . Reince, come up here. Where is Reince? Come up here, Reince. Boy oh boy, oh boy."

On that night, Trump may have thought Priebus was "a superstar, like Secretariat." But in the Trump White House, Priebus does not lead the conversation. He is trying to keep up. In the "Washington daily gossip" that Priebus was complaining to Chris Wallace about, Priebus began coming in second, or third, or fourth, behind Steve Bannon or Gary Cohn or Jared Kushner or Ivanka Trump or whoever else was calling the shots on that particular day in the White House where Priebus is, at best, a witness to history.

In a functional White House, the chief of staff position is supposed to count for something. This is the job once filled by the giants of Washington lore, the powers behind the throne who controlled the ebb and flow around presidents—advising the commander in chief, selecting staff, managing the message. But Priebus was no H. R. Haldeman to Trump's Nixon, no Dick Cheney to Trump's Gerald Ford, no James Baker to Trump's Ronald Reagan. No one could imagine this guy named "Reince" announcing as Alexander Haig (a former chief of staff, then serving as secretary of state) did following an attempt on Ronald Reagan's life that "I am in charge here." Everyone could imagine Steve Bannon doing that; in fact, everyone suspected that Bannon was in charge during those first, tumultuous weeks of the Trump presidency. It was Trump who created the speculation, with his unprecedented announcement that the Machiavellian character who served as "chief executive" of the Trump campaign would serve as "White House chief strategist and senior counselor to the president," a newly created position that, ominously for Priebus, was identified from the start as a parallel

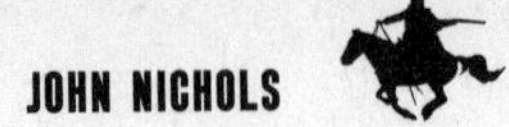

position to the chief of staff job. Priebus was a mandarin, not a powerbroker; an unthinking partisan, not a true believer. And no one doubted that Trump knew this.

Still, there were fabulists who imagined that Priebus might assert himself. Unfortunately for Priebus, they were not people who knew much about the man who was toiling as a clerk for the Wisconsin State Assembly Education Committee when Bannon was finishing a stint at Goldman Sachs and setting up his Bannon & Company investment bank. Priebus was losing a race for the Wisconsin state senate when Bannon was forging the relationship with Andrew Breitbart that scholars will eventually understand as a pivot point in the history of American media and politics.

Priebus came of age on the Wisconsin political scene that spawned Governor Scott Walker and House Speaker Paul Ryan—from neighboring counties in southeast Wisconsin, the trio knew each other from their aspiring days as Republican errand boys. But by 2004, when Walker was the elected chief executive of the state's largest county and Ryan was emerging as a "Young Gun" leader in the U.S. House, Priebus got beat by Bob Wirch, a former sweeper at the Anaconda Brass plant in the blue-collar town of Kenosha who proudly listed his profession as "factory worker." Priebus was, by then, a corporate lawyer with plenty of connections and all the campaign money he could have wanted. But Wirch, a working-class intellectual who had devoted much of his life to the labor movement, had street smarts. The Democrat swept to victory in the state senate race, even as Paul Ryan was winning reelection to the House from the same region.

Priebus got the message. He wasn't electable. So he became a backroom man, parlaying his corporate connections and fund-raising prowess into the chairmanship of the Republican Party of Wisconsin and then the Republican National Committee. The Wisconsinite elbowed aside the first African American chairman of the RNC, Michael Steele, who had presided over the party's "wave" win in the 2010 election cycle, and Priebus promised bigger things to come. But Republicans crashed and burned in the first national election cycle that Priebus oversaw, as Mitt Romney failed to displace Barack

Obama in the 2012 presidential race and Harry Reid's Democrats picked up two seats and clear control of the U.S. Senate.

Priebus, who had gingerly embraced the right-wing populist "Tea Party" movement before the 2012 election, announced after the humiliating defeat that "our message was weak; our ground game was insufficient; we weren't inclusive." Rejecting the image of intolerance that had come to define the party as anti-immigrant, anti-gay, anti-woman and antithetical to young voters. Priebus ordered an "autopsy" of the party's failings and got back a plan for a "Growth and Opportunity Project" that proposed extensive outreach to women, African American, Asian, Hispanic, LGBTQ and young voters. It also proposed a softening and shifting of party rhetoric, going so far as to endorse "comprehensive immigration reform."

"To be clear, our principles are sound, our principles are not old rusty thoughts in some book," said Priebus, who added that "the way we communicate our principles isn't resonating widely enough." The chairman acknowledged that "in many ways the way we communicate can be a real problem."

That was true enough, and 2016 Republican prospects like former Florida governor Jeb Bush and Florida senator Marco Rubio embraced the new vision Priebus and the party insiders laid out. But Donald Trump had different ideas. He dismissed Bush as "the weakest person on this stage" and the candidate of "special interests and lobbyists." He ripped Rubio as "little Marco." Trump made obnoxious comments about women, slurred Latinos, proposed building a wall along the Mexican border, outlined plans for a ban on immigration from Muslim countries and dismissed the preachers of tolerance as "politically correct fools."

It was the opposite of what Priebus wanted. But Trump started winning primaries and caucuses and eventually trounced the rest of the contenders for the party's nomination. How did Priebus react? When many of his closest allies among the party's fund-raising establishment and electoral elites were still spinning #NeverTrump scenarios, Priebus tweeted "@realDonaldTrump will be presumptive @GOP nominee, we all need to unite and focus on defeating @HillaryClinton #NeverClinton."

The party realignment that Priebus had advanced was finished. "Trump kills GOP autopsy," explained a *Politico* headline. "Republican elders drew up a blueprint for a kinder, more inclusive Republican party. Trump is tearing it apart." Priebus was cool with that. Sure, he looked like a fool, and a man without principles. But the hack is always prepared to play the fool, and to shed principles, if that is what is required to retain access to power.

While Trump continued to distrust many in the GOP establishment, the candidate who spoke openly of buying political favors with campaign checks saw something he liked in Priebus. He approved of the party chairman's flexibility when it came to the definition of what it meant to be a Republican. When Priebus arranged a Republican National Convention that short-circuited dissent and let the nominee call the shots, on everything from speakers to platform language, the relationship was sealed. And it proved to be highly beneficial for Trump.

Donald Trump had imagined himself as a potential presidential contender for the better part of two decades. He toyed with the prospect of mounting an independent campaign, going so far as to announce the formation of a presidential exploratory committee as part of a bid for the 2000 nomination of what remained of Ross Perot's Reform Party. But even Trump's enormous ego was insufficient to assure him that he would run any better than Perot had in his losing 1992 and 1996 bids. Trump knew that if he was going to get anywhere near the presidency, his name had to appear on the ballot line of a major party. He bet on the Republicans and took full advantage of a nomination process that Priebus had crafted to benefit a sufficiently well funded and prominent establishment figure but that worked just as well for a sufficiently well funded and prominent "anti-establishment" figure. When that process brought the billionaire to the brink of the nomination, Priebus helped him cross the line more gracefully than even Trump's strategists had imagined possible. That, in turn, legitimized Trump in the eyes of Republicans who were not necessarily enthused by his "New York values." Pundits spent much of 2016 talking about how Trump was dividing the Republican Party, but with vetting from Priebus and other political hacks who maintained the party infrastructure, like Sean Spicer, Trump won 88 percent of the votes of self-described Republicans (just as 89 percent of self-described Democrats backed Hillary Clinton).

Trump could not have become president without that high level of Republican support. So Priebus did his part, and the new president was appreciative: less than a week after the election, Trump named the Republican National Committee chairman as his chief of staff.

The only problem was that Priebus had actually been right about his party's image problem. And Trump, with his crude complaints about political correctness, had been wrong. Trump won the presidency in 2016 not because of his broad popular appeal but because of a narrowly focused Electoral College strategy. In that 2012 campaign where Priebus griped that "our message was weak; our ground game was insufficient; we weren't inclusive," Mitt Romney had won 47.2 percent of the vote nationwide. Trump won just 46.1 percent, one of the lowest levels of support for a Republican nominee in modern times. Fifty-four percent of Americans had opposed Donald Trump.

The defeated state senate candidate from Wisconsin was willing to change direction to facilitate a Trump candidacy even as more conscionable Republicans recognized this was the wrong candidate for their party and their country. Donald Trump said that made Priebus a "superstar." And superstar status has its rewards: a title and a fine office in the West Wing. For a hack, that's enough—even if he has to play the fool on TV.

— 19 —

SPICERFACTS

Sean Spicer

White House Press Secretary

When George Orwell's *1984* is studied in the future, English teachers may want to refer to White House press secretary Sean Spicer's remarkable briefing on January 21, 2017, at the close of the first full day of Donald Trump's presidency.

Trump had been sworn in the day before, as a commander in chief without a mandate—a candidate who lost 54 percent of the popular vote and trailed his chief opponent by close to 3 million votes. The pretender delivered an uninspired sixteen-minute inaugural address to an unimpressive crowd and then paraded through the streets of a capital city where 96 percent of the electorate had rejected him, and where evidence of enthusiasm for his inauguration gave new meaning to the term "modest."

The next morning, January 21, 2017, in the same capital city, the streets were filled by a crowd of Americans, conservatively estimated at more than a half-million, who had come to challenge the new administration's policies toward women in particular and humanity in general. These Americans marched and rallied as part of a national (and global) outpouring of opposition to this president that was so dramatic that Britain's *Guardian* newspaper headlined its report "Women's March on Washington overshadows Trump's first full day in office."

It had the makings of a nightmare scenario for the newly minted press secretary for a minority president who obsessed about his electoral dysfunction. But Spicer should have known what to do. He'd been around the block in DC, several times. A Naval War

College graduate who worked for Republican congressmen like Florida's Mark Foley before joining the Bush-Cheney administration as the assistant U.S. trade representative for media and public affairs, Spicer co-founded a lobbying firm (Endeavor Global Strategies) to represent foreign governments like that of Colombia when they were wrangling with U.S. officials. He jumped to the Republican National Committee when Reince Priebus took over in 2011, first as communications director and then as an all-around communications czar with the vaguely Bannonesque title of "chief strategist."

Spicer, one might suppose, knew how to handle ticklish situations. (With the Republican National Convention, he had even put Trump in his place a few times; for instance, when he pushed back against the presidential candidate's dismissal of U.S. senator John McCain's military record by explaining that there was "no place in our party or our country for comments that disparage those who have served honorably.") Spicer had options. Should it come up, he could have approached the crowd-size conflict from any number of directions. Or he could simply have said nothing on a Saturday night when no one was expecting the partied-out Trump team to add anything to the narrative.

Unfortunately, Trump was fretting that the legitimacy of his new presidency was in question. He had reason to worry, as even his own supporters were beginning to question the wisdom of their 2016 choices. (While Trump won 46 percent of the vote on Election Day, the Real Clear Politics average placed his approval rating at just 41.8 percent on the eve of his inauguration, and some surveys put the number as low as 32 percent.)

So Spicer was pushed out in front of the cameras to deliver a diatribe that surely merited the application of the often misapplied term "Orwellian."

Trump's man declared that "yesterday, at a time when our nation and the world was watching the peaceful transition of power and, as the President said, the transition and the balance of power from Washington to the citizens of the United States, some members of the media were engaged in deliberately false reporting."

In other words, don't believe news reports.

Spicer asserted, at length, that "photographs of the inaugural proceedings were intentionally framed in a way, in one particular tweet, to minimize the enormous support that had gathered on the National Mall. This was the first time in our nation's history that floor coverings have been used to protect the grass on the Mall. That had the effect of highlighting any areas where people were not standing, while in years past the grass eliminated this visual. This was also the first time that fencing and magnetometers went as far back on the Mall, preventing hundreds of thousands of people from being able to access the Mall as quickly as they had in inaugurations past."

In other words, don't believe what you are seeing with your own eyes.

"Inaccurate numbers involving crowd size were also tweeted," Spicer continued. "No one had numbers, because the National Park Service, which controls the National Mall, does not put any out. By the way, this applies to any attempts to try to count the number of protesters today in the same fashion."

In other words, don't accept any numbers that are not provided by an "official" source, such as, say, the Trump White House.

Then Spicer provided numbers that were deliberately chosen to produce a false impression of Trump's inauguration. The press secretary insisted that "this was the largest audience to ever witness an inauguration." To pound in his point, Spicer added a this ends the discussion assertion: "Period!"

In short order, PolitiFact reviewed the statement and the data, and headlined its report "Donald Trump had biggest inaugural crowd ever? Metrics don't show it." After reviewing the multiple falsehoods uttered by the new White House press secretary, the nonpartisan fact-checking site concluded its report with the line "We rate Spicer's claim Pants on Fire." As in pants-on-fire lying.

The following morning, an even higher-ranking Trump apparatchik, presidential counselor Kellyanne Conway, was asked by NBC's *Meet the Press* host Chuck Todd to explain "why the president asked the White House press secretary to come out in front of the podium for the first time and utter a falsehood."

"Sean Spicer, our press secretary, gave alternative facts to that," replied Conway. And so was launched the Twitter hashtag #SpicerFacts. As the months went on, Spicer repeated the performance on an almost daily basis. His "Trump can do no wrong" preachments provided the ultimate show of Republican Party loyalty to a Republican president. The same went for his biased treatment of the news outlets that asked the toughest questions, as when Spicer excluded reporters from the *New York Times,* CNN, *Politico* and several other outlets from attending a press gaggle.

What Spicer was doing was bad for journalism; the White House Correspondents' Association protested the exclusion of the reporters from the gaggle. It was also wrong for Spicer. His daily briefings became must-see viewing for the writers of comedy sketches. NBC's *Saturday Night Live* shredded Spicer by having actress Melissa McCarthy appear as an only slightly more addled and agitated version of the real thing.

McCarthy's impersonation was pitch-perfect. So perfect that, by March, the press secretary seemed to be imitating the comic imitating him. Or perhaps Spicer, whose disputes with the media dated to college days when the school paper printed his name as "Sean Sphincter," was finally losing it.

On March 7, 2017, Spicer tried to make the argument for replacing the Affordable Care Act's "Obamacare" with a Republican reform that was being referred to as "Trumpcare" by placing a copy of the final version of the original 974-page law next to the sketchy Republican substitute.

Forget about the contents, argued Spicer. "Our plan, in far fewer pages, 123 . . . so far we're at 57 for the repeal plan and 66 pages for the replacement portion . . . And remember, half of it, 57 of those pages, are the repeal part. So when you really get down to it, our plan is 66 pages long, half of what we actually even have there."

Say what?

"[Look] at the size. This is the Democrats, this is us. You can't get any clearer in terms of this is government, this is not," said Spicer, as he moved back and forth, hovering over the two stacks of paper. "And I think that part of the reason the visual is important is that when you actually look at the difference, you realize this is what big government does. . . . I think the greatest illustration of the differences in the approaches is that size."

The Spicer "size" video went viral.

The White House press secretary was getting a little weird. And that was unsettling. But what really unsettled people was that no one in the administration seemed to care. In fact, they seemed to approve.

Spicer was not off message. He was weirdly on message. His daily performances grew increasingly laughable, and by the time the administration reached its "one hundred days" mark there was already talk of getting a new press secretary. But Spicer had already set the tone. No matter how absurd his pronouncements became, he made them with the straight face of an unblinking, unquestioning loyalist, not to the truth but to his boss. And that was the point. George Orwell imagined a dystopian future in which authoritarians aspired to "reality control." What was required of mandarins was an ability "to be conscious of complete truthfulness while telling carefully constructed lies."

What Orwell anticipated would become a reality: the alternative world of #SpicerFacts.

— 20 —

THE TRUMPLICAN

Omarosa Manigault

Assistant to the President

Back in the day when Kellyanne Conway was one of Donald Trump's most effective critics on the cable-TV circuit, she clashed on CNN with Omarosa Manigault, one of the most persistent of Trump's apologists.

Things got so crazy on that March 2016 evening that Don Lemon, the host of *CNN Tonight*, had Omarosa's microphone silenced so he could regain control of a discussion about Donald Trump ridiculing the looks of Heidi Cruz, the wife of Texas senator Ted Cruz, who had emerged as the most serious of Trump's challengers for the Republican presidential nomination.

Conway kept trying to turn the discussion toward the damage Trump did to his own campaign when he made crude and sexist remarks. "Women are telling pollsters they don't appreciate a leader who has to get the last word all the time and says certain things," said Conway, who at the time identified herself as the head of "the largest pro-Cruz super-PAC."

But Omarosa, who usually goes by her first name, was not going there. She kept coming back to the clash between the candidates and to defending Trump as a stand-up guy who had every right to let rip on the Cruz family.

"Let's be honest about who created this mess!" demanded Conway, identifying Trump as the wrongdoer. Then she brought up Cruz's two young daughters and imagined them searching their mother's name on the Internet. "What do you want them to find? To see?" asked Conway.

"When they Google it, they're going to see that . . . Daddy, you haven't really been playing by the rules," snapped Omarosa, as she ticked off complaints about Cruz.

"I gave you a nice softball and you struck it out," said an exasperated Conway.

Omarosa shot back: "I'm going to speak my truth and you will never control that."

A few months later, Conway and Omarosa found themselves on the same Trump campaign team—Conway at the direction of the billionaire Mercer family, which funded her super PAC; Omarosa because Trump was her ticket back to the White House where she had once served as a Democrat. Now they work together in the Trump White House, though their roles are reversed. Conway is the no-holds-barred Trump defender, griping about reporters and promising to deliver alternative facts. Omarosa, if her job description is to be believed, is the one bringing people together around ideas and policy initiatives.

Unfortunately, Omarosa Manigault's assignment isn't going any more smoothly than Kellyanne Conway's.

Three days before Christmas, at the close of 2016, Trump named Conway to serve as a White House counselor, an ill-defined position in which the veteran campaigner was, in the president's words, charged with providing "amazing insights on how to effectively communicate our message."

Omarosa was named a few days later as assistant to the president and director of communications for the Office of Public Liaison. Omarosa had announced before her selection for the job that she would have a "huge" position in the new White House. While the Public Liaison office may not be the State Department, it's important. And her posting was not welcomed by everyone in the White House. "To the consternation of the president's chief of staff, Reince Priebus, and others, Trump has given her the same title of presidential assistant as Mr. Priebus and other senior aides—and regularly includes her in high-level strategy sessions on the budget and other matters," noted the *New York Times.*

"She is the highest-ranking African-American in the White House, and she has the ear of the president," Paris Dennard, who served as former President George W. Bush's director of outreach to African Americans, says of Omarosa. "That's a good thing." Some of the time.

For a very long time, white male presidents from both parties have sought insight and counsel regarding relations with racial and ethnic minorities. Frederick Douglass met with and counseled President Lincoln during the Civil War. Franklin Delano Roosevelt appointed dozens of African Americans to key positions in his "New Deal" administration and formed a Federal Council of Negro Affairs (known as the "Black Cabinet") to advise him during the Great Depression and World War II. A member of the council, Robert Clifton Weaver, would be appointed by President Lyndon Johnson as the first secretary of housing and urban development and the first African American cabinet member. Since the 1970s, presidents have tended to have more diverse cabinets. But cabinet members have often been less influential than White House aides and allies such as Bill Clinton's "First Friend," Vernon Jordan, and Valerie Jarrett, who served Barack Obama as assistant to the president for Public Engagement and Intergovernmental Affairs during the administration of the nation's first African American president.

While Omarosa has more political background than many Trump picks, it was not universally seen as impressive. She was, according to a 2004 *People* magazine profile, "banished from four jobs in two years with the Clinton administration."

"Ms Manigault, 43, has no policy experience, a spotty history in her previous federal positions and a resume that has cast her—inaccurately—as a university professor and a former top aide to Vice President Al Gore," observed the *New York Times* in an article headlined "Prerequisite for Key White House Posts: Loyalty, Not Experience." Along with Jason Greenblatt, a former Trump Organization lawyer now charged with forging peace in the Middle East and sorting out relations with Cuba, and Keith Schiller, a former part-time security guard at Trump Tower (and later Trump Organization

 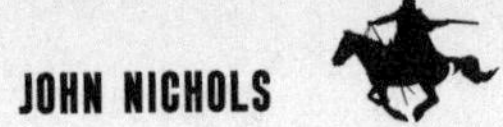

director of security) who now serves as the director of Oval Office operations, Omarosa was featured as an example of how the White House is "peppered with assistants and advisers whose principal qualification is their long friendship with Mr. Trump and his family."

"Manigault, whose star turn on 'The Apprentice' propelled the show's breakout first season, is now among about two dozen aides with the rank of assistant to the president—and one of the few with walk-in privileges for the Oval Office," explained the *Times*. The key phrase there was "star turn on 'The Apprentice.'" That's what brought her into Trump's orbit.

A combative figure on Trump's pioneering program, Omarosa was, according to *Time* magazine, "booted off *The Apprentice* in Week 9, but that was only the beginning of her reality-TV career." Trump knew a good villain when he saw one, so he invited her onto the program *Celebrity Apprentice* and then fired her again. Though she attempted other gigs, Omarosa owed her fame and fortune to Trump, and when he veered into presidential politics in 2015, she abandoned her Democratic roots and declared herself to be a "Trumplican."

Omarosa's appointment as "African-American Outreach" director for the Trump campaign did not impress Trump critics like filmmaker Spike Lee, who posted an off-center image of the reality-TV star with the message "Trump has named her his 'director of African-American Outreach.' You might know her from Trump's reality TV show, *The Apprentice*. Who's next? Step N' Fetchit? Aunt Jemina? Uncle Ben? Sleep N' Eat? Rastus? Lil' (N-word) Jim? Omarosa gonna give out free Popeye's Chicken with sides to deliver [the] black vote to Trump? YA-DIG? SHO-NUFF. #blacklivesmatter." Omarosa accused the *Do the Right Thing* director of race-baiting.

Despite Omarosa's efforts, African American voters did not flock to Trump. According to the NBC News post-election analysis: "With blacks, exit polls show Trump claimed 8 percent of the vote to the previous Republican nominee's 6 percent." Trump failed to match the double-digit finishes of Republicans like George H. W. Bush and Ronald Reagan, and there was no indication that he was renewing the historic "Party of Lincoln" appeal.

So Omarosa had her White House work cut out for her. But there were immediate questions about whether she was steering the Trump train in the right direction. "Trump respects Manigault, and in turn, she will defend him to the exclusion of all else—a trait on display in recent tense, borderline-explosive interactions with the press," explained *BuzzFeed* political writer Darren Sands, in a perceptive assessment of Omarosa's role in some of the new administration's early stumbles.

MSNBC host Joy-Ann Reid noted that "Omarosa is seen by many as the force behind Trump's arguably clumsy attempts to reach across the racial aisle." Reid pointed in particular to "the Black History Month kick-off in the Roosevelt Room, where we were treated to The Donald's delighted discovery of Frederick Douglass and where blinged-out Cleveland pastor Darrell Scott publicly negotiated between the 'top gang thugs' and the White House. And who can forget Trump's awkward visit to the Smithsonian's new African American History and Culture museum, where he once again used his public remarks to boast about his diminutive Electoral College victory and, when confronted with artifacts of American slavery, apparently remarked 'boy, that's not good'?"

Omarosa even rubbed African American Republicans the wrong way. "See what's happening right now, ladies and gentlemen—and people need to understand this very clearly—is black Republicans and black conservatives are being frozen out of the Trump administration by Omarosa Manigault," veteran Republican activist Ralph Chittams explained on his radio show. "I'm saying it. I'm going on record. It's going to cause me some problems, but this nonsense needs to stop and it needs to stop yesterday."

Darren Sands suggested that Omarosa had set herself up as a gatekeeper whose controlling nature reinforced the worst instincts of her boss. "The reality is that if you are black, or concerned with issues affecting black America, with black politics, policy, or culture, Manigault is the person standing between you and the president of the United States," Sands explained. "Trump, in fact, said it himself. Last month at the White House's African American listening

session, he listened to one person after another speak about their priorities. According to a source in the room, Trump twice asked people to follow up with Manigault. At one juncture, he pointed his thumbs outward—one at Trump loyalist Lynne Patton, and the other at Manigault. 'You talk to them,' he said."

The problem is that, when people do try to talk with Omarosa, they are hit with a loyalty test. Omarosa is not always as extreme as she appeared to be in a PBS *Frontline* documentary on the Trump campaign, which featured her declaring: "Every critic, every detractor, will have to bow down to President Trump: it's everyone who's ever doubted Donald, whoever disagreed, whoever challenged him. It is the ultimate revenge to become the most powerful man in the universe." But keen observers see little evidence that Omarosa is immune to the "get even" bitterness that infects Trump's inner circle.

"Omarosa, like Trump, brings high drama with her to the White House," observes Joy-Ann Reid. That's clearly true. And that's clearly a problem. The best aides to presidents, especially those charged with the work of easing tensions with groups that did not support their boss's election, recognize the full meaning of the "Outreach" title. It is not their job simply to push the administration line; it is their job to open up lines of communication. They know that they serve their president best by connecting him with people who come from outside his circle of acquaintance and, at least sometimes, from outside his comfort zone. Unfortunately, that does not appear to be Omarosa's style. "Omarosa," suggests Reid, "is like Trump in the way she relates to the world: as a collection of people for and against her." Unfortunately, being like Trump does nothing to make Trump a better man, or a better president.

— 21 —

THE HYPOCRITE WHO MADE HIS PARTY OF LINCOLN THE PARTY OF TRUMP

Mitch McConnell

Senate Majority Leader

Senate majority leader Mitch McConnell began his exceptionally long Capitol Hill career in the summer of 1963, when he was working as an intern for a Republican congressman from Kentucky. On August 28 of that year, he left the office to watch the March on Washington for Jobs and Freedom. Recalling that he was "overcome by the sight of the crowd, which stretched from the Lincoln Memorial to the Washington Monument," McConnell would later write that "I was too far away to hear Dr. King, but I knew I was witnessing a pivotal moment in history." Though he had grown up in "Jim Crow" Alabama, McConnell recalled that his family opposed segregation and wrote that he had known from an early age "that everyone deserved equal opportunities and a right to vote."

As a young man, Mitch McConnell wanted to be on the right side of history. After he left that first congressional office in which he had served a congressman who had opposed civil rights, McConnell asked for a position with one of the lions of the Senate: Kentucky senator John Sherman Cooper. It happened that McConnell worked with Cooper, an old-school liberal Republican, during the remarkable era when the senator championed enactment of the Civil Rights Act of 1964 and the Voting Rights Act of 1965.

McConnell has spoken and written at great length about how he was inspired by Cooper's steady support of civil rights legislation in the 1960s: "Despite the considerable opposition from back home, Senator Cooper never wavered." In his own memoir, McConnell

hailed Senator Cooper's long and courageous record of advancing "racial equality for every American citizen."

Cooper did, indeed, act as a "profile in courage" senator when he rallied fellow Republicans to support civil rights legislation, with the argument that it was their historic and moral duty as members of the "Party of Lincoln." History well records that the courageous Kentuckian played a critical role in organizing most of his party's caucus to vote with liberal Democrats to avert the stalling tactics of segregationist Democrats, and their conservative Republican allies, so that the Senate could finally speak on behalf of civil rights.

McConnell has always celebrated Cooper's legacy of statesmanship, recognizing the senator's courageous advocacy for opening up a real debate on racial justice.

Yet, when a fellow senator invoked the memory of past struggles on behalf of racial equality by reading the words of Coretta Scott King on February 7, 2017, McConnell rushed to the floor of the Senate and silenced her.

During the Senate debate on the nomination of Alabama senator Jefferson Beauregard Sessions III to serve as Donald Trump's attorney general, Massachusetts senator Elizabeth Warren referred to portions of a letter written three decades earlier by Coretta Scott King in opposition to the nomination of Sessions to serve as a federal judge. In that letter, the widow of the Reverend Martin Luther King Jr. recalled how Sessions had as a U.S. attorney prosecuted voting rights activists in Alabama and wrote: "Anyone who has used the power of his office as United States Attorney to intimidate and chill the free exercise of the ballot by citizens should not be elevated to our courts."

There was no question that what Coretta Scott King wrote was true. The courts had slapped Sessions down, as had the Republican-controlled Senate Judiciary Committee that rejected the Sessions nomination in 1986. Nor was there any question that Senator Warren was accurately recalling struggles that extended from an era that McConnell claims in his autobiography "changed the course of my life."

Yet, as Warren was recalling King's words on that Tuesday evening in the first weeks of the Trump interregnum, McConnell interrupted her and objected that "the senator has impugned the motives and conduct of our colleague from Alabama."

A shocked Warren responded: "I am surprised that the words of Coretta Scott King are not suitable for debate in the United States Senate. I ask leave of the Senate to continue my remarks." Asserting that the senator who holds the seat once occupied by Edward Kennedy had "violated Senate rules against assailing the reputation of a colleague," McConnell objected. Warren appealed but Montana senator Steve Daines, who was chairing the Senate session, interrupted her and announced: "Objection is heard. The senator will take her seat."

A pair of party-line votes sustained McConnell's draconian interpretation of the rules, which if taken to its logical conclusion could effectively silence meaningful debate on any presidential nominee who is a sitting senator.

The majority leader made no apologies for barring Warren, a former Harvard Law School professor and former vice president of the American Law Institute, from further participation in the Senate debate on whether to make Sessions the next attorney general of the United States. (McConnell's Republicans and West Virginia Democrat Joe Manchin eventually cast fifty-two votes to confirm the Alabaman, while Warren and the rest of the Democratic caucus voted no.)

McConnell claimed that Warren had to be silenced because "she was warned. She was given an explanation. Nevertheless, she persisted."

Those words were immediately embraced by Warren and her supporters as a badge of honor.

For McConnell, however, there was no honor. The man who held the seat once occupied by his mentor and hero, John Sherman Cooper, had used the awesome powers of his office in a shabby attempt to silence the recollection of Coretta Scott King's warning that entrusting Jeff Sessions to uphold the rule of law would have "a

devastating effect . . . on the progress we have made toward fulfilling my husband's dream."

Mitch McConnell shamed himself and the Senate that Tuesday night. It was not the first shaming of Mitch McConnell, the man who once championed campaign finance reform but became Washington's most ardent advocate for the big money that distorts our discourse and dominates our politics. McConnell has a long history of hypocrisy, and of using his legislative skills and connections to achieve nefarious results in a chamber he claims to revere. That makes McConnell an able ally for Donald Trump; perhaps the ablest ally that Trump has in all of Washington.

But there was still something shocking, and more than a little heartbreaking, about the sight of a seventy-five-year-old man abandoning everything he had ever stood for in order to speed up the process of rubberstamping Trump's cabinet picks.

A half century ago, when some Republicans began to toy with a strategy of abandoning their party's historic commitment to civil rights, John Sherman Cooper warned of the absolute amorality of the compromise. "In the long run, such a position will destroy the Republican Party, and worse, it will do a great wrong because it will be supporting the denial of the constitutional and human rights of our citizens."

Mitch McConnell knew Cooper was right when the late senator from Kentucky uttered those words. Undoubtedly, Mitch McConnell knows them to be right today. Yet, he has abandoned his mentor's "profile in courage" politics to join in the shameful servicing of Donald Trump's retrograde presidency.

John Sherman Cooper would be horrified by his former intern's infamy, and by the transformation of the "Party of Lincoln" into the "Party of Trump."

— 22 —

PARTY BOY

Paul Ryan

Speaker of the House

House Speaker Paul Ryan told the House Republican Caucus just one month before the 2016 presidential election that Donald Trump's shocking comments about women, as recorded on the infamous *Access Hollywood* tape, were "not anywhere in keeping with our party's principles and values."

"There are basically two things that I want to make really clear, as for myself as your Speaker," Ryan explained, in what was supposed to be a private conference call with members of the House Republican Caucus. "I am not going to defend Donald Trump—not now, not in the future. As you probably heard, I disinvited him from my first congressional district GOP event this weekend—a thing I do every year. And I'm not going to be campaigning with him over the next 30 days."

So that was it. Ryan and Trump were over and done with. The speaker stood his ground. Firmly. Unapologetically. For the better part of two weeks.

Then Ryan cheerfully announced that he had not just cast an early ballot for Trump, but that he was urging fellow Republicans to do the same.

"I stand where I've stood all fall and all summer," Ryan chirped on the Fox News show *Fox and Friends*. "In fact I already voted here in Janesville for our nominee last week in early voting. We need to support our entire Republican ticket."

Then Ryan went on to rip the Democratic nominee and to speak with considerable passion about the absolute necessity of electing a Republican Congress and a Republican president.

Once again, as he had throughout the 2016 campaign, Ryan delivered for Trump at precisely the point when Trump needed an establishment Republican to step up. For Trump, the critical final struggle of the 2016 race involved the work of getting Republicans who had soured on their nominee to "come home" to the GOP ticket. And Paul Ryan was the chief wrangler.

Despite his occasional protestations to the contrary, despite the dippy media storyline that imagined again and again and again that Ryan might break with the nominee and stand strong for the historic Republican values that the billionaire populist so ardently assaulted, the speaker invariably put party loyalties ahead of principles. He did so during the campaign. He did so during the transition. He did so when he got 217 House Republicans to back a scheme to "repeal and replace" the Affordable Care Act that Trump claimed—disingenuously, as it would never survive Senate scrutiny—as the first real legislative achievement of his presidency.

This is the essential understanding with regard to Paul Ryan: he will never stand up to Trump when it matters. Never. Paul Ryan will sacrifice any principle, any ideal, on the altar of his own ambition. And now his ambition is wedded with the Trump presidency that Ryan, to a greater extent than any other Republican, made possible. That was good for Trump when he needed Ryan to keep Republican voters in line at the close of the 2016 campaign, and that is good now for Ryan because an ill-prepared and unfocused president is ripe for manipulation by one of Capitol Hill's slyest self-promoters.

Paul Ryan wants very much to be recognized as the adult at the kids' table that his Republican Party has become. No one in the party works harder to curry the favor of the print and broadcast outlets that have for the better part of a decade formed an amen corner for the House Speaker.

Ryan endeavors to portray himself as a diligent public servant who simply wants to do the heavy lifting required to reform government and the economy, even if his "reforms" consistently involve shaping budgets and rewriting tax codes to favor the interests of the billionaires, bankers and corporate CEOs who donate so generously to the many campaign funds he manages.

Since he arrived on Capitol Hill more than a quarter century ago, Paul Ryan's heaviest lifting is always on behalf of Paul Ryan's personal ambition. Though he frequently portrays himself as an unwilling participant in the power politics of DC, Ryan invariably ends up as a vice presidential nominee, a powerful committee chair or the Speaker of the House. That does not happen by chance. That happens because no one in contemporary American politics claws and clutches and compromises more consistently in pursuit of personal power than Paul Ryan.

Ryan's power extends from the success or failure of the Republican Party that will be led for the foreseeable future by Donald Trump. So, for the foreseeable future, Ryan is going to be Trump's man on the hill. No doubt about it. No questions asked. As Washington's most determined political careerist, Paul Ryan knows that when the political winds shift he must shift with them. Still, the man's cynicism can be breathtaking.

The House Speaker pitches himself as a high priest, speaking unfortunate truths about debts and deficits; as the unforgiving foe of social spending who would willingly sacrifice Social Security, Medicare and Medicaid as we know them in order to achieve debt reduction. Ryan has branded himself well in Republican circles, so well that he has parlayed himself into contention for the key committee chairmanships, the speakership and a place on a national ticket. The congressman from Wisconsin inspires confidence among Republicans by pitching himself as the champion of an old-school Republican agenda of fiscal responsibility and balanced budgets.

But Ryan is nothing of the sort. He's actually a hypocritical big spender—at least when Wall Street, the insurance industry and the military-industrial complex call. More like Trump than he might want to admit, Ryan has been a steady voter for unconscionable health care policies, unsustainable bailouts of big banks, unfunded mandates and unnecessary wars. Few members of Congress have run up such very big tabs while doing so little to figure out how to pay the piper.

"Congressman Paul Ryan can grandstand about the debt all he wants, but at the end of the day, Ryan is a root cause of many of the

financial issues our country faces today," explained Rob Zerban, a local official in Ryan's home district who challenged the congressman several years ago. "From supporting two unfunded wars, to dumping millions of senior citizens into the Medicare Part D 'donut hole' while tying the hands of the government to negotiate prescription drug prices, and from fighting for subsidies for Big Oil that his family personally benefits from, to supporting the unfunded Bush tax cuts for his wealthiest campaign contributors, Paul Ryan's hypocrisy is astounding."

Ryan's scorching cynicism grew ever more astounding as Trump elbowed his way into contention for the Republican presidential nomination in 2016.

Everything that anyone needed to know about how Ryan would relate to Trump, as a candidate and as a president, was revealed in the fall of 2015, when Trump called for a "total and complete shutdown" of Muslims entering the United States. That was a stunning expression of the xenophobia and bigotry that had always existed on the fringe of the Republican Party but that Trump threatened to bring into its mainstream.

Paul Ryan, as the supposed adult in a room full of immature and belligerent Republicans, had a clear duty. He was the Speaker of the House, the party's immediate former nominee for vice president and a frequently boomed prospect for the presidency himself. Ryan possessed both the authority and the stature to a draw a line in the sand and declare that responsible Republicans were on one side and Donald Trump was on the other.

Yet, after Trump called for a religious test that was broadly recognized as unconstitutional, after Trump made advocacy for indiscriminate discrimination central to his candidacy, Ryan provided nothing in the way of leadership.

Rather, Ryan played the part of the indulgent parent talking about a troublesome child.

"Normally, I do not comment on what's going on in the presidential election. I will take an exception today," Ryan said on December 8, 2015, as a firestorm rose regarding Trump's crude extremism. "This is not conservatism. What was proposed yesterday is not what this party stands for. And, more importantly, it's not what this country stands for," Ryan told a Capitol Hill news conference. "Not only are there many Muslims serving in our armed forces dying for this country, there are Muslims serving right here in the House working every day to uphold and to defend the Constitution."

All true. And it was clear Ryan was talking about Trump, even if the Speaker lacked the wherewithal to call out the billionaire by name.

There can be no question that millions of Muslims are proud Americans, that they serve honorably in the military and Congress. Nor can there be any question that, as Ryan noted: "Some of our best and biggest allies in this struggle and fight against radical Islamic terror are Muslims—the vast, vast, vast majority of whom are peaceful, who believe in pluralism, freedom, democracy, individual rights."

There can be no question that Trump's religious-test bigotry is at odds with the basic premises of the U.S. Constitution and what this country has stood for at its best. That was true in the fall of 2015, and that was still true in the early days of 2017, when Trump signed an executive order that was read as a Muslim ban.

In the fall of 2015, however, there was significant uncertainty about whether Trump's extremism was at odds with what the Republican Party was coming to stand for—as the party's base was rallying around Trump in the fall of 2015, and as the party's establishment continued to provide him with forums to promote discrimination against people based on their religion and national origin.

This was where Ryan needed to step up. This was where he needed to say that conservatives could not accept Donald Trump, that Republicans could not support Donald Trump, that the Republican Party could not aid and abet Donald Trump's bigotry, and could no longer entertain the notion of making him its 2016 nominee.

Unfortunately, Ryan lacked the courage to break with Trump.

Asked at a point when Trump might still have been stopped if he would support Trump if the billionaire was nominated by the party as its 2016 candidate, Ryan responded: "I'm going to support whoever the Republican nominee is and I'm going to stand up for what I believe in as I do that."

 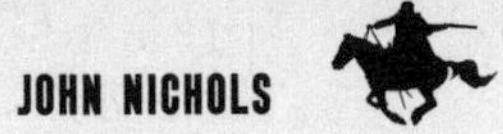

So, just to be clear, Ryan griped that Trump was not advocating for conservatism. Ryan griped that Trump did not represent what the Republican Party stood for. But Ryan would back Trump for president of the United States. That was not a break with Trump. That was Ryan providing Trump with precisely the cover the presidential contender needed at a critical point in the campaign—cover of the same sort Ryan would later provide when Republicans drafted their party platform, when they gathered for a convention the Speaker chaired and when they rallied behind their nominee in November.

Nothing aided and abetted Trump more as he sought the Republican nomination than Ryan's constant signaling that, even if Trump made Republican elites uncomfortable, the party's supposedly sober and responsible leaders would stand for Trump if he was nominated.

Ryan's words and deeds identified Trump as a troublesome but acceptable, controversial but legitimate candidate. And that was all that Trump needed, in the primary season, and in the fall to pull the party together sufficiently to prevail.

In Ryan's home state of Wisconsin, one of the three states that broke partisan pattern and backed the Republican presidential nominee in 2016 (thus providing the electoral votes that were required to secure the presidency), Trump won by less than 23,000 votes. If just 11,500 votes had shifted, Wisconsin could have gone to Hillary Clinton. With similar shifts in Michigan and Pennsylvania, a Trump presidency could have been averted.

But Paul Ryan made sure that did not happen. He told Republicans they could and should vote for Trump, again and again and again. While principled Republicans rejected Trump during the campaign, and continue to stand up to him now, Ryan cleared the way for the billionaire—not because the Wisconsinite liked Trump but because, as a fiercely sectarian political careerist, Ryan never has and never will put the best interest of his country ahead of the immediate demands of partisanship—and of Paul Ryan.

— 23 —

COMPLICIT

Ivanka Trump, First Daughter, and Jared Kushner, First Son-in-Law

The comforting notion that even cynical citizens allow themselves when assessing an authoritarian, extreme or merely cruel regime is the suggestion that a thuggish leader's wife or daughter or in-law or extended family member might somehow temper the worst impulses of the strongman. The notion is global (think "Evita"), but it is especially popular in the United States. This is where the myth machinery of media and politics strains to reimagine particular members of particular first families as quiet heroes ever at the ready to intervene on behalf of reason in otherwise unreasonable White Houses. This is about much more than First Ladies taking on charitable and educational duties, or children of presidents presenting themselves as wholesome freethinkers. This is about policy making, and unmaking; about the prospects for averting disasters and slyly advancing agendas.

Whole books are written on the topic. Plays are penned. Movies are made. There is just one problem.

The "moderating influence" argument has always required a suspension of disbelief and an embrace of false hope that can border on delusion.

So it was that Americans were constantly reminded of former First Lady Barbara Bush's pro-choice leanings, even as President George H. W. Bush packed the courts with anti-choice jurists. So it was that First Daughter Jenna Bush's internship with UNICEF was portrayed as good news, even as George W. Bush was pursuing foreign (and domestic) policies that were unhealthy for children and other living things.

So it is that Ivanka Marie Trump, the daughter of Donald Trump's first marriage to Ivana Marie Zelníčková, has emerged, with her husband, Jared Kushner, as a supposed agent of influence on behalf of liberal humanity in the shadowy recesses of Steve Bannon's West Wing. "Ivanka Trump and Jared Kushner Said to Have Helped Thwart L.G.B.T. Rights Rollback," announces the *New York Times* headline. "In Closed-Door Climate Showdown, It's Jared and Ivanka vs. Bannon and Pruitt," announces *Foreign Policy* magazine. The *Washington Times* reports: "Donald Trump unveils child-care policy influenced by Ivanka Trump." CNBC reveals a paid-family leave push with the headline "Ivanka Trump has found a cause to champion—and Democrats love it."

Why, it's almost too good to be true! Because, of course, it *is* too good to be true.

A few weeks into the Trump interregnum, *Slate*'s Christina Cauterucci actually wrote what everyone else had been thinking: "Trump and her husband, Jared Kushner, have been the subjects of so many 'leaks' pushing the narrative that they're common-sense forces of conscience in the White House, it's hard to imagine the 'leaks' could come from any source other than Trump and Kushner themselves."

Ivanka Trump is all about branding: "With her intelligence, business savvy and style, Ivanka Trump has ensured that the board room is never the board room on 'The Apprentice,'" a breathless profile from a decade ago began. "And now, with a sexy and revealing cover and photo layout for *Stuff* magazine, Ivanka lives up to the title, 'World's Sexiest Boss!'" Ivanka has sold jewelry and clothing, shoes, purses and expensive perfumes (with a "floral-oriental composition [that] has a touch of luminous fruity notes and flirtatious spices making the whole fragrant story even more exciting," coos *Fragrantica*). She has occupied the boardroom, on *The Apprentice* and in real life, developing a persona as the smart daughter who is trusted (and favored) by her father over a pair of sons who, "although outshone in many ways by their sister Ivanka," serve as the figurehead head honchos of their father's business empire during a period when *Vanity Fair* says "he won't be letting go easily, or anytime soon."

"The Trump Sons," screams the headline, "are expanding like crazy but swear it's totally legal." Unlike Ivanka, who is constantly telling tales about conversations with "My Father," Donald Trump Jr. says: "I basically have zero contact with him at this point." But a more realistic review of the relationship came on *Saturday Night Live* where, several weeks into Trump's presidency, an actor playing Donald Jr. announced: "Bottom line is, the only people making decisions regarding the Trump organization are Eric and myself." The actor playing Eric Trump interrupted to announce: "And Dad."

Ivanka Trump, the Trump child who matters, says she will "no longer be involved with the management or operations of the Trump Organization." Her "Ivanka" branded business operations are now in what even her lawyer admits is a murky trust—she's still got "veto power" over decisions and as her lawyer put it: "She has the conflicts that derive from the ownership of this brand." Those conflicts aren't going away, for Ivanka or for husband Jared, who in mid-May faced scrutiny after it was revealed that members of his family exploited their White House connection to solicit Chinese investors. Jared will always be the bigger embarrassment, but Ivanka will always be the bigger deal when it comes to the Trump White House. She's made sure of that.

While she could have stayed in New York, Ivanka decamped to Washington within days of her father's election. Her purpose? To launch her boldest project yet: serving as First Daughter to be sure and, in some assessments, as a sort of "surrogate First Lady" while Melania Trump maintains her sanity in New York. Ivanka initially suggested that she might spend a lot of time in DC but not so much time at the White House (unlike Jared, who was sworn in as an "official senior adviser" to the president). But all that changed as winter turned to spring and *Politico* announced that Ivanka "is now officially setting up shop in the White House."

"The powerful first daughter has secured her own office on the West Wing's second floor—a space next to senior adviser Dina Powell, who was recently promoted to a position on the National Security Council," the DC-insider publication announced. "She is also in

 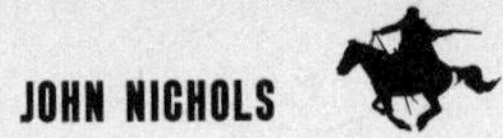

the process of obtaining a security clearance and is set to receive government-issued communications devices this week."

Ivanka's current brand is something of a theatrical production: a White House version of Dr. Jekyll and Mr. Hyde. She's the good doctor; her father is the pathetic soul who cannot control his raging id. From the very beginning of Donald Trump's White House bidding, Ivanka Trump has promoted herself (and to a lesser extent husband Jared) as the conscience of the campaign, the conscience of the transition, the conscience of the administration. But a fabricated liberal conscience does not undo the inconvenient truth of Trumpism. It simply, in the parlance of Alaskan philosopher Sarah Palin, puts lipstick on a pit bull. Ivanka may avert an executive order here, or celebrate International Women's Day there, but Muslim bans are still initiated, environmental protections are still abandoned, health care is still denied, international family-planning services are still gagged and Betsy DeVos is still in charge of dumbing down education.

People who had paid attention to the Trump family knew how the relationship of father and daughter would evolve even before the election—back in the days when the "false hope" crowd was still peddling "Donald Trump is an urbane and maybe even kind of liberal New Yorker" happy talk.

"Ivanka Trump Is Not Going to Save Us From Her Father," warned *New York* magazine in the summer of 2016. "Of course, we all know Ivanka. This is true especially in New York, where Trump's eldest daughter has become, like her father, one of the city's stock characters, albeit one whose personality is more in line with the city's current self-image than his. Where the Donald scowls and stomps and blusters around town like a fat-cat ghost from another era, Ivanka moves gracefully, with the unwavering poise she displayed in the 2003 documentary *Born Rich*, in which she was one of the few heiresses to comport herself with dignity," wrote Jessica Pressler, a savvy observer of the New York scene. "It is often noted that she is the polar opposite of Donald, the suggestion being that someone as controlled as Ivanka must be somewhat embarrassed by her circus-clown father. But no: Ivanka is 'absolutely proud to be a Trump,' as she told the makers of *Born Rich*, and shares with her father a sense of outsize ambition. On her this patrilineal zeal looks so much better, more modern: less 'Greed is good' and more 'You go, girl.'"

But, this wise writer counseled, there was about Ivanka a darker side, a willingness "to overlook ugliness in exchange for success." "She is not, as the Latin-American and Mexican version of *Marie Claire* recently begged, going to stop her father by talking to him," explained Pressler. "If she has tried to get him to tone it down, as reports have suggested, it should be pretty clear by now that she has failed . . . She is not, after 34 years of control, going to lose her cool and rebel. As Ivanka has told us repeatedly: 'Trumps play to win.' And that's what she and her husband, Jared Kushner, seem to be exclusively focused on now."

The proof of Pressler's point came several months later, when media outlets went wall to wall with the old *Access Hollywood* tape that revealed Donald Trump in full "grab 'em by the pussy" sleazy old-man mode. After a discreet silence, Ivanka released a much mentioned statement to *Fast Company* magazine in which she offered a carefully crafted acknowledgment-cum-defense of the man whose own words marked him as a sexual predator: "My father's comments were clearly inappropriate and offensive and I'm glad that he acknowledged this fact with an immediate apology to my family and the American people."

If anyone missed the point of her defenses of "my father," Ivanka explained that her dad was really just the victim of media that portrayed Donald Trump as, well, Donald Trump. "The greatest comfort I have is the fact that I know my father. Most of the people who write about him don't. I do," Ivanka told *Fast Company*. "So that gives me an ability to shrug off the things that I read about him that are wrong."

Of course, what Donald Trump said on the *Access Hollywood* bus was wrong—so wrong that the parents of young children could not let them near the news for several days at the close of what the Republican nominee for president referred to as "the very sacred election process." But here was the self-proclaimed advocate for women and children covering for the candidate at precisely the point when he needed it most. It was the stuff of the *Saturday Night Live* skit that it became some months later when actress Scarlett Johansson

 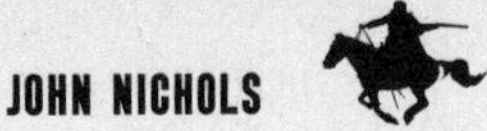

portrayed a glamorous Ivanka peddling a new perfume named "Complicit."

"A feminist, an advocate, a champion for women," says the classic commercial voiceover before asking: "But, like, how? She's loyal. Devoted. But probably should have bounced after the whole *Access Hollywood* bus thing."

Ultimately, however, it is not Ivanka who is complicit. It is those who fall for the fantasy that she is going to smooth over the rough edges of her father's presidency and make everything nice and New Yorky. Ivanka has made no secret of the fact that she is and will continue to be her father's enabler, and that her husband is, if anything, even more complicit.

Like Ivanka, Jared Kushner is ideologically pliable and exceptionally loyal to Donald Trump. An overseer of his own family's real estate empire—operating out of a skyscraper at 666 Fifth Avenue, just down the street from Trump Tower—Kushner is young and reportedly savvy. "It's hard to overstate and hard to summarize Jared's role in the campaign," tech billionaire Peter Thiel, another Trump enabler, said in 2016. "If Trump was the CEO, Jared was effectively the chief operating officer." That is somewhat overstated and rather poorly summarized: Jared played a genuine role in developing the social-media focus of the Trump campaign, but he had plenty of help from Steve Bannon, Kellyanne Conway and a rogues' gallery of hangers-on. The same goes for his position in the White House, which supposedly involves him in everything from reforming the criminal-justice system to addressing the opioid epidemic to reinventing government. As *Fortune* magazine notes: "Kushner has been given a litany of tasks, from international diplomacy to daily White House operations." Sean Spicer says he's in charge of "applying the president's ahead-of-schedule and under-budget mentality to a wide number of government operations and services—enhancing the quality of life for all Americans."

That's a tall order. And the fact that some media outlets imagine that Kushner is actually endeavoring to fill it speaks to the fabulism that continues to be embraced by those who have not figured out that neither Trump nor Kushner keeps track of everything that this "always in campaign mode" administration claims it is going to do.

The essential fact with regard to Ivanka and Jared is that they are facilitators. They help Trump get things done; but they do not define what is getting done. The president's daughter and son-in-law were, during the campaign, and remain to this day, trusted counselors for Donald Trump. They are empowered by that trust. But the counsel, to the extent that it errs toward the left of the administration's trajectory, is only rarely taken. For the most part, Ivanka and Jared are props—and in Jared's case a reported "person of interst" in the ongoing investigation into possible ties between Russia and the Trump campaign.

On the eve of Trump's inauguration, the president-elect announced that he would charge Jared, whose Orthodox Jewish family has funded controversial right-wing settlement activity on the occupied West Bank, with sorting out ancient differences between Israel and Palestine. "If you can't produce peace in the Middle East, nobody can," Trump told Jared at a festive dinner where the president-elect's cabinet picks were celebrated. Trump's aides and allies were smiling; they recognized that the president likes to talk about Kushner because he knows the guy who married his daughter a lot better than he does the people he has nominated to run things.

That does not mean that Jared won't be meeting with Israeli prime minister Benjamin Netanyahu, a Kushner family friend and associate for decades. It does mean, however, that "Jared Kushner, who has no diplomatic experience or regional expertise" (as the *Daily Beast* explained), has an exceptionally ill-defined role. So ill-defined that, after meeting with Kushner, former secretary of state Henry Kissinger said, "It's not clear to me in what way he's in charge of it, whether he's in charge of it with supervision from the White House, or whether he's supposed to be the actual negotiator. Nor has it been defined what they're negotiating about."

Jared is not going to replace Secretary of State Rex Tillerson. He can't be in the cabinet, nor can Ivanka. Nepotism rules see to that. But Jared did play a weird role, based more on personal pique than measured assessment, in shaping the cabinet, if jarring insider reports from the transition process are to be believed.

One of Trump's essential backers in the late stages of the 2016 Republican primary campaign was New Jersey governor Chris Christie,

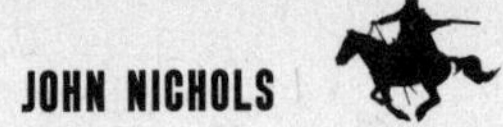

who endorsed the billionaire developer after folding his own presidential bid. Christie was a stalwart supporter, to the point of embarrassing himself with shameless displays of loyalty that made him little more than a gofer. But Donald Trump appreciates that sort of surrender and, when it came time to name a vice presidential running mate, Christie was reportedly the frontrunner. According to some accounts, the presidential candidate offered his most enthusiastic backer the number two slot. "Days before the Republican National Convention, however," CBS News reported, "Trump reneged on the deal after others in his inner circle convinced him otherwise."

The specific "others," according to several accounts of the *House of Cards* scenario, were Jared and Ivanka. A source with direct knowledge of the situation told CBS that "it was Jared Kushner, Trump's son-in-law and a key adviser, who made the final moves to seal [Indiana governor Mike] Pence's fate and oust Christie."

No problem. Christie got another gig as the head of the transition team that was supposed to put the pieces in place for a Trump presidency, with a special emphasis on building a strong cabinet. That made sense. While Christie may be a hothead with dubious ethics, he is also a sitting governor with actual experience putting together cabinets, making appointments and framing agendas. But when the Trump candidacy became the Trump presidency, Christie and the able associates he had pulled in to help organize the transition were tossed from the team. Just as the administration was embarking on its perilous journey, the people with the maps and the GPS systems were told that their assistance was no longer required. Why? Because, despite the fact that he wears cardigans and tennis shoes and affects a boyish persona, Jared Kushner can be as cutthroat and calculating as his father-in-law.

Jared "led the ouster of Christie allies from the president-elect's transition organization," explained *USA Today*, while less gentle commentators referred to the move as a "Stalinesque purge." To be clear, there are plenty of reasons to dislike Chris Christie, and plenty more to argue for his exclusion from positions of public trust. But Jared had a distinct, particularly personal reason of his own. "It all goes back to his dad being prosecuted by Christie," an in-the-know source explained.

A decade earlier, as a hard-charging U.S. attorney in New Jersey, Christie had indeed prosecuted Jared's father, Charles Kushner. After Charles Kushner was convicted on eighteen counts of witness tampering, making illegal campaign donations and tax evasion, he headed to prison for fourteen months. The prosecutor then took a victory lap. "The court of law was the great equalizer for Mr. Kushner, who had obviously convinced himself that his power, influence and immense wealth put him above the law," declared Christie, sounding populist themes that anticipated the 2016 campaign. "We are very pleased that justice was done."

Christie's prosecutorial bravado came back to haunt him, and Donald Trump, as the transition process moved into high gear. Kushner and other members of the Trump team denied that the knives were out. But as Christie allies and associates were purged one after another, Rutgers University political scientist Ross Baker, a veteran analyst of New Jersey political intrigues, told New Jersey's *Asbury Park Press*: "I have to believe it's a Kushner revenge."

"That's the only way to explain these demotions and departures," Baker explained. "I don't buy the argument that Christie flunked some kind of loyalty test. I think it's Jared Kushner's high hand behind this whole thing and it's a little bit of karma, because Christie is known for getting even with people, too."

The problem Kushner did not fully anticipate was that, when Christie and his allies were elbowed out of the transition process, months of work on the transition and decades of connections to potential White House appointees, especially in the legal and law-enforcement communities, were lost. Former congressman Mike Rogers, a key player on intelligence issues and close friend of Christie's, left the transition team when his longtime ally was booted. The chaos became ever more evident, as the void opened by the purge went unfilled. "They really have to get the train on track," argued Baker in mid-November, just weeks into what was turning into a very rocky transition. "Plus you're trying to set up an administration for someone with no governmental experience and who operates a lot on whim and impulse. People who are trying to read the crystal ball are going to find it cloudy on how this is going to look by Inauguration Day."

It was still cloudy on Inauguration Day. Thousands of executive branch positions remained unfilled, the new president's initial address to the nation and the world sounded like a "written on the back of an unpaid bill" list of personal complaints and the festivities were so dismally organized that Trump landed in the middle of a bizarre debate about inflated crowd estimates.

The mess offered a measure of the influence that Ivanka Trump and Jared Kushner bring to the Trump White House. They might temper a statement here, or unmangle a message there, but they are more a part of the pettiness and the dysfunction than they are of the solution. To some extent this is because, like Donald Trump, they lack the basic experience that is required for governing. The most charitable thing that can be said about Jared Kushner and Ivanka Trump is that they may not even know how their words and deeds prevent them from doing what they want to do.

It could be that Ivanka actually believes, as her website advises working women to believe, that "everything you need is already inside you." But that's a self-help mantra, not the agenda for the working women that Ivanka claims to champion (on her own and with Dina Powell, the former Goldman Sachs head of "impact investing" and veteran White House aide who has been charged with helping Ivanka advance an agenda of "entrepreneurship, small business growth and the global economic empowerment of women"). As author Amy Wilentz wisely observed in the *Nation*: "The fact that Ivanka is supposedly guiding women's policy shows just how little—not how much—[Trump] cares about it."

Even when Ivanka makes a seemingly meaningful move, it is often as disastrously ill-thought as Jared's apparent purging of the adults from the West Wing at precisely the moment when they were most needed. Ivanka's much heralded plan to develop a universal childcare system in the United States sounded great on the 2016 campaign trail. And it added a few good lines to Trump's first address to a Joint Session of Congress. But the plan itself is awful.

A study for the Tax Policy Center by Lily L. Batchelder, Elaine Maag, Chye-Ching Huang and Emily Horton determined "that about 70 percent of benefits go to families with at least $100,000 and 25 percent of benefits go to families with at least $200,000." Bottom line: "Very few benefits go to the lowest income families who are likely to struggle most with paying for child care."

"What kind of childcare plan gives the majority of its funding to families making over $100,000 a year?" asked the *Nation's* Michelle Chen. The answer is that what Ivanka proposed was not a childcare plan; it was a campaign slogan. And the same goes for her image as the Trump administration's moderator in chief. Ivanka Trump and Jared Kushner are not the cavalry. They are not heroes; they are children of privilege who know their place. Jared is only on the scene by virtue of the fact that he married Ivanka. And Ivanka is on the scene because her father is the boss.

This is not a meritocracy, and nothing meritorious is going to come of it. These are just a couple of New York socialites with grifter instincts. "Shop Ivanka's look from her #RNC speech" read the tweet posted after she spoke on her father's behalf at the 2016 Republican National Convention; "Is Jared Kushner Getting a 'Sweetheart Deal'?" asked the *Vanity Fair* headline two months into the Trump presidency, which went on to explain that "The First Son-in-Law's family is set to receive $400 million from a Chinese company in a deal with 'unusually favorable' terms." Like those sly con artists in all the best movies, Ivanka and Jared seek to create the impression that they are at once trustworthy and influential. But, when it matters, they are neither, as Ivanka readily admits. "I'm his daughter, so I give him my feedback, solicited or otherwise," she told ABC's 20/20 on the eve of her father's inauguration. But when ABC's Deborah Roberts asked if he actually listened to her, Ivanka acknowledged that it "depends on the day." That was Ivanka comforting herself. But it is cold comfort. As Amy Wilentz reminds us, Ivanka Trump knows full well that "her only job has been to burnish Trump's kinder, gentler side (if only he had one), to soften the Stephen Bannon blow, and to brand the new administration with a contemporary attitude toward women and women's rights, rather than the attitude of a pussy-grabbing sexual predator."

— 24 —

THE SECRETARY OF TRUMP IS ALWAYS RIGHT

John Kelly

Secretary of Homeland Security

Homeland Security secretary John Kelly is loyal to a fault. "I work for one man. His name is Donald Trump," says Kelly, when he is asked by congressional committees about the messes made by Trump and the West Wing cabal that has turned governing into chaos.

Translation: Even if Kelly disagrees with a policy, even if he has doubts about whether Trump is doing the right thing, he's not going to share those anxieties with the members of Congress who are charged with providing oversight of Kelly and one of the most powerful departments in the federal government. And the fifth secretary of the Department of Homeland Security (DHS) is certainly not going to share with the American people any concerns about the unsettling and bizarre behaviors of the president who made him part of the cabinet.

That's a far cry from the image of Kelly that was perpetuated by his advocates, and by the retired Marine Corps general himself, during the assessment of his nomination to join Trump's team. Kelly got high marks when he told the Senate Homeland Security and Governmental Affairs Committee: "I have never had a problem speaking truth to power, and I firmly believe that those in power deserve full candor and my honest assessment and recommendations."

That blunt talk fit with his image as a marine who had, during forty-five years of service in war zones from Vietnam to Iraq, earned a reputation for speaking his mind. This was the guy who, when he was asked in 2003 about how hard taking the capital of Iraq might be, answered: "Hell these are Marines. Men like them held Guadalcanal and took Iwo Jima. Baghdad ain't shit." As it happened, Iraq proved to be a heavier lift than Kelly anticipated; a decade after the invasion, he was saying: "If you think this war against our way of life is over because some of the self-appointed opinion-makers and chattering class grow 'war weary,' because they want to be out of Iraq or Afghanistan, you are mistaken. This enemy is dedicated to our destruction. He will fight us for generations, and the conflict will move through various phases as it has since 9/11."

It was Kelly's linking of border security issues with the "war on terror" that reportedly got Trump and his transition team excited about the general in the first place. While serving as head of the U.S. Southern Command, the general told a 2015 Senate Armed Services Committee hearing that "terrorist organizations could seek to leverage those same smuggling routes [in Central America and Mexico] to move operatives with intent to cause grave harm to our citizens or even bring weapons of mass destruction into the United States."

That bold language was "a little over the top" in the view of Frank Sharry, the executive director of the immigration reform group America's Voice. But members of the Senate comforted themselves with the expectation that Kelly's experience with national security issues would lead him to speak truth to Trump's power on the issues of immigration policy, deportations, border walls, Muslim bans and domestic policing that are within the purview of a Department of Homeland Security with a $40 billion budget and 240,000 employees in the twenty-three federal agencies it oversees.

After the Senate approved Kelly's nomination by a lopsided 88–11 vote on the day Trump was inaugurated, however, the general lost his voice. He did not speak truth to power. Rather, he reinforced power that would have been better served by blunt questioning and open objection.

In late January 2017, after the rollout of the president's executive order banning travel from seven Muslim countries went horribly awry—with mass protests, immediate legal challenges, judicial orders blocking its implementation and an international outcry—Kelly was called before Congress to explain the whys and wherefores

of the chaos. "This is all on me," the secretary announced, taking full blame for the failed attempt to impose a religious-test restriction on refugees and visitors that critics correctly labeled as a "Muslim ban."

That may have sounded like an honorable acceptance of responsibility when no one else in the administration was acting responsibly. But when a member of the cabinet speaks to Congress they are supposed to give a clear and accurate assessment of what has transpired. And Kelly failed to provide that. Kelly may well have approved of the ban; he told the House Homeland Security Committee in his February 7 appearance that he thought it was "entirely possible" terrorists were entering the country after the courts blocked implementation of Trump's executive order, and he griped that objections to the order were part of a "very academic, very almost in a vacuum discussion." He also repeated the White House talking point that said: "This is not, I repeat, not a ban on Muslims," even though lawyers, judges, diplomats and scholars said it was.

Despite the public apologias and explanations, however, the fact is that the Muslim ban was never "all on" Kelly. Quite the opposite. The travel ban was, by virtually all accounts, the work of White House strategists Steve Bannon and Stephen Miller. Indeed, in a *Wall Street Journal* report based on leaks from inside the administration: "Mr. Kelly was also frustrated at not knowing the details of the travel ban earlier, so he could prepare his agency to respond, according to people familiar with the matter. Mr. Trump signed the executive order that created the ban late Friday afternoon. Mr. Kelly was only informed of the details that day as he was traveling to Washington, even though he had pressed the White House for days to share with him the final language, the people said."

"The tensions between DHS and the White House have led to uncertainty at the top of an agency charged with keeping Americans safe within US borders. The agency struggled to respond to demonstrations and scenes of confusion at various airports after the immigration order," explained the *Journal*, which noted that "even though he was not involved in the order's preparation, Mr. Kelly was peppered with questions about it. Democrat Senate minority leader Charles Schumer spoke with Mr. Kelly twice at the time to press for details." The newspaper suggested that "the problems at DHS reflect a growing unease among government workers with a series of abrupt policy changes dictated by a close-knit group inside the West Wing of the White House."

Kelly did not acknowledge those tensions when he appeared before the House committee. Indeed, he downplayed press reports about clashes with Bannon and tried to paint a picture of smooth relations that strained credulity. His "I work for one man" response to questions from the committee was another way of saying that frankness was not on the agenda.

That's a problem because cabinet members do not work for one man. They are not extensions of the president. They may serve at the behest of a president, but they swear an oath to the Constitution and they have responsibilities to consult with the legislative branch as well as the executive. When they fail in that responsibility, they create problems that are greater than leaks. They may even obscure wrongdoing, or facilitate wrongheaded actions.

This is why cabinet members are not supposed to be yes-men and apologists.

Yet, Kelly sounded like just that when he was asked in early March 2017 about Trump's allegation that President Barack Obama ordered the wiretapping of Trump Tower phones during the 2016 campaign. Trump's charge was explicit and exceptionally serious. "Terrible! Just found out that Obama had my 'wires tapped' in Trump Tower just before the victory. Nothing found. This is McCarthyism!" the president tweeted on March 4. He even outlined legal remedies, tweeting: "Is it legal for a sitting President to be 'wire tapping' a race for president prior to an election? Turned down by court earlier. A NEW LOW!" and "I'd bet a good lawyer could make a great case out of the fact that President Obama was tapping my phones in October, just prior to Election!"

Obama, Trump asserted, had undermined "the very sacred election process. This is Nixon/Watergate. Bad (or sick) guy!"

There was only one problem with the charge, which the president apparently picked up from right-wing Internet chatter. As the BBC noted with regard to the charges: "They were not backed up by any evidence." None. Even if contacts with Trump aides might have been swept up as part of legitimate surveillance by U.S. intelligence agencies of international communications, there was no reason to believe that President Obama had ordered wiretapping of the campaign. It was such a stretch that, when CBS *Face the Nation* host John Dickerson pressed the president in early May on the question of whether he stood by his accusation against Obama, Trump replied defensively: "I don't stand by anything."

But John Kelly sure stood by Trump.

Kelly admitted, when he appeared on CNN on the Monday after Trump's initial tweeting of those claims about Obama, that he had nothing to add to the discussion. "I don't know anything about it," the top national security figure told CNN's Wolf Blitzer. But then Kelly went off the rails.

"If the President of the United States said that, he's got his reasons to say it," the secretary of homeland security announced. "He must have some convincing evidence that took place . . . I don't pretend to even guess as to what the motivation may have been for the previous administration to do something like that."

When Kelly uttered his "for the previous administration to do something like that" line, he was asserting that the wiretapping had either occurred or, at the least, was likely to have occurred. Yet, former director of national intelligence James Clapper was already saying that "there was no wiretap against Trump Tower during the campaign conducted by any part of the National Intelligence Community." Former CIA and NSA director General Michael Hayden was saying that there was "no body of evidence" for Trump's claim that Obama ordered those election season wiretaps. "What was claimed is inconsistent with the way I know the system works," Hayden told Fox Business's Neil Cavuto. And the *New York Times* reported that FBI director James Comey had asked the Justice Department immediately after Trump tweeted his claims to publicly reject the "assertion that President Barack Obama ordered the tapping of Mr. Trump's phones." According to the *Times*, officials said: "Mr. Comey, who made the request on Saturday after Mr. Trump leveled his allegation on Twitter, has been working to get the Justice Department to knock down the claim because it falsely insinuates that the FBI broke the law."

Kelly's response: "Jim Comey is an honorable guy. And so is the President of the United States. And the President must have his reasons." Kelly's loyalty to Trump was unyielding. And, as such, Kelly was failing Trump and the nation Kelly is supposed to serve.

"To have to go through these kinds of games that are being played right now—and they're dangerous games, where the credibility of the FBI and the credibility of our intelligence agencies are called into question—is just sending a terrible message not only to the American people but to the world," said Leon Panetta, a former CIA director and secretary of defense. "Everybody is asking: What the hell is going on in Washington, D.C., right now? When that happens it weakens us, weakens our country."

When Panetta served as Barack Obama's second secretary of defense, then-general Kelly served as his senior military assistant. Panetta endorsed Kelly as an "excellent choice" for the Homeland Security post in December of 2016. But he was not echoing Kelly's bizarre deference to Trump the following March.

"No such wiretap took place. There is no evidence to support what the president has alleged," said Panetta, who argued that "President Trump has to understand he is now president of the United States, that he won the election in last November and he became president of the greatest country on Earth. He's not the head of 'The Apprentice' now, he's not a TV personality. He doesn't have, you know, the convenience of basically saying whatever he wants to the American people and to the world without substantiating that there is any kind of truth to what he's saying."

A veteran staffer in Republican and Democratic administrations, Panetta did not merely blame the president. "So, look," he said, "presidents of the United States have a staff. They're supposed to have people around them who are able to determine what the truth is and a president who is responsible will take the time to ask that staff and the people who are working for him 'what is the truth and what can I say?'"

One of the people who is supposed to speak that truth to power, even presidential power, is Homeland Security secretary John Kelly. He swore to the Senate that he would do just that. Yet, when it came time to speak truth, to clarify, to make sure that a falsehood was not propelled forward or legitimized, Kelly failed out of an excess of loyalty. That was embarrassing for Kelly, for the administration he serves and for the country to which he owes a higher loyalty.

— 25 —

THE CAPTAIN OF THE WRECKING CREW

Alexander Acosta

Labor Secretary

The essential battleground state of the 2004 presidential campaign was Ohio, and as the election approached, supporters of embattled President George W. Bush announced an exceptionally controversial scheme to station citizen "challengers" at polling places. As a Brennan Center for Justice report explained: "Only a few weeks before Election Day, the Ohio Republican Party announced its plan to deploy thousands of citizen challengers across the state, mostly in African-American voting precincts. The announcement led to multiple voting rights lawsuits and sparked a media firestorm."

The firestorm ultimately led Ohio Republicans to abandon their initial plan. But, the Brennan Center analysts noted in their 2012 report "Voter Challengers" that "the ensuing controversy shined a national spotlight on the disruptions that partisan and discriminatory challenge efforts can cause." It also shined a light on Alexander Acosta.

Acosta wasn't Trump's first choice for the Department of Labor post. The president's initial pick was Andrew Puzder, a wealthy fast-food CEO with a record of taking fiercely anti-worker positions on issues ranging from wages to workplace safety, and an even more unsettling record as a fiercely anti-worker boss. As his confirmation hearing approached, opposition from labor unions hit a fever pitch and media outlets began to uncover more sordid stories from Puzder's past. "Maybe Mr. Puzder should quit before the public learns more about him," Massachusetts senator Elizabeth Warren wrote in late January of 2017. By early February, Puzder accepted the

 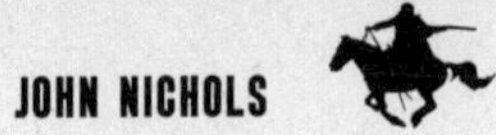

counsel, from Warren and a number of Republicans, and withdrew his name from consideration.

Trump needed a quick replacement, so he went with an insider favorite who knew his way around the Washington swamp. Acosta was an experienced government hand, with a long history of working the conservative Republican side of the aisle. When he finished Harvard Law School, he clerked for future Supreme Court justice Samuel Alito, who was then serving as a judge on the U.S. Court of Appeals for the Third Circuit. After a stint as a senior fellow with the right-wing Ethics and Public Policy Center, Acosta served for nine months during George W. Bush's first term on the National Labor Relations Board, as a conservative but relatively mainstream member. Then he was plucked from that position and appointed by Bush as the assistant attorney general with responsibility for leading the U.S. Department of Justice's Civil Rights Division.

It was in that latter role that Acosta intervened just before the 2004 presidential election in a pair of lawsuits brought by Ohio civil rights activists who argued that an Ohio law that permitted the challenging of the right of voters to cast their ballots was unconstitutional.

A former Justice Department official argued, in a McClatchy DC bureau report published June 24, 2007, under the headline "Ex-Justice official accused of aiding scheme to scratch minority voters," that Acosta's Ohio intervention amounted to "cheerleading for the Republican defendants."

So-called challenge statutes have long been a subject of controversy. A September 10, 2012, Demos study, "Bullies at the Ballot Box: Protecting the Freedom to Vote Against Wrongful Challenges and Intimidation," argued that "there is a real danger that voters will face overzealous volunteers who take the law into their own hands to target voters they deem suspect. But there is no place for bullies at the ballot box." The Brennan Center warned in an August 31, 2015, summary of its work on voting rights issues that "when challenges are used improperly, they can have the effect of intimidating voters or suppress voter participation."

One lawsuit filed by Donald and Marian Spencer, a pair of veteran civil rights activists from the Cincinnati area, argued that Ohio's

1886 "challenge statute" was what the *Los Angeles Times* in a November 1, 2004, report described as "a vestige of 'Jim Crow' laws and created the possibility of disenfranchising a voter without due process of law."

Acosta cannot have been unfamiliar with these concerns. Yet the assistant attorney general dispatched what the *Los Angeles Times* referred to as "an unusual letter brief supporting the statute." Acosta's letter urged the judge to uphold the "challenge statute" in order to maintain "the balance between ballot access and ballot integrity." "Challenge statutes, such as those at issue in Ohio, are part of this balance," wrote Acosta, according to the November 1, 2004, *Los Angeles Times* report on the Ohio controversy. "They are intended to allow citizens and election officials, who have information pertinent to the crucial determination of whether an individual possesses all of the necessary qualifiers to being able to vote, to place that information before the officials charged with making such determinations."

Acosta's letter also argued that "nothing in the Voting Rights Act facially condemns challenge statutes" because "a challenge statute permitting objections based on United States citizenship, residency, precinct residency, and legal voting age like those at issue here are not subject to facial challenge . . . under the Act because these qualifications are not tied to race."

In fact, as the *Los Angeles Times* noted: "David Maume, a sociologist at the University of Cincinnati, testified that demographic data demonstrated that a disproportionate number of Republican challengers would be placed in precincts that were predominantly African American. Maume told the judge that his analysis found that 77 percent of black voters in Hamilton County, where Cincinnati is the largest city, could face a Republican challenger on Election Day, while only 25% of white voters could encounter a challenger."

Alphonse Gerhardstein, the civil rights lawyer who represented Donald and Marian Spencer, told reporter Henry Weinstein in 2004 that the letter was "highly irregular" and noted that "the Justice Department is not a party to the case. They have not filed a motion to intervene in the case or filed an amicus brief. . . . They volunteered information that goes beyond any federal interest. It's startling

 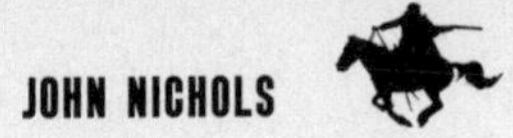

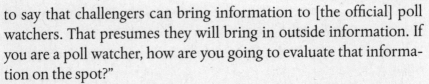

to say that challengers can bring information to [the official] poll watchers. That presumes they will bring in outside information. If you are a poll watcher, how are you going to evaluate that information on the spot?"

In 2007, the former chief of the voting section of the Department of Justice's Civil Rights Division, Joseph Rich, referred to the 2004 moves by the Ohio Republicans as a "vote caging" scheme. (The Brennan Center referred in its 2007 guide to voter caging that the practice is "a notoriously unreliable means of calling the voter rolls into question [that] can lead to unwarranted purges or challenges of eligible citizens. When it is targeted at minority voters [as it often is, unfortunately], it is also illegal.")

Robert Kengle, the deputy chief of the voting section, explained to *Talking Points Memo* in 2007 that he left his position because of the politicization of the department during the time of Acosta's leadership. It was Kengle who complained that the controversial letter brief in the Ohio case amounted to "cheerleading for the Republican defendants," and told the McClatchy newspapers in 2007 that "it was doubly outrageous because the allegation in the litigation was that these were overwhelmingly African-American voters that were on the challenge list." He was not alone in expressing concerns. McClatchy reported that "former Justice Department civil rights officials and election watchdog groups charge that [Acosta's] letter sided with Republicans engaging in an illegal, racially motivated tactic known as 'vote-caging' in a state that would be pivotal in delivering President Bush a second term in the White House."

"Acosta's letter," the McClatchy coverage explained, "is among a host of allegedly partisan Justice Department voting rights positions."

The issues raised by "challenge statutes" and "voter caging" remain a profound concern, and the subject of legal debates, as does Acosta's tenure with the Department of Justice's Civil Rights Division. Minutes after Trump announced Acosta's nomination to serve as labor secretary, Wade Henderson, the president and CEO of the Leadership Conference on Civil and Human Rights, said: "It is incumbent upon the Senate to conduct a thorough review of Alexander Acosta's record."

In a February 2017 statement released by the Lawyers' Committee for Civil Rights Under Law, the group's president and executive director, Kristen Clarke, said she was "astonished by the nomination of Alexander Acosta to serve as Secretary of the US Department of Labor." "Mr. Acosta led the Civil Rights Division at a time that was marked by stark politicization, and other improper hiring and personnel decisions that were fully laid bare in a 2008 report issued by the Office of Inspector General (OIG)," said Clarke. "The OIG found that actions taken during Mr. Acosta's tenure violated Justice Department policy and federal law. Political and ideological affiliations were used as a litmus test to evaluate job candidates and career attorneys, wreaking havoc on the work of the Division. This egregious conduct played out under Mr. Acosta's watch and undermined the integrity of the Civil Rights Division. It is hard to believe that Mr. Acosta would now be nominated to lead a federal agency tasked with promoting lawful hiring practices and safe workplaces."

Critics also pointed to a 2008 Justice Department inspector general report, which determined that, when Acosta was in charge of the division: "Attorneys hired by [one of his deputies] were more than twice as likely to be Republican or conservative than those attorneys [the deputy] was not involved in hiring." The inspector general's report concluded that the Civil Service Reform Act and DOJ policies that barred hiring discrimination based on political and ideological affiliations had been violated. Acosta and his fellow Civil Rights Division managers were singled out for failing to "exercise sufficient oversight" to guard against "inappropriate hiring and personnel practices."

Politicizing policies and hiring practices are a big deal in any circumstance, but they are an especially big deal when they threaten the Labor Department, which has long been under attack by conservatives. The Department of Labor is powerful, with a budget in excess of $12 billion, more than 17,000 employees, and a charge to protect the rights of more than 125 million workers and to assure

that 10 million employers respect those rights. It is a defining agency that sets not just the specific standards of regulations and mandates but a societal standard that is, at best, an extension of the vision former labor secretary Frances Perkins outlined when she explained in her 1934 book *People at Work*: "Very slowly there evolved from these conferences certain basic facts, none of them new, but all of them seen in a new light. It was no new thing for America to refuse to let its people starve, nor was it a new idea that man should live by his own labor, but it had not been generally realized that on the ability of the common man to support himself hung the prosperity of every one in the country."

At a time when the nature of work is being transformed by globalization, a digital revolution and automation, when wage stagnation remains an issue, when discrimination in the workplace is a pressing concern, the Department of Labor needs to be strengthened. Instead, the Trump administration has sought to cut the department's funding by $2.5 billion, or 21 percent. When the budget plan was announced in March 2017, the National Employment Law Project issued an assessment in which the cuts were described as "draconian" and Christine Owens, the project's executive director, said: "The Trump budget would gut the very job-training programs workers need to develop the skills required to compete in emerging fields and fill many of the high-paying jobs available now and projected for the future." With Alexander Acosta at the helm, a man who drew sharp rebukes for politicizing the management and work of another federal agency is positioned to make the Department of Labor more vulnerable than it has ever been in its history. Working Americans today should feel every bit as threatened as did those voters in Ohio back in 2004.

— 26 —

PUTT-HEAD

Andrew Giuliani

Associate Director for the Office of Public Liaison

Meet Andrew, a high-spirited young man from New York City who dreamed of being a professional golfer. Andrew's father was very powerful, very connected, very wealthy. And that was very fine for Andrew. He did not need a scholarship to play college golf. His way was paid to go to an elite university: "$200,000 in tuition and fees across four years" at Duke, according to *Golf Digest*. Andrew joined the Duke Blue Devils golf team, with its spiffy golf bags, spiffy leather golf club covers and color-coordinated outfits. Unfortunately, he ended up ranking twelfth out of fourteen players. And it did not help that Andrew was kind of a jerk. A teammate told *Sports Illustrated* that the kid was "rude, impolite and a disturbance to our team." The teammate recalled "a series of events, of him being rude to me and talking to me a certain way, and when I finally told him I didn't appreciate it," well, then came what *Golf Digest* called "The Flying Apple Incident."

"He threw an apple at me point-blank, and it shattered on my face," the Duke teammate said of Andrew. He threw the apple so hard that it reportedly "exploded." It was, lawyers would later argue, a "physical assault" that fit into a pattern of sometimes destructive, sometimes simply bizarre behavior. That was it: Andrew was off the varsity golf team. This upset him. It upset him so much that he sued the university and the head golf coach for, as the *New York Times* delicately explained, "dashing his dreams."

Andrew's lawyers demanded monetary damages from the university and argued in legal filings that the coach who dismissed Andrew had stolen a page from William Golding's *The Lord of the Flies*.

The legal gambit did not end well. U.S. magistrate judge Wallace Dixon reached the conclusion that Andrew's claim "slices far from the fairway" and recommended its dismissal in a ruling that included a reference to the movie *Caddyshack*. A federal judge agreed.

Because Andrew's father was famous, having just finished a run for the presidency of the United States, the story went national, as did the ridicule. Golf.com announced that the "lawsuit against the school did not make par." The *New York Post* referred to Andrew as a "Putt-Head."

What's an aspiring athlete to do? Andrew went pro. But that plan petered out eventually. So Andrew became a thirtysomething "sales intern" for CapRoc Capital in Rye, New York, where one of the "founding principles" is "understanding and managing one's liquidity is paramount."

This young man so needed a break. Something new. A job where he could realize his full potential, a job with status, a job with a title like "Associate Director" in the White House Office of Public Liaison. And so it was.

On March 6, 2017, as the Trump administration rushed to "staff up" key White House positions, the president officially announced that Andrew Giuliani would be joining a White House office that had previously employed future cabinet secretaries and U.S. senators, like Alexis Herman and Elizabeth Dole. The same office that Margaret "Midge" Costanza used in the 1970s to raise awareness about, and engagement with, a still-young LGBTQ rights movement; the same office that became Faith Ryan Whittlesey's vehicle for aligning the Reagan administration with the religious right in the 1980s; the same office that served as Valerie Jarrett's base of operations through the two full terms of Barack Obama's presidency. The announcement made headlines—bigger ones in at least some papers than for a few of Trump's cabinet picks. Unfortunately, the headlines somewhat diminished Andrew's accomplishment:

Politico: "Trump hires Rudy Giuliani's son for White House role."

New York Daily News: "Rudy Giuliani's son takes job with Trump administration."

New York Post: "Trump picks Giuliani's son for WH job."

Well, yes, Andrew is the son of former New York City mayor Rudy Giuliani, the one-time presidential candidate who threw his considerable energy into getting Trump elected in 2016. Rudy Giuliani was angling for a big job in the Trump administration, like secretary of state. But that didn't happen. All he got in the early stages of the Trump presidency was an informal assignment as Trump's "cybersecurity adviser"—and a lot of grief for going on Fox News and saying something that would come back to haunt the administration in courts of law and in the court of public opinion: "I'll tell you the whole history of it: When he first announced it, he said 'Muslim ban.'"

But, Andrew is not Rudy. Andrew is his own man. So why the dad-referencing headlines?

It was almost as if the media was suggesting that Andrew did not get a White House position, with an office and a title and a good bit of authority to influence politics and policies, based on his own merits.

But at least the independent daily newspaper at his alma mater recognized Andrew Giuliani as more than just the son of the most shameless of Donald Trump's high-profile apologists during the 2016 campaign. The *Duke Chronicle* headline on the day after it was revealed that another sinecure had been found for another family member of another Trump associate announced: "Former men's golfer who sued Duke joins Trump administration."

— 27 —

THE PRODUCT OF A JUDICIAL COUP

Neil Gorsuch

Associate Justice of the Supreme Court

Neil Gorsuch's nomination to serve on the U.S. Supreme Court was born in politics. But it was not just any politics; it was a corrupt politics that sinned against tradition and the Constitution. Nothing in Gorsuch's record of judicial service could alter the facts. Nothing in his mild-mannered "Oh goodness" testimony to the Senate Judiciary Committee could change the circumstances of his selection on January 31, 2017, as Donald Trump's nominee to serve an open-ended term on the highest and most powerful court in the land.

Gorsuch entered the process a marked man.

He was marked not by the Democrats who challenged his nomination but by the Republicans who broke the rules, corrupted the process and lied to the American people in order to make Gorsuch's nomination possible.

By all rights, Gorsuch's nomination belonged to another man, Judge Merrick Garland, the distinguished chief judge of the U.S. Court of Appeals for the District of Columbia Circuit. Able and reasoned, fully qualified in every sense, Garland was nominated on March 16, 2016, by President Barack Obama to fill the vacancy caused by the death of Associate Justice Antonin Scalia. Garland was denied proper consideration by the U.S Senate after Senate majority leader Mitch McConnell and Senate Judiciary Committee chair Chuck Grassley determined to put politics ahead of their constitutionally defined duty to provide advice and consent regarding judicial nominations.

Gorsuch knew of this wrongdoing when he was nominated; indeed, shortly after Donald Trump announced his decision, Gorsuch called Garland "out of respect." Gorsuch would later avow that he believed Garland to be an "outstanding judge" whose opinions he read "with special care."

Yet, Gorsuch sacrificed his own self-respect on March 21, 2017, when he refused to answer a simple question about the shameful treatment of Garland by the lawless partisans who had corrupted the confirmation process in order to steal a Supreme Court nomination.

The senior Democrat on the Judiciary Committee, Senator Patrick Leahy of Vermont, asked Gorsuch a simple question about Garland: "Do you think he was treated fairly by this committee, yes or no?"

"Senator," Gorsuch replied, "as I explained to you before, I can't get involved in politics. There's judicial canons that prevent me from doing that, and I think it would be very imprudent of judges to start commenting on political disputes between themselves, or the various branches."

That was a legalistic and, at the same time, shamefully dishonest answer.

When Minnesota senator Al Franken raised the issue, Gorsuch said much the same thing, adding: "There is a reason why judges don't clap at the State of the Union, and why I can't even attend a political caucus in my home state to register a vote in the equivalent of a primary."

Franken pressed him on the matter, explaining that "I think you're allowed to talk about what happened to the last guy that was nominated in your position. You're allowed to say something without getting involved in politics. You can express an opinion on this."

The senator pointed to the legitimate constitutional concerns that had been raised by the failure of the Republican-controlled Senate to even consider the Garland nomination. But Gorsuch steadfastly refused to respond.

"Senator," said Trump's nominee, "I appreciate the invitation, but I know the other side has their views of this, and your side has your views of it. That, by definition, is politics. And Senator, judges have to stay outside of politics."

True enough. Sitting judges are expected to stay out of electoral politics. But this is not about attending a caucus or writing a

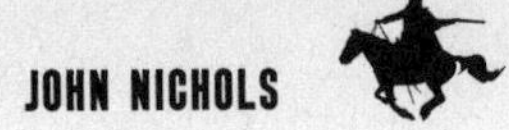

campaign check. This is about respect, or disrespect, for the process by which judges are nominated, how those nominations are reviewed and the standards by which they are confirmed or rejected. Gorsuch is not a stupid man. He knew the question he was being asked and he refused to address it, not with the purpose of avoiding politics but because his own nomination was marinated in politics.

Gorsuch's refusal to acknowledge that corruption that cleared the way for his nomination diminished him. "Judge Gorsuch himself should understand the precedent his nomination risks setting and not hide behind statements about the need to avoid politics," explained former U.S. senator Russ Feingold, a three-term veteran of the Senate Judiciary Committee who weighed the nominations of six Supreme Court justices during his eighteen years in the Senate. Of Gorsuch, Feingold said: "He should have refused the nomination. He reportedly called Judge Garland after he was nominated. If he had truly understood what is at stake, he would have called Judge Garland to say he had turned down the nomination in solidarity—not with Judge Garland personally, but with the Supreme Court and the U.S. Constitution that he says he holds in such high regard."

This was not a small matter. This was the essential matter regarding Gorsuch's nomination to serve on the nation's highest court.

The issue was not one of ideology or partisan balance.

It is true that Gorsuch is a rigid conservative—a little to the right of Scalia, but not so far off the deep end as Justice Clarence Thomas, according to analyses of their opinions. Gorsuch's roots are on the right wing of the Republican Party. His mother served as a Colorado Republican legislator in the 1970s, aligning with what at the time was described as "a group of conservative lawmakers intent on permanently changing government." A corporate lawyer, Anne Gorsuch Burford went on to serve as Ronald Reagan's much-criticized Environmental Protection Agency administrator. As a young lawyer, Neil Gorsuch was an active supporter of Republican campaigns, especially the 2000 Bush-Cheney campaign. He was active with the Republican National Lawyers' Association, a group that says its mission involves "advancing Republican ideals." Gorsuch served in George W. Bush's Department of Justice and Bush appointed

Gorsuch to serve as a judge of the United States Court of Appeals for the Tenth Circuit.

Gorsuch's career advanced on a classic conservative and classic Republican trajectory. There is no scandal in that. The court is awash in ideology and partisanship. Clearly defined conservatives and clearly defined liberals have been appointed to the bench before, as have partisan Republicans and partisan Democrats. Many of them have served well and honorably.

The fundamental problem with the Gorsuch nomination was not with the politics of the nominee, although many reasonable people opposed him because they believed Gorsuch would be unable to overcome the political biases of a lifetime. The fundamental problem was with the politics of obstruction and lying that Republicans, including Donald Trump, employed to block Merrick Garland's nomination. Within hours of Scalia's death, Senate majority leader McConnell declared that "this vacancy should not be filled until we have a new president." Senate Republicans, with Trump cheering them on, argued that Supreme Court vacancies are simply not to be filled in presidential election years.

That was a lie. The Constitution entertains no such instruction. In fact, it sends the opposite message. The Constitution does not say that presidents *may* nominate justices. It says they *shall* do so. The Constitution does not say that presidents are limited in this duty by the timing when a vacancy occurs. There is no footnote that says presidents shall only perform their duties in nonelection years. Nor is there a footnote that says members of the Senate shall only provide appropriate advice and consent when a president is in the early stages of a term. Nor is there any language that suggests that a president's nominee to the Court must parallel the ideology of the justice he or she would replace—or that of the Senate.

Yet Republican senators responded to the death of Justice Scalia by proposing to shred not just the Constitution but precedents that date from the first years of the American experiment.

American history is full of instances where Supreme Court justices were nominated, confirmed and seated in presidential election years.

On September 7, 1956, U.S. Supreme Court justice Sherman Minton penned a note to President Dwight Eisenhower, explaining that he intended to retire from the court. Minton, a former Democratic senator from Indiana who had been appointed to the Court by President Harry Truman, was in ailing health. Eisenhower responded with a note expressing his hope that Minton would enjoy his time off.

Justice Minton left the Court on October 15, 1956, as the country was focused on that year's presidential campaign and intense battles for control of the House of Representatives and the Senate. Eisenhower, the Republican nominee for a new term, had a lot on his mind. But he found time that week to fill the vacancy created by Minton's departure. As the Senate was in recess, the president simply appointed New Jersey supreme court justice William Brennan Jr. to the high court.

Justice Brennan took his place on the bench immediately. That was that. And that is a part of the history of how Supreme Court vacancies are filled in election years.

Recess appointments are rare (although Eisenhower also made initial appointments of Chief Justice Earl Warren and Justice Potter Stewart during recesses in 1953 and 1958, respectively) and are eventually followed by post-recess, post-election nominations, and confirmations (as was the case with Warren, Stewart and Brennan). But nominations and confirmations of new justices in election years are relatively common. Indeed, the authoritative *Scotusblog* notes: "The historical record does not reveal any instances since at least 1900 of the president failing to nominate and/or the Senate failing to confirm a nominee in a presidential election year because of the impending election. In that period, there were several nominations and confirmations of Justices during presidential election years."

There is ample precedent for nominations and confirmations in politically contentious periods during, or on the cusp of, presidential election years. Supreme Court justice Anthony Kennedy was confirmed in a presidential election year, gaining Senate approval just five days before the Iowa caucuses of 1988. He was sworn in six days before the New Hampshire primary. Justice Clarence Thomas was confirmed in the fall of 1991, well after candidates had begun announcing and campaigning for the 1992 race that would see President George H. W. Bush (the man who nominated Thomas) swept from office. It's worth noting that, despite the proximity to an election, and despite the fact that the Senate was controlled by the opposition party, Bush nominated a new justice who was dramatically more conservative than the man he would succeed, Justice Thurgood Marshall.

It is also worth noting that one of the greatest justices ever to sit on the Court, Louis Brandeis, was nominated by Democratic president Woodrow Wilson in 1916. It was a presidential election year that was expected to be closely contested. Brandeis was a leading progressive (some of his critics decried him as "a radical," while Supreme Court justice William O. Douglas would eventually characterize him as "a militant crusader for social justice"). Brandeis was also the first Jew named to the Court, and at a time when anti-Semitism and other forms of prejudice were so widespread and concerning that B'nai B'rith had recently formed the Anti-Defamation League. America was on the verge of entering World War I, corporations were violently suppressing labor organizing and strikes, and anti-immigrant sentiment was on the rise. Wilson had a Democratic Senate, but many of the Democrats were southern segregationists who had little sympathy for Brandeis's progressive politics. The nomination stirred plenty of contention and serious opposition, yet Brandeis was approved by the Senate on June 1, 1916. Ten days after Justice Brandeis was confirmed, Justice Charles Evans Hughes resigned from the high court in order to accept the Republican nomination against Wilson. That created a second election-year vacancy, which was filled in two months.

It may be too much to expect conscience-challenged partisans like McConnell and Texas senator Ted Cruz to acknowledge history, or to respect the Constitution. But Judge Gorsuch had a duty, as a jurist and as a man of the law, to reject false constructs, radical rewrites of history and mischaracterizations of constitutional intents and practices. Gorsuch failed in that duty when he accepted this nomination and then refused during his Senate hearing even to acknowledge the wrongdoing of those who made it possible.

Gorsuch should have recognized the wisdom of former senator Feingold's observation during the confirmation process that "we need to stop talking about the Gorsuch nomination as if it is about a single seat on the Supreme Court. This nomination, this hearing, is about a precedent that if allowed to stand will tarnish the legitimacy of our highest court for generations to come."

Instead, Gorsuch put his own political advancement ahead of a duty to the republic. And, in so doing, he extended the damage done by Republican partisans in 2016.

Gorsuch served himself.

But he also served the party with which he was aligned before he entered the judiciary. As Feingold warned: "If Republicans get away with the judicial coup they launched last year when they refused to grant Judge Merrick Garland a hearing, such a cynical political ploy could become commonplace. The GOP will apply it to lower courts. They will refuse to grant a hearing in the year before a midterm, or during the two years of a presidential race. The Supreme Court will become a permanent pawn of the GOP."

— 28 —

DONALD TRUMP'S VERY OWN MILHOUS

Mike Pence

Vice President of the United States

On October 5, 2016, in the one and only vice presidential debate of the campaign, Mike Pence grumbled about Democrat Tim Kaine's "avalanche of insults" after the senator from Virginia reviewed a litany of Trump's insulting comments about women, federal jurists, and American prisoners of war. When Kaine pressed his point on Trump's racism and xenophobia, Pence twisted the scenario once more, griping: "Senator, you whipped out that Mexican thing again."

Pence did it all with a straight face, which, some might suggest, was Nixonian. Richard Milhous Nixon's great skill as a campaigner was his ability to look into a television camera and make statements that he knew to be false. But Nixon had a measure of shame. He would sweat; he would stumble in his delivery; his eyes would go a little wild. Not Pence.

He is calm and deliberate when mouthing absolute falsehoods. Go back and watch the tapes from the campaign that made a failing governor of Indiana into the forty-eighth vice president of the United States, or watch any of the tapes of Pence defending the Trump transition or the Trump presidency. No one, not Sean Spicer, not Kellyanne Conway, not Trump himself, is as good at denying that Donald Trump said or did things that Donald Trump is famous for saying and doing. The only thing that Pence is better at is denying that Mike Pence said or did things that Mike Pence is famous for saying or doing.

But if you're putting together your own collection of Mike Pence's big lies, you should begin with the vice presidential debate.

That October 5, 2016, debate performance earned the Republican contender high marks from feckless pundits who imagine that shamelessness is a mark of political agility. But that also unsettled Americans who remember the past and fear for the future. Why? Because it was that debate that confirmed for any remaining doubters that Mike Pence really is more Nixonian than the famously disreputable thirty-seventh president.

Nowhere was this chilling detail more evident than when Pence uttered the most cynical line of a debate that was thick with cynicism. Early in the program, after Pence had danced his way around a number of straightforward questions regarding Trump's misstatements and misdeeds, Kaine tried to force open a discussion about the maybe not a billionaire's shadowy financial arrangements. Referring to Pence, Kaine said: "I am interested to hear whether he'll defend his running mate's not releasing taxes and not paying taxes."

"Absolutely I will," responded Pence, even as he absolutely did not answer the most basic questions about Trump's lack of transparency. Moderator Elaine Quijano pressed Pence: "Governor, with all due respect, the question was about whether it seems fair to you that Mr. Trump said he brilliantly used the laws to pay as little tax as legally possible." Pence's reply was more shamelessly disingenuous than anything Nixon would have dared attempt.

"Well," began Pence, "this is probably the difference between Donald Trump and Hillary Clinton and Senator Kaine. And, I mean, Hillary Clinton and Senator Kaine—God bless you for it, career public servants, that's great—Donald Trump is a businessman, not a career politician. He actually built a business."

What went unmentioned, and this is on Kaine and Quijano, is that someone else on Tuesday night's stage was a career politician.

Who might that be? Well, Mike Pence, of course. The governor may identify as a Republican and a conservative, but he is first and foremost a political opportunist of the old school who is constantly on the make, looking for the next opening to advance a career that Pence still hopes will land him in the Oval Office.

It is true that Pence gets to visit the Oval Office now and again as vice president. He wanders in to check on what loops he is being left out of by the people who actually run things. And then it's back to watching Fox and waiting for tie votes in the Senate, like the one he broke to make his "friend" (which is what career politicians call major campaign donors) Betsy DeVos the secretary of education.

That Pence is not taken overly seriously in the Trump White House was illustrated agonizingly by the Mike Flynn scandal. Flynn had met with Russian officials during the Trump transition. The retired general knew this was going to be a problem, so he lied about it. One of the people he supposedly lied to was Mike Pence, who went on TV and vouched for Mike Flynn. Then everyone who mattered at the White House found out that Flynn was lying, or maybe just confirmed what they already knew. But they let several weeks go by before doing anything about Flynn lying. Then the story hit the news and the president claimed that he had to fire Flynn because Flynn had lied to Pence. But the president had to have known about that lie for weeks, so that lie wasn't the real reason the scandal-plagued Flynn was being tossed overboard. So Pence was either a useful tool or a useful fool. Either that, or Pence was lying about being lied to. No matter. The bottom line is the same: the Flynn fiasco confirmed that Mike Pence had been reduced to an asterisk on the Trump staff list.

Pence always understood that he was an afterthought for Trump, just as Trump had been an afterthought for him.

Back in April of 2016, Pence endorsed Texas senator Ted Cruz's last-ditch attempt to prevent Trump from securing the Republican nomination. That move might have knocked Pence off Trump's vice presidential shortlist. But, luckily for Pence, he pulled a classic political careerist stunt. Even as he was endorsing Cruz, who was in the middle of a bitter fight to the political death with Trump, Pence went out of his way to avoid offending Trump.

The May 3, 2016, Indiana primary was the last stand at the ballot box for Cruz and the so-called #NeverTrump movement. It was a brutal battle that degenerated into name calling over whether Cruz's father was part of the plot to assassinate John F. Kennedy. (Spoiler alert: he wasn't.) Yet, Pence was all good with everyone. Just days before the voting, the governor announced on Indiana news radio

station WIBC: "I'm not against anybody, but I will be voting for Ted Cruz in the upcoming Republican primary."

That was about as tepid as an endorsement could get.

But Pence wasn't done. He watered things down a little more by praising the guy he wasn't endorsing. "I particularly want to commend Donald Trump, who I think has given voice to the frustration of millions of working Americans with a lack of progress in Washington, DC," he explained in the radio interview. "And I'm also particularly grateful that Donald Trump has taken a strong stance for Hoosier jobs."

That was classic Mike Pence. He would back Cruz but keep his bases covered with Trump. The frontrunner took note of the governor's carefully crafted ambiguity when Trump appeared on *Fox News Sunday* and described Pence's declaration for Cruz as "the weakest endorsement anyone has seen in a long time."

The political strongman was not offended by Pence's weakness. Rather, he recognized this obscure governor as someone who was sufficiently shameless and calculating to meet his standards. Trump confirmed this on July 14, 2016, when he announced that he had chosen the "weakest endorsement" governor to be his running mate on a ticket that prominent Republicans with common sense and/or a conscience had indicated they were unwilling to join.

Trump and Pence were made for each other—out of the spare parts of tossed-off morality and abandoned consciences.

As Indiana political analyst Andrew Downs told *Politico* at the time of the Trump announcement: "Mike Pence clearly would like to be in the White House. Everybody knows he would like to be in the White House, and one way to get there is by being the VP." So he was in, even if he supposedly disagreed with Donald Trump on, well, just about everything.

As for Trump, well, Pence wasn't his first choice. Or his second. Or his third. They had all said no. Pence wasn't even his fourth or fifth or sixth choice. In fact, Pence came after New Jersey's Chris Christie, who Trump reportedly offered the VP spot to, before he was talked out of it by soon to be ousted campaign manager Paul Manafort (who thought Pence brought more balance to the ticket than another hot-headed guy from the northeast) and, according to some news reports, Jared Kushner, who was still cranky about Christie getting his dad sent to jail.

Trump was frustrated with the whole process. But he recognized that he needed a sidekick who was sufficiently connected to corporate and conservative insiders and sufficiently deferential to the presumptive nominee.

Trump, who had gone out of his way to position himself as an outsider challenging the political establishment, found in Pence a consummate insider who was wedded to the conservative political establishment and its generous network of wealthy donors. That worked for Trump because he was still struggling to unite a Republican Party that was made up of social, economic and foreign policy wings that did not always get along. Trump had offended most of them. But Pence had spent a lifetime appealing to each of them, even at the expense of his broader appeal to mainstream general-election voters.

A political careerist raised in an Irish Catholic family that revered Democratic president John Kennedy, as a young man Pence chose a new hero, conservative Republican Ronald Reagan, and a new politics, that of the religious right. Adopting the language of the religious-right activists who were becoming the dominant force in the Grand Old Party, Pence declared himself to be "a Christian, a conservative, and a Republican, in that order."

Pence was a movement man with a personal agenda. He desperately wanted to be a politician. Unfortunately, he wasn't very good at it. At least not initially.

Two years after finishing law school at Indiana University, he was campaigning for Congress. And losing.

After two defeats in 1988 and 1990 for a U.S. House seat that combined rural and urban counties and was then represented by Democrat Phil Sharp, Pence attached himself to the "state-based free-market think-tank movement" that corporations and the Koch brothers have used to advance their agendas. As president of the Indiana Policy Review Foundation, Pence was associated with the

State Policy Network that the *National Review* in 2007 described as a group of "mini-Heritage Foundations—at the state level."

That gig gave the ambitious but unsuccessful congressional candidate the connections he needed to become a right-wing talk radio host. *The Mike Pence Show* was syndicated across Indiana at a time when Rush Limbaugh and other stars of conservative media were making talk radio the main means of communication for a new and more rigid right. To this day, Pence is a Limbaugh loyalist; after the talk radio giant announced at the time of Barack Obama's first inauguration that he hoped that the first African American president of the United States would fail, Pence announced in a January 29, 2009, interview with MSNBC that "I don't believe Rush Limbaugh has a racist bone in his body. If you're suggesting that his statement had a racist element in it, I commend you to a greater understanding of the positions he's taken. He's a man about opportunity of all Americans, regardless of race, creed, or color. That's why he's so admired and appreciated across America."

Always on the make, Pence parlayed his "think tank" and talk radio connections into a Republican nomination for Congress in 2000, won the seat and quickly began angling for positions of authority in Washington. He was a steady vote for the foreign and domestic policies of President George W. Bush and Vice President Dick Cheney. But his ambition often got the better of him. Pence bid for the post of House minority leader in a 2006 race with eventual Speaker John Boehner, but earned only twenty-seven votes from social-conservative hardliners.

In 2009, Pence was elected to the third-ranking post in the House, Republican Conference chairman. But he quickly began making noise about running for an Indiana U.S. Senate seat. Then he repositioned himself for a 2012 gubernatorial bid, which he won. A single controversy-plagued term saw Pence promoting religious-right agenda items (including a Religious Freedom Restoration Act designed to permit discrimination against members of the LGBTQ community that provoked widespread outrage and had to be rewritten); picking on refugees, immigrants, labor unions and public schools; and trying, without success, to set up a taxpayer-funded state-run news service that critics described as "the Pence News Service" and that one Indiana editor dismissed as "antithetical to the idea of an independent press."

Pence's many stumbles and conflicts made him unpopular at home. Polls had him in a tight race for reelection in 2016, leading Democrat John Gregg. The *Indianapolis Star* reported in that spring, in a May 19 article, that "[poll results] found that Pence has been unable to make up much of the ground he lost after last year's Religious Freedom Restoration Act controversy. Only 36 percent [of voters] said he should be re-elected."

The year 2016 was not shaping up as an easy one for Pence in Indiana. So as soon as word arrived on July 14 that he was Trump's vice presidential pick, the *Indianapolis Star* reported that Pence was "dropping his re-election bid in Indiana."

Why was Trump so attracted to a potential running mate who was not particularly popular in his home state?

It has a lot to do with the fact that Pence wanted the job, and that he had tended to say nice things about Trump when other Republicans had been condemning the billionaire. But it also had to do with where Pence comes from—not Indiana but the professional infrastructure established in the 1980s and 1990s by conservative political and economic elites. Toiling in the think tanks and radio studios of the right had made Pence exactly what Trump was not: consistent and connected. The governor was an absolutely steady social and economic and foreign policy conservative, who corporate CEOs and religious-right organizers alike knew they could count on to answer their call.

Pence had problems at home. But Andrew Downs told *Politico* in a July 12 article headlined "Trump flirts with unpopular Pence" that the governor's "stance on things like the Religious Freedom Restoration Act in Indiana, as well as his stance on civil rights legislation in Indiana, those are things people are criticizing but they actually are things that help solidify social conservatives within the Republican Party."

That's what Trump wanted at this point, even if he had to settle for a weak endorser.

Pence didn't get much respect. But he was cool with that. If the Trump campaign needed a Nixon, a Nixon Mike Pence would be. If the Trump transition needed a Nixon, a Nixon Mike Pence would be. If the Trump White House needed a Nixon, a Nixon Mike Pence would be. And he would do it without breaking a sweat.

PART 4

Privateers

[Private interests] had begun to consider the Government of the United States as a mere appendage to their own affairs. We know now that Government by organized money is just as dangerous as Government by organized mob.

—PRESIDENT FRANKLIN DELANO ROOSEVELT, 1936

Yes, as through this world I've wandered
I've seen lots of funny men;
Some will rob you with a six-gun,
And some with a fountain pen.

—WOODY GUTHRIE, "Pretty Boy Floyd," 1939

Half a millennium ago, the kings and queens of an old world formalized the practice of issuing letters of marque: official documents that authorized private vessels to cruise the high seas in search of foreign merchant ships laden with treasure. With a letter of marque in hand, a captain and his crew could attack, capture and plunder full-rigged ships, arrange for their "condemnation" and divide the bounty among investors, ship owners, ships officers and crews. Aside from a piece of paper conveying the "legitimacy" that extends from the royal hand, the armed brigands who fired upon, fought with and often killed the crews of targeted ships were difficult to distinguish from pirates. And when the privateers sailed into ports, they sacked cities with a purposeful precision and lethal lawlessness that rivaled the most ruthless marauders.

The new United States was not in its first stumbling moments above the employment of the seaborne skelm. But the enlightened

among the founders recognized the folly of the endeavor; the wiliest of their number, Benjamin Franklin, made a strategic argument for the elimination of the wicked game, negotiating treaties that promised "if any person of either nation shall take commissions or letters of marque, he shall be punished as a pirate." But Franklin's efforts were so frequently thwarted and undone in times of war, even by allies such as the French, that the framers of the U.S. Constitution included in their charge to the legislative branch of the new federal government an understanding that "the Congress shall have Power . . . To declare War, grant Letters of Marque and Reprisal, and make Rules concerning Captures on Land and Water."

The development of naval ships and armaments sufficient to see off assaults by smaller private vessels, and the evolution of the law of the sea (from the 1856 Declaration of Paris to the 1907 Hague Conventions and beyond), would eventually make letters of marque and reprisal historical artifacts, even if right-wing militarists continued to champion them as libertarian responses to Somali piracy just a few years ago.

But, make no mistake, state-sanctioned plundering remains, with twists of practice and legality every bit as sly as those of the ancient brigands.

The swashbucklers of old, who grabbed letters of marque and reprisal before embarking on careers of pillage, went by a name: privateer. They boarded foreign ships with official sanction and claimed their treasure under a "prize law" that legitimized what their victims understood as piracy. Today's pirates wear business suits and perfume themselves with the colognes and essences of political power. Yet, they still seek official sanction for acts of plunder. Though they do not identify as such, they are privateers, and though they do not acknowledge as much, they embrace a "prize law" mandate that is every bit as dangerous and disruptive as the state-sanctioned piracy of old. Only the convenient unfamiliarity of most Americans with the history of naval engagement and the progression of the English language obscures the tangled roots of the word they employ to describe their infamy: privatization.

Conservative "think tanks," and the politicians and pundits who imagine that the association of the word "think" with a progenitor of proposals imbues self-serving "ideas" with virtue or value, have for decades preached a gospel of privatization. They use their resources and their bully pulpits to drag dysfunctional and discredited proposals—school vouchers, "self-regulation" of industry, incarceration for profit—from the far fringes of the national discourse to the center of policy debates. And now, as befits the administration of a grifter businessman turned grifter politician, the Trump presidency is empowering the most dysfunctional and discredited of these privateers to initiate expansive policies of piracy and plunder.

No president in American history has had as much experience as Trump when it comes to collecting federal, state and local government largesse. Though Trump "portrays himself as a swashbuckling entrepreneur, shrewder and tougher than any politician, and as a leader who would use his billionaire skills to restore discipline to the federal government," the *Los Angeles Times* noted in 2011: "Trump glances over an expensive irony: He built his empire in part through government largesse and connections." As a New York City developer, Trump "sought to abuse the taxpayer and stretch the law" as he pursued massive government subsidies, says Congressman Jerrold Nadler, who represents much of Manhattan. Karen Burstein, a former auditor general of New York City who once concluded that Trump had "cheated" the city out of nearly $2.9 million, explained at a point when Trump was merely considering a presidential run that "it's extraordinary to me that we elevated someone to this position of public importance who has openly admitted that he has used government's incompetence as a wedge to increase his private fortune."

Now, Trump has been elevated to the ultimate position of national guardianship, a position with immense authority to defend the public trust, or to barter it off. With his severely underdeveloped sense of irony, the president continues to peddle the fantasy that the private sector has the answer to every challenge facing America, and that the federal government should be dramatically downsized. One

 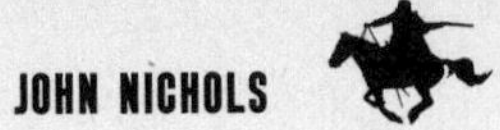

of Trump's first acts as president was to issue an executive order that froze federal hiring while maintaining a burgeoning network of private contractors that now employs roughly twice the number of full-time employees as the does the government. "Numerous studies have shown that contractors are two to three times more costly than each federal employee they replace," American Federation of Government Employees union president J. David Cox Sr. explained shortly after the president's inauguration. "President Trump's federal hiring freeze could result in more government waste if agencies are forced to hire high-priced contractors to do the work that federal employees can and should be doing."

"All Americans," declared Cox, "should be outraged that President Trump is gutting federal programs and funneling their taxpayer dollars into the hands of less-regulated private companies who answer to their corporate shareholders and not the American people."

The causes for outrage extend far beyond a single executive order. The new president's budget blueprint outlined deep cuts to domestic programs and proposals to end funding for programs to address climate change, programs to feed the poor, NPR, PBS, the National Endowment for the Arts, the National Endowment for the Humanities.

Trump may know nothing of governing. But he is not a stupid man. He is an experienced crony capitalist who well understands the money that is to be made if and when the vital responsibilities of the federal government are bartered off to the highest bidders or, at the very minimum, leased away to the energy companies that lust after the oil and coal that lies beneath public lands. That understanding defined his thinking as he assumed the presidency. When he was transitioning from a campaign in which he promised to "drain the swamp" of official Washington to a presidency in which he would expand the swamp as never before, Trump assembled a crew of privateers who were not merely enthusiastic about cutting federal jobs and contracting out the work. Many were unrelenting apostles of privatization whose assumption of positions of power inspired a flurry of telling headlines in the weeks surrounding Trump's inauguration:

Fortune: "Trump's Team Said to Be Planning to Privatize Public Broadcasting"

New York Times: "Prisons Run by C.E.O.s? Privatization Under Trump Could Carry a Heavy Price"

Wall Street Journal: "Donald Trump Considers Moving VA Toward Privatization"

Reuters: "Trump could privatize nation's air traffic controllers"

Slate: "How Trump Could Gut Public Education"

Forbes: "Trump Advisers' Plan to 'Privatize' Indian Lands"

Huffington Post: "Trump's infrastructure plan is a privatization trap"

Washington Post: "Elaine Chao emphasizes private funds for Trump's promised transportation fixes"

The *Washington Post* headline got closest to the heart of the matter, as it focused not merely on Trump but on one of his nominees for a cabinet post. There is every reason to be concerned with allegations of illicit and ongoing profiteering on the part of a president who will not release his tax returns, engages in elaborate schemes to maintain a family-owned business empire and does not seem to understand that the Constitution he has sworn to "preserve, protect and defend" charges him with a responsibility to "promote the general Welfare," as opposed to his own. But no president, no matter how nefarious, no matter how self-absorbed and self-serving, can empty the federal treasury on his own.

No president is possessed of sufficient time or energy, or authority, to fully betray the public trust in order to enrich the profiteering class that Franklin Delano Roosevelt decried as "those forces which

disregard human cooperation and human rights in seeking that kind of individual profit which is gained at the expense of his fellows."

A presidency that is inclined toward legalized larceny needs a complement of privateers, a gang of certain malefactors of great wealth, a wrecking crew waving modern-day letters of marque and reprisal as they board the ship of state. Not all Trump cabinet members and appointees will engage in careers of plunder on their own behalf. Some will do so as the extraordinarily well-compensated champions of a faux philosophy, developed by the pliant pundits of the Heritage Foundation, the American Enterprise Institute, the Cato Institute and other "think tanks" that think primarily of enriching their benefactors. The distinctions are real. Some of Trump's most prominent picks were indeed foxes-in-the-henhouse robber barons who the president was charging with oversight of the common coffers. Others are the mere servants of the robber barons: mandarins on a mission to facilitate pilfering on a grand scale. But the debate about gradations of greed ought not to obscure the broader point that the sacking of Washington has commenced. It threatens to extend across the nation, and around the world. And it may not stop there.

"You know," says Trump, "space is actually being taken over privately, which is great."

—29—

"I'VE GOT A BRIDGE TO SELL YOU"

Elaine Chao

Secretary of Transportation

When the U.S. State Department considers the corruptions of empire and avarice around the globe, it often highlights the unscrupulous practices that make governments the playthings of political and economic elites. Some less than democratic countries suffer under military rule, others struggle with rampant cronyism and still others wrestle with the ancient practice Italians call *nepotismo.* Nepotism is the stuff of scandal and conflict sufficient to collapse governments and spark people's revolutions in states that have not previously known popular governance. Its manifestations are many, but some of the most concerning cases in recent years, like the one that destabilized the French ruling class on the eve of that country's 2017 presidential election, have involved politicians who arrange sinecures for their spouses.

How might this work? Let's imagine a scenario. The powerful majority leader of a legislative chamber that must approve or disapprove executive appointments could, in collaboration with a new and ethically unconcerned president, preside over the confirmation of his wife to serve as the overseer of a massive infrastructure program involving the distribution of a trillion dollars or more in direct funding, tax breaks and other benefits to industries with which the appointing president, the confirming husband and the confirmed wife have long maintained close and profitable relations.

Now, that could never happen in the United States, a country that was ushered into being by founders like Thomas Jefferson, who preached against allowing "government of an Aristocracy

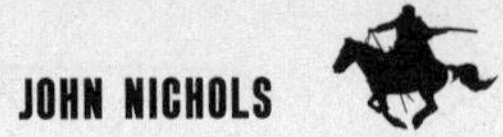

. . . riding and ruling over the plundered ploughman and beggared yeomanry" and warned that "the hereditary branches of modern governments are the patrons of privilege and prerogative, and not of the natural rights of the people, whose oppressors they generally are." Or could it?

On January 31, 2017, the U.S. Senate voted after limited debate to approve Elaine Chao as secretary of the treasury. Just about everyone in the Senate supported the return of the former deputy secretary of transportation (for two years in the cabinet of President George H. W. Bush), director of the Peace Corps (for another two years under Bush the First) and secretary of labor (for eight years in the cabinet of President George W. Bush) to the government payroll. While many Trump nominations provoked bitter debate, the discussion leading up to the Chao vote was exceptionally cordial. The *New York Times* headline on the short story about her confirmation hearing with the Senate Committee on Commerce, Science and Transportation, at which she reportedly "offered remarkably few specifics," read: "Elaine Chao Gets Cozy Reception at Confirmation Hearing." And why not? She was introduced to the committee by the leader of the Senate, the man in charge of the chamber constitutionally mandated to provide "advice and consent" with regard to presidential nominations. A photo caption noted, ever so delicately, that "Ms. Chao sat with her father as her husband, the Senate majority leader, Mitch McConnell, introduced her on Wednesday."

McConnell did not vote to confirm his wife as secretary of transportation. But that did not absolve the couple from talk of whether they might be skirting the 1967 federal anti-nepotism statute that says "a public official may not appoint, employ, promote, advance, or advocate for appointment, employment, promotion, or advancement, in or to a civilian position in the agency in which he is serving or over which he exercises jurisdiction or control any individual who is a relative of the public official." Something about introducing Chao to the relevant committee smacked of promoting or advocating her selection. But, you know, never mind.

The nepotism statute was written in 1967, after a Democratic president, John Kennedy, selected his brother Robert Kennedy to serve as attorney general in an administration where the vice president, Lyndon Johnson, used his influence as the former Senate majority leader (McConnell's position) to secure approval of said brother to serve in the cabinet (like Chao). But, defenders of Chao noted that the measure, while written broadly, had been very narrowly applied. Indeed, as Adam Bellow, author of the book *In Praise of Nepotism,* has noted, the George W. Bush administration sort of settled the issue in the 2000s when "Michael Powell, son of Secretary of State Colin Powell, became chairman of the Federal Communications Commission. Elaine Chao, wife of Sen. Mitch McConnell, became secretary of labor. Chao's chief labor attorney, Eugene Scalia, was the son of Supreme Court Justice Antonin Scalia. Elizabeth Cheney, the vice president's daughter, became a deputy assistant secretary of state; her husband became chief counsel of the Office of Management and Budget. And in a crowning act of nepotistic chutzpah, Bush acceded to Sen. Strom Thurmond's request that he appoint 28-year-old Strom Thurmond, Jr. U.S. attorney for South Carolina."

While the rules have not been aggressively applied up to this point, that does not mean that the neglect has been good for the country, or will be good. It is always wise to recall the counsel of Tom Paine at the founding of the American experiment: "A long habit of not thinking a thing wrong, gives it a superficial appearance of being right, and raises at first a formidable outcry in defense of custom." As Paine suggested, some customs are worth reexamining.

Following the announcement of Chao's nomination in November of 2016, the *National Journal*'s Josh Kraushaar tweeted about how this selection potentially "gives Trump leverage over McConnell for his infrastructure plan, which could entail more spending than GOPers [are] usually comfortable with." Matt Lewis, the conservative author of the book *Too Dumb to Fail: How the GOP Went from the Party of Reagan to the Party of Trump,* wrote that, while Chao's story was "inspirational and aspirational," and while he had interviewed McConnell in the congenial confines of an American Enterprise Institute book-release party, he entertained some "serious concerns regarding a conflict of interest for Chao's husband when it comes to dealing with her new boss."

"That's not to say that Chao isn't qualified or experienced (she is), but if Trump were looking to find a way to influence McConnell, he might come up with precisely this scenario. The conflict of interest is as follows: McConnell should be focused on the American people, the U.S. Senate, and the Republican caucus. And, in his capacity as Senate majority leader, he should serve as a check on the executive branch," wrote Lewis, who explained that "we currently have a president-elect who is viewed by many Americans as dangerously ambitious and overtly powerful. And one of the primary ways our system reins in the power of an executive is via a balance of power. Granted, this conflict existed when Chao served in the George W. Bush Cabinet—but Trump isn't Bush, and McConnell wasn't Senate majority leader then, either. As Brad Pitt's character in 'Oceans Eleven' tells George Clooney's character, 'OK, here's the problem: We're stealing two things. And when push comes to shove, and you can't have both, which are you gonna choose?'"

Lewis, to his credit, acknowledged the challenge of dealing with the intermingling of elites in the nation's capital city. "Now, it might be unfair to suggest that the incredibly accomplished spouse of the existing Senate majority leader should not be given a certain position because of her incredibly accomplished husband. (D.C. is rife with such potential conflicts of interest.) But I think it's fair to say that the American people have grown distrustful of the political dog and pony show. Chao's appointment could (at the very least) raise questions regarding McConnell's priorities, if he is accused of setting aside conservative concerns about 'Keynesian' stimulus spending plans that just happen to be endorsed by the Republican president—who just happens to have hired his wife."

Unfortunately, aside from a handful of conscientious scribblers on the margins of the discussion, Chao did not face those questions. "I mean, she's been vetted many times already because she's held multiple roles in different administrations over the years. So I'm not sure how much there is to ask," chirped Commerce Committee chairman John Thune, R-South Dakota, and for the most part, Democratic and Republican committee members agreed. "She's been at our house. We're close friends," said another committee member,

Oklahoma Republican Jim Inhofe, who did their friendship no harm by adding that "I was with her when she was secretary of Labor, and she did a great job, and she'll do a great job this time."

Thune, Imhofe and the rest of the Commerce Committee approved the nomination with a voice vote, despite the fact that even after her hearing, *Politico* reported: "Chao's personal positions on transportation issues aren't well known." The Senate backed her 93–6 (with Mitch sitting out), despite the fact that, as Reuters reported: "Chao declined to take positions on a number of issues, including whether air traffic control jobs should be privatized, concerns over the safety of shipments of crude oil by rail, foreign airlines' push to move into the U.S. market and regulation of developing technologies."

If the Senate had vetted Chao with anywhere near the seriousness that the founders intended when they established the chamber's "advice and consent" authority, the scrutiny would have revealed the real story of her "multiple roles in different administrations." It is not a story that inspires confidence in Chao's ability to stand up to Trump or to run a massive federal agency with a staff of almost sixty thousand, a budget of almost $80 billion and responsibility for managing the Federal Aviation Administration, the Federal Highway Administration, the Federal Railroad Administration and the Pipeline and Hazardous Materials Safety Administration.

When Chao ran the Department of Labor, it was a disaster for the people she was supposed to serve. The *New York Times* headline at the close of her tenure read: "Labor Agency Is Failing Workers." The U.S. Government Accountability Office (GAO) produced a report on Chao's Labor Department, which concluded that, on her watch, the agency's Wage and Hour Division was so lax that "Labor has left thousands of actual victims of wage theft who sought federal government assistance with nowhere to turn. Unfortunately, far too often the result is unscrupulous employers' taking advantage of our country's low-wage workers."

Nine of ten cases brought by a team of undercover agents posing as workers who had suffered wage theft were mishandled, according to the report on Chao's Wage and Hour Division. Kim Bobo, the executive director of Interfaith Worker Justice, a group that advocates

for low-wage workers, suggested that Chao's Labor Department had become "the wild, wild West of wage theft." Former House Education and Labor Committee chairman George Miller, the California Democrat who had asked the GAO to examine the crisis, observed at the time that "when you have weak penalties and weak enforcement, that's a deadly combination for workers. It's clear that under the existing system, employers feel they can steal workers' wages with impunity, and that has to change." An even more damning assessment came from Catherine Ruckelshaus, general counselor and program director at the National Employment Law Project: "The USDOL under Secretary Chao was not primarily in the business of enforcing the law."

Under Chao, the Labor Department did not merely shirk responsibilities. It made things worse for workers. A harrowing report by the Alicia Patterson Foundation on the period when Chao oversaw workplace safety was titled "How the Bush Administration Reversed Decades of Progress on Mine Safety." Recounting how the Mine Safety and Health Administration in Chao's Labor Department rejected "tighter rules and stricter enforcement" and "stressed cooperating with mine operators over policing them," the report concluded that "progress toward safer mines has lagged in places like West Virginia, where the death rate for miners has more than doubled since 1997 and increased by 50 percent in the last five years." An examination of the details of the 2006 Sago Mine disaster in West Virginia, which killed a dozen miners, explained that "the accident might not have proved fatal had the Bush administration not stood in the way of a number of efforts to improve mine safety."

The complaints grew so loud that, by the time Chao was finishing her stint as a Bush cabinet member, the *New York Times* wrote: "Secretary of Labor Elaine L. Chao, the only member of President Bush's cabinet to serve a full eight years, has heard a flood of criticisms that her department favored business and was lax on enforcement and worker safety." Former AFL-CIO staffer Lane Windham (now a fellow with Georgetown University's Kalmanovitz Initiative for Labor and the Working Poor) summed up Chao as "political at every turn" and said "she saw her role as labor secretary as cooperating with corporations, rolling back overtime protections, weakening enforcement of wage and hour laws, and pursuing labor organizations—especially those that had supported Democrats." John Sweeney, who led the AFL-CIO during Chao's tenure, called her the "most anti-labor labor secretary he had ever seen."

Things improved significantly at the Labor Department after Chao left, offering a none too subtle reminder that the problem was not the department but the boss. It was for that reason that concerns about her dismal record as an agency head have dogged Chao.

When Trump tapped her for the transportation post, the *American Prospect* headlined its report "The Workers' Menace Becomes the Commuters' Threat." In the *Nation* under the headline "Elaine Chao, Ruined Department of Labor, Picked to Ensure Safety of Nation's Planes, Trains, and Automobiles," Spencer Woodman noted that "the stakes might be even higher than they were eight years ago. As Secretary of Transportation Chao will oversee more than three times the number of employees that report to the Labor Secretary. And, in addition to helping allocate big dollars in infrastructure spending, Chao will also likely preside over the continuing rise of self-driving cars and trucks—a technology that could amount to the largest mechanization of jobs in recent history."

She'll even be charged with regulating drones. But don't expect Chao, who spent her off-time between administrations as a distinguished fellow with the right-wing Heritage Foundation and a director of the Wells Fargo banking conglomerate, to crack down on transportation corporations and tech companies any more aggressively than she did on wage-stealing employers. University of Texas law professor Thomas McGarity, who titled his book about Chao's time at the Labor Department *Freedom to Harm*, warns that "she's not going to be especially inclined to second-guess the industry when they say that (some new technology) will be safe."

Handing over the regulatory process to industry, whether it be through the lax enforcement of rules or the embrace of the even more lax concept of "self-regulation," is not exactly a form of privatization. But it does represent a bartering off of public responsibility via what Steve Bannon refers to as the "deconstruction of the

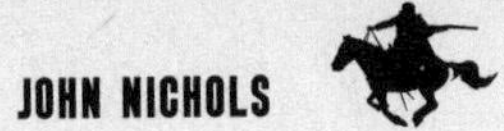

administrative state." Chao is an old hand at that, as she is at the governmental sleight-of-hand trick that can turn what is supposedly a "job creation" program into an epic privatization scam.

During the 2016 campaign, Donald Trump seized the infrastructure issue that his fellow Republicans and too many Democrats had neglected for years. Trump made the job-creating project of rebuilding American bridges, highways and airports central to his appeal to working-class voters. He ripped Reagan-quoting Republicans for their limited-government fantasies and their lack of interest in putting Americans back to work. And he tore into Hillary Clinton for her tepid proposal to allocate $275 billion in direct spending for infrastructure projects over five years, and another $225 billion for loan-guarantee programs and loans to develop infrastructure. "Her number is a fraction of what we're talking about," the newly minted Republican nominee said of the Democrat in an August 2016 interview with the Fox Business Network. "We need much more money to rebuild our infrastructure. I would say at least double her numbers, and you're going to really need a lot more than that."

That was a "wow" commitment. Trump was talking about pouring over a trillion dollars into infrastructure projects. It resonated with working families in states that had not voted for a Republican in decades and it played a critical role in making him president. He recognized this political reality in a viscerally populist inaugural address that had the new president announcing: "We will build new roads and highways and bridges and airports and tunnels, and railways, all across our wonderful nation. We will get our people off of welfare and back to work, rebuilding our country with American hands and American labor."

Democrats who had opposed Trump's candidacy suggested that the one area of agreement with the new president was on the need for a great big investment in jobs, jobs, jobs. And why not? Investment in infrastructure has historically had bipartisan support. Republican Dwight Eisenhower built the interstate highway system. Democrat Franklin Roosevelt gave the country a Works Progress Administration (WPA) and the Civilian Conservation Corps (CCC) and rural electrification. Everybody loves infrastructure! It's what we remember from great presidencies. Indeed, the Roosevelt Institute reminds us that FDR's New Deal "literally built the infrastructure of modern America, including 572,000 miles of rural roads, 67,000 miles of urban streets, 122,000 bridges, 1,000 tunnels, 1,050 airfields, and 4,000 airport buildings. It also constructed 500 water treatment plants, 1,800 pumping stations, 19,700 miles of water mains, 1,500 sewage treatment plants, 24,000 miles of sewers and storm drains, 36,900 schools, 2,552 hospitals, 2,700 firehouses, and nearly 20,000 county, state, and local government buildings."

FDR referred to all of the work that was done by the Public Works Administration, by the WPA and the CCC, to all of those roads and streets and bridges and pumping stations and firehouses and schools that were constructed in the 1930s, as "national possessions" that yield "national benefits." They were public works, built with public dollars, intended for public use and owned by the public.

The United States could use a lot more public works. The American Society of Civil Engineers estimates that, in order to meet basic demands, $3.6 trillion in infrastructure investment is needed by 2020.

Unfortunately, Donald Trump is not exactly proposing public works. Trump seemed to lose interest in infrastructure as his presidency got rolling, but when he did eventually propose a plan, it quickly became clear that this is not going to be your father's New Deal.

The primary point of Trump's infrastructure agenda has never been to do more building with American hands. The primary purpose has been to grease the palms of corporate CEOs, billionaire developers, real-estate investors and all the other Donald Trump wannabes of the private sector.

Former secretary of labor Robert Reich calls it "Trump's Infrastructure Scam." What the president is proposing, Reich explains, "is nothing more than a huge tax giveaway for the rich." To wit:

> 1. It's a giant public subsidy to developers and investors. Rather than taxing the wealthy and then using the money to fix our dangerously outdated roads, bridges, airports and water systems, Trump wants

 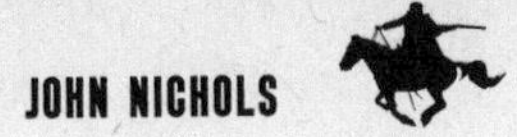

to give rich developers and Wall Street investors tax credits to encourage them to do it. That means that for every dollar they put into a project, they'd actually pay only 18 cents and we would contribute the other 82 cents through our tax dollars.

2. We'd be turning over public roads and bridges to private corporations who will charge us expensive tolls and earn big profits. These tolls will be set high in order to satisfy the profit margins demanded by elite Wall Street investors. So—essentially—we pay twice—once when we subsidize the developers and investors with our tax dollars, and then secondly when we pay the tolls and user fees that also go into their pockets.

3. We get the wrong kind of infrastructure. Projects that will be most attractive to Wall Street investors are those whose tolls and fees bring in the biggest bucks—giant mega-projects like major new throughways and new bridges. Not the thousands of smaller bridges, airports, pipes, and water treatment facilities most in need of repair. Not the needs of rural communities and smaller cities and towns too small to generate the tolls and other user fees equity investors want. Not clean energy.

Reich's criticism is echoed by Nobel Prize–winning economist Paul Krugman, who argues that Trump's "big infrastructure build" proposal "is not a plan to borrow $1 trillion and spend it on much-needed projects, which would be the straightforward, obvious thing to do. It is, instead, supposed to involve having private investors do the work both of raising money and building the projects—with the aid of a huge tax credit that gives them back 82 percent of the equity they put in. To compensate for the small sliver of additional equity and the interest on their borrowing, the private investors then have to somehow make profits on the assets they end up owning."

"In that case we haven't promoted investment at all," explains Krugman, "we've just in effect privatized a public asset—and given the buyers 82 percent of the purchase price in the form of a tax credit." That's the opposite of what FDR did. Instead of creating public works projects, Trump's plan is to have American taxpayers, via tax credits, pay for private works projects. It's a redistribution of the wealth upward that may create some transitory jobs but that effectively privatizes the most vital infrastructure of the United States.

This is why Elaine Chao, an old-school corporate conservative who used to warn Conservative Political Action Conferences about "the same old tax-and-spend crowd" that "is implementing policies that will turn our country into Europe," has had no problem aligning her future with the supposedly populist Donald Trump. This is also why Mitch McConnell, who led the opposition to a far less ambitious Obama stimulus plan in 2009, will work to get Republican senators on board for Trump's scheme. Trump's not proposing to renew the same old "tax and spend" approach to job creation, even though that approach has historically worked well for America. Instead, the president is hatching a "Robin Hood in reverse" scheme to use the government to take from the poor and give to the rich.

It aligns Bush Republicans, like Chao and McConnell, with the man who used to ridicule the Bushes and their allies as "lightweights." Nothing unites today's Republican Party like using the federal government to reward multinational corporations and billionaire campaign donors. This is, in fact, Elaine Chao's specialty. She knows exactly what her responsibility will be at the Department of Transportation. The "most anti-labor labor secretary [labor leaders] had ever seen" is more than ready to become the most anti-public infrastructure transportation secretary America has ever seen. She is already arguing that Trump's plan is the only option. "The government does not have the resources to address all the infrastructure needs within our country," Chao told senators. But, she gleefully reported that there was a lot that could be done with "innovative financing tools, such as public-private partnerships."

That doesn't sound so awful. Unfortunately, says Ronald Klain, who oversaw the team implementing President Obama's American Recovery and Renewal Act, "it's a trap."

"Trump's plan is not really an infrastructure plan," Klain explains. "It's a tax-cut plan for utility-industry and construction-sector investors, and a massive corporate welfare plan for contractors. The Trump plan doesn't directly fund new roads, bridges, water systems or airports, as did Hillary Clinton's 2016 infrastructure proposal.

Instead, Trump's plan provides tax breaks to private-sector investors who back profitable construction projects. These projects (such as electrical grid modernization or energy pipeline expansion) might already be planned or even under way. There's no requirement that the tax breaks be used for incremental or otherwise expanded construction efforts; they could all go just to fatten the pockets of investors in previously planned projects."

Corporate welfare? Check.

Fattening the accounts of investors? Check.

Bait-and-switching taxpayers with tax-cut schemes disguised as job plans? Check.

Using the good name of "infrastructure investment" to enrich private-sector profiteers? Check.

Chao swears an oath to "well and faithfully discharge the duties of the office" whenever she assumes a public position. But she has never left any doubt that her highest duty is to the private profiteers who are invariably the beneficiaries of her "service." It was slim pickings at the Department of Labor. At the Department of Transportation, Chao's ability to issue letters of marque to modern privateers is magnified a thousandfold.

—30—

THE KINGFISH OF THE QUAGMIRE

Tom Price

Secretary of Health and Human Services

The greatest secretary of what is now known as the Department of Health and Human Services in the almost seventy-year history of the agency's modern incarnation was the social and civic reformer John Gardner, who Lyndon Johnson charged with creating a "Great Society." Capitalizing on a landslide mandate from the people in the 1964 election and a supportive Congress, Johnson wanted to address the basic human needs of a prosperous nation that still knew poverty, of an innovative nation that was leading the way in curing diseases but still allowed the sick to perish for lack of care, of a technologically advanced nation that had not shared the benefits of technological progress with the whole of its population. Gardner put the emphasis on society in that "Great Society" equation, arguing for an interpretation of the American experiment that begins with the "simple, easily forgotten truth that we need one another."

"I sometimes think that history might easily say about this nation: 'It was a great nation full of talented people with enormous energy who forgot that they needed one another,'" warned Gardner, who after breaking with the Johnson administration over the Vietnam War went on to form the group Common Cause. Gardner would go on to become the great champion of civic engagement, and the great fretter about how the influence of money on our politics stifles progress. Late in life, he counseled that "we must end the indiscriminate trashing of government. Carefully targeted criticism is immensely important, but mindless trashing has made able civil servants—who constitute the majority—feel like members of a battered profession. If we want to make government better, that is not the way to do it.

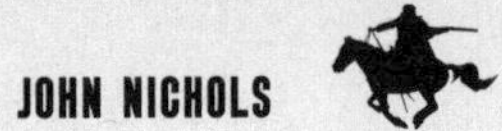

Rather we must target our efforts. We must insist, for example, that government make itself worthy of respect by eliminating the many ways in which moneyed interests coerce legislators. In a land where the Founders committed themselves to the consent of the governed, the fact that money can buy political outcomes is an obscenity. The simple rule is, 'Hold power accountable.' We can no longer tolerate any government—federal, state or local—that has created such an impenetrable web of power, money and special interest that it is no longer controllable by the electorate."

Surely, among the twenty-three secretaries of an agency that is responsible for putting a trillion-dollar budget and roughly eighty thousand employees to work on behalf of "improving the health, safety, and well-being of America," none has been so at odds with John Gardner's vision as Tom Price.

Donald Trump's secretary of health and human services is a pure reflection of the politics of special-interest influence, and self-interested denial of the public good, that Gardner decried.

A seven-term congressman from Georgia who freely admits that, as a millionaire physician, he got into politics to make sure that the views of millionaire physicians were well represented when health care policies are debated, Price has often been linked with the Association of American Physicians and Surgeons (AAPS), a group founded in the 1940s to oppose social welfare proposals in the era when Franklin Delano Roosevelt was arguing for a "Second Bill of Rights" that included "the right to adequate medical care and the opportunity to achieve and enjoy good health" and "the right to adequate protection from the economic fears of old age, sickness, accident, and unemployment." Fiercely right-wing, the AAPS says its mission is to "fight socialized medicine and to fight the government takeover of medicine." And it takes that fight to extremes, *Mother Jones* magazine noted in a 2009 piece. "As tea partiers have become the leading opposition to [President Barack Obama's Affordable Care Act], AAPS has lent credibility to their criticism of the emerging health care legislation. Before the big 9/12 rally in Washington, AAPS cosponsored a protest on Capitol Hill with the Tea Party Patriots that AAPS says attracted 1,000 physicians. The organization's president, Mark Kellen, appeared with Georgia representatives Tom Price and Phil Gingrey—GOP members of the congressional doctors' caucus—to slam the bill," explained writer Stephanie Mencimer, one of the ablest chroniclers of the Tea Party movement and its political fallout.

Mencimer detailed the deep engagement of "AAPS docs" in the anti-reform drive, noting that, on Fox News and talk radio programs, "AAPS docs often appear to offer an expert medical opinion against reform."

"Yet despite the lab coats and the official-sounding name," she continued, "the docs of the AAPS are hardly part of mainstream medical society. Think Glenn Beck with an MD. The group (which did not return calls for comment for this story) has been around since 1943. Some of its former leaders were John Birchers, and its political philosophy comes straight out of Ayn Rand. Its general counsel is Andrew Schlafly, son of the legendary conservative activist Phyllis. The AAPS statement of principles declares that it is 'evil' and 'immoral' for physicians to participate in Medicare and Medicaid, and its journal is a repository for quackery. Its website features claims that tobacco taxes harm public health and electronic medical records are a form of 'data control' like that employed by the East German secret police. An article on the AAPS website speculated that Barack Obama may have won the presidency by hypnotizing voters, especially cohorts known to be susceptible to 'neurolinguistic programming'—that is, according to the writer, young people, educated people, and possibly Jews."

Price comes across as a considerably more reasonable man than the most whacked-out of the "AAPS docs." He is a frequently genial southern-gentleman type who only occasionally goes off the rails with a speech like the 2010 Conservative Political Action Conference address in which he declared: "We must take our country back—take it back from a vile liberal agenda that is threatening everything we hold dear as Americans." But when it comes to policy, he's not just way out on the right wing (as an ardent if often factually challenged foe of abortion rights, gun control and gay rights), he's way in the pocket of the special interests that use their campaign money

 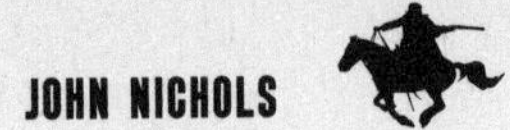

and lobbying power to warp debates about things like "improving the health, safety, and well-being of America." (In 2009, he was one of just ninety-seven House members to oppose the bipartisan Family Smoking Prevention and Tobacco Control Act, groundbreaking legislation that gave the Food and Drug Administration regulatory jurisdiction over tobacco products and the authority to regulate tobacco as the drug that it is.)

In a Washington swamp that is overpopulated with self-serving politicians, Price is the kingfish of the quagmire.

"Tom Price Is the Walking Definition of an Appearance of Corruption," explains *Slate*'s Jordan Weissmann. "First," Weissmann wrote when Price joined the Trump team, "the congressman has a habit of trading stocks in medical companies while also writing legislation that could sway those firms' fortunes. The *Wall Street Journal* recently found that Price had 'bought and sold stock in about 40 health-care, pharmaceutical and biomedical companies since 2012, including a dozen in the current congressional session.' In total, he traded shares worth $300,000. Price, a former orthopedic surgeon who now chairs the extremely powerful House Budget Committee, regularly introduces bills on health care policy and sits on the House subcommittee that oversees Medicare."

Weissmann went on to note that "his investments have included at least one very nice bargain. In 2015 Price bought discounted stock in a small Australian biotech firm, Innate Immuno, that was attempting to win Food and Drug Administration approval for a new multiple sclerosis drug. Price purchased the stock in a private offering marketed only to 'sophisticated U.S. investors' that Kaiser Health News referred to as a 'sweetheart deal.'" As of January 2017, Price was enjoying a 400 percent gain on the investment.

These details, along with a January 17, 2017, CNN report that Price "purchased shares in a medical device manufacturer days before introducing legislation that would have directly benefited the company," led Senate minority leader Chuck Schumer, D-New York, to announce that the Office of Congressional Ethics needed to "conduct an immediate and thorough investigation into these potential violations of the STOCK Act before Rep. Price's nomination moves forward."

The 2012 Stop Trading on Congressional Knowledge (STOCK) Act was enacted to combat insider trading by members of Congress, and Schumer said: "This new report makes clear that this isn't just a couple of questionable trades, but rather a clear and troubling pattern of Congressman Price trading stock and using his office to benefit the companies in which he is investing." (According to a ProPublica report published in mid-March 2017, former U.S. attorney Preet Bharara was overseeing an investigation into Price's stock trades when he was ousted from his post by President Trump.)

"The President-elect claims he wants to drain the swamp, but Congressman Price has spent his career filling it up," declared Schumer. Massachusetts senator Elizabeth Warren asked Price during his Senate Committee on Health, Education, Labor and Pensions confirmation hearing if the congressman had taken actions "to advance your plan to help the company that you now owned stock in."

"I'm offended by that insinuation," responded Price, with what keen observers will recognize as something less than a full-throated denial of any conflicts of interest.

Warren persisted. "I'm just asking: Did you buy the stock and then did you introduce a bill that would be helpful to the companies you just bought stock in?"

"The stock was bought by a broker who was making those decisions. I wasn't making those decisions," claimed Price.

Warren persisted. "Let's just be clear," said the Democrat from Massachusetts. "This is someone who buys stock at your direction. This is someone who buys and sells the stock you want them to buy and sell."

"That's not true, senator," claimed Price.

Warren persisted. "Well, because you decide not to tell them? Wink wink, nod nod? And we're all just supposed to believe that?"

Price and the Trump administration correctly assumed that the Republican majority in the Senate would accept the kingfish's lame excuses as sufficient and put him in charge of a massive federal agency with responsibility for the Food and Drug Administration, the National Institutes of Health, the Indian Health Service, the Centers for Disease Control and Prevention, the Centers for Medicare

 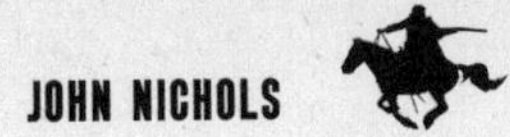

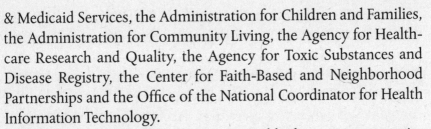

& Medicaid Services, the Administration for Children and Families, the Administration for Community Living, the Agency for Healthcare Research and Quality, the Agency for Toxic Substances and Disease Registry, the Center for Faith-Based and Neighborhood Partnerships and the Office of the National Coordinator for Health Information Technology.

But Ohio senator Sherrod Brown grabbed every opportunity to highlight the cruel ironies of this particular nomination. "Buying and selling health care stocks as a member of Congress while you're voting and helping those companies, that's bad enough," said Brown. "But what he wants to do to maybe the greatest program in American history, Medicare, is much, much worse." And there was the matter of Price's opposition not just to the Affordable Care Act but to the premise that Americans have a right to get the treatment they need when they are ailing.

National Nurses United executive director RoseAnn DeMoro echoed an observation by Vermont senator Bernie Sanders at Price's Senate confirmation hearing. Price equated the notion that an American might have "access" to buying insurance with access to actual care. "'Has access to' does not mean that they are guaranteed health care," said Sanders. "I have access to buying a $10 million home; I don't have the money to do that." "Unpack the evasions and you have the Ayn Rand–Tea Party philosophy in a nutshell," DeMoro said of Price. "You only deserve the healthcare you can buy, from private insurance companies that have a history of price gouging with multiple restrictions on the care you can receive even after paying your premiums."

National Nurses United co-president Jean Ross, RN, noted that "during his first hearing before the Senate HELP Committee (Health, Education, Labor and Pensions), Representative Price failed to provide any reassurance that he will be an advocate for the public interest, rather than the narrow interest of the corporate healthcare industry and his most conservative backers who have long threatened our vital safety net protections."

Before Price's nomination was taken up by the full Senate, Ross said it was vitally important for Price "to end the evasion of how the

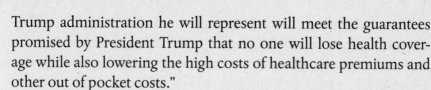

Trump administration he will represent will meet the guarantees promised by President Trump that no one will lose health coverage while also lowering the high costs of healthcare premiums and other out of pocket costs."

Senate Republicans opted against settling that issue, confirming Price on a 52–47 party-line vote on February 10, 2017. Less than a month later, Price advanced a plan to repeal and replace the Affordable Care Act that broke Trump's campaign trail promises. Price's claim that the new plan was "much better than what's out there now" provoked laughter, and tears.

The nonpartisan Congressional Budget Office reviewed the plan and determined that, were it to be enacted, 14 million more Americans would be uninsured within a year and 24 million more Americans would be uninsured by 2026. Internal White House forecasts suggested the prospect that the uninsured numbers could be even higher. Even conservative Republicans said the plan was a travesty, as it cut programs for the vulnerable in order to fund tax breaks for the wealthiest Americans. Senator Susan Collins, R-Maine, said Price's proposal "[didn't] come close to achieving the goal of allowing low-income seniors to purchase health insurance." Newspapers across the country ripped Price's plan to scuttle successful and popular Medicaid expansion initiatives.

"Thousands of Americans will die if this legislation is passed," said Senator Sanders, who decried Price's plan for "throwing 24 million Americans off of health insurance, raising premiums for older low income Americans, while giving $285 billion in tax breaks to the top 2 percent" as "disgusting and immoral."

Tom Price was undeterred. He defended massive new tax cuts for health insurance company CEOs and other benefits for wealthy people like, um, Tom Price. He blew off the concerns of ailing Americans. Brian Kline, a cancer survivor from Pennsylvania, told Price at a town hall gathering that "Medicaid expansion saved my life and saved me from medical bankruptcy." "Why do you want to take away my Medicaid expansion?" asked the retail worker who makes $11.66 an hour. The answer Kline got from the secretary of health and human services, whose net worth is listed as $13,640,071, was a

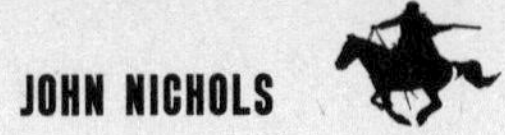

dismissive suggestion that the patient should be grateful to be getting any care at all. "It's wonderful that you have received the care that you've received," he said. "But that's not necessarily true for everybody."

Price's callous response did nothing to advance the cause of a "repeal and replace" scheme that initially crashed and burned. But the secretary kept at it, as he had throughout the Obama years. By early May, the Republican-controlled House endorsed a Price-backed proposal that many critics saw as worse than the initial plan. Price said the House majority was doing "what's right for the American people." But Sister Simone Campbell, SSS, the executive director of NETWORK Lobby for Catholic Social Justice, said Price and his allies were "preferencing the millionaires and billionaires" over ailing Americans. "The passage of the American Health Care Act (AHCA) in the House is a dangerous and irresponsible step that threatens access to healthcare for at least 24 million Americans. It violates Christian and Catholic faith teaching and the values of our nation," said Sister Simone. "The AHCA cuts $880 billion from Medicaid to give large tax cuts to the very wealthiest. This is far from the Gospel mandate to care for our most vulnerable sisters and brothers. It takes away access to healthcare for the most vulnerable and widens the gaps in inequality in our society. This vote was a vote against the millions of children, elderly, people living with disabilities, and people experiencing poverty who are supported by Medicaid."

When John Gardner headed the old Department of Health, Education and Welfare in the 1960s, he looked at the challenges facing the country and declared: "What we have before us are some breathtaking opportunities disguised as insoluble problems." He argued that government had a moral and a practical duty to find solutions so that all Americans could enjoy those opportunities.

Tom Price is different. As secretary of health and human services he doesn't fret much about solving problems. Instead, he uses government as he always has—to create breathtaking opportunities for a small circle of wealthy Americans and, in particular, for a very wealthy physician named Tom Price.

— 31 —

THE HEALTH CARE PROFITEER

Seema Verma

Administrator, Centers for Medicare & Medicaid Services

Here's a powerful federal agency that you've probably never heard of: the Centers for Medicare & Medicaid Services. Perhaps you do remember it from when it was called the Health Care Financing Administration. But probably not.

The Centers for Medicare & Medicaid Services is one of the agencies that most Americans would prefer not to think about. They hope it does nice things because, after all, Medicare and Medicaid are nice and necessary programs. And as part of the Department of Health and Human Services (HHS), the Centers for Medicare & Medicaid Services should be providing a service.

But what kind of service?

On March 14, 2017, one day after the Senate confirmed her nomination on 55–43 vote, Donald Trump's administrator for the Centers for Medicare & Medicaid Services began her tenure by sending a letter to the nation's governors announcing that she and HHS secretary Tom Price were "ushering in a new era for the federal and state Medicaid partnership where states have more freedom to design programs that meet the spectrum of diverse needs of their Medicaid population." How could they exercise that freedom? Verma suggested that they could impose insurance premiums for Medicaid and charge Medicaid recipients for emergency room visits. They could also, the letter noted, encourage recipients, no matter how sick or ailing, to get a job.

That doesn't sound very nice.

That sounds like the person in charge of Medicare and Medicaid was making health care more expensive and more difficult to obtain for some of the most vulnerable people in America.

Meet Centers for Medicare & Medicaid Services administrator Seema Verma, who was charged with reshaping Indiana's Medicaid program when Vice President Mike Pence was governor of that state. She was a crafty consultant who used waivers to get around federal guidelines and to make a tidy sum of money for herself, somewhat controversially, as the *Indianapolis Star* revealed in 2014, reporting that "the state has paid her millions of dollars for her work—amid a potential conflict of interest that ethics experts say should concern taxpayers."

"Largely invisible to the public, Verma's work has included the design of the Healthy Indiana Plan, a consumer-driven insurance program for low-income Hoosiers now being touted nationally as an alternative to Obamacare. In all, Verma and her small consulting firm, SVC, Inc., have received more than $3.5 million in state contracts," explained the paper. "At the same time, Verma has worked for one of the state's largest Medicaid vendors—a division of Silicon Valley tech giant Hewlett-Packard. That company agreed to pay Verma more than $1 million and has landed more than $500 million in state contracts during her tenure as Indiana's go-to health-care consultant, according to documents obtained by *The Indianapolis Star*."

The conflicts surrounding Verma, who made even more money as a consultant for other states (most of which had Republican governors), raised a question, the Indiana paper said: "Who is she working for when she advises the state on how to spend billions of dollars in Medicaid funds—Hoosier taxpayers or one of the state's largest contractors?"

The answer is that Verma is working for the sort of profits-first, patients-last health care system that allows people like her to, as Washington senator Maria Cantwell notes, "[make] millions of dollars in consulting fees by kicking poor, working people off of Medicaid for failure to pay monthly contributions similar to premiums."

When Verma was nominated by Trump, Dr. Robert Zarr, the president of Physicians for a National Health Program, decried the consultant as the architect of a plan that "forced impoverished Medicaid enrollees to pay dearly for care, imposing unprecedented co-payments and premiums on people with little chance of affording them; those who miss a payment are denied coverage."

The past president of the DC chapter of the American Academy of Pediatrics, who holds adjunct professorships at Children's National Medical Center and George Washington University, Dr. Zarr warned that "her actions in Indiana signal that she will inflict cruel and unusual punishment on America's most vulnerable citizens."

President Trump and House Speaker Paul Ryan did not set out to prove the concerned physician to be correct. But, as they unveiled health care "reforms" that would further empower Seema Verma's Centers for Medicare & Medicaid Services, and her cruel and unusual vision, they did just that.

—32—

THE INVESTOR WHO GOT A HIGH RETURN

Betsy DeVos

Secretary of Education

In March of 2017, the eleventh secretary of education for a nation founded on James Madison's premise that "learned institutions ought to be favorite objects with every free people" because "they throw that light over the public mind which is the best security against crafty and dangerous encroachments on the public liberty" embraced a federal budget proposal to cut $9 billion from programs that support public education. Yes, public schools would suffer. But Betsy DeVos was delighted that the Trump administration's budget blueprint called for steering $1.4 billion toward the gimmicky "school choice" programs that she had championed for decades as an alternative to public education—and that historian of education (and U.S. assistant secretary of education during George H. W. Bush's presidency) Diane Ravitch decries as a "hoax" that destroys communities and destroys public schools.

DeVos had gotten what she paid for.

Twenty years before she joined Donald Trump's wrecking crew cabinet, DeVos had explained as a billionaire campaign contributor to conservative causes that she was on a mission.

"I know a little something about soft money, as my family is the largest single contributor of soft money to the national Republican Party. Occasionally a wayward reporter will try to make the charge that we are giving this money to get something in return, or that we must be purchasing influence in some way," she wrote in an essay for the Capitol Hill newspaper *Roll Call*. After explaining that she did not always get everything that she demanded, DeVos concluded that "I have decided, however, to stop taking offense at the suggestion that we are buying influence. Now I simply concede the point. They are right. We do expect some things in return."

"We expect return on our investment," wrote DeVos, an heir to a manufacturing fortune (and the sister of Erik Prince, the founder of Blackwater USA, the private military services contractor exposed by writer Jeremy Scahill) who married into the Amway fortune. She described that "return" as Republican Party election wins and the advancement of "a conservative governing philosophy consisting of limited government and respect for traditional American virtues."

Over the next two decades, DeVos used her money to make the Republican Party an ever more outlandish critic of public education and an ever more unapologetic advocate for steering public money into discredited choice, charter and privatization schemes.

A special-interest power player who travels in the elite circles of billionaire political players like the Koch brothers and Sheldon Adelson, DeVos has used inherited wealth to buy her way into the elections of states across the country. She has done so in order to advance an agenda that is as unworkable as it is irresponsible—an agenda that has very little to do with education and very much to do with reshaping society to reflect the fever dreams of Betsy DeVos and the people she pays to share those dreams.

DeVos has never been an education "reformer," as she is frequently described. She's a right-wing political activist who entertains "Make America Great Again" fantasies about recreating the Gilded Age. It just happens that DeVos has settled on the public schools as the vehicle for advancing the societal transformation she seeks. Real reformers recognize this. When Trump nominated DeVos to serve as secretary of education, one of the most prominent education reformers in the United States, billionaire Eli Broad, wrote to senators urging her rejection. "I believe she is unprepared and unqualified for the position," explained Broad. "Indeed, with Betsy DeVos at the helm of the U.S. Department of Education, much of the good work that has been accomplished to improve public education for all of America's children could be undone."

 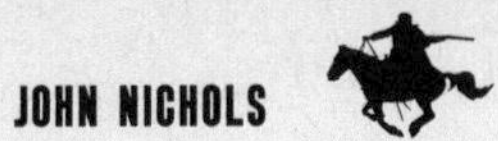

Broad supports charter schools, and he has clashed at times with teacher unions over school issues. But, as he explained in his letter: "We must have a Secretary of Education who believes in the sincere and positive reform of public education and the need to keep public schools public."

Though the Senate did not follow Broad's wise counsel, his point was well taken. DeVos is not interested in the sincere and positive reform of public education; she is interested in politics, and in using politics to engage in right-wing social engineering.

"Betsy DeVos claims she's a reformer but actually she's a privatizer. She wants everybody to be able to take their money and go to a religious school—that's her first choice," Ravitch says of the secretary of education who never attended a public school and has throughout her adult life been an ardent advocate for religious-right doctrines and the schools that teach them.

"Betsy and her husband Dick DeVos engineered a referendum in 2000 in Michigan on vouchers that failed. Then they began putting their money into charter schools. They have also put their money into states across the country through their different political PACs to elect people who are opposed to public education," Ravitch told WBEZ radio in Chicago as the DeVos nomination fight raged. "What makes DeVos an unusually bad choice for the U.S. secretary of education is that she's a lobbyist. She's not an expert in education. Since 1980, most secretaries have been governors with experiences dealing with budgets and understanding that 90 percent of the kids in their state go to public school—not to charters or vouchers. But she's an advocate that comes in with hostility to public education. She invests money into election campaigns across the country to defeat people who support their public schools, so it's a bizarre choice to say the least."

Bizarre, and dangerous.

Many of Trump's cabinet picks were critics of the agencies they were chosen to head, but DeVos was more than that. She was the leader of a movement to attack public education itself. American Federation of Teachers (AFT) president Randi Weingarten identifies DeVos as "the most ideological, anti–public education nominee put forward since President Carter created a Cabinet-level Department of Education."

Weingarten, who has worked closely with teachers and parents in states across the country, objected to the nomination of DeVos because of the billionaire's advocacy for an agenda that the AFT president said would put the focus of the Trump administration on "privatizing, defunding and destroying public education in America."

But Weingarten, who got her start teaching history and government classes at Clara Barton High School in Crown Heights, Brooklyn, kept returning to a deeper concern regarding this particular Trump designee: "DeVos has no meaningful experience in the classroom or in our schools. The sum total of her involvement has been spending her family's wealth in an effort to dismantle public education in Michigan."

That fact should have derailed DeVos, who is best understood as a political operative, not a serious thinker regarding education, and whose confirmation hearing was a train wreck. But DeVos got a narrow 51–50 pass from a Senate that included at least twenty-one Republicans who had accepted major campaign donations from the DeVos political operation. The individual donations by DeVos and her family totaled almost $1 million, coming in increments as high as $98,300 for Florida's Marco Rubio. If Rubio alone had turned against DeVos, she would have been rejected by the Senate. Instead, he hailed the nominee of the man who had humiliated him during the 2016 Republican presidential race as a champion of "educational opportunity for all."

Betsy DeVos had explained that "we do expect some things in return." And she got them.

The Department of Education gig served as a formal return. But the real value of her investments was far greater for DeVos. She bought the framing of the debate about education in the United States—by spending hundreds of millions of dollars to "help people become more open to what were once considered really radical reforms. Reforms like vouchers, tax credits, and education savings accounts" that allowed someone with her extreme views to be considered for secretary of education.

The problem, for DeVos and for America, is that she never promoted honest debate about whether her proposals would actually benefit elementary and secondary school students. She was too busy playing politics.

A former chair of the Michigan Republican Party, DeVos and her husband, Dick (a former Michigan gubernatorial candidate), have directed hundreds of millions of dollars into the ideological and electoral infrastructure that supports school privatization. While many DeVos investments were ideologically inspired as opposed to explicitly partisan, she acknowledged to the Senate that total DeVos family giving to Republican candidates and campaigns could total $200 million. "Nowhere is the impact of the DeVos family fortune greater . . . than in the movement to privatize public education," explains a People for the American Way study on how the DeVos political operation has used a family fortune to "create an intricate national network of nonprofits, political action committees and federal groups known as 527s that effectively fund the political arm of the school voucher movement."

The DeVos operation warped politics not just in Michigan but in states such as Wisconsin, where the billionaires were early and ardent supporters of Governor Scott Walker and his anti-labor allies.

Walker got $70,000 in direct contributions to his 2010 gubernatorial race from "choice" advocates. But even more money was spent on so-called independent campaigning by groups that poured hundreds of thousands of dollars into promoting Walker and his legislative allies and into attacks on supporters of public education. Walker and the other Republican governors whose exploitation of a politics of resentment gave rise to Trumpism could not have succeeded as they did without DeVos's money machine. All of this made Betsy DeVos incredibly influential at the state level years before she became incredibly influential at the federal level. But not in a good way.

One group with which DeVos has been associated, the political action committee All Children Matter, was fined a record $5.2 million by the Ohio Elections Commission after it was charged with illegally shifting money into the state to support candidates considered friendly to private-school "choice" initiatives. It was also fined for political misconduct in Wisconsin, where officials determined that the secretive group's 2006 campaigning violated campaign finance laws by expressly urging voters to cast ballots against legislative candidates who were strong backers of public education.

Those troubles led to the evolution of All Children Matter into the American Federation for Children, which has collected money from a who's who of right-wing millionaires and billionaires, including the political operations of right-wing donors Charles and David Koch. The money helped Republicans to win elections, in Michigan, Ohio, Wisconsin and elsewhere, and solidified DeVos's reputation as a go-to donor for national Republican contenders. But it has not improved education in the states. Rather, it imposed a failed ideological construct that borders on fantasy, and that has much more to do with attacking the unions that represent teachers and the infrastructure of public education than with helping students achieve their full potential. In Walker's Wisconsin, for instance, the group One Wisconsin Now noted that "we have seen her school privatization playbook in action in Wisconsin, and the result is more failure and less accountability."

"Betsy DeVos has been a driving force for the privatization of our public schools. She's used her family's wealth to reward politicians who support her agenda across the nation, including Scott Walker and Republicans in Wisconsin," said One Wisconsin Now's Scot Ross. "Being a billionaire whose hobby is underwriting campaigns to steal our public school dollars and send them to unaccountable private schools disqualifies her from being our secretary of education."

Ross was right. But in Donald Trump's Washington, where big money and insider connections matter far more than relevant experience and good ideas, Betsy DeVos got a return on her investment.

— 33 —

MR. SECRETS AND LIES

Scott Pruitt

Environmental Protection Agency Administrator

It is possible to pinpoint the moment at which "the world's greatest deliberative body" was remade by Senate majority leader Mitch McConnell to serve as nothing more than a rubber stamp for Trump's presidency, and for the fossil fuel industries that have risen to the pinnacle of their power with the billionaire's assumption of the presidency. It came on Friday, February 17, 2017.

The awful truth about Donald Trump's scandal-plagued designee to deconstruct the Environmental Protection Agency (EPA), climate science denier and corporate errand boy Scott Pruitt, was expected to be confirmed on the following Tuesday. So McConnell and the Republican Senate leaders rushed on the Friday before the whistle was blown to confirm Pruitt as the nation's new EPA administrator. In the lawless, shameless #AlternativeFacts universe that is Donald Trump's Washington, this move stood out. It was the most reckless rejection of basic responsibilities in which the Senate would engage during the transition to Trumpism, and one of the most haunting abandonments of constitutional duty in the chamber's history.

Senate Democrats tried on that Friday morning to restore a measure of order. They asked to extend deliberations on the Pruitt nomination, so that the Senate could have an informed debate. They had every reason to request the extension. On Thursday afternoon, as the Senate was beginning what would turn out to be the final (if woefully incomplete) review of the Pruitt nomination, Oklahoma County district judge Aletia Haynes Timmons found evidence of an "abject failure" on the part of Pruitt, in his role as state attorney general, to abide by the Oklahoma Open Records Act.

Timmons ordered Pruitt to release his communications with oil, gas and coal industry insiders. For two years, Pruitt had withheld more than twenty-five hundred emails with fossil fuel interests, which had been requested by an investigative-reporting group, the Center for Media and Democracy (CMD). Judge Timmons gave Pruitt's office until Tuesday, February 21, to release the emails. She also gave the office ten days to release related materials that might reveal controversial or inappropriate contacts between the hyper-partisan attorney general and interests regulated by the EPA.

Rhode Island senator Sheldon Whitehouse, a former state attorney general, raced to the floor of the Senate as the clock ticked toward the February 17 confirmation vote and explained how the emails could help to shed light on Pruitt's involvement with dark-money campaign groups that had sought to prevent open and honest debate about climate change and a host of other environmental issues overseen by the EPA. "Not only has dark money poisoned our conversation about climate change, this guy ran his own dark money operation," said Whitehouse. "His 'Rule of Law Defense Fund,' a 501 C-4 organization that does not disclose its donors, has been linked to the Koch brothers, who run one of the biggest polluting operations in the country. But we don't really know [the details of that link because] it's been kept absolutely quiet."

"There is a black hole of secrecy around this nominee's dark money operation: who he raised money from, what the quid pro quo was, what he did with it," the senator continued. "This is a question, Mr. President. This is a test of the Senate. Will this nominee ever tell us exactly what his relationship with the fossil fuel industry is? Will we get these emails in time to make an informed decision before this nomination is rammed through, one step ahead of the emails that the judge said had to be released?"

The Senate failed the test. The Pruitt nomination was rammed through in spite of repeated requests by Oregon senator Jeff Merkley and others for an extension of deliberations until after the release of the emails and an appropriate review by the chamber.

Merkley initially asked that the Pruitt vote be put off until after the release of all materials that had been withheld by Pruitt's office.

McConnell, who had not been present for most of the debate, suddenly appeared and grumbled: "I object." Senator Merkley then made a more modest request that the Pruitt vote be moved until immediately after the Senate returned from its Presidents' Day break. "I object," declared McConnell.

Every effort by Senator Merkley to set aside enough time to review the nomination of Scott Pruitt to take charge of an agency with more than fifteen thousand employees and an $8 billion budget, and to abandon the historic mission of that agency, faced a McConnell objection.

The Republican-controlled Senate finally upheld the McConnell objection to engaging in full review of Pruitt's record. A frustrated Delaware senator Tom Carper came to the floor of the chamber and declared: "We are preparing to vote here with incomplete information." And so they did, approving the Pruitt nomination by a vote of 52–46. The majority leader got his way.

The Senate rejected its constitutional responsibility to review presidential nominations before providing the "advice and consent" that is required for cabinet picks to assume their posts. In its place, the majority embraced Mitch McConnell's new standard. That standard says that, when it comes to doing Donald Trump's bidding, the Senate will proceed without respect for the facts, and the truth that might be revealed by those facts.

On the following Tuesday, the Oklahoma attorney general's office released more than seventy-five hundred pages of emails and other records it withheld to CMD. The group's analysis revealed that Pruitt had maintained a secretive relationship as the nation's most anti-environment state attorney general with fossil fuel companies, including fracking giant Devon Energy, as well as groups funded by the Koch brothers and other billionaire campaign funders.

Among the documents CMD immediately discovered were those revealing the following:

- As Oklahoma's attorney general, Pruit used template language provided by lobbyists to help advance the agendas of those lobbyists. According to the watchdog group: "The oil and gas lobby group American Fuel & Petrochemical Manufacturers (AFPM) coordinated opposition in 2013 to both the Renewable Fuel Standard Program (RFS) and ozone limits with Pruitt's office. While AFPM was making its own case against the RFS with the American Petroleum Institute, it provided Pruitt with a template language for an Oklahoma petition, noting "this argument is more credible coming from a State." Later that year, Pruitt did file opposition to both the RFS and ozone limits."

- An energy corporation drafted letters and language for Pruitt to circulate under his own name. "In a groundbreaking *New York Times* Pulitzer–winning series in 2014, Eric Lipton exposed the close relationship between Devon Energy and Scott Pruitt, and highlighted examples where Devon Energy drafted letters that were sent by Pruitt under his own name," explained CMD. "These new emails reveal more of the same close relationship with Devon Energy. In one email, Devon Energy helped draft language that was later sent by Pruitt to the EPA about the limiting of methane from oil and gas fracking."
- Pruitt plotted with corporate representatives to influence his fellow state attorneys general. "In 2013," noted CMD, "Devon Energy organized a meeting between Scott Pruitt, Leonard Leo of the Federalist Society and coal industry lawyer Paul Seby to plan the creation of a 'clearinghouse' that would 'assist AGs in addressing federalism issues.' Melissa Houston, then Pruitt's chief of staff, emailed Devon Energy saying, 'This will be an amazing resource for the AGs and for industry.'"

Headlines spelled out the truth about Pruitt:

New York Times: "The Pruitt Emails: E.P.A. Chief Was Arm in Arm with Industry"

Washington Post: "Thousands of emails detail EPA head's close ties to fossil fuel industry"

CNN: "Emails reveal Pruitt's behind-the-scenes collaboration with oil and natural gas giant"

What was revealed was scandalous. It outlined relationships that defined Pruitt as a dramatically conflicted appointee and that set the stage for Pruitt's wrecking-crew tenure at the head of an agency that he began dismantling almost immediately. Within weeks of Pruitt's confirmation, the White House (which eventually announced plans to withdraw from the Paris climate accord) proposed a budget blueprint that included a 31 percent cut to EPA funding that "slashed funding for the Clean Power Plan, international climate change programs and climate change research and partnership programs."

"Regarding the question as to climate change, I think the President was fairly straightforward. We're not spending money on that anymore," announced Office of Management and Budget director Mick Mulvaney. "We consider that to be a waste of your money to go out and do that." For his part, Pruitt was busy announcing that he did not believe that carbon dioxide was a major cause of global warming and suggesting that "there's tremendous disagreement about the degree of impact" of climate change.

Those statements were completely at odds with the overwhelming body of scientific evidence on the issues. They were also, notably, at odds with Pruitt's written testimony to the Senate in which he claimed that "I also believe the Administrator has an important role when it comes to the regulation of carbon dioxide."

"Scott Pruitt shocked the world [on March 9, 2017] when he declared that carbon pollution was not the primary driver of the climate crisis," declared Liz Perera, the Sierra Club's climate policy director. "But what was even more shocking was that he clearly and repeatedly misled Congress about his intentions on this critical issue during his confirmation process to serve as the administrator of the Environmental Protection Agency."

The Senate failed to consider the whole of Scott Pruitt's record, even though revelations about that record arrived, as had been anticipated, within days of his confirmation. "What happened [in the Senate on Friday, February 17, 2017] was an egregious cover-up, and a total abdication of the Senate's constitutional responsibility to vet nominees before voting," Senator Merkley said after the vote.

Jeff Merkley was on the losing side of that vote. But he upheld his oath to "support and defend the Constitution of the United States." Mitch McConnell was on the winning side of that vote. But in order to prevail he abandoned that oath and shamed both himself and the Senate by establishing the Scott Pruitt rule: #TheTruthBeDamned.

— 34 —

PRISTINE WILDERNESS FOR SALE, LEASE OR HIRE

Ryan Zinke

Secretary of the Interior

It was a Republican president who planted the conservation ethic in the American psyche and nurtured it by using the power of government to protect the nation's most cherished spaces from private exploitation. Theodore Roosevelt decried the ruination by robber barons of human potential, but he added: "It is also vandalism wantonly to destroy or to permit the destruction of what is beautiful in nature, whether it be a cliff, a forest, or a species of mammal or bird. Here in the United States we turn our rivers and streams into sewers and dumping-grounds, we pollute the air, we destroy forests, and exterminate fishes, birds and mammals—not to speak of vulgarizing charming landscapes with hideous advertisements. But at last it looks as if our people were awakening."

As president, Teddy Roosevelt fostered and encouraged that awakening, borrowing on the wisdom of the naturalist John Muir, and framing out intellectual and spiritual arguments for establishing national forests and parks, and for protecting rivers and mountains from the despoilers who would rob a nation of its natural beauty. "We have fallen heirs to the most glorious heritage a people ever received, and each one must do his part if we wish to show that the nation is worthy of its good fortune," observed the twenty-sixth president of the United States, who looked to the southwest and preached that "in the Grand Canyon, Arizona has a natural wonder which is in kind absolutely unparalleled throughout the rest of the world. I want to ask you to keep this great wonder of nature as it now is. I hope you will not have a building of any kind, not a summer cottage, a hotel or anything else, to mar the wonderful grandeur, the sublimity, the great loneliness and beauty of the canyon. Leave it as it is. You cannot improve on it. The ages have been at work on it, and man can only mar it."

To that end, Roosevelt used the power of his presidency in the opening years of the twentieth century to establish 4 national game preserves, 5 national parks, 18 national monuments, 24 major reclamation projects, 51 federal bird reservations and 150 national forests. "In seven years and sixty-nine days [as president]," observed presidential historian Douglas Brinkley in his book *Wilderness Warrior: Theodore Roosevelt and the Crusade for America*, Roosevelt "saved more than 240 million acres of American wilderness."

"He was the only politician we had in the White House in that period who had a biological sense of the world, who understood the need for species survival and did something about it," explains Brinkley. "When you open up a Rand McNally map and look at all the green on the United States, you're looking at TR's America."

The national parks that Roosevelt called into being were managed by the secretary of the interior, who now oversees a sprawling federal agency with authority over seventy thousand employees, hundreds of thousands of volunteers and a $12 billion annual budget for managing roughly one-fifth of the surface land of the United States. Seventy-five percent of America's federal public land is managed by the department that is home to the Bureau of Land Management, the Bureau of Ocean Energy Management, the Bureau of Reclamation (and the Office of Surface Mining Reclamation and Enforcement), the Bureau of Safety and Environmental Enforcement, the U.S. Fish and Wildlife Service, the U.S. Geological Survey, the Bureau of Indian Affairs and the century-old National Park Service.

Roosevelt's handful of parks has grown to a vast system of "national parks, monuments, battlefields, military parks, historical parks, historic sites, lakeshores, seashores, recreation areas, scenic rivers and trails, and the White House." On 84 million acres of public land, the park service maintains everything from Old Faithful geyser at Yellowstone to the Harriet Tubman National Historical Park in

Auburn, New York, established in 2016 as the 414th unit of the National Park Service. And that's nothing compared to the roughly 250 million acres, one-eighth of the landmass of the United States, that is overseen by the Bureau of Land Management that former president Harry S. Truman cobbled together when he combined the old General Land Office and the Grazing Service in 1946.

Teddy Roosevelt, who said after leaving the presidency that "there can be no greater issue than that of conservation in this country," fretted throughout his last years about the prospect that powerful interests might attempt to claw back public lands.

But how would they do that?

Perhaps by following the platform of the Republican Party that has not just abandoned the legacy of Abraham Lincoln but also the legacy of Teddy Roosevelt. The current Republican platform, the one on which President Trump and congressional Republicans were elected, announces that "the environment is too important to be left to radical environmentalists." Like, presumably, Teddy Roosevelt and Richard Nixon (creator of the Environmental Protection Agency, signer of the Clean Air Act and the Clean Water Act). The GOP platform rejects "the illusion of an environmental crisis" and dismisses many of the most serious warnings about climate change as "politicized science." It complains that the Bureau of Land Management is too slow when it comes to leasing public lands for private use and too restrictive when it comes to allowing hydraulic fracturing (fracking) of those lands. And it declares that federal ownership or management of land "places an economic burden on counties and local communities in terms of lost revenue to pay for things such as schools, police, and emergency services."

So is the Republican Party proposing to make it possible for communities across the country to lease off, or perhaps barter off, public lands? Yes, indeed. "It is absurd to think that all that acreage must remain under the absentee ownership or management of official Washington," reads the official policy of Roosevelt's Grand Old Party regarding public lands. "Congress shall immediately pass universal legislation providing for a timely and orderly mechanism requiring the federal government to convey certain federally controlled public lands to states. We call upon all national and state leaders and representatives to exert their utmost power and influence to urge the transfer of those lands, identified in the review process, to all willing states for the benefit of the states and the nation as a whole." But wait, there's more. The GOP also supports "amending the Antiquities Act of 1906 to establish Congress' right to approve the designation of national monuments and to further require the approval of the state where a national monument is designated or a national park is proposed."

Who was the radical environmentalist who signed the Antiquities Act of 1906 into law and established the model for its use? None other than Teddy Roosevelt.

Who might undo Roosevelt's legacy? Meet Ryan Zinke, Donald Trump's idea of an environmentalist.

A congressman from Montana, Zinke is a former Navy SEAL who earned some attention for calling Hillary Clinton "the real enemy" and the "anti-Christ" during the course of the 2016 campaign. He was one of the few people who openly campaigned for a place on Trump's ticket. Asked about vice presidential speculation, Zinke told the Breitbart News site—yes, Breitbart—that "I know my name has been thrown around, and I would be honored to [do] the duty in whatever capacity that is. I would be honored to do my duty. You know why? It's about making America great again." To his credit, Zinke complained before the Republican National Convention about some of the most extreme language in a party platform that he characterized as "more divisive than uniting." But his speech to the convention was a dramatically divisive address in which he declared that "together Barack Obama and Hillary Clinton brought us ISIS and brought down Benghazi. I shudder to think how many times our flag will fly at half-mast if Hillary Clinton is in the Oval Office." Trump, the congressman told the crowd, would "make America safe again."

When he stood in the national spotlight, Zinke made no effort to address environmental policy or public lands. Even when he did so at home in Montana, where he could not avoid the issues, the congressman tried to peddle a politically palatable, everything for everyone line, dismissing discussions of selling off national parks and

striking the most absurd balance possible on climate change, telling a debate crowd: "It's not a hoax, but it's not proven science either."

So who is Ryan Zinke? Where does he really stand?

When Zinke sought reelection in 2016, his Democratic challenger, former Montana state superintendent of public instruction Denise Juneau, mounted a campaign that focused scrutiny on the congressman's anything but ironclad commitment to the environment in general and public lands in particular. Juneau had plenty of ammunition.

Zinke's rating on the League of Conservation Voters National Environmental Scorecard during his first year in the House was 3 percent—80 points below that of Montana senator Jon Tester and worse than a good many Republicans.

Even as he announced that he was not an advocate for the wholesale bartering off of public lands, Zinke voted for the private exploitation of those lands, and for moves that environmentalists feared would loosen safeguards against sell-offs. He refused to recognize that, while privatization advocates certainly don't pass up opportunities for ownership, the essential goal of privateers throughout history has been pillage. And Zinke is quite enthusiastic about opening up opportunities for corporations to pillage public lands.

An ardent advocate for overturning a temporary bar on the issuance of new coal-mining leases for public lands, which was ordered in 2016 by the Obama administration's Department of Interior after it was established that there was a twenty-year coal supply available without new leases, Zinke wrote congressional legislation to direct the Department of Interior to restructure its approach on leasing issues. He also voted to initiate a 4 million acre pilot program for local management of federal lands, HR 2316 (the Self-Sufficient Community Lands Act), which was sponsored by one of the most environmentally unfriendly members of the U.S. House, Idaho Republican Raúl Labrador. The Juneau campaign explained in the summer of 2016 that "Denise is opposed to any attempt to chip away at management of and access to our public lands. Congressman Zinke cannot say the same. Both the Montana and National Republican Party platforms advocate for the transfer or sale of our land."

Zinke won a new term in a good year for Republicans, but the former Trump vice presidential prospect was not satisfied to serve the new president from a Montana House seat. He began angling almost immediately for a place on the Trump team. And he soon got that place. (It didn't hurt that the congressman's wife, Lolita Hand Zinke, was a member of Trump's transition team.)

Trump's announcement of Zinke's selection for the Department of the Interior post was typically vague—"He has built one of the strongest track records on championing regulatory relief, forest management, responsible energy development and public land issues"—but the response of environmental groups was precise: "If the task is plundering our public lands on behalf of fossil fuel empires, Rep. Ryan Zinke is the man for the job," announced Friends of the Earth's Marissa Knodel. "Representative Zinke and Donald Trump are determined to turn our public lands and waters into energy sacrifice zones. Zinke denies climate change science, and champions increasing fossil fuel development for corporate profits over the health and safety of people and the planet."

Sierra Club executive director Michael Brune said Zinke's nomination "jeopardizes the places that are so much a part of the American spirit and the backbone of the outdoor recreation economy."

"Public lands are held in trust for all of us and should be managed as an investment in the future," explained Brune. "Yet, Zinke is firmly in the past, clinging to plans to mine, drill and log public lands to benefit corporate polluters, supporting dangerous and dirty projects like the Keystone XL pipeline, and opposing efforts to clean up our air. The need to keep dirty fuels in the ground is urgent, especially on public lands. We cannot afford to have someone in charge who dabbles in climate denial."

Zinke pushed back, telling members of the Senate Energy and Natural Resources Committee that "upfront, I am an unapologetic admirer of Teddy Roosevelt." Zinke even said that Roosevelt "had it right" on some specific conservation issues. *Scientific American* reported that "with a right-wing movement to wrestle control of public lands from the federal government gaining momentum, Zinke's rhetoric offered conservationists some measure of comfort."

But it was cold comfort. As the magazine noted: "Zinke's views on easing energy development on public lands seem largely in line with his party."

The Sierra Club's Matthew Kirby, an expert on western public lands issues, was not buying the Teddy Roosevelt comparison.

"While he continues to paint himself as a modern Teddy Roosevelt," said Kirby, "his very short voting record shows him repeatedly siding with industry."

Ultimately, 170 environmental and conservation groups signed a letter urging the Senate to reject Trump's nominee because "Representative Zinke's voting record suggests he will put corporate profits ahead of conservation and public involvement. His record includes voting to turn management of public land over to industry-dominated panels, while dispensing with environmental laws in order to ramp up unsustainable logging levels, voting to strip the president of authority to designate national monuments in seven western states, and voting to block the Bureau of Land Management from limiting harm to water, air and wildlife from hydraulic fracking. Rep. Zinke even voted against designating the Arctic National Wildlife Refuge—an area of global environmental significance—as wilderness to protect it from oil and gas drilling."

At the top of that list of groups warning that Zinke's "views are out of step with the majority of Americans who want to see our public lands protected from rapacious development, endangered species conserved and a livable climate future" was the name of the Sierra Club. That's an environmental organization formed by John Muir, with whom President Theodore Roosevelt camped at Yosemite in 1903. The experience had a profound impact on the former president, who came away convinced that public lands should be "preserved for their children and their children's children forever, with their majestic beauty all unmarred."

This was an expression of the conservation ethic that Republicans once embraced. That ethic did not die with Teddy Roosevelt. It survived for decades. Through much of the twentieth century, the GOP defined itself as a party that extended from Roosevelt. But no more.

— 35 —

MARS INCORPORATED

Newt Gingrich and Robert Walker

Trump Space Advisors

President Trump announced in his January 20, 2017, inaugural address that "we stand at the birth of a new millennium, ready to unlock the mysteries of space." What Trump did not say is that his vision of space has nothing to do with the sixties-era ideal of missions "to explore strange new worlds, to seek out new life and new civilizations, to boldly go where no man has gone before," or the understanding that those missions must be undertaken with an anti-colonialist, anti-imperialist "prime directive" to avoid interference with the social development of those new worlds.

Trump was not channeling John F. Kennedy's 1962 address at Rice University, in which the thirty-fifth president explained: "We set sail on this new sea because there is new knowledge to be gained, and new rights to be won, and they must be won and used for the progress of all people. For space science, like nuclear science and all technology, has no conscience of its own. Whether it will become a force for good or ill depends on man, and only if the United States occupies a position of pre-eminence can we help decide whether this new ocean will be a sea of peace or a new terrifying theater of war. I do not say that we should or will go unprotected against the hostile misuse of space any more than we go unprotected against the hostile use of land or sea, but I do say that space can be explored and mastered without feeding the fires of war, without repeating the mistakes that man has made in extending his writ around this globe of ours."

In fact, Trump's vision is all about "repeating the mistakes that man has made in extending his writ around this globe of ours." The billionaire developer said as much during the campaign that made

him president. While Trump professes to "love NASA," he said on the campaign trail that "in the old days, [NASA] was great. Right now, we have bigger problems, you understand that. We have to fix our potholes. We don't exactly have a lot of money."

So how does Trump imagine "unlocking the mysteries of space"? And to what purpose? He's been quite clear on this front. "You know, space is actually being taken over privately, which is great," candidate Trump explained in New Hampshire in 2015. "It is being taken over; by a lot of private companies are going after space, and I like that maybe even better, but it's very exciting."

Trump has aligned himself with advocates for the exploitation of the outer limits.

In what *Politico* refers to as "a struggle for supremacy between traditional aerospace contractors and the tech billionaires who have put big money into private space ventures," Trump and his advisors know which side they are on. "The early indications are that private rocket firms like Elon Musk's SpaceX and Jeff Bezos' Blue Origin and their supporters have a clear upper hand in what Trump's transition advisers portrayed as a race between 'Old Space' and 'New Space,' according to emails among key players inside the administration," the DC-insider tip sheet explained. "Trump has met with Bezos and Musk, while tech investor Peter Thiel, a close confidant, has lobbied the president to look at using NASA to help grow the private space industry."

"It is a big fight," said former House Science, Space and Technology Committee chairman Bob Walker, a veteran Republican operative. Walker, whose lobbying firm's promotional materials identify the former congressman as "one of Washington's most influential lobbyists" and brags about being "a trusted advisor to several of the key leaders on Capitol Hill [who] is frequently invited to private meetings where policy and strategy are discussed and determined," drafted the Trump campaign's space policy and counseled the transition team on how to approach the universe. What does Walker say? "There are billions of dollars at stake. It has come to a head now when it has become clear to the space community that the real innovative work is being done outside of NASA."

Walker and other Trump allies and advisors talk up the industrialization of space and argue that policies must be reshaped so that investors won't have to worry that "they might be competing with the government." National security writer Bryan Bender reported a few weeks into Trump's presidency that "the proposals being considered by the new administration also call for a 'space industrialization initiative' in which NASA, with its $19 billion annual budget, would be 'refocused on the large-scale economic development of space,' according to the summary."

Who is counseling Trump on all things spacey? Walker, to be sure. He advised the campaign and the transition team on NASA and space issues; and once the administration was in place he continued to appear as a "Trump Space Advisor" on programs such as the *PBS NewsHour* to discuss topics like "What do the stars hold for the Trump administration?" "Trump Space Advisor" is not a formal title. *SpaceNews* refers to him as "a key advisor." Walker's still very much in the private sector, but he's very close to key players in the administration, including Vice President Mike Pence. And he is clearly in the know when it comes to decisions on space policy. It was Walker who announced in early May that the administration was reestablishing the long dormant National Space Council. "The recommendation coming out of the Trump campaign to create the National Space Council is going to happen," he announced. "It's a way of ensuring that the nation's resources are all directed towards national goals."

Walker was being modest. Since he was the key player in drafting the Trump campaign's space policy, he could just have said "my recommendation."

A line from Walker is frequently quoted in papers on commercialization of space. "Most of our laws and regulations governing space activity were written to make it easier for government to function in space," he says. "Now we need to make it easier for the private sector to undertake space development." In a preelection opinion piece, written with Peter Navarro (a business professor at the University of California-Irvine and senior policy advisor to the Trump campaign who now serves as what the *Wall Street Journal* calls "the White House's most hawkish trade adviser"), Walker stated: "Government

 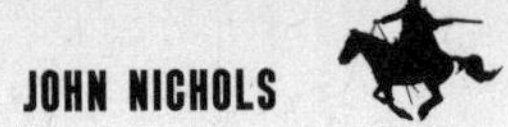

must recognize that space is no longer the province of governments alone."

The point, Walker and Navarro argued in *SpaceNews,* is to "assure that each space sector is playing its proper role in advancing U.S. interests." This notion of an "America First" space policy is a big deal with the people Trump listens to and empowers. One of Navarro's compatriots helped frame things out as a member of the so-called beachhead team at NASA, where he briefly served as White House Liaison.

Dr. Greg Autry, an assistant professor of entrepreneurship—yes, entrepreneurship—at the University of Southern California, has long been one of the nation's leading champions of commercial spaceflight, arguing that the U.S. can "establish a profitable space economy." He's also been a big champion of relying on "space assets" to win wars. "Our commitment to today's warfighters and those yet to serve demands that we maintain our space advantage over any and all adversaries," argues Autry.

An agile thinker and ardent advocate, Autry's writings give a good sense of the thinking among those who have influenced the Trump team's approach to the stars. He is all for space exploration; however, he writes: "We will not plant a flag, collect some rocks and then pack up. Our goal must be to establish an economically sustainable human presence in our Solar System." The professor comes from the business school, not the planetarium; he identifies as "a serial entrepreneur in video games, computer services, Internet content, enterprise applications, health care IT and material upcycling," and he writes about "engaging the warp power of the private sector" to launch probes and "deliver American astronauts to orbit." NASA still exists in his brave new world, but the emphasis will be on building "the new space economy."

"The cost of an investment in extremely long-term exploration and research made by a nation financing large budget deficits will be borne by multiple generations," explains the synopsis of one of Autry's major papers on interplanetary development. "The decision to burden future citizens with the cost of a public space program begs a question of intergenerational equity with both economic and environmental aspects. While these two facets are [*sic*] most often been considered in a context of dialectical opposition, space exploration offers a paradigm shift that aligns economic development with environmental stewardship by actually offering to remove human economic activity from the planet."

Autry is no "One World" or "United Federation of Planets" visionary. The co-author (with Navarro) of the book *Death by China: Confronting the Dragon: A Global Call to Action*, which was made into a documentary that the *New York Times* reviewed as "alarming and alarmist," "unabashedly one-sided" and "short on solutions," is all about "American commercial space operations and missions of exploration that leverage these entrepreneurial capabilities."

International cooperation? "[We] will never accept a secondary position in space to China or Russia," writes Autry. "Authoritarian political ideologies and state-dominated economies have no place in the future and must not spread to the stars. The U.S. must also ensure that the aging international Outer Space Treaty and other laws are interpreted in a manner that leaves commercial firms free to act responsibly in space."

The 1967 Treaty on Principles Governing the Activities of States in the Exploration and Use of Outer Space, including the Moon and Other Celestial Bodies, forms the basis for international space law. It's a roadblock to the commercialization of space, and a lot of other bad ideas, like the placement of weapons of mass destruction in the orbit of Earth, on the moon or on any other celestial body. The treaty declares that "outer space, including the Moon and other celestial bodies, is not subject to national appropriation by claim of sovereignty, by means of use or occupation, or by any other means" and it outlines a vision of space exploration by all countries for the benefit of all mankind.

There are sound arguments to be made for reexamining international space law. But this is a complicated and often frustrating endeavor, as the ongoing refusal of the United States, Russia, China, Japan and India to ratify the visionary 1979 Agreement Governing the Activities of States on the Moon and Other Celestial Bodies well illustrates. But those who would commercialize and colonize space

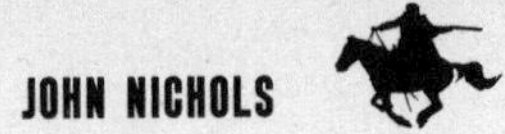

are not pointing in the right direction. And the suggestion that existing laws should be "interpreted in a manner that leaves commercial firms free to act responsibly in space" opens up the possibility of conflicts—and threats—that most Americans have not begun to imagine.

Unfortunately, Trump's inner circle invites those conflicts. One of the new president's closest allies and steadiest defenders is former House Speaker Newt Gingrich, who the *Atlantic* notes has been "touting space colonization" for more than three decades. Gingrich, who now predicts that Trump will be the "most effective anti-left" president in modern American history, made his own bid to become commander in chief in 2012. There are many explanations for why Gingrich did not become president, but there is good reason to suggest that the most striking argument against his election was argued by Gingrich himself, when he made a Trump-like call to make America great again by colonizing the moon for commercial and political purposes.

"At one point early in my career I introduced the Northwest Ordinance for space and I said when we got—I think the number is 13,000—when we have 13,000 Americans living on the moon they can petition to become a state," Gingrich told a Florida crowd before that state's 2012 Republican primary. "And I will as president encourage the introduction of the Northwest Ordinance for space to put a marker down that we want Americans to think boldly about the future." The colonization plan was ridiculed. NBC's *Saturday Night Live* sent the candidate into space and had him developing an "admoonistration" as "Newt Gingrich: Moon President." The eventual Republican nominee, Mitt Romney, turned to Gingrich during a Jacksonville debate and announced that "if I had a business executive come to me and say I want to spend a few hundred billion dollars to put a colony on the moon, I'd say, 'You're fired.'"

Romney borrowed the dismissal line from a prospective 2012 presidential candidate named Donald Trump who a few years later would claim that "space is actually being taken over privately." That's not technically true. Yet.

— 36 —

THE SECRETARY OF GENTRIFICATION

Dr. Ben Carson

Secretary of Housing and Urban Development

Dr. Ben Carson sort of wanted to be president, even if his listless debate performances and tendency to wander off the campaign trail suggested otherwise. But the man who Donald Trump shredded during the pre-primary campaign—noting that Carson had described his own temper as "pathological," Trump told CNN: "You don't cure these people. You don't cure a child molester. There's no cure for it. Pathological, there's no cure for that."—definitely never wanted to be secretary of housing and urban development. When the prospect was raised following the 2016 election, Carson's friend and frequent spokesman Armstrong Williams told Reuters: "Dr. Carson doesn't feel like that's the best way for him to serve the president-elect."

Williams explained to the *Hill* newspaper in Washington that "Dr. Carson feels he has no government experience, he's never run a federal agency. The last thing he would want to do was take a position that could cripple the presidency."

A renowned neurosurgeon who made a fortune peddling inspirational books, Carson got credit for rejecting a place in the cabinet after determining that his education, his background and his skills had not prepared him for the job. Then he changed his mind.

That put Carson in front of the Senate Banking, Housing and Urban Affairs Committee, where the nominee struggled to explain why he wanted a job for which he was unqualified. It had already been revealed that Carson had even less experience than his supporters imagined—former Arkansas governor Mike Huckabee's attempt to justify Trump's choice by describing the nominee as the

 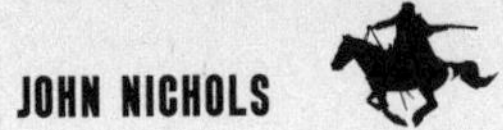

first potential Housing and Urban Development (HUD) secretary "to have actually lived in government housing" fell apart when Carson said he hadn't actually lived in government housing. But everything was cool, said Carson, because he would be sort of a CEO of HUD, delegating responsibility to capable people.

Comedian Trevor Noah sorted that one out: "Dr. Carson, I'm confused, I thought Donald Trump was the hands-off CEO, and now you're also the hands-off CEO? No, no, think about it—Donald Trump said he does not know how to do the job but he'll make sure he'll hire the best. Now Dr. Carson says that he doesn't know the job but he'll make sure to hire the best. How far down does this . . . go? Who actually knows how to do the job?"

That's a good question, because the job is actually quite challenging. HUD is an agency, as Peter Dreier, the chair of the Urban & Environmental Policy Department at Occidental College, has explained, "with a $47 billion budget that oversees federal rental assistance programs serving more than five million of the country's lowest-income households. The largest of these is the housing choice voucher program (formerly known as Section 8), which helps low-income families rent apartments in the private market. HUD also oversees a million units of public housing run by local governments, administers $5 billion in community development funds, insures the mortgages of more than one-fifth of all homeowners, and enforces fair housing laws that bar racial discrimination by lenders and landlords."

Dreier reminds us that "Carson has no experience with any of these programs—nor any experience in government at all." New York City Council Housing Committee chair Jumaane Williams has been blunter. He ripped the selection of Carson to head this particular department as a move that was "ill-advised, irresponsible and hovers on absurdity."

The absurdity was made abundantly clear when Carson appeared before the Senate Banking Committee and was asked whether Trump's real-estate empire (which has a stake in affordable housing developments) might benefit from his oversight of the agency. "It will not be my intention to do anything to benefit any American particularly," he mused. "It's for all Americans, everything that we do."

"I understand that," responded Massachusetts senator Elizabeth Warren, a committee member. "Do I take that to mean that you may manage programs that will significantly benefit the president-elect?"

"You can take it to mean that I will manage things that will benefit the American people. That is going to be the goal," replied Carson, who could have left it there. But he kept going, telling Warren that "if there happens to be an extraordinarily good program that is working for millions of people and it turns out that someone that you're targeting is going to gain $10 from it, am I going to say, 'No, the rest of you Americans can't have it'? I think logic and common sense will probably be the best way."

What Carson said there was not understood as a guarantee that scrupulous care would be taken to avoid rewarding America's developer in chief and his family.

Trump family profiteering was among the lesser concerns regarding Carson at HUD. A bigger concern, the *Washington Post* suggested, was the potential for "a collision between [Carson's] philosophical aversion to social safety-net programs and an agency that administers some of the government's most expansive programs for helping minorities and low-income people."

"Coming to lead an agency that serves the poorest people in the country with a philosophy of if people are that poor it's because they're not trying hard enough could have a big impact on the people HUD serves," fretted National Low Income Housing Coalition president Diane Yentel.

Yentel had reason to worry

As a presidential candidate, Carson dismissed initiatives to identify and address patterns of racial and income disparity in housing as "mandated social-engineering schemes" and wrote: "These government-engineered attempts to legislate racial equality create consequences that often make matters worse. There are reasonable ways to use housing policy to enhance the opportunities available

to lower-income citizens, but based on the history of failed socialist experiments in this country, entrusting the government to get it right can prove downright dangerous."

The target of Carson's wrath was one of the most important, if undercovered, civil rights and social justice initiatives of the Obama administration: a 2015 rule that required cities to "affirmatively further fair housing." The initiative sought, as the *Atlantic* noted, to give meaning to "a provision of the Fair Housing Act of 1968 that had long been mostly ignored. Under the 2015 rule, cities are required to assess whether housing in their communities is racially segregated, and then release the results of that assessment every three to five years. Cities are encouraged, through financial incentives, to set desegregation goals, establish new low-income housing in integrated neighborhoods, and track their progress on those goals."

Trump decried the rule, as did Carson, who claimed that it relied on "a tortured reading of the Fair Housing laws to empower the Department of Housing and Urban Development to 'affirmatively promote' fair housing, even in the absence of explicit discrimination." Of course, discrimination is often implicit. And if Carson had bothered to review the HUD mission statement, he would have known that the agency does not make distinctions. It simply says that HUD seeks to "build inclusive and sustainable communities free from discrimination."

Carson says something different. He argues that what housing advocates hail as a serious and needed intervention is just a repeat of "the failed socialist experiments of the 1980s" (someone should probably tell him that Ronald Reagan was president for most of that decade) and past attempts to "usher in a new era of racial utopia in America."

After Trump announced his HUD pick, New York mayor Bill de Blasio said: "Carson's utter lack of qualifications, combined with the hostility he has expressed towards fair housing and social programs, does not bode well, especially with Republicans in control of Congress and the presidency." There is good reason to accept that assessment by the mayor of the nation's largest city. So let's mark Carson down as another Trump cabinet member who is disinclined to carry forward the Obama administration's efforts to respond to existing problems. But what if Carson makes America's affordable housing crisis worse? What if he makes it a lot worse? What if the man who has no government experience is supposed to cripple an agency with a mission "to create strong, sustainable, inclusive communities and quality affordable homes for all"?

That's what scares Seema Agnani, executive director of the National Coalition for Asian Pacific American Community Development. "[What] does it mean that the worst kind of developer—one of the biggest, wealthiest, and most aggressive developers—is the boss of the boss of HUD?" she asked after Carson's nomination.

Agnani, a veteran housing activist with long experience in New York City, argues that "anything having to do with HUD or the issues in HUD's purview must be evaluated in the context of Donald Trump, the real estate magnate" and, further, she asks: "What does it mean for fair housing that a landlord with a history of fair housing violations is Houser-in-Chief? It means that Ben Carson's ignorance of fair housing law wasn't some incidental flaw—something that one might associate with the normal shortcomings of an underqualified political appointee—but rather, it is his central qualification for the job. It is license for racist landlords to discriminate more openly, for racist city leaders to more aggressively create policies and allocate resources in ways that segregate and exploit communities of color. It is the signal of the intent to dismantle fair housing as we know it." And just as worrisome, she continues: "What does it mean for HUD to have a president who has been so cavalier about conflict of interest? And who has such a long history of ties to contractors, developers, predatory investors, and a whole set of players in the real estate industry? What does this specifically mean for federally subsidized housing and infrastructure development? With the worst of the industry taking their cues from the Developer in Chief, I fear it will create a climate of graft where important and scarce federal resources will be siphoned into private pockets or will be channeled toward developments that have dubious public benefit. Any and all block grants, federal pass-throughs, and Public-Private-Partnership activities should be examined in terms of their impact on the Trump

 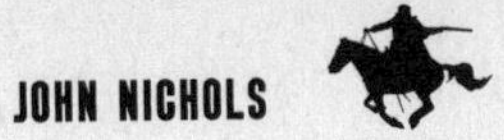

brand or their propensity to line the pockets of Trump's companies and those that he works with."

Those are not idle fears, especially those concerns about "a climate of graft" and the prospect that "scarce federal resources will be siphoned into private pockets."

The *Atlantic*'s Alana Semuels reminds us that "Trump could, for instance, focus more on privatizing public housing, and asking real-estate developers to take responsibility for revitalizing the neighborhoods around housing complexes."

Public housing projects that were constructed decades ago near the centers of major cities, at a time when upper-class and then middle-class urbanites were moving to the suburbs, now sit atop desirable real estate. Central cities are booming. Well-to-do young people are moving downtown to be where the action is; well-to-do older folks are retiring near the theater, the symphony and the waterfront. Developers with an eye for gentrification can tick off the names of public housing projects that are located on attractive parcels. HUD can make privatization seem necessary, not by selling off properties itself but by squeezing funding for local housing authorities across the country (the New York City Housing Authority gets 40 percent of its income from the federal agency), by creating incentives for sell-offs and by developing programs that suggest to cities that they have no alternative but to turn to developers. The federal government has already experimented with so-called rental assistance demonstration schemes, under which developers sign agreements to provide public housing in high-cost cities such as San Francisco. Under the Obama administration, Federal Housing Administration aides and advisors emphasized "public housing preservation . . . to ensure that the housing units are preserved and affordable for the long term." But as journalist Toshio Meronek noted in an assessment of the program in *Truthout*: "Tenants and housing rights activists are worried the program is just another step toward dismantling public housing altogether."

Meronek highlighted those concerns under an Obama administration that gave evidence of being at least somewhat sensitive to them. Under a Trump administration, however, it is hard to imagine that the sensitivities will remain. The Right to the City alliance of tenant and neighborhood groups has labeled Trump America's "#GentrifierInChief" and warns that the president's "cabinet nominations show deep allegiance to Wall Street and his intention to continue the policies of displacement, gentrification and rising rents at the expense of the American People."

Housing affordability is an issue for tens of millions of Americans, and the chief issue for millions of them. We should all be concerned when experts on housing warn us, as does Andrea Shapiro of New York City's Metropolitan Council on Housing, about the prospect that a developer-led presidential administration might radically alter housing policy to benefit landlords and real-estate developers rather than low-income families and communities. And that is exactly what Shapiro is saying when she reports that "advocates believe it is likely that his administration will attempt to privatize public housing. This would increase gentrification pressure and displace thousands of people who cannot afford housing on the private market."

In the best of worlds, a wise and experienced secretary of housing and urban development might push back against the deconstruction, the dismantling and dismembering of HUD, and of America's commitment to affordable housing. But, as was made quite clear when he was signaling that he was not up to the job, that's not Dr. Ben Carson.

—37—

THE OOPSING OF NUCLEAR WASTE DISPOSAL

Rick Perry

Secretary of Energy

Rick Perry is known for a lot of things: a fine cha-cha turn on *Dancing with the Stars,* his "[the planet is] experiencing a cooling trend" rejection of climate science and those "smart-guy" glasses he started wearing to compensate for impressions left by one of the great crash-and-burn moments in American politics.

Perry was outlining his vision for slimming down the federal government during a November 2011 Republican presidential debate. "It does the things to the regulatory climate that has to happen," the then-governor of Texas said of his agenda. "And I will tell you, it is three agencies of government when I get there that are gone. Commerce, Education, and the—what's the third one there? Let's see . . ." Perry paused. The crowd laughed. A lot.

Then-congressman Ron Paul, always a helper, filled the void: "You need five."

"Oh, five, okay," said a befuddled Perry. "So Commerce, Education, and the . . ."

The eventual nominee of the party that year, Mitt Romney, had an idea: "EPA?"

"EPA," chirped a relieved Perry. "There you go . . ."

By now the crowd was laughing harder.

Then the moderator, John Harwood, committed an act of unintentional yet devastating cruelty. He prolonged Perry's misery by asking: "Seriously, is the EPA the one you were talking about?"

"No, sir, no, sir," admitted Perry. "We were talking about the agencies of government—the EPA needs to be rebuilt. There's no doubt about that."

"But you can't," Harwood interrupted, "but you can't name the third one?"

The governor kept trying. "The third agency of government I would—I would do away with, Education, the . . ."

His fellow candidates were still trying to help: "Commerce?"

"Commerce and, let's see. I can't," said Perry. "The third one, I can't. Sorry. Oops."

Oops.

But Perry's a scrappy contender who doesn't like to leave things unsettled. Later in the debate he interrupted one of his own answers to announce: "By the way, that was the Department of Energy I was reaching for a while ago."

So it only made sense that Donald Trump—who got some unsolicited debate advice from the always enthusiastic Perry during the 2016 fall campaign (when discussing the fine points of policy with Hillary Clinton, the Texan suggested, "Peel her skin off")—would appoint Perry as energy secretary.

Never mind that those who know Perry did not see him as even remotely prepared for the position. Even among Lone Star State observers who liked Perry, there was widespread agreement with the assessment of Calvin Jillson, a professor of political science at Southern Methodist University in Texas who told the *New York Times*: "Rick Perry was pitch-perfect for Texas politics. He has very close ties to the oil industry. He is about 'the Texas way'—low taxes, low regulation. But none of that gives him the depth of knowledge needed for running the Energy Department."

Famously forgetful. Woefully unprepared. Totally tied to the industries he was supposed to regulate. Nice glasses. Turns out we all know a little about good old Rick Perry. But not many folks know this about Rick Perry: he's a pioneering champion of privatized nuclear waste disposal.

During Perry's tenure as governor, the *Texas Observer* recalls that he was a "Cheerleader for a Nuclear Waste Company."

Not long after he won his first election for governor in 2002, Perry signed legislation that cleared the way for the privatization of radioactive waste disposal in Texas.

The company that stood to benefit from that legislation was Waste Control Specialists (WCS), an outfit owned by the late Dallas billionaire Harold Simmons. Political observers remember Simmons as the funder of those 2004 Swift Boat ads that attacked Democratic presidential nominee John Kerry for doing something Donald Trump could not get around to—serving in the military during the Vietnam War. But the Swift Boat ads were just a freelance distraction from Simmons's political occupation: advancing the career of Rick Perry.

"Simmons was the No. 2 individual donor to Perry's gubernatorial campaigns, with contributions totaling $1.2 million," noted the *Observer*. "Perry's administration seemed to reciprocate," the magazine added, explaining that "in 2008 and 2009, his Texas Commission on Environmental Quality (TCEQ) appointees granted Waste Control two licenses to handle radioactive waste. One allowed Waste Control to take 3,776 canisters of radioactive residues from NL Industries, a Department of Energy (DOE) contractor that Simmons also owned. The second one gave the company the authority to bury a wide variety of state and federal radioactive waste. The company's planned West Texas dump in Andrews County was so dangerously close to nearby aquifers that three state employees reviewing the application resigned."

People who worried about the aquifers may not have been happy with Rick Perry. But people at Waste Control Specialists were thrilled with the governor. "No other state has licensed a nuclear waste facility like this, and it was all done on Governor Perry's watch," Charles McDonald, a spokesman for the corporation, told the *New York Times*. "He really understands this stuff."

Okay, so Rick Perry may not always remember whether he wants to maintain the Department of Energy (after his nomination to head the agency, he said he was learning a lot about the great work it does), but he does know how to arrange for nuclear waste burial services by a major campaign donor.

Why does this matter? The "DOE continues to focus on all things nuclear," begins the latest fact sheet from the federal Department of Energy's Office of Nuclear Energy. "Nearly two thirds of our budget still goes to maintaining America's nuclear deterrent and cleaning up the legacy of past nuclear arms development."

The fact sheet is titled "The Path Forward for Nuclear Waste Disposal."

That's right, as energy secretary, Rick Perry will be in charge of nuclear waste disposal.

Most of the DOE's $30 billion annual budget goes to maintaining the nation's nuclear stockpile and updating nuclear production. It also has a big role in monitoring, and hopefully preventing, nuclear proliferation. And, as the agency notes, "the Nuclear Waste Policy Act of 1982 (NWPA), which provides the basic policy framework for U.S. efforts to manage nuclear waste" charges the DOE with determining what to do with a whole lot of highly radioactive garbage. The waste is now stored at the power plants where it was produced, but the neighbors are restless. So the DOE has the job of figuring out how to take charge of the trash, collect it and store it in a single secure location. These are immense responsibilities with awesome consequences if anything goes wrong. President Obama took them seriously. He went with the best and the brightest, literally, when he chose energy secretaries. His first was Stephen Chu, who won the Nobel Prize in physics. His second was Ernest J. Moniz, the former chairman of the Massachusetts Institute of Technology (MIT) physics department (where he kept watch on the linear accelerator at MIT's Laboratory for Nuclear Science).

Rick Perry never directed a linear accelerator program or won a Nobel Prize. Nor has he ever been thought of as an expert on climate science, green technologies or any of the other issues that might concern an energy secretary, a fact noted with some discomfort by groups that monitor the work of the Department of Energy. "If the consequences weren't so dire, it would be humorous that the Senate just confirmed Rick Perry to lead the Department of Energy—the agency he couldn't recall by name when asserting he wanted to eliminate it," Sierra Club executive director Michael Brune observed

after the Senate voted 62–37 to give the Texan the job on March 2, 2017. "Beyond that, Perry's financial interests in major energy projects run counter to his responsibility to manage the Department of Energy's activities impartially. The Department of Energy is now in the hands of someone who promotes dirty fossil fuels rather than the advancing clean energy market all the while ignoring the climate crisis."

"Unlike the preeminent physicists who ran the department for the last eight years, Perry lacks the knowledge and experience to run the DOE," says Damon Moglen, a senior strategic advisor to Friends of the Earth. "The absurdity of trusting former-Gov. Perry to clean up the nation's nuclear weapons facilities speaks to the clueless nature of the Trump administration."

But perhaps the Trump administration is not so clueless as it seems. Perhaps Perry's "experience" could be just what is required by an administration that sees as its mission the "deconstruction of the administrative state." Where better to show a true commitment to Steve Bannon's mission than by bartering off responsibility for nuclear waste to the highest bidder—or the highest campaign donor?

Perry could do just that.

In 2016, the *Texas Tribune* reported that Waste Control Specialists had applied for a federal license to accept "spent nuclear reactor fuel, much of it highly radioactive" at a "temporary storage site" on the grounds of its fourteen-thousand-acre site that Perry helped it get going as governor. "The application seeks a 40-year license to take in up to 40,000 metric tons of higher level waste in eight phases, with the possibility for 20-year renewals going forward," reported the *Tribune*.

There were skeptics. Friends of the Earth reviewed the details of the proposal and dubbed it as a plan for a "dump" that "would be little more than a parking lot on which casks of the highly radioactive waste would have to be stored."

"The WCS location is close to the Ogallala Aquifer, the nation's largest aquifer, which lies beneath eight states. What if our water becomes contaminated?" said Karen Hadden, director of the Texas-based Sustainable Energy & Economic Development coalition. "Rather than store this radioactive waste on an exposed parking lot in West Texas, it should remain at the power plant where it was generated or nearby until a scientifically viable isolation system for permanent disposal can be designed and built."

Tom Smith, the director of Public Citizen's Texas office, picked up on the transportation theme when he said: "This plan is all risk and no reward, not only for the states of Texas and New Mexico, but for the whole country, and it should be halted immediately. People across the country should be concerned because putting this waste on the nation's railways would invite disaster. The amount of radioactive waste on a single train car would contain as much plutonium as the bomb dropped on Nagasaki. Radioactive waste moving through highly populated cities across the country could be targeted for sabotage by terrorists or could cause catastrophe in the event of an accident."

As it happens, accidents can happen. "In June 2016, two trains in Texas collided head-on at 65 miles per hour, creating a huge fireball and causing at least two deaths," noted Hadden. "What if one of these trains had been hauling radioactive waste? Real world accidents sometimes exceed modeling. The risky transport of radioactive waste across the country and the plan to dump it on people in West Texas without the resources to fight back should be halted immediately. We do not consent to being put at radioactive risk."

No need to fret, said Rod Baltzer, the president and CEO of Waste Control Specialists, who explained that "we've got a unique environment and a unique state, and I think they understand the risks and the technical challenges. But they also know that with the proper regulatory oversight and the proper technology that you can overcome those."

So who would provide that "proper regulatory oversight"? The Nuclear Regulatory Commission officially accepted Waste Control Specialists' application two weeks after Donald Trump became president. That approval began a review process that is expected to conclude in about two years. And here's the interesting part: "for the project to go forward, the Department of Energy would have to assume the title to, and liability for, the spent nuclear fuel stored at the site," explained the *Texas Tribune*.

Congress may have to weigh in with a few winks and nods. But Public Citizen's Tom Smith takes us to the bottom line: "The U.S. Department of Energy will write the rules that will determine where this waste can be stored."

Someone from MIT's Laboratory for Nuclear Science? A winner of the Nobel Prize in physics? Nope.

After President Trump announced his nominee to serve as energy secretary during the term when the question of whether the disposal of nuclear waste will be privatized, Waste Control Specialists spokesman Chuck McDonald announced that "from our perspective, from the perspective of the nuclear radioactive waste disposal industry, it's a benefit to have Rick Perry's experience at the Department of Energy." Oops.

— 38 —

THE SECRETARY OF CORPORATE AGRIBUSINESS

Sonny Perdue

Secretary of Agriculture

There is a good argument to be made that Donald Trump, New Yorker from birth and urban to his core, did not even know the United States had a secretary of agriculture when he decided to run for president. Though Trump swept farm country in the election of 2016, winning more than 90 percent of the nation's rural counties, that was not because the Republican presidential nominee offered a coherent program for the renewal of regions that have been battered not just by agribusiness consolidation but by the deindustrialization of small towns and small cities. Trump ran well because the Democratic Party of Franklin Roosevelt and the Agricultural Adjustment Administration, the Farm Security Administration, the Civilian Conservation Corps and rural electrification forgot how to speak to farm families and voters in small-town America. Hillary Clinton did not even show up to campaign in key farm states, while Trump made the trip. There is no evidence to suggest, however, that he paid attention to anything but his own voice.

So it was that, as the president-elect and his transition team "staffed up," there was a glaring omission. No one was nominated to head the Department of Agriculture, a sprawling agency with a $155 billion budget and a staff of more than a hundred thousand, in the immediate aftermath of the election. November passed and no one was named. December passed and no one was named. As Trump's inauguration approached in January, media outlets began to note that no one had been designated to lead the department that oversees

everything from rural development to soil conservation to natural resources preservation to food safety to food stamps to nutrition labeling to determinations about whether consumers have a right to know whether they are being sold genetically engineered food.

Iowa senator Chuck Grassley, a Republican who was embarrassingly loyal to Trump on most issues, tweeted about how it was frustrating to read about the failure of the Trump team to accomplish the "PRETTY SIMPLE" task of picking a secretary of agriculture. Finally, one day before Trump's inauguration, the president picked a career politician who had spent much of his adult life in Atlanta to fill the post. Once the announcement was made, however, Trump promptly forgot about the nominee and the position. Even as Trump and his aides complained (and complained and complained) about Senate Democrats "slow-walking" the president's nominees for cabinet and subcabinet posts, the Trump administration never bothered to send its nominee's paperwork to the Senate in January, or February or the first weeks of March. "They don't seem to have a reason as to why his name hasn't come up," griped Senator Grassley as the clock ticked onward. Vox headlined a March 8 assessment of the mess: "The weird mystery of the Trump administration's agriculture secretary vacancy: Sonny Perdue's stalled confirmation, not explained because nobody knows what's happening."

There was no mystery. Sonny Perdue was an afterthought, a nominee nominated for a post to which someone had to be nominated. He met the baseline standard established by the Trump transition team ("a mild-mannered and reliably conservative politician who campaigned vigorously for Trump," as *Modern Farmer* magazine noted) and he had the added bonus of being very well liked by the bosses of Monsanto, Conagra and the other agribusiness combines that maintained a particularly pecuniary interest in the department he was slated to head. But Perdue excited zero enthusiasm among small farmers and the tens of millions of nonfarmers whose lives are influenced by the Department of Agriculture.

"We'd love to see Perdue really support rural farmers and Americans, by supporting the farmers who are farming in a responsible way. But as Naomi Klein said, the Trump cabinet is a 'corporate coup d'état.' Perdue, from all appearances, fits right in with the rest of the millionaire and billionaire corporate cronies tapped by Trump to run the country," observed the Organic Consumers Association (OCA), which noted that Perdue was a millionaire businessman, not a working farmer. "Perdue may have impressed Trump by showing up for his job interview wearing a backpack and a tie with little tractors on it," explained the OCA assessment. "But most farmers are smart enough to see through Perdue's phony concern for rural farmers, no matter how he dresses it up."

Tom Colicchio, the co-founder of Food Policy Action, was equally dismissive. "Sonny Perdue's record on food policy is light on substance and poor on action," said Colicchio. "We need strong leadership to reform our food policy, promote affordable, nutritious and safe food, fight hunger, safeguard our lands and clean water, and protect our farmers and farm workers, not someone who is weak on oversight and in the pocket of Big Ag."

"While he may have grown up on a family farm," observed *Modern Farmer* writer Brian Barth, "Perdue is clearly more of an industrial agriculture and agribusiness guy."

In reality, he's more of a "politician guy" who has made a lot of money moving back and forth through the revolving door between elective offices and corporate suites. As Georgia's Republican governor, Barth notes: "Perdue was not known for a focus on agriculture or rural issues." In response to what the *Atlanta Journal Constitution* referred to as an "epic drought, threatening the region's water supply," Sonny Perdue urged Georgians to pray for rain.

To the extent that Perdue caught the attention of a Trump transition team packed with fossil-fuel industry advocates, it may have been because of his attacks on the Environmental Protection Agency and the Clean Air Act and his mockery of what he once termed "ridiculous" coverage of climate change. "It's become a running joke among the public, and liberals have lost all credibility when it comes to climate science because their arguments have become so ridiculous and so obviously disconnected from reality," the Georgia conservative wrote in a 2014 *National Review* article. Or, perhaps, the alt-right contingent on the Trump team was excited

by an aspect of Perdue's gubernatorial record highlighted by Think Progress: "As Governor, Perdue delighted neo-Confederates by signing legislation permanently making April 'Confederate History and Heritage Month' in the Peach State and issued proclamations that honored 'the more than 90,000 brave men and women who served the Confederate States of America,' and falsely suggested that 'many African-Americans both free and slave' voluntarily served in the Confederate armed forces."

It was certainly not Perdue's ethics that gained him a job overseeing one of the largest agencies in the federal government. "In his campaign, President Trump promised to 'drain the swamp' in Washington. But his nominee for secretary of agriculture, former Georgia Gov. Sonny Perdue, is mired in ethical lapses, self-dealing and back-room deals that raise troubling questions about his fitness to run the department," observed Colin O'Neil, the agriculture policy director of the Environmental Working Group (EWG), whose investigation of Trump's Department of Agriculture pick revealed that, as governor, Perdue:

- refused to put his businesses in a blind trust;
- signed state tax legislation that gave him a $100,000 tax break on a land deal;
- received gifts from lobbyists after signing a sweeping order to ban such gifts;
- filled state agencies and boards with business partners and political donors;
- allocated state funds to projects that benefited companies he created after his time in office.

Reviews of Perdue's record focused particular attention on his habit of accepting substantial farm subsidies—more than $278,000—while serving in Atlanta as a legislator and governor. "In his first two years as governor, Perdue received a sizable payment through the peanut buyout program, as well as direct payments for wheat—both likely as a result of him being a landowner, not necessarily a farmer. Although he had a financial interest in farms, there is scant evidence that he was 'actively engaged' in farming, which is now an eligibility requirement for subsidy recipients," wrote O'Neil, who asked: "Was Perdue like thousands of other city slickers whose land ownership made them eligible to receive subsidies that should be flowing to family farmers?"

It was not just Perdue's city-slicker stylings that troubled the folks who took the former governor's nomination more seriously than did the Trump administration. It was the Georgian's very long and very intricate alliance with corporate agribusiness, not just as a politician doing the bidding of corporate interests but as an actual living, breathing corporate interest. "Perdue has started or been associated with well over a dozen agribusiness companies and limited liability corporations: Houston Fertilizer and Grain Co. in 1976; Perdue, Inc., a trucking company, in 1993; Perdue Family Limited Partnership, LLC in 1996; and AGrowStar, LLC, a grain buying company, in 1999," recounted the EWG report "Trump Agriculture Nominee Brings the Swamp to Washington." The report noted that "in his last year as governor, Perdue's attorneys created four companies, including Perdue Business Holdings, Inc.; Perdue Management Holdings, LLC; Perdue Properties, LLC; and Perdue Real Estate Holdings, LLLP. Since leaving office, he has created at least two new companies—Perdue Partners, LLC, and Perdue Consulting Group—and he also serves as secretary for the Georgia Agribusiness Council."

Perdue has set himself up as what *Modern Farmer* refers to as "among the many middlemen in the international commodity foods chain." That's rewarding for Perdue but it is not so good for working farmers or rural communities.

A *New York Times* assessment of Perdue was headlined "Ethical Lapses Trail President's Nominee for Agriculture Department." Ethical lapses are always concerning, but they are especially concerning when they are revealed in a nominee to serve as secretary of agriculture, a position that has so much direct authority over decisions regarding what interests are served by the department's massive budget and its extensive regulatory apparatus.

Describing the Perdue selection as "a clear signal that [the Trump administration] plans to prioritize corporate interests over

 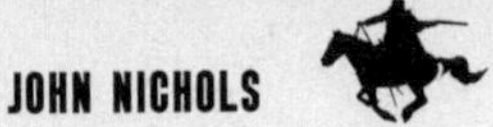

communities—in this case rural, agricultural communities," Pesticide Action Network policy director Kristin Schafer complained that "as a politician in Georgia, Perdue consistently received significant donations from large agribusiness interests. We expect him to cater to giant industrial producers—even though they represent a small percentage of growers across the country that USDA should be serving. The well-being of small family farmers—particularly farmers of color, women farmers and the fast-growing segment of agriculture pursuing sustainable production—will undoubtedly continue to be overlooked." The watchdogs at *New York* magazine blog *Grub Street* explained that Perdue "also took about $330,000 in contributions from Monsanto and other agribusinesses for his campaigns" and added that "the GMO lobby group Biotechnology Innovation Organization even named him its 2009 Governor of the Year."

The Organic Consumers Association's assessment of the Perdue record is damning: "He supports factory farms, pesticides and genetically engineered crops. In 2009, he signed a bill into law that blocked local communities in Georgia from regulating factory farms to address animal cruelty, pollution or any other hazard." Under Trump and Perdue, the group suggests, the Department of Agriculture "will likely let companies like Monsanto dictate food, agriculture and environmental policy."

Close ties to corporate agribusiness put Sonny Perdue on the wrong side of a host of food and farm issues when he was governor. He erred, invariably and aggressively, on the side of bigness, consolidation and the factory farming that diminishes our food system rather than diversity, competition and the family farming that realizes the mission of a Department of Agriculture that veteran food and farm writer Kelsey Gee reminds us was founded to "procure, propagate, and distribute" safe and healthy food for all Americans. "If you're curious what's in store for food & agriculture in President Trump's America, interesting to watch Georgia's evolution since 2003," Gee wrote after Trump named his secretary of agriculture. When Perdue was elected governor of that state in 2002, it had 49,311 farm operations. The year after Perdue finished his tenure, it had 42,257 operations. "That's a 17 percent drop in farm operations, compared to a nationwide downturn of just 1 percent," noted Gee.

While sales were up, the measure of diversity and small-farm resilience declined in Perdue's Georgia at a dramatically more rapid rate than it did nationally.

"There are two ideas of government," William Jennings Bryan explained 120 years before Sonny Perdue was named as the nation's thirty-first secretary of agriculture. "There are those who believe that, if you will only legislate to make the well-to-do prosperous, their prosperity will leak through on those below. The Democratic idea, however, has been that if you legislate to make the masses prosperous, their prosperity will find its way up through every class which rests upon them. You come to us and tell us that the great cities are in favor of the gold standard; we reply that the great cities rest upon our broad and fertile prairies. Burn down your cities and leave our farms, and your cities will spring up again as if by magic; but destroy our farms and the grass will grow in the streets of every city in the country."

What Bryan said remains true. The great cities still rest upon our broad and fertile prairies. And, in an age of climate change and automation, of ill-thought globalization and constant dislocation, the evolution of small farms and small towns matters more to the future than ever before. Unfortunately, in debates over rural life and rural development, Sonny Perdue has always favored the policies that make the well-to-do prosperous and barter the future off to Monsanto.

— 39 —

THE WEED WHACKER

Ajit Pai

Federal Communications Commission Chairman

Donald Trump, who has never been shy about demanding that the media do his bidding, now has the power to shape the rules that define the future of newspapers, broadcast media and the Internet. Trump's appointees are already employing the regulatory-agency equivalent of executive orders to gut programs that would ensure net neutrality, expand broadband access, guard against consolidation of media ownership and enforce disclosure of sources of spending on political ads. "This is what government by billionaires and special interests looks like," says Michael Copps, who served for eight years on the Federal Communications Commission (FCC) and completed his tenure as the FCC's acting chairman.

Within days of assuming the presidency in January 2017, Trump named Ajit Pai as his FCC chair. A former associate general counsel for the Verizon telecommunications conglomerate, Pai was one of the FCC's five commissioners during the Obama era. In that role, he often dissented against consumer-friendly regulations, robust market competition and diversification of media ownership. Now, as FCC chair, Pai has moved rapidly to undo Obama's FCC legacy, reversing or weakening measures that had begun to restore the commission's commitment to regulating on behalf of the public, rather than the corporate, interest.

Pai speaks Trump's language, promising to "fire up the weed whacker" to shred regulations that media corporations and the right-wing media echo chamber have long opposed. He also mimics Trump's disdain for democratic processes and procedures. Pai and his aides have employed "delegated authority"—a claim of power to act without public input, hearings or votes by the full commission—to advance their agenda. In one case, they killed the FCC's guidance to broadcasters on "shared service" agreements, an initiative to guard against media companies operating two or more stations in markets where there is supposed to be competition. In a second case, Pai pulled the FCC's set-top-box proceeding, which would have brought competition to the cable market by enabling independent manufacturers to sell the set-top boxes that otherwise are provided by cable companies.

Pai also undermined a program to protect prisoners from profiteering off their calls home and scrapped a plan to expand broadband access for low-income families. "Rather than working to close the digital divide," Mignon Clyburn, a Democratic commissioner who remained on the FCC after Trump assumed the presidency, said of the latter move, "this action widens the gap." Pai rejected a report from the FCC's Homeland Security Bureau on cybersecurity risk reduction, prompting FCC watchdog Dana Floberg of Free Press to accuse him of "willfully ignoring reports and analyses that don't bolster his preferred agenda of scaling back the FCC's congressionally granted power." Pai also withdrew a requirement that noncommercial stations file data that helped the FCC monitor the diversity of media ownership, and he set aside orders that made it easier for the FCC to sanction broadcasters that violate the agency's political advertising disclosure rules.

Pai has been an outspoken foe of net neutrality, the first amendment of the Internet that guarantees the free flow of information without censorship or corporate favoritism. With Trump's backing, and that of a Congress whose Republican leaders rarely say no to telecom giants, the new FCC chair moved before the finish of the new president's first one hundred days to throttle digital democracy, outlining what the *New York Times* described as "a sweeping plan to loosen the government's oversight of high-speed internet providers, a rebuke of a landmark policy approved two years ago to ensure that all online content is treated the same by the companies that deliver broadband service to Americans." Former FCC commissioner Copps warned that "by reopening the FCC's historic 2015 Open

Internet Order, the FCC is jeopardizing core protections for online free speech and competition. Chairman Pai appears more interested in currying favor with cable and telecom industry lobbyists than in serving the millions of Americans who wrote and called to urge the commission, during the original rule-making, to provide strong protections against online blocking, throttling, or censorship."

"Chairman Pai is kissing the ring of the Big Money lobbyists who too often call the shots in the Trump Administration," declared Copps, who now works with Common Cause and other groups seeking to defend an open Internet. "Ending net neutrality would be a body blow to the open dialogue upon which successful self-government depends. It would be a red light for democracy and a green light for cable and telecom giants to control where we go and what we do on the internet."

The assault on net neutrality was not the only body blow to the democratic discourse proposed by the Trump administration. Through formal actions by what will be a Republican-controlled FCC for as long as Trump is president, and by the granting of waivers that allow corporations to get around cross-ownership and joint-sales rules that were designed to maintain competition in local television markets, the FCC could end up facilitating media mergers and monopolies at the national and local levels that diminish competition and narrow the debate. It's not just the Trump's FCC that is out to downsize the discourse. In addition to zeroing out funding for the National Endowment for the Arts and the National Endowment for the Humanities, the Trump team's initial budget blueprint called for cutting all funding for the Corporation for Public Broadcasting (CPB). At present, the CPB funnels roughly $445 million a year of federal money to the nearly fifteen hundred public radio and television stations of the NPR and PBS networks, as well as to community stations around the country. A tiny portion of the federal budget, this $445 million makes a life-and-death difference for rural and small-town radio and TV stations that are indispensable sources of news and intelligent programming.

That's the point, of course. Trump ally and former Speaker of the House Newt Gingrich has long attacked public and community broadcasters that provide an alternative to the dust storm of alternative facts that has blown across America since the Gingrich-backed Telecommunications Act of 1996. That measure, a classic example of what goes wrong when corporations and self-serving politicians of both parties write the rules to serve campaign donors rather than citizens, unleashed a wave of ownership consolidation that shuttered radio newsrooms, silenced local talk and welcomed the big-media syndication frenzy that made Rush Limbaugh ubiquitous and coverage of state capitols and school boards scarce.

At a time when the United States should be supercharging public and community media to prevent development of news deserts where the only "information" comes from partisan corporate outlets, Trump and White House chief strategist Steve Bannon are dusting off the playbooks of the 1990s. Schemes to weaken competition and diversity, to create one-size-fits-all "newsrooms," to set-up digital fast lanes for subsidized content and slow lanes for democratic discourse—all were proposed back then. But they were beaten back by popular movements that built remarkable left-right coalitions and forged innovative legal strategies that surprised their wealthy and powerful opponents. When the George W. Bush administration advanced a media-consolidation agenda, the outcry from 3 million Americans who contacted the FCC played a critical role in preventing it, according to then-commissioner Copps. When the FCC asked for public comment on a controversial net neutrality proposal in late 2014, they received nearly 4 million responses, almost all supporting stronger federal regulation. The voice of the people was heard and, in February 2015, the FCC voted in favor of robust net neutrality, and the robust democracy that might eventually extend from it.

Now, everything that the people accomplished could be undone by an FCC chairman who once represented telecommunications conglomerates as a lawyer and who now represents them as a regulator. "They're coming for all of it," Free Press president Craig Aaron says of the Trump administration's agenda. "They're coming for net neutrality. They're coming for every protection for citizens and consumers."

— 40 —

THE FORECLOSURE KING

Steven Mnuchin

Secretary of the Treasury

The secretary of the treasury is not a bookkeeper. There is no requirement that the head of the department created by Alexander Hamilton keep tabs on the nation's finances wearing a green eyeshade, with one hand hovering over a calculator at all times. But there is some general expectation that the secretary of the treasury should have a facility with numbers.

So it was a little troubling when Steven Mnuchin, the man Donald Trump tapped to serve as the seventy-seventh secretary of the treasury, forgot to disclose $95 million of his own assets on Senate Finance Committee disclosure documents, and also neglected to mention that he was a director of a tax-avoiding investment fund located in the Cayman Islands. And another one in Anguilla.

"I think as you all can appreciate, filling out these government forms is quite complicated," explained Mnuchin.

So complicated that Mnuchin never discovered errors involving an amount of money comparable with the entire budgets of several Pacific Island nations. "This was not self-corrected," noted Oregon senator Ron Wyden, the ranking Democratic member of the Senate Finance Committee, where Mnuchin appeared to say "my bad" on the day before Trump was inaugurated. "The only reason it came to light was my staff found it and told you that it had to be corrected," explained an exasperated Wyden.

"Any oversight was unintentional," said Mnuchin, who marveled about "the amount of paperwork" that was required to snag a cabinet post.

Well, gosh, yes, filling our government forms and keeping track of large sums of money can get kind of complicated. But there's also kind of an expectation in that regard for the man or woman who is entrusted with responsibility for a Department of the Treasury where the secretary is expected to serve as "the principal economic advisor to the President" and to play "a critical role in policy-making by bringing an economic and government financial policy perspective to issues facing the government."

"The Secretary," the agency explains, "is responsible for formulating and recommending domestic and international financial, economic, and tax policy, participating in the formulation of broad fiscal policies that have general significance for the economy, and managing the public debt. The Secretary oversees the activities of the Department in carrying out its major law enforcement responsibilities; in serving as the financial agent for the United States Government; and in manufacturing coins and currency. The Chief Financial Officer of the government, the Secretary serves as Chairman Pro Tempore of the President's Economic Policy Council, Chairman of the Boards and Managing Trustee of the Social Security and Medicare Trust Funds, and as U.S. Governor of the International Monetary Fund, the International Bank for Reconstruction and Development, the Inter-American Development Bank, the Asian Development Bank, and the European Bank for Reconstruction and Development."

That's bound to involve government forms.

Lots of paperwork. Quite complicated.

Mnuchin's inability to master the basics should have raised red flags for the Senate, which has a duty to make sure that nominees are up to the tasks they are given. But Utah senator Orrin Hatch, the chairman of the Senate Finance Committee, which has the largest jurisdiction of any committee in either House of Congress, overseeing more than 50 percent of the federal budget, was unconcerned.

"Objectively speaking, I don't believe anyone can reasonably argue that Mr. Mnuchin is unqualified for the position," chirped Hatch. "If the confirmation process focused mainly on the question

of a nominee's qualifications, there would be little, if any, opposition to Mr. Mnuchin's nomination."

Hatch and the Republicans suspended the rules to dismiss opposition objections and approved Mnuchin's nomination 14–0 on February 1. Within two weeks, the full Senate had approved Mnuchin on a 53–47 vote, and the guy who we are assured is a whiz with numbers, as long as the forms aren't too complicated, was secretary of the treasury.

The only thing is that, despite what Hatch said, there was a powerful sense on the part of serious observers of financial issues, and of existential threats to the republic, that Mnuchin was not just unqualified. He was uniquely unqualified.

Yes, Trump's pick was a second-generation Goldman Sachs executive who had parlayed his good fortune into a career in high finance and low entertainment (a Mnuchin "side business," RatPac-Dune Entertainment, financed films like *Storks* and *Get Hard* and *The Conjuring 2*). He lived large: the twenty-one-thousand-square-foot Mnuchin mansion in Bel Air was valued at $26.5 million. And he was worth a lot of money: $400 million—oops, strike that, $495 million. He had also, as someone who had once been identified mainly with Democrats, served ably as the national finance chairman of his friend Donald Trump's 2016 presidential campaign.

But Steve Mnuchin really isn't a swamp-draining kind of guy. Wyden called him "greedy" and "unethical." Illinois senator Tammy Duckworth objected that "whether illegally foreclosing on thousands of families, skirting the law with offshore tax havens or helping design tactics that contributed to the 2008 financial crisis, Steve Mnuchin made a career—and millions of dollars—pioneering increasingly deceptive and predatory ways to rob hardworking Americans of their savings and homes." New Jersey senator Robert Menendez said: "He was part of the cadre of corporate raiders that brought our economy to its knees."

Tough crowd.

Unfortunately, the critics were right. Mnuchin, the Goldman Sachs kingpin who in the 2000s branched out into hedge fund management, hit the big time when he led an investment group that bought the California-based residential lender IndyMac, which had been placed in receivership by the FDIC and owned $23.5 billion in commercial loans, mortgages and mortgage-backed securities, for a deep discount. They renamed it OneWest Bank. And then Steven Mnuchin's bank did some very bad things.

CNN reported that "OneWest developed a reputation as a 'Foreclosure Machine,' and Mnuchin himself has been dubbed the 'Foreclosure King.'" After a memo from the office of the California attorney general alleged that OneWest engaged in "widespread misconduct" to boost foreclosures, including the backdating of mortgage documents, the network noted: "The nonprofit watchdog Campaign for Accountability called on the Department of Justice to investigate OneWest for 'using potentially illegal tactics to foreclose on as many as 80,000 California homes.'"

A ProPublica investigation revealed that "since the financial crisis, OneWest, through Financial Freedom, has conducted a disproportionate number of the nation's reverse mortgage foreclosures." ProPublica found numerous examples where Financial Freedom "had foreclosed for legally questionable reasons. The company served several other homeowners at their homes to let them know they were being sued for not occupying their homes. In Florida, a shortfall of only $0.27 led to a foreclosure attempt. In Atlanta, the company sought to foreclose on a widow after her husband's death, but backed down when a legal aid attorney sued, citing federal law that allowed the surviving spouse to remain in the home."

Alys Cohen, a staff attorney for the National Consumer Law Center in Washington, DC, reviewed the details from Mnuchin's tenure and said: "It appears their business approach is scorched earth, in a way that doesn't serve communities, homeowners or the taxpayer."

How scorched? A California Reinvestment Coalition analysis determined that OneWest was responsible for 39 percent of foreclosures on government-backed reverse mortgages nationwide from 2009 to 2014, yet it serviced only around 17 percent of those loans.

None of the revelations made Mnuchin sound like the right person to be heading a federal department that takes as its mission stewardship of U.S. economic and financial systems. Describing Mnuchin as someone who "spent two decades at Goldman Sachs helping the bank peddle the same kind of mortgage products that blew up the economy and sucked down billions in taxpayer bailout money, before he moved on to run a bank that was famous for aggressively foreclosing on families," Massachusetts senator Elizabeth Warren said: "His selection as Treasury Secretary should send shivers down the spine of every American who got hit hard by the financial crisis."

Warren was even more upset when the *Columbus Dispatch* revealed that Mnuchin's testimony to the Finance Committee that his firm did not engage in the controversial practice of robo-signing mortgage paperwork (signing stacks of foreclosure documents without properly reviewing them) was, um, untrue. The paper reported widespread evidence of aggressive foreclosure practices, including robo-signing in the Buckeye state. "The guy is just lying. There's no other way to say it," said Bill Faith, executive director of the Coalition on Homelessness and Housing in Ohio. "People were bamboozled into signing these mortgages," Faith added. "We watched this train wreck happen. It's been devastating, not only to the people who got caught in this kind of scheme, but also to people who happened to live in the neighborhood . . . It's scary that he's going to be treasury secretary."

The conflict over Mnuchin's truthfulness had some skeptics wondering about whether the befuddled nominee really was confused by those financial disclosure forms. But there was no question regarding the robo-signing testimony. "You know, in this town nobody wants to use the word I'm going to use," said Ohio senator Sherrod Brown when it came time to vote on the Mnuchin nomination. "They want to say it was a half-truth or it was not quite right or fabricated. No. What Mr. Mnuchin did is he lied."

"Mnuchin profited off of kicking people out of their homes and then gave false testimony about his bank's abusive practices," said Brown. "He cannot be trusted to make decisions about policies as personal to working Ohioans as their taxes and retirement."

Former Ohio attorney general Marc Dann worries a lot about that. Dann specializes in representing the victims of wrongdoing by big banks, and he says he is troubled that a man whose firm was a "major offender" that "caused unbelievable devastation in people's lives" is now in a position to undermine the 2010 Dodd-Frank Wall Street Reform and Consumer Protection Act that allowed victimized borrowers to sue reckless and irresponsible banks.

Dann is right to worry. In written testimony to the Senate, Mnuchin argued that "it has been over six years since the passage of Dodd-Frank and it seems like an appropriate time to review all of the regulations from Dodd-Frank to understand their impact on the market, investors, small businesses and economic growth."

Mnuchin says he wants to "strip back parts of Dodd-Frank" because, the *New York Times* reports, as with those financial disclosure forms he had so much trouble filling out, the secretary of the treasury finds all those regulations on banks and protections for consumers "too complicated."

—41—

THE FOX GUARDING THE HENHOUSE

Jay Clayton

Chairman, Securities and Exchange Commission

When Donald Trump announced his nominee to head the powerful Securities and Exchange Commission (SEC), watchdogs started to wonder whether the president had confused his mission. Instead of "draining the swamp" of Wall Street–tied influence peddlers, he seemed to be stocking it with even bigger fish. Trump's SEC pick was Jay Clayton, a lawyer for the most powerful investment bankers on Wall Street who listed his specialties as "public and private mergers and acquisitions transactions, capital markets offerings, regulatory and enforcement proceedings, and other matters where multidisciplinary advice and experience is valued."

"Jay Clayton, the Sullivan & Cromwell partner tapped by Trump, outlined his clients—and his potential conflicts—in a filing to the U.S. Office of Government Ethics that he signed in January," explained a Bloomberg assessment when Trump announced the nomination. "If confirmed by the Senate, Clayton would have to recuse himself for one year from matters involving [his law firm] Sullivan & Cromwell and companies he represented. He also would be barred from ever weighing in on a specific business deal or an investigation that he worked on as a lawyer. At least one of Clayton's clients, Valeant Pharmaceuticals International Inc., has disclosed that it's being investigated by the SEC. Pershing Square, another Clayton client, is among Valeant's biggest investors."

The recusals were a serious concern for senators who thought it might be useful to have a fully functional SEC led by an engaged and involved chair. "Holding Wall Street firms accountable is a major job of the SEC's mission and the SEC chair needs to be able to participate in those enforcement actions . . . Not on the sidelines when former clients and Wall Street firms are able to skate free," complained Massachusetts senator Elizabeth Warren, who told the nominee when he appeared before the Senate Banking Committee that "the conflicts raised a very serious concern about your nomination."

Other senators were concerned about what Clayton might do when he wasn't recused.

Senator Sherrod Brown, the Ohio Democrat who has made it his mission to take on the power of the banking combines and investment houses that are supposed to be regulated by the SEC, said: "It's hard to see how an attorney who's spent his career helping Wall Street beat the rap will keep President-elect Trump's promise to stop big banks and hedge funds from 'getting away with murder.'"

Over at *Rolling Stone*, Matt Taibbi argued that the elephant in the room was wearing an "I work for Wall Street" T-shirt. Clayton did not have a record of cracking down on bad banking practices; he had a record of helping banks avoid crackdowns. "He represented Goldman Sachs when the firm received a $5 billion capital infusion from Warren Buffet during the September 2008 meltdown. He also represented Barclays during its malodorous acquisition of the assets of Lehman Brothers, an episode one lawyer described to me years ago as 'the greatest bank robbery you never heard of,'" wrote Taibbi. "That Clayton has been a devoted legal slave to the usual Wall Street monsters over the years is obviously concerning, though not terribly unusual."

Obviously not.

On April 4, the Banking Committee voted 15–8 to recommend Clayton's confirmation, with three Democrats—Jon Tester of Montana, Mark Warner of Virginia and Heidi Heitkamp of North Dakota—joining the Republicans in supporting Trump's man. A month later, the full Senate backed Clayton by a 61–37 margin, with ten Democrats joining fifty-one Republicans in voting to approve a nominee who a former congressional aide told Taibbi would serve as "the most financially conflicted SEC chairman in history."

— 42 —

SWIMMING IN THE GOVERNMENT SACHS SWAMP

Gary Cohn

Director of the National Economic Council

When Donald Trump sat down on May 4, 2017, with the editors of the *Economist* magazine, he was accompanied by National Economic Council director Gary Cohn and Treasury Secretary Steven Mnuchin. They listened attentively as their boss made a fool of himself.

The president explained that he was a free trader and a fair trader.

He explained that he was all about negotiation but that some things were not negotiable.

He said he was against deficits but more than ready to run deficits in order to give out tax breaks while at the same time making massive investments to spur economic growth. Bloating out the deficit is cool, sometimes, "because [the combination of tax cuts and spending hikes] won't increase it for long," Trump explained to the editors. "You may have two years where you'll . . . you understand the expression 'prime the pump'?"

"Yes," said his inquisitor from the *Economist*, who was obviously familiar with the common term for the sort of governmental interventions that John Maynard Keynes (1883–1946) proposed to avert, or at the very least address, recessions and depressions.

The president continued. "We have to prime the pump," he said.

The *Economist* editor allowed as how "it's very Keynesian," but Trump did not get the joke.

The president really wanted to make sure that the editors knew what he was talking about. "Have you heard that expression before, for this particular type of an event?" he asked.

"Priming the pump?" asked the editor.

"Yeah, have you heard it?" asked the president.

"Yes," said the editor.

"Have you heard that expression used before? Because I haven't heard it," said Trump. "I mean, I just . . . I came up with it a couple of days ago and I thought it was good. It's what you have to do."

Gary Cohn, the former president and co-chief operating officer of the Goldman Sachs investment banking empire, who had left his previous position with a $285 million severance package in order to bring a measure of coherence to the young Trump presidency, was very quiet. Presumably, Cohn knew about priming the pump and John Maynard Keynes and all that. But he just let the president talk himself out. The interview ended and Trump went off to fret about FBI director James Comey, who he would fire a few days later. Cohn went back to running the economy.

Donald Trump had in February of 2016, when he was campaigning in South Carolina before that state's critical Republican primary, warned that voters should reject Texas senator Ted Cruz because "the guys at Goldman Sachs . . . have total, total control over him—just like they have total control over Hillary Clinton." By February 2017, however, Trump had a different view altogether. As the new president of the United States he was busy appointing a graduating class of Goldman Sachs alumni to top positions in his administration:

- Secretary of the Treasury Steven Mnuchin
- Deputy Secretary of the Treasury Jim Donovan, the managing director at Goldman Sachs's Private Wealth Management Division, who Mnuchin tapped to oversee the radically transforming $13.8 trillion market for treasury bonds. Donovan's client list at Goldman Sachs included Bain Capital and Mitt Romney, whose presidential campaign Donovan served as an economic policy advisor.
- Deputy National Security Advisor Dina Habib Powell, a former Goldman Sachs managing director, partner and global head of the Office of Corporate Engagement, who was initially brought into the Trump administration as "Senior Advisor to

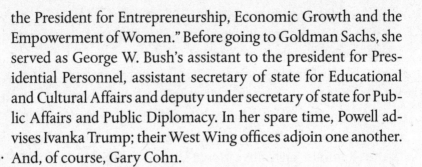

the President for Entrepreneurship, Economic Growth and the Empowerment of Women." Before going to Goldman Sachs, she served as George W. Bush's assistant to the president for Presidential Personnel, assistant secretary of state for Educational and Cultural Affairs and deputy under secretary of state for Public Affairs and Public Diplomacy. In her spare time, Powell advises Ivanka Trump; their West Wing offices adjoin one another.
- And, of course, Gary Cohn.

Though he accepts the director of the National Economic Council title, Cohn is broadly recognized as Trump's "chief economic advisor." That's kind of a big deal. DC gossip columnists and commentators who delight in palace intrigues like to imagine that Cohn is the leader of a team of internationalists who square off against a team of protectionists for influence in the West Wing. Sometimes they get excited because it seems like Cohn and his crew have captured the president's attention and begun to place their input on the administration. But then Trump jets off to Wisconsin to tout his "Buy America, Hire America" agenda and the pundits get confused.

People who recognize how Goldman Sachs has always operated know that Cohn and his compatriots have things covered, even if they sometimes have to listen to Donald Trump brag about how he came up with Keynesian economics.

Cohn is, in fact, aligned with a West Wing faction known as the "New Yorkers" that includes Dina Powell, Jared Kushner and Ivanka Trump, among others. The *Forward* newspaper says he strides through the White House with "the swagger befitting a banking titan." And he is surely influential. But there are other influential people in the West Wing, and one of their factions is led by a fellow named Steve Bannon.

Now, here's the interesting part: for all the talk of long knives and petty feuds, Bannon is not quite so different from Cohn as the fevered coverage of White House positioning might suggest.

Bannon was also a Goldman Sachs investment banker. He worked in the Mergers and Acquisitions Department during the "greed is good" 1980s. Determining that more greed would be even better, he left Goldman to go even deeper into the game as the head of Bannon & Company, a boutique investment bank that specialized in media financing and eventually ended up with a stake in the TV show *Seinfeld*.

Bannon is a frequent critic of Wall Street who played a critical role in framing the final Trump campaign ad that featured an image of Goldman Sachs CEO Lloyd Blankfein as the candidate decried "a global power structure that is responsible for the economic decisions that have robbed our working class, stripped our country of its wealth and put that money into the pockets of a handful of large corporations and political entities." He has an ally in Peter Navarro, the China-wary director of Trump's newly created National Trade Council, who warned in a March 5, 2017, *Wall Street Journal* op-ed that the persistent U.S. trade deficit "would put US national security in jeopardy." It was once thought that, on the trade issues so central to Trump's campaign, Bannon and Navarro (and to a lesser extent Robert Lighthizer, the former Reagan aide who is the new U.S. trade representative) might steer the Trump White House away from the influence of the Goldman Sachs and Wall Street axis, which has contributed so many cabinet members and economic "advisors" to so many administrations of both parties that it is now referred to as "Government Sachs."

But as the Trump administration took shape, Bannon seemed to be distracted and Navarro was increasingly marginalized. AFL-CIO trade specialist Thea Lee told the *Financial Times* in early March of 2017 that "at the moment it appears that the Wall Street wing of the Trump administration is winning this battle and the Wall Street wing is in favor of the status quo in terms of US trade policy." As the investment bankers arrayed themselves throughout the administration, on every side of every issue but always around core "deconstruct the regulatory state" strategies that invariably reward Wall Street, it became clear that the "factions" were not really at odds, at least not sufficiently at odds to change the economic equations that matter to Main Street. As the influential financial blog *Zero Hedge* reminds us, if there is a conflict over economics in the White House, "Goldman is winning."

Afterword

AVERTING THE TRUMPOCALYPSE

A little patience, and we shall see the reign of witches pass over, their spells dissolve, and the people, recovering their true sight, restore their government to its true principles. It is true that in the meantime we are suffering deeply in spirit, and incurring the horrors of a war and long oppressions of enormous public debt . . . And if we feel their power just sufficiently to hoop us together, it will be the happiest situation in which we can exist. If the game runs sometimes against us at home we must have patience till luck turns, and then we shall have an opportunity of winning back the principles we have lost, for this is a game where principles are at stake.

—THOMAS JEFFERSON, 1798 letter on building an opposition to the Alien and Sedition Acts and to John Adams's abuses of power

When Justin Trudeau became the twenty-third prime minister of Canada in November of 2015, he announced an unprecedented cabinet. "This group—men and women totaling 30 in all—included new Canadians and members of the first peoples of this land, a woman who is just 30 years old, and three men who have reached the age when most Canadians retire," explained the Canadian Broadcasting Corporation report. "For justice minister, Trudeau chose Jody Wilson-Raybould, a member of the We Wai Kai Nation. Another of his ministers, Maryam Monsef, just 30 years of age, fled Afghanistan as a child with members of her family to escape the Taliban. She becomes the minister of democratic institutions. There are five ministers of South Asian descent. There are two with disabilities. And yes, there are 15 women and 15 men, not including Trudeau, although gender parity is only part of the story. Women also hold senior positions, among them Chrystia Freeland in Trade, Wilson-Raybould in Justice and Catherine McKenna in the newly renamed Environment and Climate Change."

That there was a department that acknowledged climate change in its name offered an indication of how distinct Trudeau's project in Canada was from the one launched fourteen months later in the United States by Donald Trump. Trudeau was not elected as a radical change agent and most of his appointees remained too invested in the neoliberal compromises of our times. But the emphasis was on making government work. Trudeau was not governing based on some Steve Bannon theory about "deconstructing the administrative state" or the denial fantasies of American Environmental Protection Agency administrator Scott Pruitt. The new Canadian government was not constructed with an ulterior motive. It was not packed with greedheads and grifters, blank-stare ideologues and partisan hacks, Koch brothers mandarins and the campaign donors who have bought their way into the Trump White House.

Trudeau did not suggest that he was all-knowing, that he alone could meet Canada's challenges. He made it clear that he would rely on the members of his Cabinet. He proudly empowered them to color outside the lines, to push limits, to improve upon his ideas. The son of one of Canada's greatest political figures, Justin Trudeau had forged his own career as a parliamentarian before taking the lead of his Liberal Party and waging a campaign that promised to renew Canada's sense of purpose.

Even before that campaign produced a landslide victory for Trudeau, he was thinking long and hard about how best to govern. He thought, particularly, about strengthening the government he would lead by surrounding himself with a cadre of brilliant individuals who were ready to learn, to legislate, to lead in their own right. "This is going to be a period of slight adjustment for a number of people in the political world in Canada," the new prime minister announced as he introduced his team, "because government by cabinet is back." He was calling not for blind loyalty but for broad vision. Even those who did not embrace the whole of that vision were encouraged to imagine that their country might be unified and strengthened by an engaged and caring government.

Americans should be furious that Donald Trump has cheated their country out of the opportunity to have faith in their government and

hope in its possibility. They should be enraged with this president and the people he has surrounded himself with: gross incompetents and stupefied partisans, dirty dealers and self-absorbed schemers, cruel executioners of inhumane policies and the defenders of the indefensible. Trump has not assembled a cabinet; he has assembled a wanted list of unindicted co-conspirators. Around himself in the West Wing, where he freely admits that power is centralized and jealously guarded, Trump swims in a right-wing fever swamp of conspiracy theorists and crackpots. One of his top advisors wears the badge of a Hungarian group that collaborated so closely with a Nazi-aligned government during World War II that the State Department keeps it on a list of "Organizations Under the Direction of the Nazi Government of Germany." His closest advisor quotes from the texts of European fascists and is portrayed on *Saturday Night Live* as the Grim Reaper.

Despite Trump's own authoritarian impulses, however, he too governs by cabinet. It is just a different sort of governing, rooted not in the hope of making government work but in the determination to dismantle it. His cabinet members, aides and assistants form a crew of wreckers that have scrambled aboard a sinking ship of state to grab whatever is not nailed down. Trump will often direct the dismantlement. But when he is not directing, his appointees know how to carry the project forward on their own. And a few, like Secretary of Education Betsy DeVos and Secretary of Health and Human Services Tom Price, have schemes even more nefarious than those of their president.

While there are already conflicts within the Trump White House, and while there will be more, Trump has not created a "team of rivals" administration. He has surrounded himself with sycophants and Svengalis, mandarins who have the apologia ready even before the boss gets caught and cruel calculators who are ever ready to initiate the next high crimes and misdemeanors.

For citizens, watching from a nation that did not vote for this president (54 percent of ballot-casting Americans opposed Trump's election in 2016) and that certainly did not vote for this presidency

(Trump gave little indication of who he would surround himself with if he prevailed on Election Day), this can be confusing, confounding, dizzying, horrifying.

But Americans cannot look away from the crisis. Americans cannot simplify or diminish the circumstance in which we find ourselves. We have to accept that this is now about so much more than a man. Trump became president because of the obsession of our political and media elites with a dumbed-down, personality-driven imagining of American politics. Even now, many in the media continue to obsess about the strongman and his lies, as opposed to the federal machinery of deceit that now manufactures false premises, alternative facts and fake news on an industrial level. Yet, their obsession cannot be our obsession. It is impossible to understand (let alone challenge) Trump the president without understanding the Trump presidency—the whole of what he has created, the whole of what this book has examined.

What, then, is the duty of a citizen in times such as these? And what is the duty of the enlightened media and the visionary political leaders who would embrace and extend that duty?

The first response must always be solidarity. It is not enough to care about what Trump or one of Trump's agencies is doing to you and yours. It is necessary to recognize that, with thousands of appointees in place, with the full apparatus of government at its command, with all the resources of the wealthiest nation in the world in its possession, this beast will have enough tentacles to wrap around every one of us.

Only the fool imagines that the damage done by a presidency that begins with a Muslim ban will not soon produce more bans touching more people, more assaults on rights, more restrictions. An injury to one will become an injury to all, and it is cruel delusion to duck and cover. The hope for America is found in a resistance that goes first to the airport when Muslims are being barred and then to the workplace or the school where immigration raids are being carried out, to the school where Betsy DeVos's grand schemes are tearing apart the promise of education for all, to the clinic where Tom

Price's mangling of the health care system is denying care to those who need it most, to the countryside where Scott Pruitt's rejection of science threatens sacred lands.

Standing in solidarity, standing in resistance matters. And if it is an intersectional solidarity, a "one for all and all for one" resistance, then the potential for victory is far greater than people imagine. The initial Muslim ban was blocked at the airports and in the courts. Mike Pence had to be called in to rescue Betsy DeVos's nomination because even a few Republican senators rejected her—after their constituents demanded that they do so. Trump's most noxious initial cabinet pick, fast-food CEO Andy Puzder, had to withdraw himself from consideration after a mass movement challenged and exposed him. Mike Flynn was hounded from his national security advisor position because a free press reported his wrongdoing. Jeff Sessions was forced to recuse himself from inquiries into the Trump campaign because of the revelation that he had lied to the Senate. When Sessions abandoned his recusal and aided and abetted Trump's firing of FBI director James Comey in early May, the outcry was so loud that even Republicans in Congress heard it.

Every act of resistance matters, but it is a full-spectrum resistance that matters most. It is not enough to hope that Donald Trump will be hounded from office or simply lose interest; as this book explains, his vice president is every bit as conflicted, every bit as cruel, every bit as dangerous—and a good bit more doctrinaire and edgily partisan. It is not enough to hope for, and work for, an election result that takes power from a Paul Ryan or a Mitch McConnell, although that disempowerment is surely critical to the eventual delivery of the republic from its current peril.

What is necessary is a broader and deeper resistance that identifies all the wrongdoers, all the collaborators and conspirators within and around the Trump presidency, and that holds them to account. Infrastructure matters, and kicking the underpinnings out from under Donald Trump will hasten his fall. The founders of the American experiment wisely established an impeachment process for holding to account lawless presidents. But presidents were not the only errant executives they considered.

Article II, Section 4 of the Constitution of the United States announces that "the President, Vice President and all civil Officers of the United States, shall be removed from Office on Impeachment for, and Conviction of, Treason, Bribery, or other high Crimes and Misdemeanors." Jeff Sessions is a civil officer. Betsy DeVos is a civil officer. Scott Pruitt is a civil officer. Steve Bannon is a duly sworn civil officer, and so are Trump's men at the FCC and the SEC and all the other agencies that this presidency is mangling as it seeks to deconstruct the administrative state. As Neil Gorsuch told Patrick Leahy: "Senator, no man is above the law." And we are best served by a resistance that demands accountability from every department head, from every commissioner, from every counselor and advisor.

This book seeks to identify some of the most serious subjects of concern, some of the most likely targets for investigation and censure. But the Trump administration is a moving target, and the ongoing work of watchdog groups is essential. Public Citizen has stepped up. The group's Corporate Cabinet project (www.corporatecabinet.org) is an essential tool. The Trump Transition Watch initiated by the American Civil Liberties Union (https://www.aclu.org/feature/trump-transition-watch) is invaluable, as is the detailed examination of the backgrounds of specific Trump appointees by the Southern Poverty Law Center. The Center for American Progress has produced great investigative reports at Trump Cabinet Watch, while the Natural Resources Defense Council's Trump Watch monitors assaults on the environment. Citizens for Responsibility and Ethics in Washington is all over this administration on issues of ethics and conflicts of interest.

Information is vital. Acting on information is even more vital. And people are acting. Few members of congress in this country can hold a town meeting without attracting an overflow crowd. The next step is to make sure that, when Trump cabinet members and appointees travel, they too are met and challenged.

Americans are going to be busy over the next several years, holding the Trump presidency to account and holding their country together. But at a certain point Americans must dream. We have a right to demand that this administration do no harm. But we have a

right, as well, to demand that American politics evolve beyond the game of chance that gave us Donald Trump and his wrecking crew. Along with voting rights and campaign finance reform and gerrymandering reform and Electoral College elimination, Americans should pursue a new vision for how presidencies are configured.

In most democracies, political parties seek power not merely on the basis of personalities but on the basis of ideas that are outlined, and often costed and budgeted, in party manifestoes that are far more serious and detailed than the platforms that are quickly approved at American political conventions and then even more quickly abandoned. Parties in other countries give scope and meaning to their promises by identifying who will be in charge of major departments and agencies when the party comes to power.

The "opposition bench" is well known and outspoken in countries such as Great Britain, and it gives definition to that opposition. For years, Ralph Nader has argued that American presidential candidates should name their cabinets before they are elected, and that the fall campaign should feature debates involving not just the presidential and vice presidential contenders but party leaders who are identified with specific issues and missions: health care, education, food and farming, war and peace. Nader was always right, but the chaos and corruption of the Trump administration argues more strongly than ever for consideration of the "opposition bench" approach as a tool for opposing the Trump presidency.

Americans need to hear a steady critique of Trump appointees by informed and engaged leaders who might suggest themselves as potential replacements for those they are holding to account. The point is not just to oppose but also to imagine alternatives, to speak of the next America where that which has been broken can be repaired and where the work that has been neglected can finally begin. As Rebecca Solnit reminds us, hope in a time of darkness is powerful, and healing. It dissolves the spells of errant presidents and their cruel cabinets, it helps the people to recover their true sight and throw off chains of hatred and division, it restores government to its true principle—the service of the people. It teaches the genius of resistance and solidarity, and it transforms that resistance and solidarity into a new politics strong enough to assure that this country will never again surrender its future to a madman and his minions.

The horsemen will be dispersed.

The Trumpocalypse will be averted.

Source Notes

A Note on How to Use This Book

My parents gave me a new edition of Arthur M. Schlesinger Jr.'s book *The Imperial Presidency* (Houghton Mifflin, 1974) when I was a child. That says a lot about them, and about my upbringing. But it remains the best book for beginning a consideration of the expansion of presidential powers and the scope and character of the executive branch. Willard Sterne Randall writes brilliantly about how Washington and Jefferson shaped the presidency in his books *George Washington: A Life* (Holt Paperbacks, 1998) and *Thomas Jefferson: A Life* (Harper Perennial Modern Classics, 2014). John Dean's essay on Trump appeared on January 20, 2017, on Justia's Verdict website as "Inauguration Day 2017—Trump's Dangerous Ego Trip." For some fine writing on Trump and Berlusconi, read Alexander Stille's "Donald Trump, America's Own Silvio Berlusconi," the *Intercept*, March 7, 2016. You will find a fine reflection on James Madison's views regarding an informed citizenry—"FOIA Post (2008): Celebrating James Madison and the Freedom of Information Act"—on the U.S. Department of Justice website.

Betsy DeVos and the Malice Domestic: An Introduction to the Trumpocalypse

Franklin Delano Roosevelt referred to the "malice domestic" in his address at the San Diego Exposition, October 2, 1935. It can be found in many places, including the terrific American Presidency Project website assembled by Gerhard Peters and John T. Woolley: http://www.presidency.ucsb.edu. "Their malice may be concealed . . ." is found in Proverbs 26:26. The *Los Angeles Times* editorial "Putting Scott Pruitt in charge of the EPA risks irreversible damage to the planet" appeared February 4, 2017. The *New York Times* editorial "President Bannon?" appeared January 30, 2017. I wrote about the phenomenon and philosophy of Trumpism for the *Nation* in a number of pieces, including "It Really Is That Bad: So now we must get very good at saying 'no' to Trumpism," published November 9, 2016. Walter Dean Burnham's essay "By co-opting an ultra-right wrecking crew, Donald Trump is sending the US back to the 1920s" can be found on the very useful London School of Economics US Centre blog (http://bit.ly/2jgK23G). Elizabeth Warren tweeted her impression of DeVos from @SenWarren. Diane Ravitch's "An Open Letter to Senator Lamar Alexander About Betsy DeVos" appeared January 22, 2017, on *Huffington Post*. Trump's statements about his cabinet picks can be found on the Trump Transition Team at https://greatagain.gov/. Budgets and staffing levels for

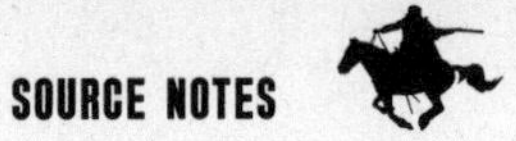

the various cabinet agencies are in constant flux; for this book I tried to use the figures cited by the departments themselves, which give a fair sense of their size at the point when Trump was filling posts. Trump's odd reference to DeVos was detailed by the *Washington Post*, January 23, 2017, "President Trump signs executive order for Betsy DeVos's nomination." Video and transcripts from the DeVos confirmation hearing, and those of other nominees, can be found at the terrific CSPAN website: https://www.c-span.org/congress/. It's all archived and easily searched. Also, the Senate committees themselves provide many valuable resources on their websites. Randi Weingarten issued her statement on DeVos on November 23, 2016. *Politico*'s assessment of the cabinet picks, "Trump rewards big donors with jobs and access," appeared December 27, 2016. Madison's words are collected in *The Letters and Other Writings of James Madison* (Lippincott & Co., 1865). The *Economist*'s assessment of the new president appeared as "The Republicans: Time to Fire Trump" on February 27, 2016.

Part I: Wicked Messengers

Henry Wallace's essay "The Danger of American Fascism" appeared in the *New York Times*, April 9, 1944. John Dean spoke to the *Atlantic*'s McKay Coppins for the January 17, 2017, piece "'He Is Going to Test Our Democracy as It Has Never Been Tested': Why Nixon's former lawyer John Dean worries Trump could be one of the most corrupt presidents ever—and get away with it." I have written a great deal about the actual breakdown of the 2016 presidential vote and the attempts to spin it by Donald Trump and his associates; a good sum-up can be found in "Donald Trump Has No Mandate—Sad! He pretends to be a strongman to compensate for his weaknesses," the *Nation*, January 19, 2017. The full exchange between Peter Alexander and Trump can be found in "Remarks by President Trump in Press Conference," made available February 16, 2017. The Cuomo-Spicer clash aired on CNN, December 15, 2016. Bannon's most revealing discussion of Trump and Trumpism was at the 2017 Conservative Political Action Conference, and it was summed up well by the *New York Times* piece "Stephen K. Bannon's CPAC Comments, Annotated and Explained," February 24, 2017. Evan McMullin's piece "Trump's Threat to the Constitution" appeared in the *New York Times*, December 6, 2016. Dean's comments are from his "Inauguration Day 2017—Trump's Dangerous Ego Trip" piece.

The Investors: The *New York Daily News* wrote up the Mercer party: "President-elect Donald Trump suits himself by not dressing up for extravagant Long Island costume party," December 4, 2016. A fine Bloomberg *Politics* review, published December 1, 2016, was titled "Trump 'Villains and Heroes' to Mingle at Annual Mercer Costume Party." The always brilliant Jane Mayer's assessment appeared in the *New Yorker* as "The Reclusive Hedge-Fund Tycoon Behind the Trump

Presidency: How Robert Mercer exploited America's populist insurgency," March 27, 2017. David M. Magerman's piece "The Oligarchy of the 0.001 Percenters" appeared on the philly.com website March 1, 2017. The Campaign Legal Center summed up its concerns in a December 2, 2016, statement: "New Evidence of Illegal Compensation to Steve Bannon by Mercer-Backed Super PAC." Matea Gold's excellent piece "The Mercers and Stephen Bannon: How a populist power base was funded and built: The wealthy GOP donors and Trump's chief strategist collaborated on at least five ventures" appeared in the *Washington Post*, March 17, 2017. Philip Bump's "The rise of GOP mega-donor Rebekah Mercer," another fine piece by the *Post*'s Philip Bump, was published September 14, 2016. I also spoke with a number of GOP fund-raising specialists for insights regarding the Mercers.

The Jacksonian Democrat: Michael Wolff's revealing *Hollywood Reporter* interview appeared November 18, 2016, as "Ringside with Steve Bannon at Trump Tower as the President-Elect's Strategist Plots 'An Entirely New Political Movement.'" Juan Cole's commentary "Translating Trump's inaugural Speech from the original German" was published January 21, 2017, on his Informed Comment (www.juancole.com) website. The *Post*'s Robert Costa published "Bannon calls Trump's speech 'Jacksonian'" on January 20, 2017. The Asawin Suebsaeng piece "Steve Bannon Pushed Trump to Go Full Andrew Jackson" was published March 16, 2017, by the *Daily Beast*. The Trump interview with Fox's Tucker Carlson took place March 15, 2017. A long piece on Bannon and Evola was published February 10, 2017, by the *New York Times*: "Steve Bannon Cited Italian Thinker Who Inspired Fascists." *AlterNet* writer Ben Norton's assessment, "President Trump's right-hand man Steve Bannon called for Christian holy war: Now he's on the National Security Council," appeared January 30, 2017. "Indian-Killer Andrew Jackson Deserves Top Spot on List of Worst US Presidents" was published February 20, 2017, by the Indian Country Media Network. Dylan Matthews's "Andrew Jackson was a slaver, ethnic cleanser, and tyrant. He deserves no place on our money" appeared on the Vox site, April 20, 2016. The Hermitage's reflection on Jackson and slavery is found at http://thehermitage.com/learn/mansion-grounds/slavery/. The *USA Today* piece "Change in $20 bill feels like a slight to some in Andrew Jackson's home state" was published April 24, 2016. Trump's remarks at the Hermitage were delivered on March 15, 2017, and like all official addresses by the president referenced in this book can be found at www.whitehouse.gov.

The Spinster: The detailed *Washington Post* review of the *Access Hollywood* tape was published October 8, 2016, as "Trump recorded having extremely lewd conversation about women in 2005." *Huffington Post*'s Daniel Marans wrote about the Melania Trump timeline the same day. Paul Farhi wrote about Conway and other pundits for the *Washington Post* in the May 27, 2000, piece "The Voice of Experience? Um, Not Exactly Television." Ryan Lizza wrote for the *New Yorker* about George and Kellyanne Conway in the October 17, 2016, piece "Kellyanne Conway's Political Machinations: Can the first woman to run a Republican Presidential campaign reform Donald Trump?" Conway's *What Women Really Want: How American Women Are Quietly Erasing Political, Racial, Class, and Religious Lines to Change the Way We Live*, written with Celinda Lake, was published in 2010 by Atria Books. Conway's interview with Chris Matthews appeared on MSNBC on October 9, 2016. Dana Bash and Abigail Crutchfield reported on Conway's contortions on October 25, 2016, in a CNN piece: "How the GOP's first female presidential campaign manager manages Donald Trump." Bannon spoke about Conway's contribution with Molly Ball for the piece "Kellyanne's Alternative Universe," which appeared in the April 2017, issue of the *Atlantic*, as did Frank Luntz. Conway's interview with Chuck Todd took place on January 22, 2017. It was one of the defining moments of the Trump presidency, in that it contributed the term "alternative fact" to the lexicon.

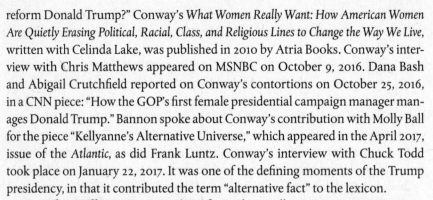

He Who Will Not Be Questioned: Stephen Miller's jarring appearance on CBS's *Face the Nation* took place on February 12, 2017, the same day that he appeared on the other Sunday morning talk shows referenced here. Senator Coons made his comments about Miller on the MSNBC show *Morning Joe*, where Joe Scarborough also discussed the White House aide's appearances. The *Chicago Tribune* ran a fine piece, "Stephen Miller, teleprompters and journalistic credibility," by Brendan M. Lynch, a lecturer at the University of Kansas William Allen White School of Journalism and Mass Communications, on February 21, 2017. Lisa Mascaro wrote a profile of Miller, "How a liberal Santa Monica high school produced a top Trump advisor and speechwriter," for the *Los Angeles Times* on January 17, 2017. That piece provides tremendous insight and detail regarding Miller's high school days, while a *Charlotte Observer* piece from February 14, 2017, "Relishing a fight: Stephen Miller's meteoric rise from Duke to the Trump White House," provides insights regarding his Duke days. "The rise of Stephen Miller: From Sessions' aide to Trump's inner circle" is the Howard Koplowitz piece, published January 19, 2017 on AL.com, that provides so much background and insight regarding the Sessions-Miller connection. *Politico* magazine profiled Miller as "The Believer" on June 27, 2016, and began to draw out the Bannon connection, as did the *Atlantic's* February 4, 2017, piece "How Stephen Miller's Rise Explains the Trump White House: The young policy adviser became the public face of Trump's controversial travel ban—and is paying the price for it." Jared Taylor's article "I Was There" appeared January 21, 2017, on his American Renaissance website. The *New York Times* piece "Stephen Miller Is a 'True Believer' Behind Core Trump Policies" appeared February 11, 2017.

The Jihad Whisperer: The *Forward*, one of my favorite publications since I was a youth, has done groundbreaking reporting on Sebastian Gorka, as it has on many aspects of the Trump administration that relate to the concerns of Jewish Americans. The *Forward* has done dozens of pieces and several have influenced the discussion significantly, including Dan Friedman's "Top White House Adviser Wears Nazi Collaborator Medal" on February 13, 2017, and the exclusive March 16, 2017, report by Lili Bayer and Larry Cohler-Esses: "Nazi-Allied Group

Claims Top Trump Aide Sebastian Gorka as Sworn Member." An important background piece was Keno Verseck's June 6, 2012, essay for *Der Spiegel*: "Hungary Rehabilitates Far-Right Figures: Hungary's right-wing extremists are becoming increasingly self-confident. They are now openly paying tribute to Miklós Horthy, Hungary's anti-Semitic regent during the interwar period, erecting a statue and renaming a town square in his honor. Even some members of Prime Minister Viktor Orbán's Fidesz party support the new trend." So, too, does Raphael Patai's *The Jews of Hungary* (Wayne State University Press, 1996) and a November 1, 2006, *Jerusalem Post* piece: "Nazi-linked flag surfaces in Hungary: The red-and-white striped Arpad flag may best capture the aggressive mood of Hungarian politics today." *BuzzFeed* added detail to the Gorka–Vitézi Rend controversy with a March 17, 2017, article: "Top Trump Adviser Sebastian Gorka Denied a Report That He Belongs to a Nazi-Allied Group." That same day, *USA Today* reported: "Organizations call for Sebastian Gorka's resignation for ties to far-right group." Gorka's responses to charges of anti-Semitism in the Trump White House were the subject of a February 7, 2017, Jewish Telegraphic Agency article, "Trump aide: Holocaust statement criticism is 'asinine,'" and he spoke about the Vitézi Rend controversy for a March 16, 2017, piece in the *Tablet* magazine: "Sebastian Gorka denies a report of his affiliations with Vitézi Rend." Gorka's writing for Breitbart is archived at http://www.breitbart.com/author/sebastian-gorka/. *Newsweek*'s Jeff Stein summed up Gorka's background and views, and his style, in a February 23, 2017, piece titled "Listen to Controversial White House Terrorism Adviser Sebastian Gorka's Angry Call to a Critic." Stein's piece highlighted questions being asked about Gorka's training and skills by experts in the field of counterterrorism. Historian and soldier Adrian Weale has written a good deal about questions regarding Gorka at adrianweale.com.

The Leopard That Did Not Change His Spots: President Trump announced the selection of Sessions to serve as attorney general in a November 18, 2016, statement: "President-Elect Donald J. Trump Selects U.S. Senator Jeff Sessions for Attorney General, Lt. Gen. Michael Flynn as Assistant to the President for National Security Affairs and U.S. Rep. Mike Pompeo as Director of the Central Intelligence Agency." David Duke is very active on social media. His initial statements on the Sessions pick came in the form of tweets from his @DrDavidDuke account, which encourages visits to his www.davidduke.com website and features the slogan "Fight for Western Civilization." He tweeted about the Sessions pick and his admiration for Sessions, Flynn and Bannon on November 18, 2016, and regularly tweeted and posted messages on his website about Sessions during the confirmation process. He wrote a web editorial: "Trump appoints men who will take America back!" Media Matters for America followed the Duke reaction closely, with pieces such as "'Great News!': White Nationalists See Sessions' Attorney General Confirmation As Major Step Toward Achieving Their Racist Goals," on February 9, 2017. On January 30, 2017, *Mother Jones* published "White Nationalists on Twitter Sure Do Love

 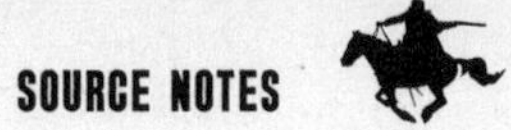

Jeff Sessions: He's their favorite Senator, by a long shot." The *Los Angeles Times* examined the "Klan without robes" in a March 1, 2016, article: "Ku Klux Klan 'without robes' makes headlines, but influence fading, anti-hate group says." The Southern Poverty Law Center tracks white nationalist and neo-Nazi extremism and has, of late, kept a close watch on connections between extremists and Trump aides and allies, with pieces such as the March 1, 2017, analysis: "Breitbart Under Bannon: How Breitbart Became a Favorite News Source for Neo-Nazis and White Nationalists." The SPLC has watched the rise of new social-media projects and websites such as the Daily Stormer, with pieces such as "Blog Wars: The Daily Stormer and Its Racist Frenemies" (March 10, 2015) and "Eye of the Stormer: Propelled by the Trump campaign and a new focus on the 'alt-right,' the Daily Stormer is now the top hate site in America" (February 9, 2017). The Daily Stormer piece "Jeff Sessions Confirmed: We are One Step Closer to Complete Control" appeared February 9, 2017. The *Washington Post* did a good sum-up of how Sessions responds to race issues on December 2, 2016: "Jeff Sessions's comments on race: For the record." Adam Serwer's *Atlantic* piece "What Jeff Sessions's Role in Prosecuting the Klan Reveals About His Civil-Rights Record: Defenders of Trump's choice for attorney general have cited an Alabama lynching case as evidence of his commitment to racial equality. The real story is more complicated" appeared January 9, 2017. The Grio has the Coretta Scott King letter at http://thegrio.com/2017/01/11/coretta-scott-king-opposed-jeff-sessions-in-1986-letter-to-congress/. The *New York Times* obituary of Albert Turner, "Albert Turner Is Dead at 64; Strove for Civil Rights in South," appeared on April 15, 2000, and included a number of quotes from prominent Alabamans reflecting on his epic struggles for civil rights and voting rights. The *New York Times* article on the rejection of the Sessions nomination for federal judge, "Senate Panel Hands Reagan First Defeat on Nominee for Judgeship," appeared June 6, 1986. For details on opposition to the 1986 nomination, see the *Times* story "Senator Urges Withdrawal of Judicial Nomination," March 20, 1986. For details of opposition by pro-choice groups to the Sessions nomination for AG, see "Planned Parenthood Urges Full Senate to Reject Sessions' Nomination," February 8, 2017. For details of concerns expressed to the LGBTQ community, see "Antigay, Right-Wing Jeff Sessions Will Sail Through Atty. Gen. Confirmation," the *Advocate*, January 9, 2017. A telling *Politico* story on Sessions opposing Obama judicial nominees, "Sessions questions Kagan's 'honesty,'" appeared June 29, 2010. I covered Sessions a good deal during the 2016 Trump campaign, and spoke with him after he delivered the nominating speech at the RNC. The *Washington Post* reported on the controversy of Sessions's Senate testimony, "Top Republicans call on Sessions to recuse himself; Dems call for resignation," on March 2, 2017. Reid Cherlin's excellent VICE News article "'The world is on fire': At a 2014 party at the 'Breitbart Embassy,' Steve Bannon promised a remaking of America" appeared February 15, 2017. The *New York Times* piece "Jeff Sessions, as Attorney General, Could Overhaul Department He's Skewered" appeared November 18, 2016. Evelyn

Turner wrote a powerful opinion piece, which appeared February 7, 2017, in *USA Today*: "I tried to help black people vote. Jeff Sessions tried to put me in jail." The Alabama Conference of the NAACP issued many statements opposing the Sessions nomination, beginning on November 19, 2016, and continuing through his confirmation; they are archived at http://www.alnaacp.org. There were a number of good stories on Sessions blocking African American judicial picks, including "Did Jeff Sessions block integration of south Alabama federal courts?" (*Birmingham News*, January 6, 2017), "Jeff Sessions Has a History of Blocking Black Judges" (*Mother Jones*, January 9, 2017) and "5 Reasons Why Jeff Sessions' Confirmation Matters to the Black Community" (*Essence*, January 10, 2017). The "Statement of SPLC President Richard Cohen on the nomination of Senator Jeff Sessions for attorney general," issued November 18, 2016, was one of many statements and articles produced by the group opposing the nomination. For a good summary of opposition to the Sessions nomination, see "Advocates Delver 1 Million Petition Signatures to the Senate to Stop Jeff Sessions," issued February 7, 2017, by the Leadership Conference on Civil and Human Rights. I wrote about the Susan Collins defense of Jeff Sessions for the *Nation* on January 10, 2017: "Susan Collins Just Disgraced Herself at Jeff Sessions's Confirmation Hearing." Evelyn Turner spoke to CNN for a powerful January 9, 2017, piece, "Woman prosecuted by Jeff Sessions can't forgive." *Salon* reported February 27, 2017: "Jeff Sessions drops DOJ lawsuit against discriminatory Texas voter ID case, reverses 6 years of litigation."

The Lawman Who Forgot Which Side He Was On: Sessions appeared before the Senate Judiciary Committee in January 2017. A video of the critical questioning by Senator Franken was posted by the *New York Times* on March 2, 2017, as "Jeff Sessions's Testimony on Russia Contacts." It can be found at https://www.nytimes.com/video/us/politics/100000004967157/sessions-i-have-recused-myself.html. The *Washington Post* story "Sessions met with Russian envoy twice last year, encounters he later did not disclose" was published on March 1, 2017. The *Hill* did a good sum-up of the ensuing controversy on March 7, 2017: "Franken: Sessions 'perjured himself.'" I wrote on the firing of Comey for the *Nation* on May 10 in a piece headlined "Trump Fires Comey, Putting the Country 'On the Verge of a Constitutional Crisis.'" Abby Phillip's *Washington Post* piece "Trump met in the Oval Office with Sessions and Rosenstein about Comey on Monday" appeared May 10, 2017, as did the NBC News piece "Who Is Rod Rosenstein, the Man Who Swung the Ax on Comey?" Background on Rosenstein and insights from Marylanders can be found in the fine reporting of the *Baltimore Sun*, especially in pieces such as the April 25, 2017, article "With bipartisan support, Maryland's Rosenstein heads to Washington as No. 2 in Justice Department." The *Sun* also did the best coverage of the Senate's questioning of Rosenstein, in pieces such as "Democrats grill Rod Rosenstein on Russia," published March 7, 2017. An interview with Elizabeth Warren on the Comey firing and related issues was broadcast May 10, 2017; the transcript can be found online at http://www.cnn.com/TRANSCRIPTS/1705/10/

 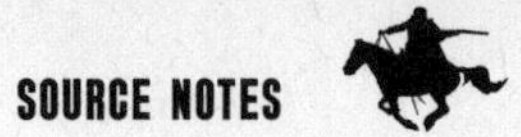

cnr.07.html. ABC News chief White House correspondent John Karl reported May 11, 2017, on Rosenstein's reaction in a piece headlined "Deputy AG Rosenstein was on the verge of resigning, upset over WH pinning Comey firing on him." Rosenstein's memo on Comey was widely circulated; an easy online source can be found on the *Atlantic*'s website at https://www.theatlantic.com/politics/archive/2017/05/rosenstein-letter-annotated/526116/.

"The King of Voter Suppression": The "ALEC Exposed" series was published July 12, 2011, by the *Nation*. The Center for Media and Democracy maintains an important website at www.alecexposed.org. I wrote about many of these issues in a May 17, 2016, *Nation* article headlined: "Wisconsin Republicans Were 'Giddy' About Making It Harder to Vote." The American Civil Liberties Union released several assessments and alerts regarding Kobach's selection for the commission, including a May 11, 2017, statement headlined "Trump Voting Commission is a Sham." The Lawyers' Committee for Civil Rights Under Law condemned the launch of the commission in a May 11, 2017, statement. The McClatchy article on Kobach, "Civil rights groups fume over Trump's choice of Kobach to head voter fraud panel," appeared May 11, 2017. PolitiFact reviews of Trump's statements on voter fraud can be found at http://www.politifact.com/personalities/donald-trump/statements/byruling/pants-fire/. Ari Berman's *Nation* article "Trump's Commission on 'Election Integrity' Will Lead to Massive Voter Suppression" was published May 11, 2017. The *New York Daily News* report on Kobach, "Trump picks controversial figure to head voter fraud investigation," was published May 11, 2017.

Part II: Generals and CEOs Searching for Monsters to Destroy

Eleanor Roosevelt wrote about freedom in her 1960 book, *You Learn by Living*, which was republished in 2011 by Harper Perennial. The Eisenhower quote is from the less-noted section of his 1961 "Farewell Address to the Nation," better known as the "Military-Industrial Complex" speech. There are many fine biographies of John Quincy Adams, although there are many more to be written about this remarkable statesman. I like Harlow Giles Unger's *John Quincy Adams* (Da Capo Press, reprint edition, 2013) and, especially, Paul Nagel's *John Quincy Adams: A Public Life, a Private Life* (Harvard University Press, 1999). The full July 4, 1821, speech—"An address delivered at the request of a committee of the citizens of Washington: on the occasion of reading the Declaration of Independence, on the fourth of July, 1821"—was published that year in pamphlet form by Davis and Force. Read more about Colin Powell's "Pottery Barn Rule" in Kathy Gilsinan's fine September 30, 2015, article for the *Atlantic*: "The Pottery Barn Rule: Syria Edition. Colin Powell on his famous 'you break it, you own it' view of war, and how it's nice to have a doctrine named after you." Kristina Wong wrote a good piece, "Trump says he wouldn't take use of nuclear weapons 'off the table,'" for the *Hill* on March 30, 2015; another important assessment came on September 28, 2016, when Robert Windrem and William Arkin put together "What Does Donald Trump Really Think About Using Nuclear Weapons?" for NBC. Shane Goldmacher's article "Why Trump Is So Obsessed with Generals" appeared in *Politico* December 9, 2016, while Andrew Bacevich discussed the question on *Democracy Now!* on December 16, 2016. David Graham's article "Are Trump's Generals Mounting a Defense of Democratic Institutions?" appeared January 31, 2017, in the *Atlantic*. Fred Kaplan, the author of *Dark Territory: The Secret History of Cyber War*, wrote for *Slate*, March 15, 2017, on the subject "The Grown-Ups Are Locked Out: Trump is depriving Tillerson, Mattis, and McMaster of any real influence or support." Phillip Carter spoke with *Politico* on all these issues and also has written extensively on a variety of military issues at the Center for a New American Security website: www.cnas.org.

The "Mad Dog": I have been writing for several decades now about civilian control of the military, in books and magazine articles. For some background, consider "Will Civilians Control the Military?" a piece I wrote for the *Nation*, May 9, 2006, on President Bush's nomination of air force general Michael V. Hayden to direct the Central Intelligence Agency. Richard Kohn's "An Essay on Civilian Control of the Military" was published in 1997 by the American Diplomacy project, which works in cooperation with the University of North Carolina–Chapel Hill's College of Arts and Sciences and its Curriculum in Peace, War and Defense, and with the Triangle Institute for Security Studies. Phyllis Bennis's essay "Civilian Control Is Fundamental" appeared in *USA Today* on December 6, 2016. Richard Fontaine and others commented on the Mattis nomination in the Associated Press's "Trump to nominate retired Gen. James Mattis to lead Pentagon," published December 2, 2016. The *Atlantic* published the "16 Most Hair-Raising General Mattis Quotes" on July 9, 2010, while *Politico* produced "9 unforgettable quotes by James Mattis" on December 1, 2016. Mattis quotes are a favorite meme on Twitter and Facebook. London's *Daily Telegraph* produced a fine profile, "General James 'Mad Dog' Mattis, Donald Trump's pick for secretary of defence," on December 2, 2016. The Mattis Senate roll-call vote, and those for other nominees, can be found at www.congress.gov. You'll find details of the U.S. House wrangling over the Mattis nomination in the article "Thornberry charges Trump team with 'short-sightedness' for pulling Mattis from hearing" from Inside Defense, January 12, 2017. Senator Gillibrand issued a number of statements on the Mattis nomination; they're archived at www.gillibrand.senate.gov. She spoke about the nomination with the *Hill* in "Gillibrand doubles down on opposing waiver for Mattis after meeting," January 4, 2017.

The Deputy Secretary for Boeing: CNN Pentagon correspondent Barbara Starr reported extensively on the Flournoy prospect, in pieces such as "Mattis, Trump team clashed over Pentagon appointment." *Politico* magazine featured Flournoy in its February 27, 2017, forum: "Trump's Alpha Male Foreign Policy." There was extensive coverage of the Shanahan pick in the *Seattle Times*, where

Boeing maintains a major manufacturing presence; "Trump taps Boeing executive Pat Shanahan for deputy secretary of defense" was published March 17, 2017. The *Chicago Tribune*'s detailed piece on Shanahan was headlined "Trump selects rising star at Boeing for No. 2 at Pentagon" and was published March 16, 2017. The Trump budget blueprint, "America First: A Budget Blueprint to Make America Great Again," can be found at www.whitehouse.gov. The *Washington Post* piece "Trump nominates Boeing executive for Pentagon's second-in-command" appeared March 16, 2017. *Stars and Stripes* has also reported extensively on Trump's Pentagon picks, with articles such as "Trump nominates Boeing executive to be Pentagon's second-in-command," March 16, 2017.

The Director of the Office of the Military-Industrial Complex: Trump's address to the joint session of Congress was delivered February 28, 2017. For background on the budget and Mulvaney's statements about it, see www.whitehouse.gov. *Politico* profiled Mulvaney, with charts and lots of background, in the piece "Meet Mick Mulvaney, Trump's pick to run OMB," December 19, 2016. For more on the "Shutdown Caucus," see "Trump Picks Mick Mulvaney, South Carolina Congressman, as Budget Director," December 16, 2016. For more on McCain and Mulvaney, see "John McCain to oppose Mick Mulvaney, Trump's budget director pick," *Washington Post*, February 15, 2017. The Rock Hill, South Carolina, *Herald* reported extensively on Mulvaney's land deal and the controversy surrounding it; a good deal of background can be found in the piece "Republican hopeful Mulvaney defends past land deal," published October 8, 2010. Stanley Smith's letter "Councilman tells Edenmoor story" appeared October 27, 2010, in the Florence, South Carolina, *Morning News*. Vox reported on Mulvaney's "research" line in the piece "Trump's budget director pick: 'Do we really need government-funded research at all': Mick Mulvaney suggested Zika science is uncertain, so we shouldn't bother to fund it," January 24, 2017. ThinkProgress writer Aaron Rupar examined the conflicts between Trump's and Mulvaney's statements in "Trump promised to save entitlements. His budget director pick wants him to break his vow: If President Trump goes along, it'll break a promise candidate Trump made repeatedly," January 24, 2017. CNN's "Here's what Trump's budget proposes to cut" appeared March 16, 2017. A *Politico* magazine assessment, "Trump's Cuts: The Good, the Bad and the Bizarre," published March 17, 2017, was also very well done. Associated Press reported on Mulvaney's climate-change remarks on March 16, 2017, in the article "White House calls climate change efforts 'a waste of your money.'" *Democracy Now!*'s report on the Meals on Wheels mess appeared March 17, 2017. For background on Meals on Wheels and statements about it, visit www.mealsonwheelsamerica.org. Jeff Merkley emerged as one of the most outspoken critics of the values behind the Trump budget, as did Barbara Lee, who says: "As a social worker and a senior member of the House Budget and House Appropriations Committees, I know that the federal budget is a moral document. Sadly, President Trump's budget outline once again confirms that his priorities and values are deeply out of step with the American people." Examples of the contradictory messages from Trump on Pentagon spending can be found in the transcript of his October 4, 2015, interview on NBC's *Meet the Press.* A review of Mulvaney's over-the-top statements regarding Trump's Pentagon promises can be found in a February 28, 2017, piece I wrote for the *Nation*: "Donald Trump Goes All In for the Military-Industrial Complex: The president's address signaled his plans for domestic austerity and military bloat." Eisenhower's "The Chance for Peace" address was delivered to the American Society of Newspaper Editors on April 16, 1953. The National Priorities Project assesses U.S. military spending as compared with spending by other countries; its "U.S. Military Spending vs. the World" review can be found at https://www.nationalpriorities.org/campaigns/us-military-spending-vs-world/.

The Absolutist: The Michael Flynn fiasco was well detailed by the *New York Times* in its piece "Flynn's Downfall Sprang From 'Eroding Level of Trust," which appeared February 14, 2017. General McMaster's groundbreaking book, *Dereliction of Duty: Johnson, McNamara, the Joint Chiefs of Staff, and the Lies That Led to Vietnam,* was published by HarperCollins in 1997 and remains available in a Harper Perennial edition; McMaster has written commentary pieces for major newspapers and magazines and lectured a good deal on military issues. Vox highlighted General McMaster's record and the enthusiastic response to his selection in "H.R. McMaster, Trump's pick for national security adviser: a brief guide," February 20, 2017. As an example of the warm response the McMaster pick received, check out *Washington Post* columnist Jennifer Rubin's "Why McMaster is ideally suited to head the National Security Council," February 20, 2017. Dr. Steven Metz's thought-provoking review of *Dereliction of Duty* appeared in the autumn 1997 edition of the journal *Parameters.* General McMasters's rejection of the term "radical Islamic terrorism" was examined in a February 25, 2017, piece by Chas Danner for *New York* magazine: "In Break With Trump, National Security Adviser Pans the Use of 'Radical Islamic Terrorism.'" Dr. Steven Metz's much discussed February 24, 2017, *World Politics Review* article was headlined "Does McMaster Pick Mean Trump Will 'Go Big or Stay Home' in Using Military Force?" Peter Baker asked in a February 25, 2017, piece: "Will Trump Take 'Brutally Forthright' Advice From McMaster?" George Packer asked on February 22, 2017, in a *New Yorker* piece: "Can a Free Mind Survive in Trump's White House?" Andrew Bacevich wrote on February 21, 2017, for the *American Conservative* about "The Duty of General McMaster: As he takes charge of U.S. grand strategy, he must be a blunt, candid truth-teller."

The Koch Brother: I have been writing about the Koch brothers and groups they have created and funded, such as the American Legislative Exchange Council, for the better part of two decades. For background on the Kochs, I recommend visiting the Center for Media and Democracy's www.alecexposed.org website. Also, I recommend Jane Mayers's writing on the Kochs for the *New Yorker* and her fine book *Dark Money: The Hidden History of Billionaires Behind the Rise of the Radical Right*

(Doubleday, 2016). My interview on the Kochs and ALEC with *Fresh Air*'s Terry Gross can be found at http://www.npr.org/2011/07/21/138537515/how-alec-shapes-state-politics-behind-the-scenes. The *Washington Monthly* identified Pompeo as "The congressman from Koch Industries" in a March 21, 2011, article. The *Washington Post*'s "Pompeo draws liberal groups' ire," published March 20, 2011, also detailed the Koch connection. Lisa Graves of the Center for Media and Democracy wrote "Koch Candidates? Where Is the Koch Machine Spending in 2016 So Far," published June 14, 2016, at www.prwatch.org. Many media outlets detailed Pompeo's tough stands on a host of issues, including the U.S. response to Edward Snowden; one of the best was "America's next spy chief, Mike Pompeo, would be Trump's 'tough on terrorism' man" by the McClatchy Washington Bureau, November 18, 2016. The Human Rights Watch response to the nomination, "Reject Pompeo for CIA Director," was issued January 21, 2017. The Center for Food Safety report "Koch Industries and Monsanto Team Up to End Your Right to Know" was issued April 3, 2014. A useful report on Pompeo's campaigns and the Kochs, "In Wichita, Pompeo and Tiahrt Vie for Koch Backing," was published June 23, 2014, by the Center for Responsive Politics. The *Politico* report "Koch Industries Backs Pompeo" was published July 7, 2014.

The U.S. Ambassador to the American Anti-Choice Movement: Former U.S. ambassador to the UN Samantha Power delivered her speech to the Atlantic Council on January 17, 2017. The Vox report of the speech, published January 18, 2017, declared: "Samantha Power's diagnosis of the threat from Russia is brilliant. Her solutions aren't." Senator Chris Coons posted the video of his questioning of Haley on his official website, www.coons.senate.gov, and on January 18, 2017, circulated the transcript as "Senator Coons questions Gov. Nikki Haley, nominee for U.N. Ambassador: Senator Coons asks Gov. Haley about her views on Russia, the Iran deal, human rights, and NATO." The January 5, 2017, "Cabinet Exit Memo" by Samantha Power is archived at https://2009-2017-usun.state.gov/remarks/7643. The Republican Party platform was approved July 18, 2016, by delegates to the Republican National Convention in Cleveland. The International Women's Coalition report on Haley's nomination, "Nikki Haley: Trump's Choice for US Ambassador to the UN Is a Poor Choice for a Bold Women's Agenda," was published January 18, 2017. The October 26, 2016, WIS-TV report on Haley's sort-of endorsement of Trump was titled "Gov. Nikki Haley voting for Donald Trump only for policy reasons." A July 10, 2015, *Politico* report on the South Carolina flag controversy was headlined "Nikki Haley's star rises as rebel flag comes down: The experience of the past three weeks can only help the South Carolina governor break through into national politics." The LifeNews.com report "President-Elect Donald Trump Names Pro-Life Gov. Nikki Haley as UN Ambassador" appeared November 23, 2016. The LifeSiteNews.com report on January 26, 2017, was headlined "Pro-life Nikki Haley's confirmation as ambassador could lead to UN reining in abortion promotion." Senator Shaheen's questioning of Haley during the Senate

Foreign Relations Committee hearing, as well as Senator Booker's, is archived by CSPAN and can be viewed at www.https://www.c-span.org/video/?421753-1/un-ambassador-nominee-governor-nikki-haley-testifies-confirmation-hearing. *Slate*'s assessment of Haley as an "odd choice" for the UN post was published November 23, 2016, in the article "Trump Picks Nikki Haley, Who Called Him 'Everything a Governor Doesn't Want in a President,' for U.N. Ambassador." Charles Tiefer's November 23, 2016, piece for *Forbes* was titled "Trump's Choice of Nikki Haley Is a Slap to the U.N. and Pandering to Asian-Americans."

"Part and Parcel of an Organized Army of Hatred": The Trump rally in Jerusalem received quite a bit of attention from Israeli outlets, including the *Times of Israel* in "Trump tells Jerusalem rally he'll 'make Israel, US safe again'" (October 26, 2016), as well as in American publications such as the *Forward*, which headlined its piece by Naomi Zeveloff "Down to the Dog Whistles, Donald Trump's Jerusalem Rally Could Have Happened in Idaho" (October 26, 2016). Once David Friedman was nominated for ambassador, many more outlets reviewed the rally speech, including *Haaretz*, which headlined its December 16, 2016, piece "Trump's Envoy to Israel: We'll Break With 'anti-Semitic' State Dept., Move Embassy to Jerusalem." There have been many fine profiles of Huma Abedin, including *Vanity Fair's* big February 2016 article, "Is Huma Abedin Hillary Clinton's Secret Weapon or Her Next Big Problem: The loyal aide has spent decades at the presidential contender's side with unparalleled access. But with a powerful Republican senator raising questions about her role in the Clinton-era State Department, Abedin finds herself the latest victim of the Stop Hillary movement." The *Washington Post* Fact Checker reviewed the false statements about Abedin on August 25, 2016. PolitiFact Wisconsin reviewed Duffy's statement on September 14, 2016, headlining its conclusions "No evidence to back claim that top Hillary Clinton aide Huma Abedin has ties to Muslim Brotherhood." J Street set up a special section on its website to highlight opposition to the nomination and ran a "Stop Friedman" campaign that featured the "American Jewish Clergy Reject David Friedman" letter and a letter from former U.S. ambassadors to Israel: "Holocaust Survivors Raise Concerns About Trump's Choice for US Ambassador to Israel, David Friedman" was sent February 14, 2017. The *Haaretz* analysis by Chemi Shalev, "David Friedman, Trump's Radical-right Ambassador, Makes Netanyahu Look Like a J Street Lefty: It's a good thing ambassador-designate David Friedman will have diplomatic immunity; otherwise he might get arrested for incitement," was published December 18, 2016. *Haaretz* published the Judy Maltz article "Fund Headed by Trump's Israel Ambassador Pumped Tens of Millions Into West Bank Settlement: Rabbi heading yeshiva supported by David Friedman's organization called on soldiers to resist orders to evacuate settlements" on December 16, 2016. A statement from American Muslims for Palestine, "AMP staffers arrested protesting David Friedman's hearing at Senate Foreign Relations Committee," was released February 17, 2017. The February 17, 2017, Jewish Telegraphic Agency report on Friedman's

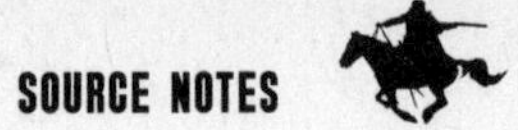

hearing was headlined "J Street Israel boss rejects David Friedman's remorse for 'kapos' remark." *Haaretz* reported on February 18, 2017, that "In Unprecedented Step, Reform Jewish Movement Opposes Trump's Pick for Israel Envoy: David Friedman lacks both the 'basic qualifications' and 'temperament' required by the position of Israel envoy, the largest Jewish movement in North America says." The Union of Reform Judaism statement "Reform Jewish Movement Opposes David Friedman's Nomination for U.S. Ambassador to Israel" was released the day before. CNN's Fareed Zakaria spoke of Trump's "surreal" lack of preparation in a February 15, 2017, interview with network colleague Don Lemon.

With the Russians, Too? Warren Zevon released "Lawyers, Guns and Money" in 1978. His jaundiced worldview might have allowed him to imagine a President Trump, but he would have been gobsmacked by Trump's appointees. *USA Today* summed up the Department of Commerce nominee with a November 30, 2016, piece headlined "Wilbur Ross: From 'king of bankruptcy' to face of American business." The November 24, 2016, *New York Times* article "Wilbur Ross, Billionaire Investor, Is Said to Be Trump's Commerce Pick" provided plenty of insights. The January 5, 2006, *New York Post* piece on the Sago Mine disaster appeared as "N.Y. Exec Knew of Problems: Ex-Honchos." A very detailed, very good *Los Angeles Times* article, "Meet Wilbur Ross, who once bailed out Trump in Atlantic City and is now his pick for Commerce secretary," was published December 8, 2016. The SpacePolicyOnline.com website headlined its January 24, 2017, report of the Senate confirmation process "Ross Promises Support for NOAA Weather and Climate Research." The McClatchy investigative piece by Kevin G. Hall appeared December 20, 2016, as "Trump's pick for commerce secretary shares a business circle with Putin associates" and stands as one of the best examples of investigative reporting on Trump cabinet picks. An important piece by the *Guardian*, "Deutsche Bank examined Donald Trump's account for Russia links: Bank looked for evidence of whether loans to president were underpinned by guarantees from Moscow, Guardian learns," was published February 16, 2017. The February 16, 2017, letter by the senators was reviewed in a number of news reports, including McClatchy's February 16 piece, "Trump commerce pick Wilbur Ross faces new Russia questions," and the *Guardian*'s "White House accused of blocking information on bank's Trump-Russia links: New commerce secretary Wilbur Ross's response about possible links between Bank of Cyprus, Russian agents and Trump officials wasn't released to Senate," published February 27, 2017. Booker's February 27, 2017, letter and the March 10 letter by the senators ("Booker, Markey, Blumenthal, Udall, Baldwin Urge Secretary Ross to Respond to Unanswered Questions on Russian Banking Ties") can be found at https://www.booker.senate.gov/?p=press_release&id=558. For more on CEPR's Revolving Door Project, go to http://cepr.net/blogs/cepr-blog/trump-appointments-and-transparency. The *New York Times* report on the Ross confirmation and Schumer's complaints was published February 27, 2017, headlined "Wilbur Ross, a Billionaire Investor, Is Confirmed as Commerce Secretary."

The Fossil-Fuel-Powered Dollar Diplomat: I wrote extensively about George Norris, Robert M. La Follette and other critics of dollar diplomacy in my 2004 book, *Against the Beast: A Documentary History of American Opposition to Empire* (Nation Books). *Fighting Liberal,* the autobiography of George Norris, was initially published in 1945 and republished in 2009 by Bison Books. The Senate letter on ethics concerns about the holdings of Trump administration members was sent December 13, 2016. *US News and World Report* published an excellent assessment of the Tillerson nomination, "Trump selects Tillerson for State, dismissing Russia ties," on December 12, 2016. Congressman Pocan released his "Tillerson Spent Career Putting Profits of Exxon over Country's National Interests" statement on December 13, 2016. CBS News produced its review of the Tillerson hearing, "Senator Menendez: 'Beyond My Imagination' That Tillerson, Trump Never Discussed Russia," on January 11, 2017. The senator's statement, "Sen. Menendez to Tillerson: 'put patriotism over profit' and support robust sanctions against Russia," was released the same day. Andrea Mitchell's NBC report, "Rex Tillerson of ExxonMobil Expected to Be Named Trump's Secretary of State: Sources," appeared December 11, 2016. Tracy Wilkinson wrote a fine assessment of the proposed State Department cuts, "Trump budget slashes State Department, but top U.S. diplomat doesn't object," for the *Los Angeles Times* on March 16, 2017. A Reuters review of official reaction to the cuts, "Tillerson says State Department spending 'simply not sustainable,'" appeared the same day. The Freedom House statement "Slashing U.S. Foreign Aid Would Weaken Security, Undermine Democracies" was issued on March 16, 2017.

Part III: The Hacks

Edmund Morris's visionary biography *The Rise of Theodore Roosevelt* was published in 1979 by Coward, McCann & Geoghegan. Elliot Richardson rejected a State Department job in the 1940s because he feared that he would become a DC careerist; he wanted to engage in electoral politics and democracy. I have written for many years, and in many venues, about the abandonment by the Republican Party of its historic mission. Some of the ideas in this section were originally scoped out in the piece "When the Republicans Really Were the Party of Lincoln: What happened to the party that fifty years ago played such a vital role in passing the Civil Rights Act?" the *Nation,* July 2, 2014. Frederick Douglass wrote a good deal about the Republican Party in the book *Life and Times of Frederick Douglass.* The Douglass papers at the Library of Congress contain many of his speeches on the Republican Party, as well as details of his engagements and frustrations with Republican leaders. Cleve R. Wootson Jr. wrote about Trump and Douglass for the *Washington Post* on February 2, 2017: "Trump implied Frederick Douglass was alive. The abolitionist's family offered a 'history lesson.'" *Democracy Now!* devoted a February 3 program to the topic: "Does Donald Trump Think Frederick Douglass Is Alive? Douglass's Great-Great-Great-Grandson Clarifies." The *Hill*'s February 1, 2017, article featuring many of the responses to the Trump incident was headlined "Trump remarks on Frederick Douglass spur questions on social media." On the passing of former senator Mathias, Robert Semple Jr. wrote a fine *New York Times* piece on January 26, 2010: "A Responsible Man." Michael O'Donnell's fine piece on the passage of the Civil Rights Act for the April 2014 issue of the *Atlantic* was titled "How LBJ Saved the Civil Rights Act: Fifty years later, new accounts of its fraught passage reveal the era's real hero—and it isn't the Supreme Court." Kenneth Reich's knowing obituary of Senator Kuchel, "Ex-Sen. Kuchel Dies; Last of State's GOP Progressives," appeared November 23, 1994, in the *Los Angeles Times*. Geoffrey Kabaservice's 2012 book, *Rule and Ruin: The Downfall of Moderation and the Destruction of the Republican Party from Eisenhower to the Tea Party* (Oxford University Press), is the most instructive book ever written on the internal battles of the Republican Party from the 1950s onward. John Avlon wrote an excellent June 20, 2008, essay that was broadly circulated: "How the Party of Lincoln Was Left Behind on Civil Rights." Dana Milbank's excellent column "In which Trump discovers some guy named Frederick Douglass" appeared February 1, 2017, in the *Washington Post*. Douglass delivered his excellent speech to the Bethel Literary and Historical Society in Washington, DC, April 16, 1889.

Secretariat Stumbling: I have covered Reince Priebus, a fellow Wisconsinite, for many years, back to when he was a losing candidate for the state senate. Priebus was a guest on *Fox News Sunday* with Chris Wallace on February 19, 2017. It was, by any measure, one of the most revealing interviews of the Trump era. Wallace's approach was fair, yet necessarily aggressive. Trump spoke about Priebus at some length early on the morning of November 9, 2016, when he claimed victory. Chris Whipple's book *The Gatekeepers: How the White House Chiefs of Staff Define Every Presidency* (Crown, 2017) offers a good sense of the role of chiefs of staff. Michael Wolff's revealing *Hollywood Reporter* interview with Bannon appeared November 18, 2017. Priebus's "our message was weak; our ground game was insufficient; we weren't inclusive" press conference was held March 18, 2013, at the National Press Club. "Trump Kills the Autopsy," wrote Kyle Cheney on March 4, 2016, for *Politico*. Robert Wirch, the man who beat Priebus, still serves in the Wisconsin state senate as a proud progressive Democrat.

Spicerfacts: George Orwell's novel *1984* was first published in 1949; it experienced a boom in sales after Donald Trump's election. I wrote many pieces on the 2016 election results and the question of whether Trump earned a mandate, including a January 19, 2017, *Nation* editorial, "Donald Trump Has No Mandate—Sad!" The transcript of Spicer's January 21, 2017, statement can be found at https://www.whitehouse.gov/the-press-office/2017/01/21/statement-press-secretary-sean-spicer. Transcripts of Spicer's other briefings, which are referenced in this and other chapters, can be found at www.whitehouse.gov/the-press-office/. The

Guardian profiled Spicer on January 22, 2017, in a piece headlined "Sean Spicer: brash brawler in frontline of Trump's 'war with the media'—period: The White House press secretary used his first briefing to berate the 'shameful' press but may find it hard to represent a master who communicates via Twitter." PolitiFact's review, "Donald Trump had biggest inaugural crowd ever? Metrics don't show it," was published January 21, 2017. The *Washington Post* report on February 24, 2017, was headlined "White House blocks CNN, New York Times from press briefing hours after Trump slams media." NBC *Saturday Night Live* clips are archived at http://www.nbc.com/saturday-night-live.

The Trumplican: Omarosa, Kellyanne Conway and Don Lemon appeared together March 25, 2016, on CNN. *Mediaite* wrote it up as "'Stop!' Don Lemon Snaps at Omarosa, Abruptly Ends Segment on Trump." The *New York Times*'s assessment of Omarosa and other Trump hangers-on who got big White House jobs, "Prerequisite for Key White House Posts: Loyalty, Not Experience," appeared March 14, 2017. *People* headlined its April 8, 2004, profile "Omarosa's Long History of Being Fired." The *New York Daily News* wrote up the "Spike Lee, Omarosa feud on social media" on July 19, 2016. You will find NBC exit polls and analysis at http://www.nbcnews.com/storyline/2016-election-day/election-polls-nbc-news-analysis-2016-votes-voters-n680466. Historic exit polls are found at the Cornell University Roper Center site: https://ropercenter.cornell.edu/polls/us-elections/. The brilliant Darren Sands *BuzzFeed* piece "The Outsider: Best known for her turn on *The Apprentice*, Omarosa Manigault—a former Democrat turned "Trumplican"—now holds an important position inside the White House. Her rise has sent black Republicans into an existential crisis as they find themselves trying to get a seat at the table" appeared March 9, 2017. The always brilliant Joy-Ann Reid wrote "Why Does Everybody Seem to Hate Omarosa Manigault?" for the *Daily Beast* on March 3, 2017.

The Hypocrite Who Made His Party of Lincoln the Party of Trump: McConnell's autobiography, *The Long Game: A Memoir*, was published by Sentinel in 2016. A biography of McConnell, by Alec MacGillis, was published in 2014 by Simon & Schuster; it's titled *The Cynic*. A lovely obituary of former senator Cooper, "John Sherman Cooper Dies at 89; Longtime Senator From Kentucky," appeared February 23, 1991, in the *New York Times*. Clarice James Mitchener's *Senator John Sherman Cooper: Consummate Statesman* was published by Arno Press in 1982. Cooper was one of the greatest senators in American history; my friends George McGovern and Gaylord Nelson spoke more highly of him than they did of most Democrats. The clash between McConnell and Senator Warren occurred on the Senate floor February 7, 2017. The Coretta Scott King letter and related materials were posted by the great *Washington Post* reporter Wesley Lowery at https://www.washingtonpost.com/news/powerpost/wp/2017/01/10/read-the-letter-coretta-scott-king-wrote-opposing-sessionss-1986-federal-nomination/?utm_term=.ff7a3f199aa5.

 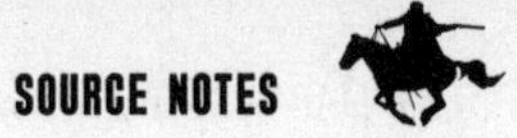

Party Boy: I have covered Paul Ryan since the start of his career. We come from the same place and know a lot of the same people. The *Daily Beast* wrote about the audio of Ryan's discussion with caucus members before the election in a March 13, 2017, piece: "TROUBLE IN PARADISE: Breitbart Leaks Audio of Paul Ryan Dumping Donald Trump: In a previously unheard audio recording, House Speaker Paul Ryan is heard telling fellow Republicans that he would not defend the embattled presidential candidate—then, or ever." Ryan appeared on Fox News, November 1, 2016, to announce he had voted for Trump. Rob Zerban was featured in my August 9, 2012, piece: "Paul Ryan? Seriously?" ABC News summed things up very well on December 8, 2015, with the headline "Paul Ryan Denounces Donald Trump Plan on Muslims but Will Still Support Party Nominee."

Complicit: Media outlets regularly highlighted Ivanka Trump's and Jared Kushner's interventions during the Trump transition and the early days of the Trump presidency, with pieces such as the *New York Times*'s February 3, 2017, piece "Ivanka Trump and Jared Kushner Said to Have Helped Thwart LGBT Rights Rollback." But *Slate*'s Christina Cauterucci called it "BS" with her March 13, 2017, piece: "Ivanka Trump is no centrist bridge-builder on paid leave and child care." *Access Hollywood* breathlessly profiled Ivanka in the August 15, 2007, piece "Ivanka Trump Struts Her 'Stuff.'" A March 5, 2017, *Vanity Fair* article reported "The Trump Sons Are Expanding Like Crazy But Swear It's Totally Legal: Their latest ventures include a new, more affordable chain of hotels in cities along the campaign trail." *Vanity Fair* profiled the Trump children in its February 2017 issue and asked: "Can Donald Jr. and Eric Trump Really Run the Family Business? Although outshone in many ways by their sister Ivanka, Donald Trump Jr. and his brother Eric are thoroughly their father's sons. Charting their battles, to the inevitable lawsuits in their wakes, William D. Cohan investigates whether the boys can handle the empire." NBC's *Saturday Night Live* answered on March 4, 2017. *Politico* reported on March 20, 2017: "Ivanka Trump set to get West Wing office as role expands." Jessica Pressler's July 10, 2016, *New York* magazine piece, "Ivanka Trump Is Not Going to Save Us From Her Father," was spot on. It set the tone for the wisest coverage of Ivanka. James Kirchick's *Los Angeles Times* op-ed "Ivanka Trump is not going to save us," published December 29, 2016, was smart and bold in its analysis. And Amy Wilentz's February 1, 2017, story for the *Nation*, "What Can Ivanka Trump Possibly Do for Women Who Work? For insight into how the first daughter will manage her signature issue, look no further than her brand's website," was simply brilliant. *Fast Company*'s October 17, 2016, piece had the perfect headline: "Ivanka Trump Doesn't Flinch: As she leads her brand into its next stage, Ivanka reveals how she's navigating the drama around her father's presidential campaign." *Saturday Night Live* called Ivanka "Complicit" on March 12, 2017. Jared Kushner's machinations were recounted by Bob Jordan, *Asbury Park Press*, on November 16, 2016, in the article "Trump son-in-law Kushner reportedly settling Christie score in transition." (The Jordan piece highlighted Ross Baker's knowing insights.) CBS News announced on October 30, 2016, that "Donald Trump Offered Chris Christie Vice President Role Before Mike Pence, Sources Say." The Tax Policy Center featured the report "Who Benefits from President Trump's Child Care Proposals?" on February 27, 2017. "Trump's Childcare Plan Will Only Help the Rich," read the headline on Michelle Chen's very fine March 14, 2017, report for the *Nation*. Ivanka Trump appeared on ABC's 20/20 on January 19, 2017, to say: "I'm his daughter."

The Secretary of Trump Is Always Right: The February 7, 2017, *Los Angeles Times* piece "Homeland Security secretary says a border wall won't be built all at once" reported ably on Kelly's appearance before the congressional committee. For a sense of how Kelly was presented as a blunt-talking nominee, see the December 7, 2016, *New York Times* article "Donald Trump Picks John Kelly, Retired General, to Lead Homeland Security." The *Times* editorial board summed up the dichotomy with a March 8, 2017, editorial headlined "Secretary Kelly Is Missing in Action on Immigration." Kelly's 2015 Senate testimony was summed up in a broader *Los Angeles Times* assessment of border issues published December 31, 2016: "A changing border: Barricades won't solve tough new challenges at the Southwest frontier." The *Wall Street Journal* reported on January 31, 2017, that "Homeland Security Chief and White House Clash: John Kelly has resisted picking immigration foe Kris Kobach as his deputy, and is frustrated over the travel ban's rollout." Kelly appeared on CNN, March 6, 2017, where he was grilled by Wolf Blitzer. Blitzer interviewed Panetta on March 8, 2017. The *New York Times* reported on March 5, 2017: "Comey Asks Justice Department to Reject Trump's Wiretapping Claim."

The Captain of the Wrecking Crew: The Brennan Center for Justice report "Voter Challengers," by Nicolas Riley, was published August 30, 2012. The Demos study "Bullies at the Ballot Box: Protecting the Freedom to Vote Against Wrongful Challenges and Intimidation" was issued September 10, 2012. I wrote about the meltdown of the Puzder nomination for the *Nation* in several pieces, including "The Resistance Prevented Puzder From Becoming Labor Secretary," which appeared February 15, 2017. Senator Warren's "quit while he's ahead" Facebook post on Puzder appeared January 26, 2017. Wade Henderson's statement can be found in "Civil and Human Rights Coalition Urges Thorough Review of Secretary of Labor Nominee Alexander Acosta," which was issued by the Leadership Conference on Civil and Human Rights on February 16, 2017. The Lawyers' Committee for Civil Rights Under Law statement was issued the same day. McClatchy DC Bureau Report published its meticulously reported "Ex-Justice official accused of aiding scheme to scratch minority voters" story on June 24, 2007. Henry Weinstein's Los Angeles Times article "Justice Department Joins Election Legal Fight in Ohio" appeared November 1, 2004; Weinstein was way ahead of the rest of the press corps in reporting this vital story. Talking Points Memo's "TPM Muckraker" published a pair of important pieces detailing Robert Kengle's concerns: "Bush Appointee 'Led by Power'" (April 26, 2007) and "Former DoJ Official: I Left Due

 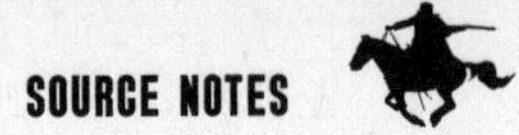

to 'Institutional Sabotage'" (April 30, 2007). "An Investigation of Allegations of Politicized Hiring and Other Improper Personnel Actions in the Civil Rights Division" was issued by the Office of the Inspector General (OIG) and the Office of Professional Responsibility (OPR) on January 13, 2009. Frances Perkins's *People at Work* was published by John Day in 1934. Learn more about FDR's secretary of labor from the Frances Perkins Center; they have a great website at http://francesperkinscenter.org/life-new/. The National Employment Law Project's assessment of threatened cuts, "On President Trump's Budget Proposal," was issued March 16, 2017.

Putt-Head: The *New York Times* reported on July 25, 2008: "Forced Off Duke's Varsity Golf Team, Giuliani's Son Files a Lawsuit." *Sports Illustrated* was all over the story, with pieces like "Sue Devils: A peek inside Giuliani v. Duke" on August 4, 2008. Jim Gorant wrote "Notebook: Giuliani v. Duke: A teammate's view" on July 30, 2008, while a notable *Golf Digest* piece published June 1, 2008, was headlined "Andrew Giuliani . . . Unruly brat or good kid who just wanted to play golf at Duke?" The *New York Post* "Rudy's Putt-Head" piece appeared July 25, 2008. Trump's naming of Andrew Giuliani to the White House post was broadly reported, especially in New York media, on March 6. The Duke *Chronicle* piece on the appointment of the "former men's golfer" appeared March 7, 2017.

The Product of a Judicial Coup: I covered the Garland and Gorsuch nomination fights extensively for the *Nation* and wrote a number of pieces that challenged the false claim that Supreme Court nominations cannot be taken up in presidential election years in articles such as "This Is Precisely the Right Time for the Senate to Consider Judge Garland's Supreme Court Nomination," published June 22, 2016. A fine historical review of the Brandeis nomination fight, "Louis Brandeis confirmed as Justice, 100 year [sic] ago today," was published June 1, 2016, by the National Constitution Center. Find background on the Senate Judiciary Committee's hearing with Neil Gorsuch at the committee's site: www.judiciary.senate.gov/. The *Washington Post* report "Franken presses Gorsuch on Garland snub, same-sex marriage" was published March 21, 2017. The People For the American Way assessment of Gorsuch's right-wing stances, "The Dissents of Judge Neil Gorsuch: Far to the Right and Out of the Mainstream," was written by Elliot Mincberg and published in February 2017. The Republican National Lawyers Association detailed Gorsuch's involvement with the group in "RNLA Statement on the Nomination of Judge Neil Gorsuch to the Supreme Court," issued January 31, 2017. For more on Supreme Court nominations in election season, check out the fine work of Amy Howe, who on February 13, 2016, published her piece "Supreme Court vacancies in presidential election years" on the essential *Scotusblog*, at http://www.scotusblog.com/2016/02/supreme-court-vacancies-in-presidential-election-years/.

Donald Trump's Very Own Milhous: *Time* magazine published a full transcript of the vice presidential debate on October 4, 2016. For more background regarding the debate, visit the Commission on Presidential Debates site at http://

www.debates.org/. A good review of Pence's problems with General Flynn, "Pence: I was 'disappointed' with Flynn," was produced February, 20, 2017. The group Every Voice, which does great research and analysis on money-in-politics issues, published "Mike Pence: Tiebreaker, DeVos Money Taker" on February 7, 2017. A look at Pence's endorsement of Cruz, "Indiana governor: 'I will be voting for Ted Cruz,'" appeared April 29, 2016, in the *Chicago Tribune*. *Politico* produced a number of good articles on Trump's considering of Pence; "Trump flirts with unpopular Pence: Some home state Republicans would be glad to see the Indiana governor abandon his re-election bid for a VP slot," from July 12, 2016, was especially useful, as was "The old cassettes that explain Mike Pence: Donald Trump's running mate learned everything he needed to know about politics from behind a studio mic," from July 20, 2016. I covered the Republican nomination process from start to finish, along with the vice presidential selection process and the Republican National Convention and traveled to Indiana several times to examine Pence's record. The *Indianapolis Star* wrote extensively about Pence's home state political challenges in pieces such as "Latest poll: Race for governor remains tight," published May 20, 2016.

Part IV: Privateers

FDR spoke of "government by organized mob" in perhaps the greatest political speech of his career, an address delivered on October 31, 1936, at Madison Square Garden in New York City. Woody Guthrie's outlaw ballad "Pretty Boy Floyd" was written in 1939. *The Papers of Ben Franklin,* collected by Ellen R. Cohn, published by Yale University Press, contain many of Franklin's writings (and machinations) regarding letters of marque and reprisal. The interested scholar will find a wealth of material on maritime law, the Paris Declaration Respecting Maritime Law and more in the Yale Law School Legal Scholarship Repository. For more on contemporary discussions of letters of marque, see *Politico,* April 15, 2009: "Ron Paul's plan to fend off pirates." The *Los Angeles Times* reported May 11, 2011, that "Trump has thrived with government's generosity: The potential presidential candidate and opponent of big government has relied on tax breaks and federal funding to build his real estate empire." The piece closely examined his New York deals and doings, providing great insights from Karen Burstein and others. The American Federation of Government Employees declared on January 23, 2017, that "President Trump's Federal Hiring Freeze Will Cost Taxpayers and Hurt Americans." Pieces on Trump and privatization appeared frequently in the media during the Trump transition. The *Washington Post* piece "Elaine Chao emphasizes private funds for Trump's promised transportation fixes" appeared on January 11, 2017, around the time of Chao's Senate confirmation hearing. FDR spoke of "human cooperation" in his great August 9, 1934, address in Green Bay, Wisconsin.

"I've Got a Bridge to Sell You": The U.S. Department of State's Bureau of International Narcotics and Law Enforcement Affairs publishes a *Guide to Anti-Corruption Policy and Programming* that includes a section on "Nepotism in Appointments." For a flavor of France's problems in this regard, see the *New York Times*, February 3, 2017: "Fillon Scandal Indicts, Foremost, France's Political Elite." Thomas Jefferson wrote to George Washington on April 16, 1784, warning about "the patrons of privilege and prerogative." The *New York Times* piece "Elaine Chao Gets Cozy Reception at Confirmation Hearing" appeared January 11, 2017. NPR provided good background on the federal anti-nepotism law in a November 18, 2016, report: "Jared Kushner and the Anti-Nepotism Statute That Might Keep Him From the White House." Adam Bellow's piece in the July/April 2003 issue of the *Atlantic* was headlined "In Praise of Nepotism: Americans censure nepotism on the one hand and practice it as much as they can on the other. There's much to be said for "good" nepotism, the author argues—which is fortunate, because we're living in a nepotistic Golden Age." Matt Lewis's piece "Elaine Chao's Appointment: Sign of Diversity or Nepotism?" appeared in *Roll Call* on November 30, 2016. *Politico* reported January 24, 2017, that "Commerce committee gives Chao the nod," while the Reuters report on her confirmation, "U.S. Senate approves Chao to lead Transportation Department," appeared February 1, 2017. Steven Greenhouse's report "Labor Agency Is Failing Workers, Report Says" was published March 24, 2009. In 2009, inspired by concerns about the issues with the Labor Department, California congressman George Miller introduced the Wage Theft Prevention Act; he continued to press for investigations and studies of wage theft. Spencer Woodman's great piece for the *Nation*, "Elaine Chao, Ruined Department of Labor, Picked to Ensure Safety of Nation's Planes, Trains, and Automobiles: Under her leadership, the Department of Labor routinely ignored complaints about wage theft and workplace safety," published November 30, 2016, highlighted many of the ongoing complaints and concerns about Chao's management style. The Alicia Patterson Foundation report "How the Bush administration reversed decades of progress on mine safety" was published in 2011. When Chao was finishing at the Labor Department, the *New York Times* published the January 9, 2009, piece "Elaine L. Chao, Departing Secretary of Labor, Fends Off Critics." Lane Windham wrote for the *American Prospect* on December 5, 2016: "The Workers' Menace Becomes the Commuters' Threat: Elaine Chao, Bush's labor secretary, is Trump's pick for transportation." Trump appeared August 2, 2016, on Fox Business to talk infrastructure. FDR spoke about "national possessions" when he dedicated Boulder Dam on September 30, 1935. The latest American Society of Civil Engineers estimates on infrastructure can be found at www.asce.org. Robert Reich explained "Trump's Infrastructure Scam" at www.robertreich.org, while Paul Krugman wrote about the issue in the November 19, 2016, *New York Times* blog "Infrastructure Build or Privatization Scam?" Ronald Klain's piece "Trump's big infrastructure plan? It's a trap" appeared November 18, 2016, in the *Washington Post*.

The Kingfish of the Quagmire: Stanford's February 1, 2002, reflection, "John Gardner, founder of Common Cause, engineer of President Lyndon B. Johnson's 'Great Society' program, dead at 89," provides a great sense of this remarkable man's accomplishments, as does the 2001 PBS tribute: "John Gardner: Uncommon American." Stephanie Mencimer is always great, but her November 18, 2009, piece for *Mother Jones,* "The Tea Party's Favorite Doctors," was masterfully reported and written. CNN reported on Price's CPAC speech in a February 19, 2010, piece: "Price welcomes 'Party of No' label." *Slate* writer Jordan Weissmann's piece "Tom Price Is the Walking Definition of an Appearance of Corruption" appeared January 17, 2017.

CNN reported that same day that "Trump's Cabinet pick invested in company, then introduced a bill to help it." On March 17, 2017, ProPublica reported that "Fired U.S. Attorney Preet Bharara Said to Have Been Investigating HHS Secretary Tom Price." RoseAnn DeMoro wrote a January 19, 2017, column that appeared on Common Dreams: "Access to Buying Insurance Is Not Health Coverage." NNU decried the lack of scrutiny of Price, and issued a January 23, 2017, statement: "Nurses Urge Senate Finance Committee to Scrutinize Tom Price." The transcript of Price's wrangling with cancer survivor Brian Kline on March 15, 2017, can be found on the CNN website: http://www.cnn.com/TRANSCRIPTS/1703/15/se.01.html.

The Health Care Profiteer: You can learn a little more about the Centers for Medicare & Medicaid Services at the agency's website: www.cms.gov. The March 14, 2017, statement from HHS announced: "Secretary Price and CMS Administrator Verma Take First Joint Action: Affirm Partnership of HHS, CMS, and States to Improve Medicaid Program." The *Indianapolis Star* investigation, published August 25, 2014, was headlined "Seema Verma, powerful state health-care consultant, serves two bosses." Concerns expressed by Senator Cantwell and others were reported March 13, 2017, in the *New York Times* article "Health Policy Expert Is Confirmed as Medicare and Medicaid Administrator." Dr. Zarr's statement was issued December 2, 2016, by Physicians for a National Health Care Program as "Doctors group calls on Trump to rescind nominations of Price, Verma to key health care posts."

The Investor Who Got a High Return: Robert W. McChesney and I wrote a good deal about DeVos in our book *Dollarocracy: How the Money and Media Election Complex Is Destroying America* (Nation Books, 2013). I have also covered her machinations at the state level for the *Nation* over many years. Diane Ravitch wrote a great book on so-called choice initiatives: *Reign of Error: The Hoax of the Privatization Movement and the Danger to America's Public Schools* (Vintage; reprint, 2014). Source Watch maintains a detailed background file on DeVos at http://www.sourcewatch.org/index.php/Betsy_DeVos. Jane Mayer examined "Betsy DeVos, Trump's Big Donor Education Secretary" in a piece for the *New Yorker* published November 23, 2016. Jeremy Scahill's *Blackwater: The Rise of the World's Most Powerful Mercenary Army* was published by Nation Books in 2007. Scahill spoke about DeVos and Prince on *Democracy Now!* on January 18, 2017. The *Los Angeles Times* reported on

Eli Broad's opposition to DeVos in a February 1, 2017, piece: "Betsy DeVos 'is unprepared and unqualified' to be Education Secretary, Eli Broad says." Ravitch explained her opposition to DeVos in a WBEZ radio interview, "The Future of Public Education If Trump Becomes Privatizer-In-Chief," on December 7, 2016. The American Federation of Teachers issued a November 23, 2016, statement: "AFT President Randi Weingarten on Nomination of Betsy DeVos as Secretary of Education." *Huffington Post* explained "Here's How Much Betsy DeVos and Her Family Paid to Back GOP Senators Who Will Support Her" in a February 2, 2017, article subtitled "It's good to be a donor." I wrote about the DeVos spending in the states for the *Nation* in a May 9, 2011, article: "Learning the Fitzwalkerstan Way: Wisconsin's Walker Pushes Privatization of Education: The governor who has led the fight to bust unions and cut public services now steps up as the pointman for privatization of education—and his own political ambitions." We examined the All Children Matter case in Ohio in *Dollarocracy*. One Wisconsin Now's November 23, 2016, statement on DeVos was headlined "Trump's DeVos Appointment Means More School Privatization, More Failure, Less Accountability: Being a Billionaire Whose Hobby Is Underwriting Campaigns to Steal Public School Dollars for Unaccountable Private Schools Disqualifies Her to Be Our Secretary of Education."

Mr. Secrets and Lies: Friends of the Earth produced a solid summary of concerns about Pruitt in their February 17, 2017, statement: "Friends of the Earth Will Hold Accountable Senators Who Voted for Pruitt." The Center for Media and Democracy investigated Pruitt thoroughly and aggressively, revealing many of their findings and concerns in a January 18, 2017, piece by Nick Surgey: "Scott Pruitt: Trump's Pick for EPA." Background on the court case involving Pruitt's emails and records can be found in "Court Orders EPA Nominee Scott Pruitt to Release Emails," published February 16, 2017, by CMD. The *New York Times* offered a sense of the chaotic Pruitt debate and vote in its February 17, 2017, piece "Senate Confirms Scott Pruitt as E.P.A. Head." But it really is worth watching the key portions on CSPAN, which archived the fiasco at https://www.c-span.org/video/?424132-1/us-senate-confirms-epa-nominee-advances-commerce-nominee. The details of the Pruitt emails were reviewed in the February 22, 2017, CMD article "Oklahoma AG Releases 7,564 Pages in Response to CMD Request." CNN reported on EPA cuts March 16, 2017, in the piece "Trump budget chief on climate change: 'We consider that to be a waste of your money.'" The Sierra Club released a review of Pruitt's conflicting statements on March 13, 2017: "Pruitt Repeatedly Misled Congress—Three Strikes You're Out!"

Pristine Wilderness for Sale, Lease or Hire: The National Park Service highlights "Theodore Roosevelt and Conservation" at its parks and in its promotional materials, especially his argument that, more than a century ago, Americans were "awakening" to the need to preserve wilderness areas. Douglas Brinkley's great book of Roosevelt's conservation legacy is *The Wilderness Warrior: Theodore Roosevelt and the Crusade for America* (Harper Collins, 2009). He spoke about it in an August

2009 interview: "Teddy's crusade." Zinke's rage at Hillary Clinton was detailed in a January 31, 2014, piece for the *Hill:* "House candidate calls Clinton 'Antichrist.'" Zinke's self-advocacy was detailed in a May 25, 2016, Breitbart piece: "Commander Ryan Zinke Backs Donald Trump for President: 'I Want to Be Part of Team Making America Great Again.'" Montana Public Radio reported July 19, 2016, on Zinke's bombastic Republican National Convention speech. CNN reported January 17, 2017, on "Trump Cabinet picks on climate change." When Zinke stepped down as an RNC delegate in the summer of 2016, the *Billings Gazette* examined his stances on environmental issues in a July 15, 2016, piece: "Zinke resigns delegate post over public lands disagreement; still will speak at RNC." Montana Public Radio produced an August 8, 2016, report: "Analyzing Zinke and Juneau's Public Lands Positions." The *Missoulian* reported November 28, 2016, that "Trump names Zinke's wife Lolita to VA landing team." *National Parks Traveler* described responses to the Zinke nomination in a December 15, 2016, article: "Montana Congressman Picked to Be Interior Secretary." The Sierra Club issued its December 13, 2016, statement as "Sierra Club Criticizes Zinke Nomination for DOI," while Friends of the Earth launched a "Tell the Senate: Block Ryan Zinke from leading the Department of the Interior" campaign. *Scientific American*'s report "Public Lands and Environment under Interior Nominee Zinke: A Mixed Bag: Trump's appointment to oversee America's parks and federal lands has pledged to protect them and public access while undoing federal regulation" was published January 20, 2017. The February 6, 2017, letter to senators from the environmental and conservation groups was titled "Oppose Ryan Zinke for Secretary of the Interior."

Mars Incorporated: Like most new presidents, Trump slipped a space reference into the inaugural address he delivered January 20, 2017, although it was largely missed amid all the talk of "carnage." Referred to as the "Moon speech," John Kennedy's September 12, 1962, speech was formally titled "Address at Rice University on the Nation's Space Effort." The *Washington Post* reported on Trump's space-is-not-the-place sentiments in a November 11, 2015, article: "Donald Trump tells 10-year-old that 'space is terrific' but potholes are more important." The *Boston Globe* headlined its piece from the same day "Trump loves NASA, but backs privatization of outer space." *Politico*'s Bryan Bender reported February 9, 2017, on the "Trump advisers' space plan: To moon, Mars and beyond: A push for privatization is inspiring a battle between aerospace contractors and the new breed of tech entrepreneurs." The *Week* reported February 9, 2017: "President Trump reportedly wants to monetize space." Bob Walker is the executive chairman of the DC firm Wexler|Walker and the chairman of the industry-friendly Alliance for Transportation Innovation (ATI21) advisory board. *SpaceNews* reported January 22, 2017: "Trump administration assigns first political appointees to NASA." *Wired* reported January 20, 2017, on Trump's space appointments and the *Atlantic* wrote January 3, 2017, about "The Most Vulnerable NASA Missions Under Trump: Reading the tea leaves on the president-elect's space policy." Dr. Greg Autry's October

15, 2017, article for *Forbes* was headlined "Space Policy 101 for Clinton and Trump." The United Nations has an Office of Outer Space Affairs and interstellar treaties can be found at its website: http://www.unoosa.org. Britain's *Telegraph* newspaper reported January 26, 2012, on Newt Gingrich's "Northwest Ordinance for Space" speech: "US election 2012: Newt Gingrich calls for US moon base: At a Florida rally, Republican presidential contender Newt Gingrich takes a giant leap into the future as he promises a permanent American colony on the moon 'by the end of my second term.'" *Saturday Night Live* parodied Gingrich's "admoonistration" on February 4, 2012. Associated Press reported January 26, 2012, that "Romney Mocks Gingrich's Plans for Moon Base."

The Secretary of Gentrification: The *Hill* reported November 15, 2016, that "Carson [is] not interested in serving in Trump administration." The *Los Angeles Times* announced the same day that "Former presidential candidate Ben Carson says he won't join Trump's Cabinet because he has no government experience." CNN reported November 12, 2015, that "Trump likens Carson's 'pathology' to that of a child molester." Mike Huckabee's claim that Carson had lived in public housing was clarified on December 7, 2016, with a report headlined "Ben Carson didn't live in public housing." Trevor Noah reflected on Carson's Senate testimony on the January 12, 2017, edition of Comedy Central's *The Daily Show*. The always brilliant professor Peter Dreier, who has written extensively about HUD and housing issues, penned a very fine piece for the *American Prospect*: "Why Trump Picked Ben Carson as HUD Secretary: Donald Trump's "edifice complex" explains his ill-advised choice of the completely inexperienced Ben Carson to head the Department of Housing and Urban Development." The *Washington Post* assessment, published December 5, 2016, was "HUD job to pit Carson ideology against long-standing housing policy." The National Low Income Housing Coalition issued its "Statement from Diane Yentel, President and CEO of the National Low Income Housing Coalition, on President-elect Trump's Appointment of Ben Carson to Lead the Department of Housing and Urban Development" on November 23, 2016. Dr. Ben Carson wrote about housing policy in a July 23, 2016, piece for the *Washington Times*: "Experimenting with failed socialism again: Obama's new housing rules try to accomplish what busing could not." The *Atlantic*'s Alana Semuels explored the same issues more deeply, and more sensitively, in her November 29, 2016, article, "The Future of Housing Segregation Under Trump: The president-elect is skeptical about many of the Obama administration's attempts to give minorities access to better homes." Seema Agnani wrote about "The President as Developer-in-Chief" on January 13, 2017, for *ROOFLINES*, the *Shelterforce* blog. Toshio Meronek has written ably about poverty issues and the piece "Privatizing Public Housing: The 'Genocide of Poor People,'" published March 13, 2015, by *Truthout* is just one example of this. Right to the City's "#GentrifierInChief" assessment appeared December 7, 2016, on Medium. Andrea Shapiro wrote about HUD and housing issues in a December 2016 essay, "Housing Under Trump: Bizarre and Scary," that appeared on the Metropolitan Council on Housing website: http://metcouncilonhousing.org.

The Oopsing of Nuclear Waste Disposal: The *Washington Post* report from November 10, 2011, summed things up: "Rick Perry stumbles badly in Republican presidential debate." The video is worth a another viewing (ABC News, November 9, 2011, "Rick Perry's Debate Lapse: 'Oops'—Can't Remember Department of Energy"): http://abcnews.go.com/blogs/politics/2011/11/rick-perrys-debate-lapse-oops-cant-remember-department-of-energy/. The *Texas Observer* has been all over the nuclear disposal story, with pieces like "Is Rick Perry Cheerleading for a Nuclear Trans-Texas Corridor?" (April 4, 2014) and "Get Ready, America: Rick Perry's Environmental and Energy Record Is Awful: During his 14 years as governor, Perry attempted to fast-track permits for 11 coal plants and supported building a radioactive waste facility in West Texas" (December 14, 2016). The *New York Times* picked up on the nuclear waste debate in a January 18, 2017, piece: "'Learning Curve' as Rick Perry Pursues a Job He Initially Misunderstood." You'll find lots about nuclear waste at www.energy.gov and in DOE assessments like "The Path Forward for Nuclear Waste Disposal" (March 24, 2015). The March 2, 2017, "Sierra Club Statement on Rick Perry's Department of Energy Confirmation" does a good job of detailing concerns about Perry's new role, as does the Friends of the Earth statement from the same day: "Perry unfit to serve as Secretary of Energy." The *Texas Tribune* site featured the April 28, 2016, Medill News Service story by Marisa Endicott: "West Texas Site Applies for Nuke Waste License: The company operating a low-level nuclear waste dump in West Texas on Thursday applied for a license to begin accepting highly radioactive spent nuclear fuel." A Public Citizen statement, "License Application for Dangerous West Texas High-Level Radioactive Waste Dump Is Now Open for Public Input," was issued January 30, 2017.

The Secretary of Corporate Agribusiness: The Pew Research Center produced a savvy report on the rural vote, "Behind Trump's win in rural white America: Women joined men in backing him," which was released November 17, 2016. The Vox piece, by Matthew Yglesias, appeared March 8, 2017, as "The weird mystery of the Trump administration's agriculture secretary vacancy: Sonny Perdue's stalled confirmation, not explained because nobody knows what's happening." The *New York Times* article on the Perdue selection appeared January 18, 2017, as "Sonny Perdue Is Trump's Choice for Agriculture Secretary." *Modern Farmer* reviewed the Perdue nomination in a January 19, 2017, story: "Former Georgia Governor Sonny Perdue nominated as USDA Secretary." The January 24, 2017, Organic Consumers Association statement was headlined "Trump's Pick for Ag Secretary Has 'Bigly' Ties to Big Ag and Big Food." The Food Policy Action assessment of January 18, 2017, was issued as "FPA Statement on the Sonny Perdue USDA Secretary Announcement." Perdue's May 8, 2014, article for *National Review* grumbled about how "Conservatives are acting like liberals." ThinkProgress reported on January 2, 2017, that "Trump could name Agriculture Secretary whose

drought strategy was to pray for rain: Former GA Gov. Sonny Perdue is the latest white male with Confederate sympathies to be considered for a cabinet slot." The Environmental Working Group report "Trump's Agricultural Nominee Brings the Swamp to Washington" was released March 8, 2017. The *New York Times* reported on it that day in a front-page story headlined "Ethics Questions Dogged Agriculture Nominee as Georgia Governor." The Pesticide Action Network statement of the Perdue pick, issued January 19, 2017, declared "Nominee for Secretary of Agriculture is the wrong choice for farmers." The *Grub Street* report on Perdue, published January 23, 2017, listed "5 Reasons Why Food Experts Are Worried About Trump's New Agriculture Secretary." Kelsey Gee, Jacob Bunge and Jesse Newman wrote a savvy *Wall Street Journal* report, published January 19, 2017, that was headlined "Agriculture Secretary Nominee Sonny Perdue Known for Promoting Trade: Former Georgia governor has fans in Farm Belt and agribusiness." William Jennings Bryan delivered his "Cross of Gold" speech to the Democratic National Convention in Chicago on July 9, 1896. Despite what Steve Bannon tries to suggest, it proposed a very different populism from that of Donald Trump.

The Weed Whacker: I wrote and talked a lot about Trump and the media during the 2016 campaign, and I always tried to keep focused on the structural issues that helped to create an opening for Trump. My March 10, 2016, piece for the *Nation*, "How We Got Trumped by the Media: They're so obsessed with "The Donald" that they can barely be bothered to cover the other candidates, much less the important issues," summed up a lot of my thinking, as did a March 16, 2016, appearance I did on *Democracy Now!* that was pitched as "Donald Trump & His Enablers: John Nichols Calls Out Trump-Obsessed Media for Wall-to-Wall Coverage." I share many of the concerns expressed by former FCC commissioner Michael Copps in a piece he wrote March 22 titled "Deconstruction"; it can be found at www.commoncause.org. The *New York Times*, on February 5, 2017, did a piece: "Trump's F.C.C. Pick Quickly Targets Net Neutrality Rules." It was a good, smart take. But the key to understanding Trump's FCC chair, Ajit Pai, is that he has a broadly pro-corporate agenda that extends well beyond high-profile issues such as net neutrality and media cross-ownership. That's why I appreciate the serious assessments of all the areas that Pai had meddled in. Free Press, a group I have been involved with since its launch, has I believe done a very good job in examining the broad spectrum of issues. I commend a number of assessments by Free Press staffers and allies, including Dana Floberg's "New FCC Chairman Ajit Pai Is Off to an Orwellian Start," which appeared February 7, 2017, and Tim Karr's "The President's Attack on Public Broadcasting Puts Him at Odds with the American People," from March 16, 2017. Joseph Torres, the senior external affairs director for Free Press, and Malkia Cyril, the executive director of the Center for Media Justice and the co-founder of the Media Action Grassroots Network, wrote an important piece on March 16, 2017: "The Resistance Must Be Digitized." My piece on Trump's proposed defunding of public broadcasting, "Trump's Plan to Eliminate Public

Broadcasting Would Hurt Listeners in Trump Country: Stations that serve rural areas neglected by corporate media would lose their funding," appeared in the *Nation* on March 16, 2017. There is resistance within the FCC. For a sense of it, read the *Variety* piece "FCC Commissioner Mignon Clyburn Blasts Chairman Ajit Pai Over 'Friday News Dump,'" which appeared February 3, 2017. I wrote about chairman Pai's assault on net neutrality in the *Nation* in a piece headlined "Trump's FCC Has Begun Its Attack on Net Neutrality," which appeared April 26, 2017. My colleague and friend Victor Pickard is also writing ably on these issues; check out his May 5, 2017, *Nation* piece: "It's Not Too Late to Save Net Neutrality From a Captured FCC." For the latest on the struggle, visit www.freepress.net.

The Foreclosure King: The January 19, 2017, *New York Times* piece pretty much says it all: "Steven Mnuchin, Treasury Nominee, Failed to Disclose $100 Million in Assets." Oregon senator Ron Wyden was the hero of the hearings on Mnuchin, and the *Los Angeles Times* report from January 19, 2017, "Sen. Wyden hammers Mnuchin, saying it's 'a real stretch' he'd work for all Americans as Treasury secretary," gives a powerful sense of why Wyden was so impassioned. The *Washington Post* report from November 30, 2016, "Trump's Treasury pick Steven Mnuchin is behind some of Hollywood's biggest movies," provides a lot of the Mnuchin backstory. *Time* did a good report on Mnuchin as the "Foreclosure King" on January 19, 2017: "Here's Why Treasury Nominee Steve Mnuchin Has Been Called the 'Foreclosure King.'" The Campaign for Accountability issued its statement on Mnuchin January 6, 2017: "CfA Calls on Federal Authorities to Investigate Steven Mnuchin's OneWest Bank for Fraud." ProPublica did an outstanding report, which was published December 27, 2016, with the headline "Trump's Treasury Pick Excelled at Kicking Elderly People Out of Their Homes: When Steven Mnuchin ran OneWest, the bank aggressively and in some cases, wrongly, foreclosed on elderly homeowners with reverse mortgages. The bank had a disproportionate share of such foreclosures." The National Consumer Law Center's "Statement Regarding Nomination of Mnuchin as U.S. Treasury Secretary" was issued November 30, 2016. The California Reinvestment Coalition's (CRC) strong statement, "CRC Responds to GOP Senators Ramming Through Steve Mnuchin's Nomination This Morning," was issued February 2, 2017. More CRC statements on Mnuchin are at http://www.calreinvest.org/news. The *Columbus Dispatch* report "Trump treasury pick Mnuchin misled Senate on foreclosures, Ohio cases show," published January 29, 2017, is an example of investigative reporting at its best. Reporters Alan Johnson and Jill Riepenhoff did exemplary work, as did *Columbus Dispatch-Washington Bureau* writer Jessica Wehrman with her February 4, 2017, piece, "Mnuchin's denials don't match record." The *Dispatch*'s highlighting of the concerns of former Ohio attorney general Marc Dann regarding threats to banking reforms was especially valuable. The *New York Times* wrote about the Trump team's targeting of reforms in a smart, important November 30, 2016, article: "Trump's Economic Cabinet Picks Signal Embrace of Wall St. Elite."

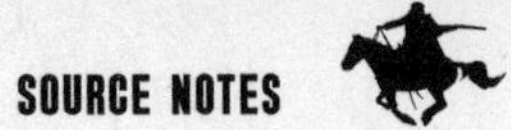

The Fox Guarding the Henhouse: Public Citizen has been in the forefront of the effort to focus attention on Jay Clayton's corporate connections. See its Clayton profile at http://corporatecabinet.org/. As usual, Matt Taibbi got to the heart of the matter with his January 5, 2017, *Rolling Stone* piece: "Trump Nominee Jay Clayton Will Be the Most Conflicted SEC Chair Ever: America's incoming top cop on finance is literally married to industry." The "Brown Statement on President-Elect Trump's SEC Nominee Jay Clayton," issued by Senator Sherrod Brown on January 4, 2017, offers an example of how a watchdog senator approaches an unacceptable nominee. Senator Elizabeth Warren's website features video of her questioning Clayton at: https://www.warren.senate.gov/?p=video&id=1551. It is definitely worth watching. Fox Business reported March 23, 2017, that "Trump's SEC Pick Clayton Gets Warren Tongue Lashing." There's also a fine *Politico* report on Warren and Senator Bernie Sanders going after Clayton, "Warren, Sanders seize on SEC nominee to attack Trump," which was published March 22, 2017.

The Government Sachs Swamp: The *Economist* released the transcript of its interview with President Trump on May 11, 2017. *New York* magazine assessed the fiasco with a Jonathan Chait piece published the same day: "Donald Trump Tries to Explain Economics to *The Economist*. Hilarity Ensues." To learn more about the economic thinking of John Maynard Keynes, which is something Donald Trump really ought to do, consider Keynes's 1936 book *The General Theory of Employment, Interest and Money*. And check out Paul Krugman's June 6, 2015, *New York Times* comment: "Why Am I A Keynesian?" Massachusetts senator Elizabeth Warren has worked hard to focus attention on the Trump administration's Goldman Sachs connections; CNN did a good report, "Elizabeth Warren probes Goldman Sachs' ties to Trump White House," on February 10, 2017. MarketWatch toted up the Goldman Sachs nominee in a February 13, 2017, report: "Another Goldman Sachs veteran may join the Trump White House, report says." The *Forward*'s savvy take, "Gary Cohn Leads White House 'New Yorker' Wing Against Team Bannon," was published March 21, 2017. The inimitable William Greider reported March 17, 2017, for the *Nation* that "Trump Is Fighting a New Trade War—and This One Is Intramural: A nasty White House battle has broken out between right-wing nationalists and globalist financiers." On March 10, 2017, *Zero Hedge* ran the report "'Civil War' Breaks Out at White House over Trade . . . And Goldman Is Winning." It concluded with the line "In retrospect, those who said Trump will ultimately do Wall Street's bidding, may have been correct all along."

Afterword

The Jefferson quote is from his letter to John Taylor (June 4, 1798) after the passage of the Alien and Sedition Acts, which is found in *The Writings of Thomas Jefferson* (G.P. Putnam's Sons, 1892). I have covered a number of Canadian campaigns and wrote a good deal about Justin Trudeau's campaign and formation of a government for the *Nation.* His book *Common Ground* (HarperCollins, 2015) gives a good sense of Trudeau's thinking on many issues. The CBC report "Justin Trudeau begins his bold experiment in 'government by cabinet,'" by Chris Hall, appeared November 5, 2015. Regarding his centralization of power, Trump angrily rejected the premise of a *Saturday Night Live* skit that portrayed him as disengaged: "I call my own shots, largely based on an accumulation of data, and everyone knows it," he tweeted. "Some FAKE NEWS media, in order to marginalize, lies!" More details about Sebastian Gorka's Vitézi Rend tie can he found in Lily Bayer's and Larry Cohler-Esses's "What Is Vitézi Rend, The Ally of The Nazis That Sebastian Gorka 'Joined,'" in the *Forward,* March 16, 2017. The *Saturday Night Live* Grim Reaper skit was aired February 4, 2017. The references to Betsy DeVos and Tom Price relate to their long-term advocacy for changes in education and health care policy, especially DeVos's work with various "choice" groups she has funded. The exchange between Leahy and Gorsuch took place during the Senate Judiciary Committee hearing on March 21. A good example of Ralph Nader's advocacy for a different approach to forming cabinets can be found in *Crashing the Party: Taking on the Corporate Government in an Age of Surrender* (St. Martin's Press, 2002). An updated version of Rebecca Solnit's great book on activist engagement, protest and resistance, *Hope in the Dark: Untold Histories, Wild Possibilities,* was published by Haymarket Books in 2016. Read everything Rebecca Solnit writes!

Acknowledgments

Alessandra Bastagli, my editor at Nation Books, encouraged me to take this project on. I am so glad she did. My editor at the *Nation*, Katrina vanden Heuvel, was absolutely on board and supportive; she is a brilliant comrade whose fierce commitment to the search for truth in an age of "alternative facts" is inspired—and inspiring. Many of the profiles in this book had their start in *Nation* articles. Others began even earlier, in my coverage of Paul Ryan, Reince Priebus and others for the great progressive newspaper of Madison, Wisconsin: the *Capital Times*. A number of members of Congress were encouraging and pointed me in the right direction as I started examining the Trump team; I especially appreciate the insights I have gained from congressmen Mark Pocan, Keith Ellison, Gwen Moore and Barbara Lee, and from Senators Bernie Sanders, Tammy Baldwin and Sherrod Brown. I cannot begin to express how much I appreciate the work of watchdog and activist groups that encouraged me to look at particular nominees and to dig deeper in particular areas. I'll mention Public Citizen, the Center for Media and Democracy, Free Press, Friends of the Earth, the National Family Farm Coalition and National Nurses United, although there are dozens of other groups that merit attention. I hope I have succeeded in highlighting their work in this book. My friends Bob McChesney, Steve Cobble and John "Sly" Sylvester were, as always, possessed of the wry humor and knowledge necessary to be great sounding boards. So, too, were my late friends Ed Garvey, Ted Shannon, Kathy Ozer and Sandy Pearlman, who shared the spirit of this book before their deaths. Lastly, I want to pay tribute to my wife, Mary, a great investigative reporter with the Center for Media and Democracy, and an even greater partner, and to my daughter, Whitman, who has a rage for justice. Oh, and thanks to Nikki, Iris and Hope for taking me to the Sister March in Madison. It was awesome.

Index

About the Author

© ROBIN HOLLAND

John Nichols is the national affairs writer for the *Nation* magazine and a contributing writer for the *Progressive* and *In These Times*. He is also the associate editor of the *Capital Times*, the daily newspaper in Madison, Wisconsin, and a co-founder of the media-reform group Free Press. A frequent commentator on American politics and media, he has appeared often on MSNBC, CNN, Fox News, NPR and BBC, and has frequently lectured at major universities on executive power and the need for presidential accountability. The author of ten books, Nichols has earned numerous awards for his investigative reports, including groundbreaking examinations (in collaboration with the Center for Media and Democracy) on the Koch brothers and the American Legislative Exchange Council.

The Nation Institute

Founded in 2000, **Nation Books** has become a leading voice in American independent publishing. The imprint's mission is to tell stories that inform and empower just as they inspire or entertain readers. We publish award-winning and bestselling journalists, thought leaders, whistleblowers, and truthtellers, and we are also committed to seeking out a new generation of emerging writers, particularly voices from underrepresented communities and writers from diverse backgrounds. As a publisher with a focused list, we work closely with all our authors to ensure that their books have broad and lasting impact. With each of our books we aim to constructively affect and amplify cultural and political discourse and to engender positive social change.

Nation Books is a project of The Nation Institute, a nonprofit media center established to extend the reach of democratic ideals and strengthen the independent press. The Nation Institute is home to a dynamic range of programs: the award-winning Investigative Fund, which supports groundbreaking investigative journalism; the widely read and syndicated website TomDispatch; journalism fellowships that support and cultivate over twenty-five emerging and high-profile reporters each year; and the Victor S. Navasky Internship Program.

For more information on Nation Books and The Nation Institute, please visit:

www.nationbooks.org
www.nationinstitute.org
www.facebook.com/nationbooks.ny
Twitter: @nationbooks